515

# STEMMING THE TIDE

## Winston S. Churchill

This volume, uniform in format with the earlier collections, contains the 50 most important speeches that Winston Churchill made during the first two years after his triumphant return to office as Britain's Prime Minister.

This time he took over responsibility for an England officially at peace; but in the uneasy world situation the decisions to be made were no less grave, the policies to be set no less important, than in the opening phases of the last war. The shifting events called for subtlety rather than heroics, and the tenor of these speeches reflect that change. However, the strength and boldness of thought and the vigor of expression remain as Churchillian as ever.

riod covered by the volume Mr. Churchill's visit to nd the United States, when ed his brilliant address to Congress in Washington, eath of King George VI to r. Churchill paid his magibute in a broadcast to the in previous volumes, Ranurchill has contributed a oduction.

# STEMMING THE TIDE

## SPEECHES
### 1951 AND 1952

BY

WINSTON S. CHURCHILL

EDITED BY
RANDOLPH S. CHURCHILL

HOUGHTON MIFFLIN COMPANY, BOSTON
THE RIVERSIDE PRESS, CAMBRIDGE
1954

FIRST PUBLISHED
IN THE UNITED STATES, 1954

Library of Congress catalogue card number: 53-9258

*Set in 11 pt Bembo type and printed*
*in Great Britain by*
THE SHENVAL PRESS, LONDON AND HERTFORD
F.353

# INTRODUCTION

THE SPEECHES contained in this volume were delivered in the years 1951 and 1952. This period was of exceptional political interest both at home and abroad. The General Election of 25 October 1951, which ended six years of Socialist rule and led to the formation of the new Conservative administration, stands out as a milestone in the post-war years. These two years were also marked by the accession of a new Sovereign in Britain and by the restoration to power in the United States of the Republican Party after twenty years of opposition.

As in all the previous volumes of Mr Churchill's speeches, nothing has been omitted on the score of political convenience. Mr Churchill's views from week to week on domestic and foreign affairs are set down as they were delivered and the discriminating reader will note the integrity of political thought displayed in changing circumstances, whether the speeches are delivered as Leader of the Opposition or as Prime Minister. In both roles Mr Churchill shows himself a national rather than a party leader; and while these pages record powerful platform polemics and many an enjoyable rough and tumble in the House of Commons this book is presented to the public with the conviction that the dominant accent is nearly always that of statesmanship rather than of party politics.

The year 1953 sees Mr Churchill, at the age of seventy-seven, having out-lived all his political contemporaries. Rosebery, Balfour, Asquith, Lloyd George, Bonar Law, Birkenhead, the three Chamberlains, Baldwin, MacDonald, Bevin, Cripps, Mussolini, Hitler, Roosevelt, and now Stalin, have all been called to what we must hope is a better world. Mr Churchill remains, in the fullest flower of his political life and at the opening of another great chapter in a political career which, half a dozen times in the last forty years, was thought by many shrewd judges to be ended. In sixteen months the new Government has achieved a considerable recovery at home and it is not impossible that before this current chapter of his career is ended, Mr Churchill will have achieved his dearest wish, of making an effective contribution to the establishment of an honourable and enduring peace. Such hopes may be chimerical, but no one can read these pages objectively without concluding that he would regard this as the crown of his life's work.

RANDOLPH S. CHURCHILL

24 *March* 1953

# CONTENTS

vii

# CONTENTS

# CONTENTS

# CONTENTS

# IRON AND STEEL INDUSTRY

## A SPEECH TO THE HOUSE OF COMMONS
### 7 FEBRUARY 1951

---

*9 January—Modifications made to the Groundnuts plan in East Africa.*

*Sir John Balfour appointed British Ambassador to Spain; the previous Ambassador was withdrawn in December 1946.*

*17 January—Mr A. Bevan, previously Minister of Health, appointed Minister of Labour.*

*Mr Isaacs, previously Minister of Labour, appointed Minister of Pensions.*

*Mr Marquand, previously Minister of Pensions, appointed Minister of Health.*

*31 January—Death announced of Kim Chek, Commanding General of North Korean Forces.*

*Dr Vargas sworn in as President of Brazil.*

*Political Committee of United Nations by 44 votes to 7 with 9 abstentions brands Communist China as an aggressor. The British Government's representative votes in favour of the resolution.*

*2 February—France signs agreement with India ceding the territory of the free city of Chandarnagore. Arab States, except Jordan, sign a security pact.*

*5 February—First General Election on Gold Coast.*

---

[*7 February 1951*

Here this afternoon we find ourselves at a major stumbling-block to national unity and to national safety, and it is surely only right that the House of Commons should show itself capable of surveying the position with composure, firmness and a clear eye. I do not expect that we shall reach any measure of agreement—that is one of the tragedies of the times in which we live. Who is responsible for forcing this disruptive issue upon the House? [HON MEMBERS: 'You.'] It is certain that if the Government had not fixed the vesting date for steel at almost the earliest moment at which the statute permitted, there would be no debate on this subject here this afternoon.

But it may also be asked of us on these benches: 'Why don't you submit in silence instead of raising controversies at a time of national crisis?' Suppose you see a man walking towards a precipice, compelled by some deep and dark motive, and even at the risk of controversies you ask him to stop, are you in the wrong to do it? Or was he wrong in walking towards the gulf? That also is one of the issues which we must weigh tonight.

In our view on this side of the House, the fixing of the vesting date of the Iron and Steel Act for 15 February, when any date in this year would have been within the limits of the statute, was, having regard to the moment when the decision was announced and to the surrounding circumstances, a deed of partisan aggression. It was bound to cause widespread rupture of national unity by party politics at a moment when unity and safety ought to come ever more together. I do not bear the burden, through the Amendment which I have placed on the Order Paper, for raising this issue now. The Government have the power, they have the initiative, they have thrust this policy upon the House, and our reaction is natural, inevitable and salutary.

I do not consider that any question of principle or of finality presses the Government at this time to enforce steel nationalization. The issue is not one of national control of a key industry, because both sides of the House, like ownership, management and labour in the steel industry itself, could easily agree upon the proposal set forth in the Report of the Economic Committee of the Trades Union Congress to their Brighton Congress, about which I spoke to the House last time we debated the matter.

There is, I suppose, no prime, vast, complicated industry in the country, in the direction of which from a practical point of view men of goodwill and good sense, however seated in the House or inflamed with party strife or working in the industry, can more easily find agreement than on this question of steel. The Conservative Party and the Liberal Party stand—[Interruption.] Have a jeer at them. Why do not hon Members opposite jeer at them? Some hon Members opposite may find themselves in a much smaller party one of these days. The Conservative Party, and I believe, the Liberal Party stand on the proposal of the Trades Union Congress which is thoroughly acceptable, alike to the management and the ownership of the steel industry.

MR DODDS (Dartford): This time it has taken the Liberals two days or more to make up their minds as to what they should do.

MR CHURCHILL: I hope the hon Gentleman may be called in the debate, though I shall not be able to make any special representations on his behalf. As to finality. Not to enforce steel nationalization now is not to say there never will be steel nationalization. If the Government and the Socialist Party choose to come into line themselves, there would be no reason why they should not, when circumstances are less grave and menacing, resume their theoretical movement for the nationalization of iron and steel. [An HON MEMBER: 'Thank you very much.'] I am not at all disturbed by interruptions, having experienced them almost before many hon Members opposite were born. They are nearly always an advantage to the speaker. He has many advantages in reply.

As long as there is a good working arrangement there is no reason why the Socialist Party should not press their doctrinal point when the time comes, and giving way or postponing now would in no way weaken their ideological integrity. No one could hold it against them that they had abandoned their principles by adopting for the time being the trade union solution. The principle of nationalization is not, I submit, involved. But even if it were it might well await a period in our affairs when our lives and existence as one of the leading branches of human society were not in jeopardy.

I earnestly hope that I shall be granted full liberty of debate on this occasion. As to being booed—this was an experience which in nearly fifty years of the House of Commons I have never previously endured, and indeed it was an exhibition which I have never witnessed employed against anyone in all the Parliamentary storms through which I have lived. [*Interruption.*] I can quite understand the feelings of shame which actuate the hon Gentleman. Let me reassure him. I can only say, sir, that if it is any relief to hon Gentlemen opposite at any time in my remarks to indulge in such an expression of their feelings, I hope you, Mr Speaker, will give the fullest latitude and flexibility to your interpretation of the rules of order.

I propose, sir, if I am allowed, to reduce this bitter and dangerous controversy to the simple limits within which it now confronts us. First, let me say I am astonished that the Prime Minister, with his responsibilities which I have never seen so personally concentrated and overwhelming, should go out of his way to add this new harsh burden to the many burdens which he bears, and to the many troubles and tangles through which he has to find his way, and in which he claims responsibility for guiding our country. Was there ever a moment in our history when there was less need for a Prime Minister, who ought to try to act in the name of the nation—not merely half the nation—to open up all this formidable field of trouble and discord among us? No one would reproach him if he said: 'I am still resolved upon the nationalization of iron and steel but I feel that at the present time we have enough problems, and many of these problems can only be settled by the co-operation of the mass of our whole people. I have to ask others to make sacrifices. I will make one myself.' That would, I am sure, have been the right course for a man who has the controlling power of the country in his hands.

What I am seeking for and, if I can find it, what I will examine at this point are the motives or impulsions—they cannot be called compulsions—that have led the Prime Minister so obdurately to take on his overburdened shoulders this new additional task which provokes and challenges so much ill will, and which must do him and his party and our country so much harm in so many ways. We are told: 'We have a mandate from the nation for the nationalization of iron and steel now. We put it in our 1945 manifesto. We carried it with our majority through the House of Commons in that same Parliament. It could have been delayed by the House of Lords, but we have dealt with that; and now after the second election'—I hope I am stating the case fairly—'we have not only placed our Bill upon the Statute Book, but we have had majorities of never less than six in favour of its immediate enforcement. Who then should challenge our right?'

Let us look into this mandate argument. The 1945 election was not fought on steel. If what I have heard is to be believed—and I am pretty sure of its truth—steel was only added as an afterthought to the already extensive programme which was proposed by the Socialist Party. Mines, railways, some aspects of transport, and services like electricty and gas opened up a very large field for the activities of a single Parliament already burdened with all the perplexities of the aftermath of a terrible struggle and the transition from war conditions to what we all then hoped would be an era of unchallenged peace and freedom.

I do not admit as democratic constitutional doctrine that anything that is stuck into a party manifesto thereupon becomes a mandated right if the electors vote for the party who draw up the manifesto. [*Interruption.*] We are all allowed to have our opinions about constitutional matters. If that principle is accepted, why not shove a dozen more items in? One can always leave them out if there is not time, or circumstances change. But is it not for our convenience to have a lot to play with, and surely it costs nothing to a party seeking a change or a new deal? Why not add the word 'etc.'? I ask the Lord President and the Chief Whip, why not add the word 'etc.' in the list of planks in the party platform? We could then be told: 'Do you not see these letters "etc." written at that point in our party manifesto? Does that not give us the right and impose upon us the obligation to do anything we please?'

At the last election steel played no prominent part in the manifestos and propaganda of the Socialist Party. The Conservative and Liberal Parties, on the other hand, declared their vehement opposition to it.

[*Interruption.*] I do not want to interrupt the right hon Gentleman the Minister of Labour.

THE MINISTER OF LABOUR [MR ANEURIN BEVAN]: The right hon Gentleman babbles quite a lot.

MR CHURCHILL: The repeal of the Act was thus one of the main issues in the domestic sphere of the Opposition parties together, and they had a majority—I am sorry to rub this in—of one-and-three-quarter million voters over those who voted, consciously or unconsciously, for the nationalization of steel.

But we are told: 'The numerical vote of the people at a General Election is not a relevant fact. Who cares for the numerical vote?' The test, we are told, is: What is the vote of the House of Commons in the new Parliament resulting from the polls? Perhaps hon Members opposite will please cheer. They had better learn the doctrine, or they may fall into the errors of diversionism or even distortionism. On this matter of the test in the House, the Government majority has fallen to as low as six. How vain to call this a mandate which leaves the Government of the day no choice but to go ahead with this unwise and untimely doctrinal Measure. If the Lord President of the Council had not had the happy thought to abolish university representation in breach of the agreement to which he was a party, at the Speaker's Conference in 1944, even this paltry majority would have been lacking. So where is the mandate?

THE PRIME MINISTER [MR ATTLEE]: Were the university seats all pocket boroughs of the Conservative Party then?

MR CHURCHILL: They certainly were not, but it was because the right hon Gentleman and his hon Friends thought they were that they abolished them. We all recall the remarks of the Secretary of State for Scotland on the subject at that time.

So I say, where is the mandate?—not in the 1945 programme, not in the vote of the people in 1950, nor in the House of Commons votes here in our present distressed assembly. It certainly does not, I think, await the Socialist Party when they are forced, as they will soon be, to appeal to the electorate. There is no mandate which is not an abuse of the term, and no obligation whatever on the Prime Minister and the Government to proceed with what I believe in their hearts they know to be an unwise and unfortunate Measure. Events have cast upon the Government fearful responsibilities which they seem to have willingly accepted. No one who has the welfare and even the safety of the country at heart would do other than respect them if they laid aside every impediment and strove only for national survival against perils which no man can measure, and which grow ever nearer and ever more grave.

I cannot recollect any more strange jumble than that into which Parliament has been plunged by the bringing forward now of the Iron and Steel Act. Ninety-two firms have been chosen out of the whole iron and steel industry. They represent about half the labour employed, but they dovetail, penetrate and permeate all the rest in such a manner as to affect and disturb the whole. No principle has governed the selection of those firms who should be in or out. When the Minister of Supply was asked in February 1949 how he arrived at the split-up of the industry, he said:

'We have found this the most convenient and practical method of achieving our purpose. . . . Our purpose is to get the preponderant parts of the basic sections of the industry with a substantial and proportionate and appropriate part of the finishing processes.'

But that is not a principle. It is the negation of a principle. It is merely the expression of a personal purpose and an individual point of view. Anyone can say, 'This is appropriate', or 'This is proportionate', and his opinion will no doubt in certain cases deserve consideration. But here we have the mass of this vast and infinitely complex business, upon which not only our economic life, but possibly even our physical existence, depends, and it is cut in twain in a rough-and-ready way on no principle but the arbitrary personal judgment of a Minister, and for no purpose but party politics at a moment of grave danger.

It is commonplace to say that the steel industry has served, and is serving, us well. It is expanding production, especially in exports; its prices are cut lower than in almost any other country; it has nearly half a century of peaceful progress and goodwill between the management and the wage earner—a great measure of common comprehension exists among them today; it has a well defined and established relationship with the State, including the fixing of prices and the direction and emphasis of effort. All this we have achieved here in the British steel industry. It should be taken as a model. Why should it be turned topsy-turvy? Why this industry, of all others, and now, at this time, of all others? These are surely questions which have often been asked and they embody one great question which we must try to answer here tonight.

I talk of the disruption of the iron and steel industry advisedly. [An HON MEMBER: 'Where?'] I shall explain that. Custom and experience have set clear boundaries to the industry. These were perhaps most sharply defined in the days of the wartime Iron and Steel Control, and this experience has particular relevance to defence. That control defined the iron and steel industry as stretching from iron ore production up to an immense variety of steel products, which I shall not try to enumerate. This same area of the industry came under the control or the post-war Iron and Steel Board; and over it the Ministry of Supply at present has long exercised extensive powers of control. The powers of control have been accepted willingly.

On the industry's side, the firms have similarly been organized for the provision of common services such as imports, the consideration of development plans, arrangements to meet the requirements of consuming industries, statistics, etc. The Iron and Steel Federation covers the whole range of steel processes. The Joint Iron and Steel Council deals with common services in relation to the foundry pig iron and iron foundry industry. These organizations have been developed for many of the very purposes specified in the Iron and Steel Act and have enabled the Ministry of Supply to carry out, in relation to the whole of the industry, the responsibilities which the Act now seeks to throw upon the new State Corporation controlling only a section of the industry. Is that not a very rough thing to do?

The second main feature of the Act is that it gives the Minister powers to give directions to the Corporation and particularly mentions the duty of agreeing with him programmes of development, training and research. In all these fields of activity the industry is at present working on programmes agreed with, or satisfactory to, the Ministry of Supply. These programmes are in full course of achievement and, unlike any programme that can be drawn up by the new Corporation, they relate to the whole output of the industry and not merely to the arbitrarily selected sections.

The third subject on which programmes under the Act have to be agreed with Ministers is research. Here again, the industry is already well in the van. It has the largest industrial research organization of any industry in the country. I have seen no criticism made by any Government spokesman that there is something lacking and that it is urgently necessary to proceed with some new type of organization for the purposes of research. But here again this organization relates to the whole production of all the firms in the country, and the working out and establishment of some separate research arrangement for the ninety-two scheduled companies can only cause confusion and certainly cannot be hastened by making February 15 the vesting day.

There is one recent proof of the growing efficiency of the British steel industry in its relation to coal. Every day we are exhorted to save coal and at the same time to increase production. It seems almost incredible that the steel industry should have been able to do both. In the last two years—1949 and 1950—it has increased its production by more than $1\frac{1}{2}$ million tons, from about $14\frac{1}{2}$ million tons to over $16\frac{1}{4}$

million tons, but—and note this—without making any increased demand upon our nationalized coal supplies. Could we have a greater service to the Government? Could there be a truer measure of economic efficiency, progress and refinement? Every supporter of coal nationalization on the benches opposite should be grateful to the steel industry and to the Executive of the Steel Federation for the example they have set.

Prices rise around us daily in every quarter, but when the railway freights went up last summer and many firms and all the nationalized industries responded nimbly, the British steel industry swallowed the dose, and have apparently digested it. They made no increase. They took it in their stride. This increased production by private enterprise without drawing more upon nationalized coal, this maintenance of an effective and profitable selling price without any increase to the public at home or any loss of competitive power abroad, ought surely to be regarded as a friendly and beneficent exploit by every Member who voted for coal and railway nationalization.

But what is their reward? The industry is to be plunged into deepening confusion at a moment when harmony, smooth working and well-known contacts and organization are more than ever vital. Sir, it is a crazy deed. We claim on this side that a cruel discord has been needlessly and wantonly thrust into our anxious and critical affairs. We affirm also that if it is carried out and enforced, this Act will be a deep and major injury to the whole process of rearmament. The iron and steel industry is the core of national rearmament. There are many other things that matter, some perhaps even more, but as a broad, fundamental element in the whole process of national rearmament, a smooth-running, efficient steel industry, under experienced and capable management, is not only paramount, but indispensible.

I have long sought for the true explanation of the strange decision of a Cabinet containing several experienced men to choose so early a vesting date for steel at the very moment when they were appealing for the help and co-operation of all parties in the national rearmament and defence. The conjuncture seemed perverse and unnatural in the extreme. I see no alterative but that this is a manoeuvre for party purposes of a complex but, none the less, obvious character. The Socialist left wing have to suffer much nowadays. They have to vote £4,700 million of additional expenditure for rearmament; they have to support voting with the Americans in branding China as an aggressor; they have to vote for the rearmament, within limits, of Germany to defend herself and to take part in general European defence; they have to call up nearly 250,000 men from the Class Z Reserve—although they compromise by making it for only fifteen days, which if it does no good, cannot do much harm; they have had, through the policy of the Foreign Office, to support Egypt against Palestine with weapons sorely needed here at home.

They have had to do a lot of things they do not like, and which are contrary to their native promptings. Their leaders felt they could be held together only by the bringing forward of this specific cause of party antagonism which would appeal to the strong, inherent, factional emotions which range below the Gangway. I repeat what I said the other day, that this unpatriotic step is being taken by the Prime Minister to placate this unhappy tail. [HON MEMBERS: 'Nonsense.'] Hon Members opposite will not get out of it all by laughing.

What defence does the right hon Gentleman suppose that this will give him at the bar of history, or even before his fellow countrymen in the near future, if the British and United Nations' sky continues to darken? I have had my share of responsibilities in public life. While my strength remains I would not shrink from bearing them again, but it is no extravagance of rhetorical expression if I say that I would rather be banished from public life for ever than be responsible for the action which the Prime Minister is taking in asking the House to vote for the February 15 vesting date tonight. I earnestly trust that Parliament will restrain him. So tremendous a situation, such awful hazards, such an unworthy contribution—I can hardly believe that the Attlee who worked at my side for more than five years of a life and death struggle is willing to have his reputation injured in this way.

I feel emboldened to hope that, perhaps, the worst will not happen. Perhaps we can hear more from the Minister of Supply. Is it, I ask him, a fact that, instead of this inadequate and almost absurd Corporation taking over the direct control of sections of the steel industry in the near future, so far as rearmament is concerned, the existing body, that has served us so well, which comprises not only the ninety-two firms to be nationalized, but, at least, 400 others, may be allowed to carry on its vital service to the whole industry and to the nation? I know he is going to follow me, and I hope that he will deal with this matter. Will they be allowed to carry on, not only for a few transitional months, but for an indefinite period? How else can the Minister of Supply work out the intricate and comprehensive plans for rearmament—now overdue, the prime responsibility for which falls upon him and upon his Department?

So far as it goes and so long as it lasts any movement in this direction would represent a concession not only to our views, wishes and arguments, but, even more, to the brutal and urgent necessities of defence

9

with which the Government are confronted, and which, whatever they say, they will have to obey. If there is any foundation for what I have said, I hope that the Minister will tell us. If not, he should, surely, contradict me when he speaks, for if it be true that this indefinite continuance of control of the Iron and Steel Federation is to be maintained indefinitely—if it be true—it cuts the ground from under his own feet, and all the more is our action vindicated; and our intention to vote against the vesting of steel will be strengthened and not weakened by the course which may be forced upon the Government through physical facts. However, we shall, perhaps, hear more about this later.

But, I ask, what is the point of persisting in the transfer of ownership at this moment? It can only be, as I have said, a party point of the narrowest character. To give the nation no more control than it has already over the whole industry, we have merely to pay out about £300 million of stock, which must be manufactured by the Chancellor of the Exchequer, to persons who are now investing their money in a business in which they have confidence and which has served us all so well.

Let us, therefore, look closer into the question of the acceleration of the act of vesting now to be imposed upon us. What is all this hurry for? Surely it would be wise and reasonable, even now, to postpone the vesting, at least within the latitude allowed within the Act? The Government always led us to believe that there would be a period of approximately nine months between the appointment of the Corporation and the vesting date. I have all the necessary quotations here from speeches by Lord Hall in another place and by the Minister of Supply at that Box. So far, the Corporation has been in existence for only four months.

Another five months could easily have been allowed—nine was the figure always mentioned—and much might have happened in that time to settle the outstanding difficulties. If in 1949 it was thought that vesting should not take place until nine months after the appointment of the Corporation it is surely unreasonable, in the infinitely more complex and disturbing conditions of today, to attempt to vest within four months. The Minister of Supply dwelt upon the feature of the Act that gives him latitude; he said that there may be industrial or political developments which may make it harmful for the iron and steel industries to transfer on that date, in which case the Minister of Supply has power to postpone the date of general transfer. What foresight! And what a waste of foresight! The Prime Minister and his Government have resolved to enforce the vesting date and to disdain at the earliest moment the latitude which their own Act allowed them.

This decision has brought in its train a host of troubles which can only be ended by a General Election, for which we shall continue to strive without a day or night's cessation. It has brought many stresses and losses upon us which are unfair. Let me give an instance or two. Out of the ninety-two firms that are to be nationalized over half are not publicly quoted securities and the rest are publicly quoted. The publicly quoted companies are to be bought out at their Stock Exchange value at the dates prescribed. Some of them have had very hard treatment. Those who have suffered most have often been those who had taken most thought for the future and been very sparing in the distribution of dividends, in response to appeals made from the Government benches. This has told against them. But the private companies, over half the ninety-two, were accorded the right to appeal to arbitration—a similar right being exercised, of course, by the Minister.

We on this side have always maintained that the Stock Exchange value for publicly quoted securities is not a fair basis of compensation. At the same time, those securities which are not public quoted and have had to be assessed by agreement between the firms and the Minister of Supply, are being much more equitably dealt with than the publicly quoted securities. Under the terms of the Act, both classes of security are supposed to be valued on the same basis, but how does it all work out? For example, in the case of the twenty-four larger public concerns whose shares are publicly quoted, the compensation represents 75 per cent of the book value of the net assets.

In the case of the nine private companies for which agreements have already been made by the Minister of Supply——

MR JOHN HYND (Sheffield, Attercliffe): All your pals are asleep behind you. [*Laughter.*]

MR CHURCHILL: Hon Gentlemen opposite only degrade themselves by behaving in that fashion. It only degrades the reputation of the Socialist Party by showing that they do not know how to listen to a careful argument. It is not the good opinion of hon Gentlemen opposite that I seek to gain, but this place is meant to be a place of serious and careful argument. On a great matter of this kind the Socialist Party would not be so restless and distressed if their guilty consciences were not troubling them so. I am sorry to have to take up more time than I meant, but I shall have to repeat myself. [HON MEMBERS: 'Get on with it.'] I shall not hurry if I am interrupted in that fashion.

In the case of the twenty-four publicly quoted concerns the compensation represents 75 per cent of the book value of the net assets. In the case of the nine private companies for which agreements have already been made by the Minister of Supply the compensation represents 162 per cent of the book value of the net assets.

Let me test this also in relation to profits for the latest year. In the case of the publicly quoted companies referred to, £20 per annum of profit is to be compensated by £100 of Government stock, whereas in the case of the non-quoted companies referred to £20 per annum of profit is to be compensated by almost £200 of Government stock. I am bound to assume that the Government hold that the agreements of the Minister of Supply have been reached on the basis of fair value, otherwise the Minister would have, as he has a right to do, sent them to arbitration. But on this assumption the unfair treatment of the publicly quoted companies, with their thousands of small shareholders —quite small people—actuated by 'public greed', to use the foul term which the Minister of Labour has recently contributed to our discussions, is now fully exposed by the Minister himself. I say, without hesitation, that the public companies and their shareholders have been far more severely treated than the private companies.

What is this new dispensation under which we have now to live, and into which the steel trade is to be plunged? The modern world, with all its varieties, has, I think, produced a no more curious figure than that of the millionaire Socialist, or Socialist millionaire. Here is a type, very rare, but when it appears, very potent. We have a type of mentality in the Socialist millionaire which reconciles the most violent denunciation of the capitalist exploitation of the proletariat with the fullest enjoyment of its fruits. There are a few in every country. Herr Krupp, who was and may be again, a millionaire, and was certainly a Nazi Socialist, is a case which springs to the mind. There are some in France, and perhaps some in Italy.

Mr Hardie, the master of the Government Corporation—[*Interruption.*] Hon Gentlemen opposite cannot bear to hear argument. Believe me, people read about all this, and it only does the party opposite harm. Not that I regret it. I only regret it from the point of view of the life of the House of Commons between the two great parties. We know the great responsibility the party opposite has to bear and the great support they have in many quarters.

Mr Hardie, the master of the Government Corporation set up to manage the ninety-two firms now to be nationalized, and inevitably to dominate and derange all the rest of this immense and intricate industry, is certainly one of these rare birds, the millionaire Socialist. We have here a successful business man, a past master of monopoly, who has made an immense fortune by 'private greed', and who without in any way relinquishing it has become a convinced Socialist adherent. His arrogant behaviour as a servant and tool of the Government will certainly be the subject of continuous attention, unless all is swept out of our thoughts either by graver catastrophies, or by new Government decisions, or by a happy release from the needless hardships that are forced upon us.

The head of the Steel Corporation and the Minister of Supply who is to follow me—and I hope I am not exaggerating his fortune—are working together. But here in Britain we have the unique spectacle of two Socialist millionaires, and it really is a record—a brace of these rare birds on the same job. I hope that the wage-earning masses will be able to look into this as the months pass by, for it really deserves their careful thought. It is always something to hold a world record. We have lost a good many of them in late years, but we have at least created and captured this one—a brace of the same kind, on the same job, one in office and one out. No wonder the representatives of the toiling millions, as hon Members opposite like in their dreams to call themselves, the planners of the Socialist welfare state—'fair shares for all'—no wonder they do not want an election in the near future. No wonder the Prime Minister agitates himself about a single vote, and threatens to bring home a Minister from the other end of the world, regardless of what he deems to be in the public interest. At all costs keep away from the people: that is their maxim today. When I survey the story in all its scope and all its viciousness, I cannot at all wonder that it is the prevailing thought of Ministers and followers alike in the party opposite.

The Lord President of the Council referred the other day to the need to end uncertainty about the steel industry. How can the act of vesting, which the House is asked to approve tonight, diminish uncertainty when the political parties opposed to nationalization had a large majority vote at the last election, and seem almost certain to have a much larger one at the next? I am forced to repeat again that should the Conservative Party be successful in a General Election—which cannot be long delayed however tightly and even passionately Ministers may cling to their offices—we shall at once repeal the Steel Act, and adopt the compromise solutions which the Trades Union Congress have themselves set before us. The fate of the steel industry must in any case turn on the vote of the nation and the uncertainty will continue till that vote has been recorded.

We have rarely seen or felt such a stroke of gratuitous, improvident spite against the whole, long-suffering, faithful community, which bears us all up upon its bruised and lacerated shoulders, than this vesting date of steel nationalization a week from tomorrow, and the fact that this should be driven through now, in the hour of danger, is an example of the cynical and spiteful mood in which our affairs are conducted, and which is indeed worthy of the formal censure of the House.

# DEFENCE (GOVERNMENT POLICY)

A SPEECH TO THE HOUSE OF COMMONS
15 FEBRUARY 1951

---

*8 February—It is reported that Admiral Fechteler is to be appointed Supreme Naval Commander North Atlantic*

---

[*15 February* 1951

Order read for resuming Adjourned Debate on Question [14 *February* 1951]:

'That this House approves the policy of His Majesty's Government relating to Defence contained in Command Paper No. 8146.'— [*Mr Shinwell*.]

Question again proposed.

MR CHURCHILL (Woodford): I beg to move to leave out from 'House', to the end of the Question, and to add instead thereof:

'while supporting all measures conceived in the real interest of national security, has no confidence in the ability of His Majesty's present Ministers to carry out an effective and consistent Defence policy in concert with their allies, having regard to their record of vacillation and delay'.

I do not intend this afternoon to make a detailed examination of the Defence position, and I shall not on this occasion ask for a Secret Session. We feel that the issue between us requires to be set before the nation on broad and general lines, to which I shall endeavour to adhere. The Motion before the House asks us to 'approve' the White Paper which represents the latest version of the Government's Defence scheme. I very much regret to say that I and those for whom I speak feel it impossible, after the best examination we could give to these proposals, to record an unqualified vote approving the military methods and proposals of the present Government in these affairs. When, at the beginning of the Parliament—on March 16 last year—a similar request was made to us to approve a White Paper on Defence, I asked the Prime Minister to substitute for the word 'approves' the words 'takes note of'. Such a step, I said, on our part, as voting afterwards proved, might be regarded hereafter as to some extent committing us to sharing, albeit indirectly, in the Government's responsibility. The Prime Minister agreed to the substitution of the words 'takes note of' for 'approves', and there was no need for a Division.

14

We considered very carefully whether this procedure could be repeated today, or whether, if the Prime Minister refused the substitution of 'takes note of' for the word 'approves', we should divide on that issue. We rejected this course for two reasons. We feel it necessary, firstly, to reaffirm in positive terms our resolve to support 'all measures conceived in the real interest of national security', and secondly to declare our want of confidence in the ability of His Majesty's present Ministers to carry out an effective Defence policy, especially under the unfortunate conditions now prevailing in our country. On this, we shall take the opinion of the House tonight.

It is very likely, and I fully recognize it, that the terms of our Amendment will have the effect of inducing the pacifists and other dissentients on the benches opposite to express their approval of the measures which the Government now propose. That may do them some good; it can certainly do the country no harm. We therefore prefer the method of direct challenge to what might have been represented as a Parliamentary manoeuvre. Should our Amendment be defeated, we should have placed our views on record, and we should not oppose the vote on the main Question when put in due course from the Chair. [*Interruption.*] It is just as well that hon Members should hear what course of action is intended to be taken by a party almost as numerous as their own, for the convenience of the House, and especially for hon Members who have so little experience of it.

Since March last—I was referring to what we did on March 16— much has happened abroad, and the Government have made large changes of policy. The White Paper of March, of which we took note, has been superseded by successive editions of the Government's defence plans. The extensive rearmament programme now before us is the third version we have had. The first was when we parted at the end of July, when fighting in Korea was already in full swing. On this occasion, the Minister of Defence [Mr Shinwell] made very alarming disclosures to the House about the overwhelming Russian strength in Europe, and also confirmed to a large extent the detailed assertions which I had made upon the Soviet armaments on land, on sea and in the air. The Minister of Defence, who, no doubt, is doing his best according to his lights, then proposed an interim expenditure of £100 million, and we separated with a Division for the Summer Recess.

A few days later, and without any new facts being presented, or indeed existing, a far larger set of proposals was adumbrated. That is not a word I like, but it seems to me appropriate to the Government action at this moment, and, on the whole, the best and most accurate word to adopt. A far larger set of proposals was adumbrated, but the

Government refused to call Parliament together until the beginning of September, and an uneasy interlude followed. When we met in September, the new plan which they put before us was for the expenditure of £3,600 million spread over three years, and for raising the term of National Service to two years.

The Prime Minister appealed to us on that occasion for national unity on defence, and I replied, on behalf of the Conservative Party:
'We shall, on this side, of course, support the Motion. . . . We shall vote for it, and we shall help to resist any Amendment . . . to it. We shall also support the Bill to extend . . . military service which is to be introduced. Several points may well arise upon that Bill for discussion in Committee, but I should hope that it can be passed through this House . . . in a single day.'
This was in fact done, and its effect must have been beneficial to our friends and Allies all over the world.

The Prime Minister acknowledged this, I should remark in passing, by announcing the very next day, or almost the very next day, that the vesting date of steel nationalization was fixed for 15 February. I do not suggest that we should be governed in our actions on Defence by a single episode of that character. It was, none the less, a milestone in the history of this Parliament. [*Interruption.*] I am glad that hon Members are agreed. Nothing could have been done to make national unity more difficult, and, combined with the uncertainty about the date of the impending General Election, on which the Prime Minister has given no indication of his wishes, it creates most unhappy and most unsuitable conditions in our country for the solution of our national problems, alike of Defence or of Foreign Policy. The responsibility for this, in my opinion, rests with the Prime Minister in a degree unusually direct and personal.

Since then, the Government have moved from the considered demand for the £3,600 million to be spread over three years, which was put before us in September, and they give us this new White Paper on Defence, which we are now asked to approve. This makes a new estimate of £4,700 million, equally spread over three years, and also provides for the fifteen days' call-up and several other measures. Evidences and examples of the ineptitude and incompetence of the Government are brought almost daily glaringly before us. We are convinced that the mismanagement exhibited in civil and domestic affairs extends also to the military field, and that that is the growing opinion of the nation. Therefore, we feel it impossible to do as we did in September, and are bound to place on record an Amendment which sets forward the exact position which we occupy.

MR SYDNEY SILVERMAN (Nelson and Colne): Although you were in favour in September?

MR CHURCHILL: Yes, but things have happened since September, and I am in principle in favour now of the whole of these demands, subject to their correct examination. I think that is perfectly reasonable. But they are entirely new demands; they are a new version, an after-thought, and a reconsideration of the facts which were long before Parliament and the public, and which simply arise out of requests which I will mention before I sit down.

Let me now illustrate by a few major examples the mismanagement of our Defence Forces, which is the gravamen of our charge. For this purpose I must go back, to some extent, into the past.

MR SHURMER (Birmingham, Sparkbrook): Do not go too far back.

MR CHURCHILL: If I went too far, I should come to that period of complete victory over all our enemies which was at that time thought to be a subject of general rejoicing. But I am not going back so far as that. After the end of the war, on 22 October 1945, I urged the Government to speed up their demobilization plans, which the National Government had made, so that as early as possible in 1946 the Forces should be reduced to definite ceilings pending the work of settling peacetime requirements. I gave the following figures: Army, 1,000,000; Navy, 150,000; Royal Air Force, 400,000—Total, 1,550,000.

If these suggestions had been accepted, two or three million men might have been spared the ordeal of standing about needlessly under arms at a time when they were not wanted, when no new dangers appeared upon us and when at least £1,000 million might have been saved from the expense to which we were put, quite apart from the loss in delaying our getting into our stride on domestic production. The £1,000 million could have been used to take proper care of the immense mass of those serviceable weapons which have a long life and take a long time to make. Instead of this, much that would be of high value today was dispersed, destroyed, sold or given away.

I do not agree with the Minister of Defence in his view which he expressed a little while ago, that troops should only be sent into action with the latest weapons. That is no doubt the ideal and what we would all like, but it has never happened in any war that has ever taken place.

THE MINISTER OF DEFENCE [MR SHINWELL] rose——

MR CHURCHILL: I am not arguing with the right hon Gentleman. [HON MEMBERS: 'Give way.'] I have all the afternoon before me in which to unfold the arguments I wish to make and, consequently, I am not at all restive under interruptions. Any serviceable weapon is better than no weapon at all.

MR SHINWELL: It may be a small point, but the right hon Gentleman was accusing me of saying something which I have never said at any time. I did not say we should not send men into battle unless they were equipped with the most modern weapons; I said we ought to ensure that when men are sent into battle they are well equipped.

MR CHURCHILL: They would have been a great deal better equipped if a wiser process had been followed. The squandering and destruction of what might have been carefully put away in care and maintenance and thus preserved for use should other trouble come, was a lack of foresight. [*Interruption.*] I never said anything about the Lord President of the Council, although I have no doubt that he had as much to do with it as anybody else, and much more than his right hon Friend the Minister of Defence on his right flank. [HON MEMBERS: 'Get on with it.'] I shall not attempt to be hurried at all; I shall take my time in dealing with every interruption, because I feel I have a perfectly legitimate right to unfold this case in my own way.

In the United States, in spite of many temptations, less improvidence was shown, especially in respect to warships. I may remind the House again that the figure for the Services which I mentioned of 1,550,000 is double that to which the Forces were later reduced. And even now, according to the Defence Minister's speech of yesterday, it will not be until 1952 that an overall figure of 900,000 can be reached. I say this because this has been made an accusation against me. I think it was the Under-Secretary of State for Foreign Affairs who made that attack the other day. I sent him some figures correcting it, which he had not the courtesy to acknowledge. I agree that the mistakes made at the beginning put us on the wrong line, but no British Government in time of peace has ever had the powers that Socialist Ministers have wielded, or the resources they have consumed.

In 1946, they took the step, with our full support, of introducing National Service in peacetime. First, eighteen months was the term, then twelve months, and then eighteen months again, according to the changing winds. Now it is two years. Before the late General Election, I said to the House that the principle which might help us in economizing our money and our manpower, and in getting better value from the sacrifices demanded, would be to take fewer men and to hold them longer. We all know how that was used at the election. Nevertheless, we have supported the Government in their further steps. Undoubtedly, the two years' service was far more suited to our dangers and to our special problems than anything else they proposed before. If it had been introduced in 1947 or 1948, when the skies began to darken—and we should certainly have supported the Government—

how much better off we should be in effective military formations today!

One has the feeling that if the position has been studied by the Minister of Defence and other Ministers responsible—and they have changed often, not always for the better—very good solutions might have been reached. But the Government deal in words, in declarations, in projects and in schemes which seem to indicate impressive action. Alas, it is mainly on paper—committee to committee, declaration to declaration, one edition after another of their proposals for National Defence. But with the control they have demanded over our manpower, and with the vast sums of money voted so constantly by the House, it ought to have been possible to produce a substantial and efficient army. I do not say an adequate army, but a substantial and efficient army. But what has happened? With Defence Estimates of nearly £1,000 million a year for five or six years, and with their unprecedented control of manpower, they have produced so few effective tactical units that when the Korean trouble broke out and it was necessary for us to send a token force—I have never advocated sending more than a token force—to Korea under the authority of the United Nations, it took over three months to produce even a brigade group of good quality. But talk and waste and muddle have robbed the nation of the results of resources which, whether adequate or not, Parliament at their request conferred upon the Government on a very large scale.

Another subject of grave complaint is the inability of the Government to produce any atomic bombs of our own in the five-and-a-half years which have passed since the war. When we remember how far we were ahead, and how we were able to deal on equal terms with the United States, it is indeed depressing to feel that we have been outstripped by the Soviets in this field. I take the opportunity of repeating now my request that the document I signed with President Roosevelt in the war should be made public at an early date. We must not forget that by creating the American atomic base in East Anglia we have made ourselves the target, and perhaps the bull's-eye of a Soviet attack. On March 28, last year, I said in Parliament:

'If, for instance, the United States had a 'stockpile' of 1,000 atomic bombs—I take the figure as an illustration merely; I have no knowledge of any sort of kind of what they have—and Russia had fifty, and we got those fifty, fearful experiences, far beyond anything we have ever endured, would be our lot.'

I say the total failure of the Government to hold its own and to keep up development——

THE PRIME MINISTER [MR ATTLEE]: The right hon Gentleman

really ought not to mislead the country on a matter like this. He knows perfectly well it was by his agreement, and the agreement of the Government of which I was a Member, that the development of the atomic bomb and the making and everything took place across the other side of the Atlantic, and it is utterly untrue to suggest there has been a failure to develop it here. It is entirely wrong of him.

MR CHURCHILL: At the end of the war we resumed full freedom to make the atomic bomb ourselves. The only reason we did not make it during the war was that we were under air bombardment. We had not got a safe place here and the United States therefore had the facility and the credit of making it. At the end of the war we were perfectly free to resume manufacture. Is not that correct?

THE PRIME MINISTER: Certainly, I have answered 'Yes'. I am sorry if the right hon Gentleman cannot hear me. I said 'Yes'.

MR CHURCHILL: Then what is the complaint about what I have said, that in the five-and-a-half years no success has rewarded our efforts in making it?

THE PRIME MINISTER: The right hon Gentleman is quite wrong. There has been successful development. He is not producing any evidence whatever to show that, given the resources and possibilities over here as compared with the resources they have in the United States of America, we could have done more than we have done now.

MR CHURCHILL: What is the meaning of that interruption? I say we have not succeeded in making the atomic bomb completely in this country in the five-and-a-half years since the war. Does anybody challenge that? [*Interruption.*] All right, find something to cheer at if you can.

MR SHINWELL: Is not the right hon Gentleman satisfying the enemy? [HON MEMBERS: 'Sit down.'] I am asking a question. When the right hon Gentleman makes the declaration that we have done nothing in the production of an atomic bomb in five-and-a-half years— [HON MEMBERS: 'No, he did not.']—that is what he implied—[HON MEMBERS: 'No.']—is he not giving satisfaction to the enemy in making that declaration?

MR CHURCHILL: If I were wrong, the Government would readily correct me. If I am right it is more important for people to know the facts than it is for the Russians, who are constantly doing their utmost. And after all, we have of course the aid of the United States to look to in the matter, which I quite agree is incomparably greater than anything we could have done.

I said when we met last year:

'The decision to form a front in Europe against a possible further invasion by Soviet Russia and its satellite States was at once grave for us and also imperative. There was a school of thought in the United States which held that Western Europe was indefensible and that the only lines where a Soviet-satellite advance could be held were the Channel and the Pyrenees. I am very glad that this view has been decisively rejected by the United States, by ourselves and by all the Powers concerned in the Brussels Treaty and the Atlantic Pact. I find it necessary to say however, speaking personally, giving my own opinion, that this long front cannot be successfully defended without the active aid of Western Germany.'

The Prime Minister immediately denounced this view as irresponsible, but he has now adopted it—'in principle', I must say. When the Foreign Secretary went to America in September last, he said to the reporters who asked him on landing whether German troops should not be integrated into the Atlantic Pact Force:

'I do not think that is the way to bring Germany back into the comity of nations.'

A few days later he was converted by the American arguments and it became the official policy of the Socialist Government.

That was the policy reiterated by the Prime Minister last Monday. With many of his arguments we on this side of the House will agree. But he was also anxious to deprive them of as much meaning and reality as possible by stressing various conditions. Let me give two of them:

'Obviously, the rearmament of the countries of the Atlantic Treaty must precede that of Germany. Second, I think the building up of forces in the democratic State whould precede the creation of German forces.'

These conditions if strictly enforced would undoubtedly involve a delay of two or three years. The realization of this had no doubt eased the Prime Minister's difficulties with his own party. It was no doubt designed to placate his tail. It is one of those compromises which do not arise from any measurement of the realities or practical facts. There is great danger in trying to have things both ways. It almost always results in falling between two stools. Safety is not to be found in searching for the line of least resistance.

So much for this question of the German Army. Then there is the European Army. All these months, eight of which are since the fighting began in Korea, have been marked by the Government doing what they can, behind the scenes, to discourage the French from their plan of a European Army. On 12 September, in our debate on the £3,600 million plan—it was as late as that—I said:

'The Prime Minister has spoken . . . scornfully about a European Army . . . and about the Germans being included in our Western defence system. Where does he stand about these matters now? . . . Is he still opposed to Germans being armed as a part of the Western defence forces or as part of an armed German police force; or does he still think the only Germans to be armed are the Communist Germans, whom the Soviets have formed into a powerful Army in the Russian zone?'

I said that six months ago. I am glad to see that in some respects the normal process of belated conversion to the obvious is going forward.

There is no doubt that a European Army will be formed as a part of the Atlantic Army, and I trust that a German contingent will take its place in the European Army on honourable terms. The conference that starts today in Paris is of great importance and all efforts to build up a defensive front against Russian Communist aggression in Europe will benefit from it, and I set great hopes upon it. It is a direct issue between the two sides of the House this afternoon, though not a major issue, that although our vital interests are intermingled with those of our continental allies, Britain should be represented at this conference only by an observer. I say to the Prime Minister—beware how you continue this half-hearted policy.

I place my hopes in General Eisenhower's efforts, and I was very glad to see the courageous support which he and Mr Truman have received from Mr Dewey, the Republican candidate at the last Presidential election. But it might well be that if the United States were convinced that no effective European Army including a German contingent could be formed within the Atlantic Pact Army, the school of thought which regards the defence of Western Europe as impossible and looks to the Channel and the Pyrenees as the only lines where a stand can be made, might again come into favour, and they would certainly be supported by the Hoover-Taft body of opinion in the United States.

If that were so, we should certainly have the vacuum which the Prime Minister condemned on Monday. Nothing is easier than to get this vacuum. We have only to break down the hopes of making an effective front in Europe to produce it. In that case all the civilization of Western Europe and the democratic way of life would have to come to terms with the Soviets, and we should see a process of Communist infiltration and control begun which would end, as the Prime Minister seemed to argue—and I agree with him—in Western Europe suffering the same fate as Czechoslovakia. If the Soviet menace, which is now on the Elbe, were to advance, possibly without fighting, possibly under some kind of agreement, to the Channel or even to the Rhine, the danger to this island would be very great. It might not be possible for the Russian armies to cross the Channel, but their air power might enable the descent of paratroops to be made in numbers hitherto unprecedented and, I think, hitherto not taken into practical calculation. We should be under continued bombardment from rockets and other pilotless missiles, and the growing stock of Russian atomic bombs might well render the ports by which we live and breathe unusable.

There is also the Russian U-boat danger which is so much greater, both in numbers and in the improved types which science has created, than was the German at the beginning of the late war. I dealt with this matter at some length when I spoke in the House at the end of July. I shall not attempt to repeat that argument today but, since the Minister of Defence was so haughty when the subject was mentioned yesterday by my right hon Friend the Member for Bromley [Mr H. Macmillan].

I will quote what I said on 27 July last:

'Reliable naval reference books estimate the present Russian U-boat fleet at 360, divided no doubt, between the Pacific and the West, of which between 100 and 200 are ocean-going and capable of high speeds. These seem to me very large figures, and I am not at all accepting them as final figures, but what is the truth about them? I do not see why the Minister of Defence should not give us his best estimate, considering the information which has been given about other portions of the Russian forces.'

And considering that, if his information happened to be correct, it would be nothing new to the Russians to learn the facts about their own forces, I could not understand why he could not give some figure nor see any reason at all why he should not give an estimate of the number of U-boats available in just the same way as he gave the number of divisions, the number of tanks and the number of aircraft.

Even if only a half or a third of these figures were available, we should be confronted with a danger of the first magnitude on the seas. Secrecy is used as a shield to cover the Government shortcomings, but I have no doubt that the main facts of our naval construction are well-known to the general staffs of Europe and certainly to the Russians who have many ways of obtaining information about the work going on in our shipyards and dockyards. We were told by the Parliamentary Secretary to the Admiralty on 25 October that this year's conversion programme of fleet destroyers to anti-submarine frigates had been doubled. That statement was very much on the same lines as those followed in so much of his speech by the Minister of Defence yesterday. Doubled from what? In this case it has been ascertained, only from the public statements, that they were doubled from three ships to six.

MR SHINWELL: 'Doubled' is what the right hon Gentleman used to say.

MR CHURCHILL: It is undoubted that in my long life I have used the word 'doubled'. The only additions to the new construction announced last March are forty-one new minesweepers and some small craft. Is that sufficient, when we consider the enormous increase both in output and in numbers with which we should be confronted in Russian U-boats over those of the Germans, which, at the outset of the last war, were such a very great immediate preoccupation to us?

When we reflect that the menace that we shall have to meet from the modern Soviet U-boats may be anything from five to ten times as great as what we suffered then, before we brought our vast flotillas and anti-submarine fleets into being in the last war, then this subject is one which leaves me deeply anxious, and I do not think the House should let it pass idly from its mind. Since the war many ships have been sold or scrapped, among them 4 aircraft carriers, 148 destroyers, 90 frigates and 214 motor torpedo-boats. Should war come—which God forfend—the wholesale scrapping and selling of vessels which would have been of value in this sphere of anti-submarine defence, where numbers are of the utmost importance will, I say, subject those responsible to very severe and direct accountability.

Take another instance of the kind of compromise system in which the Government revel—taking away with one hand what is given with the other, making a parade of what appears to be large action while, at the same time, giving it a form which deprives it of much of its usefulness. I mean, of course, the decision to call up 235,000 men from the Z reserves for fifteen days' training in the summer months. There is a widespread feeling that the Government have succeeded in striking the exact balance which combines the maximum disturbance and cost with the minimum of practical military advantage. But anyhow, the Government have to all intents and purposes, presented Parliament with an accomplished fact. Their plan is virtually in operation. The Secretary of State for War said last night:

'Our warning notices, which give the dates on which the men will be wanted, begin to go out from the War Office tonight.'

The programme of camps and permanent staffs for the coming summer is, no doubt, fully drawn up. To attempt to modify such a plan at this stage, when the training season is so close at hand, would certainly cause confusion; but there was nothing to prevent the Government producing their plans before the end of last year. Nothing at all need have prevented them from thinking these matters out and presenting them, when there would have been time to have had them debated, and any decision to amend and improve them could have been taken. But they present us with an accomplished fact.

I shall not, therefore, attempt to deal with the details of this scheme. I shall content myself with quoting a leading article in yesterday's *Manchester Guardian*, which I commend to the noble Lady the Member for Anglesey [Lady Megan Lloyd George], who is now discharging the duties of the leadership of the Liberal Party, and who has certainly a right to speak with freedom upon these defence matters, because she voted with the Chamberlain Government before the late war in support of introducing a system of National Service, of conscription, when the present Prime Minister distinguished himself by leading his party into the Lobby to vote against it. I commend to her these words of the *Manchester Guardian*:

'The Government has had the courage to call up for three months a small number of fighter pilots and aircrew reservists, so as to train them on the latest available planes (though these are already obsolescent). It has not had the courage to carry out any comparable Army scheme. Instead a great number of Class Z men will be called to camps, given uniforms, allowed a brief glimpse of the latest guns and tanks, and sent home again. Unless some new announcement is made the men will go home without knowing whether they will be wanted next year or for any further training.'

A new announcement was, however, made yesterday, and an assurance has been given that these men will not be called upon again except in the case of an emergency. Where then is the possibility of making any effective welding together of the reservists into cadres to which they belong, let alone reviving a sense of military comradeship and association? For all these purposes the fifteen-day proposals seem to have no meaning. In fact, the Secretary of State for War said last night:

'The public, however, have been a little apt to think that individual refresher training was the main, or even the sole, purpose. I would put it . . . probably fourth of the purposes, important as it is.'

In other words, which I remember hearing years ago at the Admiralty, a saying which was the definition of a naval officer's cruise: 'There and back.' That is a very fair description of what is to happen to the reservists who are to be called up in large numbers, and——

MR SHINWELL: The right hon Gentleman is talking a lot of nonsense.

HON MEMBERS: The Minister cannot take it.

MR CHURCHILL: Let me return to the *Manchester Guardian*—I choose this paper because it does not belong either to the Labour or to the Conservative Parties. It belongs to a middle party—a party which, in this matter, takes an impartial view. [An HON MEMBER: 'So did the right hon Gentleman once upon a time.'] In an article to-day the *Manchester Guardian* states:

'And the limelight yesterday shone on a farce. Mr Shinwell gave an assurance that the men recalled this summer will not be wanted for similar training in future years, and he dropped a broad hint that the number of men to be recalled this year would be reduced. It looks as if the Government had got very cold feet about its Class Z scheme. The farce is that men will be called up for fifteen days, given uniforms, marshalled into units and then sent home—never to return, unless war comes. The training they receive is bound to be negligible, for few will be physically in first-class condition, their previous experience will differ, and they will probably not be allowed more than a look at the latest weapons. Units will be built up to strength, only to be broken down again. The prospect for commanding officers is appalling. By the time they are beginning to know the many new faces in their units the men will be departing, never to be seen again.'

In the situation in which we now are there is a danger in dealing in shams and pretences—[HON MEMBERS: 'How long?']—not only because they mislead us here at home—[HON MEMBERS: 'How long?']—

MR SPEAKER: Order. These continual interruptions should not take place. After all, the final speech tonight may be somewhat provocative, and how am I to call the other side to order if the Government side is disorderly now?

MR CHURCHILL: I certainly do not feel called upon to propose an alternative time so that hon Members opposite may go round from door to door trying to make political capital out of it, but if the Government had proposed a longer period of training we would certainly have supported them, and if we were responsible we would face our obligations, as is our duty. In the situation in which we now are there is a danger in dealing in shams and pretences, not only because they mislead us here at home but because they will be used as justification for additional real measures taken in cool calculation and in design by our potential opponents on the Continent. The Government produce this small mobilization, but they do not know what other measures will be balanced against it: measures which will be real measures and not measures that have to be subjected to the tests of public opinion or free elections; measures taken with all that design and purpose with which we feel ourselves confronted, and which, the more we are confronted with, the more we are deeply impressed with the formidable character of the dangers which lie before us.

I have had the opportunity several times of seeing in conditions of grave business some of these commissars who form the oligarchy in the Kremlin and their chiefs, and I can tell you that these men are apt to form designs and to carry them out, and that when confronted with farces and shams they very often retaliate by strong and real measures. We are playing with fire when we pretend that we are taking very large steps, and we may only bring the very evils which we all hate nearer by this pretence. This is, in fact, another instance of getting the worst of both worlds. How can we approve—and 'approve' is the word we stick at—and thus accept a certain amount of responsibility for a measure of this kind, which seems designed to thread its way through political difficulties rather than add appreciably to our security?

The Minister of Defence said yesterday that the danger of war had become more acute in the last few months. I follow these matters as closely as I can, and I am not aware of any facts which justify this assertion. On the contrary, I think that the gigantic measures for re-armament adopted by the United States—the declaration of a state of emergency, 10,000 million dollars additional taxation, twenty-seven months' military service and the appointment of General Eisenhower—have all improved the chances of the rearmament of the free democracies, and the formation of a European front which will be a real deterrent upon Soviet Communist aggression in Europe; they have all improved the chances of this being achieved before the vast American superiority in the atomic weapon has been overtaken by the Russian stockpile. If any important facts have occurred justifying the statement made by the Minister of Defence about the increased danger of war they should be imparted to the House, if necessary in Secret Session. To make a statement of that kind is to give, I think, a wrong view, apart from causing alarm.

I return, in conclusion, I am glad to say—as no doubt hon Members opposite are also glad, or they ought to feel glad that I am nearly at the end of my remarks—to the direct issue that is before us. The figure of expenditure, about which we shall presently hear the Chancellor of the Exchequer, has been raised to £4,700 million over three years without, as I have said, any new changes or reasons of a fundamental character being adduced. Last year, in March, July and September, I stated the full story, so far as it was possible in public, and I do not know of any decisive facts which have occurred to alter it. The fundamental issues were not created by the United Nations interventions in Korea. They have only been brought more violently and more vividly before the masses here and in every country by these exciting and varied events which fill the newspapers from day to day.

Still less have the basic facts of the European peril been altered in the interval, after the third or fourth versions, if we take in the March White Paper. If the proposals now submitted to us are right, they would have been more right, in the sense of being more timely—and here is where time is vital—six or eight months ago, or, better still, much earlier. The Government have been in full control; they have had all the national resources at their disposal for nearly six years; their responsibilities for telling the truth to the country and giving the necessary leadership and guidance are grave, and it is by their whole conduct of our military and foreign affairs that they must be judged. Although most people feel that things are getting worse, it is not true that the basic situation has changed. All that has happened is that the Government have felt themselves forced into making a further interim scheme. They are not dealing with the realities of the situation any more now than on former occasions.

We are witnessing a process of gradual education of those who ought to know best and who have all the power, but who have to reach agreement by an endless series of compromises among themselves and with their military advisers. All we are dealing with here today is a new state of mind in those who have so long held our fortunes in their hands. It is hard to imagine a situation which gives fewer chances for the British nation to make the best of its resources and authority, and thus play the great part which might be open to us of preventing the drift into a third world war with all its indescribable, immeasurable, unimaginable horrors and perils.

# THE CONSERVATIVE CASE FOR AN ELECTION

A PARTY POLITICAL BROADCAST
17 MARCH 1951

---

16 *February—Defence Estimates presented to Parliament: Navy £278,500,000; Army £418,800,100; Air £328,750,000.*

6 *March—A Three-Power Declaration in Germany authorizes Federal Government to establish Foreign Ministry; Dr Adenauer appointed Foreign Secretary on 15th.*

7 *March—In Korea the UN forces open a general offensive on 55-mile front; Seoul recaptured by South Korean forces 14th.*

9 *March—Mr Herbert Morrison appointed Foreign Secretary in place of Mr Ernest Bevin; Mr Bevin appointed Lord Privy Seal; Viscount Addison appointed Lord President of the Council.*

17 *March—The Vatican announces the excommunication of all Roman Catholic members of the Czechoslovak Government and all priests supporting the Government.*

---

[17 *March* 1951

We have suffered a serious loss in the departure of Mr Bevin from the Foreign Office. After nearly eleven years of continuous service of the most arduous character it was felt that for some time past he was breaking under the strain. Although I differed from him in his handling of many questions, I feel bound to put on record that he takes his place among the great Foreign Secretaries of our country, and that, in his steadfast resistance to Communist aggression, in his strengthening of our ties with the United States and in his share of building up the Atlantic Pact, he has rendered services to Britain and to the cause of peace which will long be remembered. As his war-time leader I take this opportunity to pay my tribute to him and to his devoted wife.

My friends, our country is in a position of danger and perplexity. Abroad, things are bad, and we are becoming ever more divided at home. At a time when it would take our whole genius and united strength to cope with our troubles and ward off our perils, we are more sharply and evenly separated than I can remember in a long life. In 1940, you remember that, at the time of the Battle of Britain, everyone could see our danger was very great. In my opinion the dangers which many of us cannot see are even greater now. But then we were

29

a united people—now we are absorbed in party strife. I am not going to pretend that all the faults are on one side. It takes two to make a quarrel. But I submit to you that the prime responsibility must rest with the Government of the day. They have the initiative and the power. They create the situations and present the issues, and the Opposition parties react to them as best they can.

When Parliament was recalled last September, there was, I think, a chance of this House of Commons having a longer and more useful life than will now be its fate. The Prime Minister proposed to us the first version of the great rearmament schemes—£3,600 million in three years—and he asked for the institution of two years' compulsory military service. In spite of our party differences, I asked the House to pass the measures almost in a day, and thus send a message of national unity on defence and foreign policy around the world. This was done, and if the Prime Minister had met us in a similar spirit our home politics might well have taken a better turning. However, within a week of receiving our support in this effective manner, Mr Attlee astonished us by the announcement that he was proceeding at once to carry out the Steel Nationalization Act. This was playing at party politics with a vengeance. There was a perfectly good working compromise put forward by the Trades Union Congress under which owners, employers and men in the steel industry could have worked happily together. But the Prime Minister brushed this aside and used the nationalization of steel as a means of increasing the antagonism by which his party live and thus placated his own extremists. By this act of partisanship he destroyed whatever chance there was of friendly co-operation in the present Parliament. I have no wish to be too hard upon Mr Attlee. He certainly has a lot to bear. I sincerely trust his health will stand the strain. I resented Mr Stalin calling him a warmonger. I thought this was quite untrue. It was also unfair, because this word 'warmonger' was, as you have no doubt heard, the one that many of Mr Attlee's friends and followers were hoping to fasten on me whenever the election comes—they were keeping that for my especial benefit. Stalin has therefore been guilty, not only of an untruth, but of infringement of copyright. I think Mr Stalin had better be careful or else Mr Silverman will have him up for breach of privilege, or something like that.

Obviously we approach an election. Parliamentary democracy rests upon elections. But prolonged electioneering is not good for Britain. We have already had fifteen months of election fever. That would try the strongest constitution. It was hoped that the election a year ago would give a decision one way or the other, but instead it produced almost exact equality. Since then we have had a Government representing a minority of the electors trying to conduct all our grave and critical affairs without a normal working majority in the House of Commons. All their work is cut out in keeping their heads above water from day to day: indeed, I might say from night to night.

Parliamentary debate has become largely meaningless. All the time the two great party machines are grinding up against each other with the utmost energy, dividing every village, every street, every town and city into busy party camps. Each party argues that it is the fault of the other. What is certain is that to prolong the process indefinitely is the loss of all. After all, no nation possesses in common such long gathered moral and social treasures. No nation is more accustomed to practical methods of give and take from day to day, and few countries have at the present time—let me remind you—to look mortal dangers more directly in the face. Naturally, we all ask the question, are we really to go on all through the spring, summer and autumn with this struggle in Parliament and strife in the constituencies? Democracy does not express itself in clever manoeuvres by which a handful of men survive from day to day, or another handful of men try to overthrow them. Once it can be seen that a great new situation or great new issues lie before us, an appeal should be made to the people to create some governing force which can deal with our affairs in the name and in the interest of the large majority of the nation.

An entirely new situation is now before the country—there is the tremendous policy of rearmament. Why was this not mentioned by the Government at the General Election? All the essential facts were known to Mr Attlee and his colleagues. The outbreak in Korea six months later merely showed the public what was well known to the Government. The Government knew as well as they do now the menacing strength of the Soviet armies and air force and U-boats. They knew what had happened to Poland and to Czechoslovakia and in the Russian zone of Germany. They knew perfectly well that to make an efficient army for Britain with its numerous overseas requirements two years' service was needed. Why did they not propose it? Why did they not even mention it? The operative responsibility was theirs. They were seeking a new mandate. It is for them to answer that question. Why did they not do it? Mr Baldwin, as you may remember, was censured for not having warned the country as Prime Minister in 1935 that rearmament was necessary. Mr Baldwin knew that, had he done so, he would have been violently attacked by the other side. But Mr Attlee had not even that excuse, because he knew that the Conservative Party would support him if he asked for their support, not only upon rearmament but on the increase of the military service to two years. He did not do so. Thus, the present Parliament was elected on a basis quite different from that which now exists. Here, apart from all other arguments, is a plain case for consulting the people on the new issues.

Should there be an immense rearmament? We say 'Yes'—but if so, are the Ministers, who now have it in hand, having regard to their proved incapacity, the men to be trusted with it? The most disturbing and harmful condition in our domestic politics is the uncertainty about when an election will come. This keeps party strife at its keenest point. The Prime Minister has deliberately aggravated this evil. 'The election will come,' he says, 'at the right time,' meaning, of course, the right time for him and his party. Of this he is to be the sole judge. Any day, therefore, we may be plunged into all this tumult of electioneering. Both sides must be continually prepared. All our problems at home and abroad are made more difficult by this uncertainty. Yet Mr Attlee's policy seems to be to prolong it to the utmost limit in his power.

This magnifies party interests and organization out of all proportion to national affairs. It keeps everything on edge. Every word spoken has to be tested by the controversial use that might be made of it. It cannot be good for our public life. It cannot strengthen our position in the world. It harms the whole of our business. No one can compute the loss in money and prosperity, yet we are led to believe that the Government intend to go on until the last possible minute, prolonging all these strains and stresses. It is more than plain that they have lost the confidence of the nation, but the plainer it becomes the more obstinately and desperately they cling to their offices on the chance that something will turn up. They seek to prolong this hateful and costly uncertainty. We seek to bring it to an end. It is in the national interest that it should come to an end and that a broad-based Government resting on a clear and strong majority should come into power. We need a Government unhampered by narrow doctrinal party dogma or by the interests of any particular class. We need a Government able to address itself with a fresh eye and calm resolution to all our problems and deal with them on their merits. Certainly it is not an inviting prospect for any new Government to have to face. The more the consequences of devaluation make themselves remorselessly felt, the harder will be our lot. There are some who argue that we should leave the burden in the hands of those who have so largely brought it into being. 'Let them reap where they have sown': that is what is said. I hold, on the contrary, that it would be unpatriotic to allow the present degeneration to continue.

Look at the dangers to world peace which come from a weak, divided and largely disregarded Britain. Look at the way we are treated by so many countries whom we have helped in days not long gone by. The Conservative and Unionist Party have therefore made up their minds on national rather than on party grounds to do their utmost to bring about an appeal to the nation at the earliest moment, and to use to the full our parliamentary and constitutional rights for that purpose. What happens at home, my friends, is in our hands. We cannot control what happens abroad. We have an influence—we might have a much greater influence. But the supreme decisions are outside our power. It is, however, within our power to reach a solid, stable, coherent settlement at home. If we did, we should not only be much stronger and therefore much safer, but we should have far more power to shape and lever the movement of events towards our goal.

What is our goal? What is our hearts' wish? It is very plain, it is very simple. It is only the hearts' desire of all the millions of ordinary men and women with their hard workaday lives, all the peoples still outside the totalitarian curtain all over the world—only their hearts' desire: freedom and peace. The right to be let alone to lead our own lives in our own way, under our own laws, and give our children a fair chance to make the best of themselves. It is not wrong for anyone to ask for that. It is not much for Britain to ask. We did our best to fight for it, in the late war; for a whole year we fought alone. When at last all our enemies surrendered we thought we had won it—won it at least for a lifetime. But now it seems that we are again in jeopardy. We are in a sad, sombre period of world history where no good-hearted, valiant Russian soldier, worker or peasant; no hard-pressed, disillusioned German family; no home in the war-scarred democracies of Western Europe or in our own islands we have guarded so long, so well, or far across the Atlantic in mighty America—no household can have the feeling after a long day's faithful toil that they can go to sleep without the fear that something awful is moving towards them; and this is what has come to us after all our efforts and sacrifices, and come upon us at a time when, but for the thoughtlessness of the free democracies and the organized designs of the Kremlin oligarchy, expanding science, like a fairy godmother, could have opened the gates of the Golden Age to all.

I do not suggest that any one country or any party in any country has the power or the virtue to sweep away this nightmare which darkens ever more in our deep confusion and unrest. But there are a great many nations who are trying very hard and it ought to be our earnest resolve that Britain should play her part, and her full part, in saving mankind from the two hideous alternatives thrust before us—Communist tyranny or annihilating war.

My friends, I have traced for you in these few minutes tonight the outlines of this strange and awe-inspiring world picture, and everyone around every table or fireside who is listening to me here in our island and beyond it—because many are listening—will, I feel, be asking themselves: what ought we to do to make Britain strong and splendid so that we can play our true and real parts once again in the defence of human rights and dignity, founded as they can only be upon justice and peace? Surely our duty shines clear and plain before us. Surely we ought not to let the inevitable difficulties of our party strife prevent our rising to our full majesty and becoming once again one of the foremost champions and guides of the free world.

I have a long experience and this has come into my mind. In critical and baffling situations it is always best to recur to first principles and simple action. Trust the people, go to the people, let the people have their say. Let there be a General Election where they can express their will—where they can express their will through a Parliament worthy of what is strongest and best in our race. It is for this that we are resolved to strive. Goodnight!

# COMPLAINT OF PRIVILEGE

A SPEECH TO THE HOUSE OF COMMONS
21 MARCH 1951

---

18 *March—Treaty setting up 'European Coal and Steel Community'*
*(Schuman Plan) signed in Paris.*
20 *March—General Eisenhower announces appointment of Field-Marshal*
*Lord Montgomery to be Deputy Supreme Allied Commander in Europe.*

---

[*21 March* 1951

*Question proposed:*
*'That the matter of the complaint of the hon Member for Nelson and Colne*
*concerning the conduct of the hon Member for Sevenoaks in handing over to*
*the Bishop of Rochester a letter he had received from his constituent, the Rev*
*O. Fielding Clarke, M.A., B.D., be remitted to the Committee of Privileges.'*
*—[Mr Silverman.]*

No one can complain of any violence in the temper or tone of the
speeches in which this Motion has been introduced to the House. The
hon Member for Nuneaton [Mr Bowles], who seconded it, referred to
my great and unique age in this House, and that was also a subject of
interest on the Ministerial Front Bench a little while ago. I remember
well that my father—if we are to go back into the past—called Mr
Gladstone 'An old man in a hurry'. That was in the year 1885, and
sixteen years later Mr Gladstone was engaged in forming another
Administration. I do not want to suggest that such a precedent will be
repeated, for that would dishearten hon Members opposite.

I have listened to a great deal that the hon Member for Nelson and
Colne [Mr S. Silverman] has said, with a great deal of sympathy for his
general principles, but I am bound to say I do not think he dealt with
the actual issue before us. Mr Speaker, on March 13, ruled that there
was no prima facie case to refer to the Committee of Privileges. The
House has a perfect right to reverse Mr Speaker's Ruling, but the step
is a serious one, and I do not remember it happening in my time—an
immense period, far longer even than that of the Father of the House.
It is quite open to a Member to put down a Motion on the Order
Paper such as we have tonight, but I contend that it could not be
carried without implying stultification of Mr Speaker's Ruling. My

submission to the House is that Mr Speaker's Ruling was right. There was no prima facie case then, there is not now a prima facie case; still less is there a case, not prima facie but, as it were, to a certain extent, pre-judged by the decision of the House.

Let us look into this question of Privilege. Privilege means Parliamentary Privilege. It is a privilege which protects Parliament, its Members, its officers, its witnesses, counsel, people who appear before it or its Committees, and also petitioners. It is a Parliamentary Privilege protecting this House and those who take part in it. It does not protect or refer to the electors or the general public. The hon Member for Nelson and Colne may shake his head. He had better be careful not to shake it too much. That is a fact. Privilege is not instituted to protect the universal suffrage electorate. They can protect themselves if they get a chance. It is to protect the House and Members of Parliament.

The electorate and the general public have their rights under the ordinary law, and they have their votes—quite an important thing. The Motion by the hon Member for Nelson and Colne is based upon the assumption that the House should use its Privilege to protect a correspondent who wrote to my hon Friend the Member for Sevenoaks [Mr John Rodgers] from some real or supposed injury. I say that Privilege was never instituted or intended for such a purpose. It is to protect us and those who have to deal with us, and not to protect the vast mass of the nation outside.

The correspondence of a Member with his constituents or other persons is regulated by the existing law of libel, blackmail and that sort of thing. That is the law. The correspondence of a Member is also governed by good taste, good faith, and respect for private and confidential matters. If these aspects come before the public or the electors in any constituency it is for them to judge, and unless the conduct of some Member of the House, in the course of his Parliamentary duties, or the conduct of the Chair, or other matters directly connected with Parliamentary proceedings are involved, no question of Privilege arises. It is no good not liking it, because I am quite certain that it is a solid, established fact, upon which this matter rests and stands.

It is true that the Court of Criminal Appeal, in the case of *Rex v. Rule*, in 1937, held that a Member of Parliament—I use this case because it is a good illustration of how the matter stands—to whom a written communication was addressed by one of his constituents, asking for his assistance in bringing to the notice of the appropriate Minister a complaint of improper conduct on the part of some public official acting in that constituency in relation to his office, had sufficient interest in the subject matter of the complaint to render the occasion of such a publication a privileged occasion. But, here, the word 'Privilege' refers to privilege under the common law. It has nothing whatever to do with Parliamentary Privilege, which is the only thing with which we are concerned on this Motion.

How could the Court of Criminal Appeal pronounce on a question of Parliamentary Privilege? There is, therefore, I submit, no case, prima facie or otherwise, on this issue that is before us. It is ordinary privilege and does not come under Parliamentary Privilege at all. Nor is any ruling by any court relevant in the slightest degree to our affairs.

MR S. SILVERMAN: I quite appreciate the point the right hon Gentleman is making, but does he remember that in the last Parliament the House of Commons, with his consent, treated as cases of Privilege those of Mr Garry Allighan and Mr Evelyn Walkden where the only breach of Privilege alleged was that they communicated, without authority, to a third party, information which had come to them only because they were Members of Parliament?

MR CHURCHILL: I cannot pretend to argue the merits and details of this extremely complicated case, but what I do stand on is that Parliamentary Privilege is to protect Parliament and its Members and not to protect the general public.

For 250 years the House has conformed to the Resolution, passed in 1704, that it would not extend its privileges. It is very remarkable how strong and rigidly that principle has been carried out. There is, however, a wide right of interpretation. Now we are asked by the hon Gentleman, not in one case only but in another case which he raised, and we may be asked in many others, greatly to widen the interpretation of Privilege and to bring the ordinary correspondence of any Member of Parliament within the ambit of Privilege. I am sure that that would be a grave and most unwise departure from our proceedings. It would appear to entitle constituents to write libellous statements to their Member, and plead immunity on the grounds that their communication was privileged in the Parliamentary sense, which overrode the ordinary sense of the common law.

Apart from this it would involve Parliament in almost endless embarrassment and work, and the raising of so-called 'Privilege cases' arising out of a Member's correspondence might become a fertile cause of obstruction, and would certainly cast an undue burden not only upon the Chair but upon the Table. I cannot conceive anything that would be more inconvenient or more unworkable in practice than the fact that any issue, of any body, at any time in this House arising from the ordinary correspondence which we have to discharge in such great volume, might be raised as a matter of Privilege, and then referred to the Committee of Privileges to decide or examine in the utmost detail. We would ruin a valuable and vitally important protection, on which the dignity, power and freedom of the House rests if we cast upon it these cataracts of irrelevant and absurd issues.

No difficulty about the correspondence of Members has been experienced in our present practice in the fifty years that I can recall. The right of a Member at his discretion to send a letter or show a letter from a constituent to any other person cannot be a matter of Privilege. If it were we would be imposing a special and invidious responsibility and disability upon them not open to others. I must be careful how I deal with this matter. At any moment my conduct might be called in question, and I might be called before the Committee of Privileges. Someone might write a most improper or demanding letter. Is that to be within the Privilege of Parliament? If it is, it is putting a curb and a burden upon Members.

If the House accepts the view that Mr Speaker's Ruling was correct and that there was no prima facie case, the question of the injury, if any, to the Vicar of Crockham Hill does not arise. It has gone. It was no breach of Privilege and there is no prima facie case. We are not concerned with the matter, no Parliamentary Privilege being involved. The bishop is not involved, and my hon Friend the Member for Sevenoaks, who has left the Chamber, is not involved. I would not, in ordinary circumstances, have attempted—because I do not wish to take up the time of the House unnecessarily—to discuss the local and special aspects of this case, but the circumstances are somewhat peculiar. I dwell in the diocese of the Bishop of Rochester, I am a parishioner of the Vicar of Crockham Hill and I am a constituent of the hon Member for Sevenoaks. Therefore, it makes for me what is called, in racing parlance, a triple event.

Naturally, I know something about the local position. I should be very sorry if it were to be thought that, with all his extravagances and improprieties, as I hold them, the Vicar of Crockham Hill does not try to do his work and to make a contribution. I agree with what has been said about the dangers of irony and sarcasm, but I am certain that there are many phrases in the letter which, taken from their context, would be very injurious but which, read in the general scope of the letter, merely indicate an extravagant mood and a desire to use words and language beyond the power of words and language to carry. This led him into saying things which were very painful and which, for people less instructed than we are in this House, including the hon Member who moved the Motion, might very well darken their counsel and cause them pain and distress.

I turn to the hon Member for Sevenoaks. I take a special interest, as his constituent, in how he conducts his correspondence. I may say that the idea that all constituents, that is to say universal suffrage constituents, should be protected from any consequences that might conceivably arise out of any letter that they write to their Members is, on any interpretation of the Privilege rule in respect of correspondence, an absurd idea. If everything that was written down were to impose a great question of Parliamentary Privilege upon us, it is quite possible that a call upon the telephone or a personal interview might result in all kinds of things. After all, we know the kind of world in which we are living, and it is very dangerous to put undue pressure upon normal actions because we might easily create abuses that otherwise would not have occurred.

One thing is important—I am not admitting the relevance of this point to the main argument—and that is that Members of Parliament should be careful, in dealing with a letter from a constituent, not to get that constituent into trouble which might cost him his livelihood, unless criminal or libellous considerations are involved. What did my hon Friend the Member for Sevenoaks do? He wrote to the bishop, and he sent this extraordinary document, which, evidently, was not written to be published. It has seen the light of day far beyond the hopes of its author. What did my hon Friend do? He wrote to the bishop. The Church of England differs from most of the important religious institutions in having no power to discipline its priests or ministers in their opinions and doctrines. Jews, Presbyterians, Baptists, Methodists, all have the power, exerted by the authority of the religious community or by the congregation, to discipline or change their ministers, but the Church of England has not that power.

A bishop is without power to remove from his living a clergyman of whose views or doctrines he disapproves. The highest authority in the Church has no power. That is why persons like the Dean of Canterbury can do a great deal of harm with impunity. I am not at all inflicting any sort of stigma upon the Vicar of Crockham Hill by comparing him in the slightest degree with the Dean of Canterbury. Neither can the parishioners have the right or power to relieve themselves of a priest whose character, opinions or doctrines they resent. I am not sure that it might not in the long run turn out that freedom in a healthy community will be found to be the best solution of all difficulties; but still, there is no comparison. The only way in which parishioners can express their feelings is by not attending the religious services in the church of the priest concerned. Crockham Hill church is nearly always empty. There is no doubt about that, although the vicar makes special efforts by special classes and so forth. I am in no way impugning his character or the efforts he makes, but there is no doubt of what the action of the parishioners would be if they had the same power as is possessed by many other communities and congregations.

This bishop who was appealed to in this case has no power to do anything, except one thing. He has the right, and I think he has the duty, to wrestle spiritually with the Minister. That is the worst sanction that can be invoked in the proceedings between my hon Friend and the bishop, who has the power to apply all the resources of reason and persuasion, moral and spiritual. Why should they not be turned on? We all have the right to wrestle spiritually with one another when the proper time comes. I may even make myself the agent, in the short time left to me, of converting the hon Member for Nelson and Colne to a proper outlook on the way of life. Nothing was done that could possibly injure this vicar in his worldly affairs, in his office or in his pitifully small stipend.

My hon Friend was quite right to write to the bishop and send the letter to the bishop. [HON MEMBERS: 'Oh.'] I will tell the House why, because it is one of the things we might vote about tonight. My hon Friend had a duty to his constituents, who are the parishioners of this priest and who suffer the inconvenience—some of them—through the lack of religious administration and through their dislike of his opinions, of having to go to some other church which may be much further off. Perhaps that has not occurred to the hon Member for Nelson and Colne. That has not troubled him. The hon Member for Sevenoaks was only discharging his duty to his constituents in endeavouring to induce the bishop to use his moral and spiritual authority to remove the evil. How illogical and absurd it is for all the supporters of the Motion to work themselves into a state of indignation and fury at the alleged ill-usage of the Vicar of Crockham Hill as a correspondent writing to his Member when they have heard nothing about the suffering of hundreds of constituents—200 families are involved—who are deprived to a large extent of the religious comfort and services to which they are entitled.

I will not keep the House much longer. I could say a great deal, but I think I have made the point very clearly. But I will say one thing. We were all much impressed by the declaration of the Leader of the House the other day about his position as Leader of the House, his not being identified with any party, his responsibility to the House as a whole, and so forth. Now we have passed out of the realm of words into the realm of action, and I should like to know what he is going to do tonight. I think he should tell us. We have heard that the Government are not putting their Whips on in the ordinary way in favour of the Motion. I should have thought that it was their duty to vote against the Motion, as we shall certainly do, but if they are going to leave it to their followers to vote exactly as they please, how are they going to vote themselves? Is the Leader of the House going to vote for something which he knows is incorrect in procedure, or is he going to vote against it? How is he going to deal with his colleagues on the subject? I do not want to add to the many complications that he has at the present time, but, at any rate, I think it is his duty to tell the House exactly how he proposes to vote upon his Motion.

As far as we are concerned, we shall not, in these circumstances, put on the party Whips. On the merits, in perfect freedom and after full consideration of the arguments, some of which I have ventured to bring before the House tonight, we shall, I think, vote against the Motion on the grounds that no case of Privilege arises and also because we think that it is the duty of the Member to act for all his constituents —not only for those who write to him—and to be guided as a general rule in so doing by the greatest good of the greatest number.

*Note.* The motion for remitting the matter to the Committee of Privileges was defeated by 284 votes to 255.

# BUDGET PROPOSALS AND ECONOMIC SURVEY

A SPEECH TO THE HOUSE OF COMMONS
10 APRIL 1951

---

22 *March—The Persian Senate approves unanimously the decision to nationalize the oil industry.*

26 *March—Conference of American Foreign Ministers opens in Washington.*

27 *March—Belgium decides to release Generals von Falkenhausen, Reeder and Bertram.*

29 *March—US enters into agreement with France for establishment of American air base at Châteauroux.*

31 *March—The financial year closes with an ordinary Budget surplus of £720 million.*

2 *April—General Eisenhower assumes effective command of Atlantic Treaty forces in Europe.*

10 *April—Mr Gaitskell presents the Budget for 1951–2: income tax increased 6d.; purchase tax increases; tax on distributed profits increased; petrol tax increased; charge in Health Service for denture work and spectacles; old age pensions increased.*

---

[10 *April* 1951

I think I shall be expressing the opinion of the whole House if I pay our compliments to the Chancellor of the Exchequer upon the lucid, comprehensive statement which he has made to us this afternoon, and upon the evident lack of hatred or malice which I felt was apparent while he was unfolding his proposals. We have had what is, upon the whole, an objective statement, and the proposals which have been made, for all the difficulty which attaches to many of them, have been designed as he himself claimed, as an honest attempt to solve the problems which lay before him. I have listened to many Budgets in this House, and have even contributed five myself. I am bound to say that I feel the right hon Gentleman has placed himself, by his opening statement this afternoon, in a good position to conduct the long and severe debates we shall no doubt have on many aspects of the policy. I would not like to turn to criticisms without saying that again I feel sure that the whole House would wish to send a message of goodwill and encouragement to Sir Stafford Cripps. [HON MEMBERS: 'Hear, hear.'] If he is heavily burdened by affliction at the present time, it is largely because of the devoted manner in which he has endeavoured to serve the public. As one who has differed from him fundamentally in many ways, and worked with him as a trusted comrade in many others, I feel that the few words I have spoken might well carry the message of the House across the seas to him.

The speech to which we have just listened can, of course, only be considered in relation to the sombre background against which it stands. Here I cannot expect any longer to carry with me approving glances from those who sit opposite. After all, this is the seventh Budget which has been opened since the Socialist Party have become masters of our affairs.

THE SECRETARY OF STATE FOR FOREIGN AFFAIRS [MR HERBERT MORRISON]: Oh!

MR CHURCHILL: I was quoting the Attorney-General. We dwell in the aftermath of devaluation. I cannot help feeling that that dark shadow hangs over us now. It has increased by nearly a third the working and productive effort needed from Britain to make the exports out of which our vital supplies and raw materials have to be bought. The Chancellor referred to this. I have not his actual words, but they certainly stressed the fact that this 30 per cent devaluation of our national products, relative to what we get in return, was a very heavy burden, and that weighs upon us all the time. There are no doubt other causes at work, but it is this hard, dominant fact of the aftermath of devaluation which impinges upon us at the present time. Much of the life energy of our island, already over-strained when the war ended, drained away from this cause, and also from unrequited exports and from lavish expenditure.

Those who hold that taxation is an evil must recognize that it falls upon this country in a most grievous manner at the present time, continually burdening the mass of the nation and continually clogging—or, at any rate, hampering our efforts. There is to be an increase of taxation. I am not at all concerned today to examine even cursorily the detailed proposals which the Chancellor has made, but taxation is to be increased; it is to be heavier still. Naturally, many people will feel that the issue should be argued out very tensely as to whether other economies in Government expenditure might not have relieved us from the need of applying new burdens and new taxation. Of course, we know the times are difficult. The Prime Minister told us the other day that the price rises were due to world causes, but almost in the same breath he claimed the whole credit for full employment for his own party. Everything that is bad is due to world events; everything that is good is due to the Socialist Party. That may be a very comforting theory, but I feel bound to warn the Chancellor of the Exchequer that it is not one which we can adopt as the basis upon which our debates on the Budget and the Finance Bill will be conducted.

If we take the whole period of the rule of the Socialist Party. I think it is fair to say that the mismanagement of our finances over the whole period tells the same tale, or almost the same tale in different terms, as the mismanagement of our defences. We must not be led by the agreeable presentation which the right hon Gentleman has given us of these proposals into any weakening in our conviction of the grave financial position in which this country stands and of the very heavy drains which have been made, not only upon its accumulated wealth made since the war, but also upon the incentives and resourcefulness by which our future daily bread can be earned.

Of course, it is quite true to say that there has been a great increase in production, a steady annual increase, but compared to capitalist, free enterprise United States, the increase has not been on anything like the same level. If we take the whole period of Socialist rule, we must see that during this costly period we have fallen from the position which we held at the end of the war in almost every sphere of our activities and reputation at home and abroad. The Chancellor of the Exchequer is not primarily responsible for this; he bears his share of collective responsibility.

We shall, of course, study and consider with great attention the proposals which are now put before us. I should not attempt—I would not try even cursorily—to examine in these few remarks the proposals in detail or to judge them on the spur of the moment. It is our duty, however, to subject, not only the Budget, but the whole of our financial and economic position, to severe and searching examination, and we shall not fail to do it in the weeks and months which lie ahead. One thing, however, is clear, and that is that the necessary money for rearmament has got to be provided and that the House of Commons is the sole authority which should do its best to find the least harmful manner. I shall certainly conclude, as I began, by thanking the Chancellor for what I think everyone will recognize was a remarkable Parliamentary performance and which will, I trust, make the foundation upon which a high reputation as a Chancellor of the Exchequer—we are all in the club together—may be expected to rest.

# CUTLERS' FEAST

A SPEECH AT THE CUTLERS' FEAST, SHEFFIELD
17 APRIL 1951

---

11 *April—Dismissal of General MacArthur announced by President Truman; Lieut-Gen Ridgway appointed C.-in-C., UN Forces in Korea.*

13 *April—The Coronation Stone, which was removed on Christmas Day 1950, is returned to Westminster Abbey.*

14 *April—Death of Mr Ernest Bevin, Lord Privy Seal and former Foreign Secretary.*

---

[17 *April* 1951

It is nearly forty years since I last spoke at a Cutlers' Feast. I was at the Admiralty and I said: 'I am proud to come to Sheffield which, though a considerable distance from the sea, nevertheless contributes an essential part to the naval security of our country.' I wish I could add to that by saying that we were as secure in the air tonight as we were on the sea forty years ago. Here again I may quote: 'But we must be prepared. We must be ready for all eventualities. It is good to be patient; it is good to be circumspect; it is good to be peace-loving. But that is not enough. We must be strong. We must be self-reliant, and, in the end, for all our party politics, we must be united.' I could say all that tonight, for here we are again 'forty years on'.

The continued vitality and progress of your ancient and famous city springs from craftsmanship and new ideas applied to the production of steel. There is a long story in the past about craftsmanship and how much you and we all owe to the Trade Guilds. There is hardly any direction in which craftsmanship counts for more than in the field of alloys and special steels. But craftsmanship alone might have stagnated. Sheffield has had the fortune and genius to nourish a succession of pioneers and leaders whose names are household words in industry. Bessemer drove compressed air through molten iron and created steel. From that we moved on to the Siemens 'Open Hearth' and modern steel. Mushet invented self-hardening of steels. To Hadfield we owe the manganese steels which are the basis of bullet-proof sheets and shrapnel helmets, and thus brought armour back to a world which had reluctantly discarded it. Brearley invented stainless steels—a great convenience if sharpness is not lost, for after all the purpose of a knife

45

is to cut. The stainless steels led to heat-resisting steels which have made the modern jet engine possible. To these names of Sheffield pioneers we must also add—Vickers, Brown, Girth, Jessop and Tozer—the men who built up the great steel firms.

What is the characteristic that all these craftsmen, pioneers and industrialists have had in common? Surely it is the individual effort of hand and brain, and the development of free and independent enterprise. It would be hard to find a city to whose life these qualities have made so great a contribution as Sheffield, which I am told, today produces 14 per cent of our total steel production and 70 per cent of our alloy steel. If these qualities were lost all would be lost. Those who seek to plan the future should not forget the inheritance they have received from the past, for it is only by studying the past as well as dreaming of the future that the story of man's struggle can be understood.

As the new rearmament programme develops the country once again will look increasingly to Sheffield to satisfy its special requirements. They must look not only to the large firms among you but also to the small. The small are no less a permanent and essential part of the structure of any industry than the large. Many people are misled nowadays by the cult of bigness for bigness sake. One of the efforts of nationalization is to make the big more powerful. But the life of Sheffield has grown from the efforts and triumphs of individuals and all the inexhaustible variety of human initiative. To lose this would be fatal.

Often when the conditions which have made possible the growth of a city have passed away there is decline. The world is full of these examples. But it is not so with Sheffield. You have shown yourselves for generations supremely adaptable to new uses and to technical changes. That is the secret of your success and survival: adaptability, contrivance, inventiveness, dependence on freedom to initiate, a chance to push out for the prizes of the future and take the risk of losing without sending in your bill to the Chancellor of the Exchequer. Everything that restricts this vital freedom is a deadly threat to Sheffield and to our islands.

We live in an age of mass production. But mass production can only be kept healthy and vital by the continued refreshment of new processes. At present, although you are nationalized by law the authors of this policy have not chosen to take the practical, working management out of the skilled, experienced hands of the Iron and Steel Federation. The Steel Corporation vulture hovers in the sky with its two grasping claws, Uniformity and Monopoly. It has not dared to swoop and its life may be short. Meanwhile, Sheffield must have good courage and, adhering faithfully to its tradition of craftsmanship and progress, drive ahead in tireless resilience. The old Guilds were founded on a slowly-achieved combination and compromise between friendly rivalry among their members on the one hand and on the other the sense of solidarity arising from members of a common trade. There has been unending argument. Some have stressed the need for solidarity. Others, swinging to the other extreme, have questioned the need for competition. Through your remarkable institution you have kept to a very large extent the proper balance and have not only maintained Sheffield in a healthy expansion, but may claim to be a model for every other industry and city in our islands.

I do not wish to talk party politics tonight, but at a Cutlers' Feast it is quite impossible to avoid some occasional references to steel, and, alas, steel has been plunged into the very centre of party strife. But there is one cardinal rule for the British nation (and the English, we may mention them sometimes), 'Never despair.' That word is forbidden. Our fortunes and our fate are in our hands. I end where I began forty years ago. Standing here tonight, I hope I shall express our true conviction that although perfect solutions of our difficulties are not to be looked for in an imperfect world, and although persistent disagreement as to method is inevitable, and not necessarily unhealthy, yet in our own British fashion, which no one else understands, we shall in our lifetime make a notable advance and hold our ground at every point. To that work all parties in their turn can and ought to contribute. If they do so simply and sincerely according to their lights, then the nation, which is far greater than all the parties put together, will have no reason to doubt or fear its future.

# NORTH ATLANTIC (SUPREME COMMANDER)

A SPEECH TO THE HOUSE OF COMMONS
19 APRIL 1951

---

18 *April—The President of Portugal, Marshal Carmona, dies, aged* 81.

---

[19 *April* 1951

As this matter concerns both our country and the United States, I hope I may have your indulgence, Mr Speaker, if I say, I think on behalf of all parties and every hon Member, with what deep regret we have received the news this morning of the death of Senator Vandenberg, a great American statesman whose sure balance of mind and lofty disinterested pursuance of large purposes won him the respect of all parties in his own country and of all parties in our islands here.

Now I come to the business of the afternoon, and I hope the House will permit me to range rather widely over this extensive topic. In the event of war with Soviet Russia, two dangers would menace the defence of free Europe and our own life here. The first is the large number of U-boats, far more than the Germans had at the beginning of the late war, of an improved German type and of vastly increased underwater speed and endurance. The second is, of course, the mining peril at all our ports and all free European ports. This mining attack required from us in the late war nearly 60,000 men and more than 1,000 vessels, sweeping and watching ceaselessly under hard conditions. Every kind of device was tried, and, in the main, mastered by us, but now we must expect ever more subtle scientific inventions to prevent detection and clearance by sweeping or explosives. There is no doubt that the whole of this process is being studied and developed by the Soviet Government, aided by German science and German brains. Our means of keeping alive, and the power of the United States and of ourselves to send armies to Europe, depend on our mastering these two problems.

I am sure that no one knows so much about dealing with U-boats in the Atlantic and the mine menace around our shores and harbours of any kind as the British Admiralty, not because we are cleverer or braver than others, but because, in two wars, our existence has depended upon overcoming these perils. When you live for years on end with mortal danger at your throat, you learn in a hard school. 'Depend upon it,' said Dr Johnson, 'if a man is going to be hanged in a

48

month, it concentrates his mind wonderfully.' During these two recent wars, as First Lord of the Admiralty or as Minister of Defence, I studied from week to week the hopeful or sinister curves upon the charts, and nothing ever counted more with me than their movements. It is the kind of experience, prolonged as it was, which eats its way into you. The late U-boat war lasted nearly six years. I say that to take the control of this process out of Admiralty hands would, I am sure, be a grave and perhaps a fatal injury, not only to ourselves, but to the common cause.

I would begin by asking where, in fact, did this idea of a Supreme Commander for the Atlantic originate. What were the reasons for the acceptance and enforcement of so radical a change from the system which had proved itself in the recent long years of war to work effectively? What would be the powers, apart from the imposing title, of the American Supreme Commander of the Atlantic? Our coastal waters and the English Channel are not under him. It is in the White Paper. He could not move warships and flotillas from the Eastern Atlantic Zone without disrupting or changing all the intricate business of receiving convoys and keeping the ports open.

Then, what about merchant ships? The Prime Minister told us the other day:

'That is really another matter altogether. The allocation of our merchant fleet is, of course, under the Government of this country.'

Well, the merchant fleet can no more be considered apart from the escorts than the escorts can be considered apart from the merchant fleet. What powers will the Supreme Commander have over the American Navy Department? Can he transfer ships from the Pacific to the Atlantic? Surely not? He might make representations, but they would be settled by the American naval authorities, no doubt after consultation with the British Admiralty. Could he move naval forces from the North Atlantic to the South Atlantic? Is, in fact, the South Atlantic under his command at all? Could he take ships from the South Atlantic or from the Mediterranean and bring them into the Eastern or the Western Atlantic Zones?

It would be quite impossible for him to settle any of these matters, even if he had the authority on paper, except after consulting the United States Navy Department and the British Admiralty. We are told that his appointment is necessary to avoid the ocean war being conducted by a committee composed of twelve Powers, such as was set up under the Atlantic Pact. But whoever imagined that the intricate handling of the U-boat and mining war could be entrusted to a committee of twelve Powers, most of whom have contributed little or nothing to the common stock? It would not be fair to a distinguished and capable officer, like Admiral Fechteler, to cast all the nominal responsibility upon him when, in actual practice, he could not have real power. There is no doubt whatever that the business of bringing in the convoys safely to Europe can only be settled by an officer, whatever his nationality, seated at the Admiralty, and having immediately under his orders the executive Officer Commanding the Western Approaches and the merchant shipping which is the object of the enemy's attack, and whose safety is the whole object of the operation.

The White Paper, which I had the time to read, makes strange reading. Paragraph 25 says:

'The Atlantic command will include an Eastern and a Western area. The Eastern area, which is obviously the more vital so far as this country is concerned, will be under the command of a British Admiral in association with Coastal Command of the Royal Air Force. This British Admiral will be the Commander-in-Chief, Home Fleet, an appointment at present held by Admiral Sir Philip Vian.'

But what has the Home Fleet got to do with the U-boat and mining menace? It has very little to do with them. Of course, when it comes out from its harbours into the ocean it has to look after the convoys and protect them against U-boat attack, and, of course, when it stays in, it sometimes lends the flotillas of the Western Approaches some flotillas of its own. But the Home Fleet, in wartime, dwells mainly at Scapa Flow, and only comes out to deal with enemy surface raiders.

In this imaginary war, to which I am addressing myself, we have, of course, to look at the facts with which one is confronted. The Russians have some modern cruisers, but they have no fast capital ships like the *Scharnhorst*, the *Gneisenau*, the *Bismarck* and the *Tirpitz*, and they can have none in the next two or three years—two, anyhow. How is it then proposed that the Commander-in-Chief of our Home Fleet is to control the movement of convoys in the Western Approaches? The routes to be followed by convoys entering or leaving Britain must be arranged from the British Admiralty. Are the merchant ships sailing from British ports to be given their orders from America, and, if so, how can the American Commander be informed of all that is going on from hour to hour? Fancy presenting us with a plan whereby an American admiral, seated in Norfolk, Virginia, has the supreme command of the Atlantic, although the business of the reception of the convoys and bringing them in through the U-boat and mining attack, must be mainly over here and is vital to us all. I repeat that the Supreme Commander of the Atlantic, if there is one, whatever his nationality, should be situated here.

Of course, since the war stopped, changes in military science have been continued. The power of the air grows ceaselessly. Even at the end of the war, it was at least equal to that of the naval forces at sea. But the movement of convoys on the sea is a matter for naval directions, and in Great Britain the air forces allotted to their defence must conform to a comprehensive plan prepared, in the first place, by the Admiralty. This important fact was recognized when, from the outbreak of the last war, the operational control of the Coastal Command of the Royal Air Force was vested in the Admiralty. It is not clear from the White Paper whether this policy is intended to be applied in the future. Paragraph 25 of the White Paper says:

'The Eastern area . . . will be under the command of a British Admiral in association with Coastal Command of the Royal Air Force.'

Is there then to be no American air contribution to this Eastern Zone? Surely, information of this might have been given to us. It is a serious omission on the part of those who drew up this document.

Let me return to the first point I am making, that there is no need for a Supreme Commander of the Atlantic. That is the point which I submit to the House. The overwhelming weight of British naval opinion supports the view that there is no need to appoint a Supreme Commander of the Atlantic.

COMMANDER PURSEY (Hull, East): Nonsense.

MR CHURCHILL: I will affirm and sustain my statement. Admiral Andrew Cunningham, a very great sailor——

COMMANDER PURSEY: A bath-chair warrior now.

MR CHURCHILL: I think the hon and gallant Gentleman might, at any rate, lay off his sneering snarls when naval officers of great distinction have their names mentioned in the House. Admiral Andrew Cunningham used the expression that it would be 'a fifth wheel in the coach'. Admiral Tovey, who commanded the Home Fleet for a long time, and had a very important action at sea, and Lord Cork and Orrery have spoken in the same sense. I have here a letter, which I am authorized to read, from Sir Percy Noble, who has not hitherto expressed himself in public, but who has unequalled credentials, because he managed the business himself with success last time. It says:

'My dear Mr Churchill: From experience in the last war—first in command of the Western Approaches and then as one of the Combined Chiefs of Staff—it is my opinion that there is no need for a Supreme Commander in the Atlantic at all. In 1942, when I was at Liverpool, Admiral of the Fleet Sir Dudley Pound discussed this very question with me, and we agreed that such a form of command was not only unnecessary, but might (and probably would) impose an undue strain on the already very complex system of wireless and other communications.

'When I was in Washington in 1943 the whole of our machinery for controlling the North Atlantic convoys was again re-examined by Admiral King and myself with Admiral Sir Henry Moore, who was at that time the Vice-Chief of the Naval Staff in London. Had it then been considered wise to introduce a change in the system, it is probable that a British officer would have been selected for this Supreme Command as Britain and Canada were providing almost the whole of the escorting forces in that area. However, we decided that no change was necessary.

'Great Britain is the "receiving end" of the Atlantic life-line and the jumping-off place for forces entering Europe.

'In view of certain statements to the contrary which have appeared in the Press, I feel it is worth mentioning that in my experience no serious confusion ever arose in regard to the exercise of control by the methods we employed in the last war.'

That is not an opinion which should be dismissed in contemptuous terms. It is not an opinion which should be ignored, and I am sure our American friends with whom Admiral Noble worked so intimately will give it full weight in considering this matter now under discussion between us. My first submission, therefore, to the Committee is that there is no need for the appointment of a Supreme Commander in the Atlantic.

Let me now approach the question from another angle. We all rejoiced when General Eisenhower was appointed Supreme Commander of the Armies of the Atlantic Powers. There is no man in the world who can do that job so well. Although the American troops under his command will only be a fraction of the whole of the European forces which are needed—and far less than the French Army which, if France and Europe are to live, must be reborn—yet everyone was contented, and has been more contented every day since his appointment. It was a great shock however to most of the fifty millions in our islands when they learned that a United States admiral was also to be put in command of the Atlantic and of a large proportion of our Fleet employed there.

During the war the life-lines across the Atlantic fell in an overwhelming degree to the care of the Admiralty. We were always most anxious for the Americans to extend their zone eastwards towards us, even during the first two years of the struggle when we were alone and they gave us magnificent help. But in 1942, after they had come into the war, their major theatre in that war—I say that war—was inevitably and rightly in the Pacific. They suffered terrible losses in the massacre of shipping through their own inexperience of dealing with the U-boat. The 'U-boat paradise'—the Germans called it—took a terrible toll of their own eastern coast in 1942, and hard-pressed though we were ourselves, we were very glad to send them all the help we could in creating their convoy and escort system. They did not suffer to any serious extent from the mining danger. But the climax of the U-boat war was reached in 1943, and during this struggle nearly the whole business was managed and the burden borne by Britain and Canada. In fact it was by agreements reached between the British and American Governments, the Combined Chiefs of Staff Committee, and between the Admiralties, that Britain and Canada assumed full responsibility for the protection of all trade convoys, apart from American troop convoys, in the North Atlantic, and the American naval contribution fell by agreement to a little more than two per cent of the total. This was the period when the U-boat attack was decisively broken by all the means that were available.

We have become relatively, I regretfully admit, a weaker Power since those days—not only on the seas. Nevertheless, we have the experience, we have the art. Our latent resources in trained sea-faring personnel are out of all proportion to what we have presented in recent years. We need, of course, American aid. So does the whole world. We need aid particularly in the air at the reception end, but I can find no valid reason for subordinating Great Britain in the Atlantic Command. The responsibility should be shared on equal terms and with equal status between the two chief naval Powers. That is my submission.

We are told we are to have the sole command of British coastal waters and of the English Channel. We are not told what 'coastal waters' means. The First Lord of the Admiralty in another place spoke of the Americans 'commanding in deep waters'. What does that mean? Does that mean up to the 100-fathom line, or what? I had better give way if the right hon Gentleman the Minister of Defence wishes to answer.

THE MINISTER OF DEFENCE [MR SHINWELL]: I am very anxious not to interrupt the right hon Gentleman because I am intensely interested in what he is saying, but he must take into account what appears in the White Paper about the control of the Eastern Atlantic.

MR CHURCHILL: I was coming to all that, but I was talking of the coastal waters. I ask what that means because the Eastern Atlantic like the Western is under supreme American command. It is the coastal waters alone that are reserved for Great Britain and I am asking if they end at the 100-fathom line. [HON MEMBERS: 'The Minister does not know.'] In any case the area is severely restricted round our own coast, and the line that is drawn, be it the 100-fathom line or not, like the line that will be drawn across the Atlantic in no way corresponds to any boundary which applies to U-boat attack. The English Channel is reserved to us. It is surely not more vital to the integrity of the reception of convoys than the Bay of Biscay or the waters between Icelan and Ireland, or the North Sea, or the Arctic approaches to and from North Russia. It is all one story, and one story that can only be intelligently told from one place.

Let me turn now to another aspect—sentiment. Sentiment should not rule in war, but neither should it be forgotten or overlooked. I am sorry that the Prime Minister is not here and still more sorry for the cause of his absence, but I must state the case. He plays too important a part in it to be omitted from any coherent discussion. He certainly does not understand British sentiment about the Navy. Going back a long time, I admit, to 27 March 1936—it was on the same subject and living in the same discussion—the Prime Minister said, according to the *Daily Herald*—from which I take the report:

'We shall have to give up certain of our toys—one is "Britannia rules the Waves".'

This was certainly a misquotation. As has been often pointed out, it is, 'Britannia rule the Waves'—an invocation not a declaration of fact. But if the idea 'Rule Britannia' was a toy, it is certainly one for which many good men from time to time have been ready to die.

No one can doubt that it was a great shock and even an affront—quite unintended by the United States—to the whole nation when, following on an American general's supreme command in Europe, which we all welcome, we were told that an American admiral would have supreme command of the Atlantic. It was also a shock to see that our Prime Minister had so little knowledge and even less feeling in the matter. However, the United States themselves should consider the sentiments of others in executing their great mission of leading the resistance of the free world against Communist aggression and infiltration. It should not be possible for their enemies to say that they are grasping the supreme command everywhere—on the land, in the air, on the sea. Moreover, it is not true; that is not their wish or their desire. To create this superfluous supreme command of the Atlantic would be a psychological mistake, making things harder than they are already. Of course, it plays right into the hands of the Communist propagandists and their fellow travellers who declare, in their lying fashion, that we have all been bought up by Wall Street and the almighty dollar. Why make them this present in the discussion when the matter is not, as I have said, of real and fundamental importance? It would, I think, have been a natural thing in sentiment, and also on practical and technical arguments, to have shared the Atlantic Command with equal status between the Admiralty and the United States Navy Department.

I am quite sure it was not the wish of the American people or their government to treat us roughly in this matter, or to make an issue of it at all. When I made my protest I received most active and sincere and widespread American support. It is a trouble into which they have been brought, not at all by their own decision or desire but through other reasons which I will presently indicate. I have heard the argument used—and it is even suggested in the last sentence of paragraph 28 in the White Paper—that we shall get much more out of the Americans by letting them have the command, even though it is mainly nominal. That, I think, is a train of thought unworthy of the dignity of both our countries. It implies that the Americans are willing to be fooled by being flattered and that the British have no pride if they can get more help. We should dismiss such arguments from our thoughts. But still we can see the traces of them on the last page of the White Paper. The issue, I think, should be settled between comrades and brothers in common danger and on a self-respecting moral basis, and with the sole desire and resolve to find the best way of winning victory and salvation from our dangers.

It is true, no doubt, that the United States has a larger fleet than we have—double, we are told—in ships in commission, and a great preponderance in the air. Also, they have wisely and carefully kept in 'mothball' many scores of war vessels which we have improvidently scrapped, sold or given away. Thus, they have a larger material reserve. Broadly speaking, it can be said that the supreme command in war goes naturally with the size of the forces involved, and I accepted and affirmed that rule in the late struggle.

THE PARLIAMENTARY AND FINANCIAL SECRETARY TO THE ADMIRALTY [MR JAMES CALLAGHAN]: It may be quite true that the Americans have a much larger material reserve, but I suggest to the right hon Gentleman that they do not possess a proportionately larger material reserve than we have compared with their active fleet.

MR CHURCHILL: It is rather difficult to work out these rule-of-three sums. [Laughter.] Hon Members opposite laugh at that; that is all they are fit for. Why should they laugh because I am not prepared to argue that question of whether it is a proportionately larger reserve? It is a grave and foolish thing to cast away valuable ships at the end of a war. It is much better to keep them, even if you do not want them, in care and maintenance, and then you can never tell when they will turn out to be useful. I have not worked it out in proportion, but at any rate the Americans have a far larger material reserve than we have.

I was saying that, broadly speaking, the supreme command in war goes naturally with the larger forces. I think that may be taken as the rule. Nevertheless, in the campaign of Tunis we did not hesitate to allow our armies to remain under General Eisenhower's command, although we had eleven divisions in action to the Americans' four. On the other hand when, later in that year, the United States asked for an American supreme commander to have control both of the 'Overlord' campaign in France and also of the Mediterranean, I refused to agree, and although there were tense arguments the matter was settled agreeably, as so many other matters were settled between us, and it was settled without any ill-feeling. How was this accomplished? It was accomplished by the personal relations between the Heads of Governments and, of course, was based upon the continued comradeship and intercourse of our Combined Chiefs of Staff Committee. I shall come back to this institution before I sit down, but the conclusion I now draw is that commands in particular operations and in various theatres are not necessarily regulated merely by the size of the forces locally involved.

In estimating the size of these forces one must not only consider the relative naval strengths of the fleets and flotillas and aircraft squadrons as they now stand. I know we are in a temporary eclipse, but we are capable of a far greater and more rapid development of strength in the naval sphere than almost any other country. Besides the warships of all kinds, there is the Mercantile Marine. We must not forget them, or the sacrifices the merchant seamen made in the struggle—many of them sunk three or four times with their ships, but always going back. We may have let our Navy down, but it can be revived. We have not let our Mercantile Marine diminish. On the contrary——

MR CALLAGHAN *rose*——

MR CHURCHILL: The Parliamentary Secretary is a subordinate Minister of the Government and he should not interrupt from the Front Bench. We have not let our Mercantile Marine diminish. On the contrary, here are the figures. [*Interruption.*] I think I have the right to put forward the case for the potential contribution which Britain can make to war and transport on the seas. The United States have 12,400,000 tons of merchant shipping in use and 14,000,000 tons in reserve. They have 250,000 tons under construction. Great Britain has 16,600,000 tons in use, or 19,600,000 if the Commonwealth and Empire are added, and 2,000,000 tons under construction, some of it for foreign account. Moreover, we have far larger reserves of merchant——

MR SNOW (Lichfield and Tamworth): Damned old fool.

COLONEL GOMME-DUNCAN (Perth and East Perthshire): On a point of order. Is it in order for an hon Member to refer to the right hon Gentleman as 'a damned old fool'?

THE CHAIRMAN: It is certainly not in order.

MR SNOW: I beg to withdraw that statement and to apologize but, of course, the right hon Gentleman has been extremely provocative.

HON MEMBERS: Get out.

MR CHURCHILL: I always accept an apology here.

MR SNOW: Will not the right hon Gentleman follow my example and apologize to my hon Friend?

MR IVOR OWEN THOMAS (The Wrekin): May I call attention to the fact that this whole incident arose from——

THE CHAIRMAN: It was within the hearing of all Members of the Committee, and there is no point in calling attention to it now.

MR THOMAS: On a point of order. Is it in order for the right hon Gentleman to refer to an hon Member of the Committee as somewhat subordinate to another—[*Laughter*.] Let hon Members wait for the whole of it—and, therefore, not entitled to the same consideration as a Member of the Government? Are not the rights of every Member on the Floor of the Committee equal?

THE CHAIRMAN: I do not think any procedural objection can be taken to the right hon Gentleman's reference to the Parliamentary Secretary to the Admiralty. [HON MEMBERS: 'Oh.'] But it is, of course, true that the hon Gentleman is the chief Minister of the Admiralty in the House.

MR CHURCHILL: Well, I understood that the Minister of Defence was going to take responsibility for the case today; and everything is relative in importance, and consequently, compared with the Minister of Defence, the hon Gentleman must accept the position of being subordinate; although let me make it quite clear that this is the first time that I have ever heard the word 'subordinate' regarded as un-Parliamentary or even as almost an obscene expression. However, the 'damned old fool' has accepted the apology.

I was saying that, moreover, we have far larger reserves of merchant seamen than the United States; we have a much larger merchant fleet; and I say that that is not a negligible contribution to the solution of the problems we have to settle between our two great, friendly countries. This very serious mistake arises from the fault of planning from the bottom instead of planning from the top. When the top are incompetent to plan or give guidance, the process naturally begins from the bottom. We suffer from the fallacy, *deus ex machina*, which, for the benefit of any Wykehamists who may be present, is 'A god out of the machine'. There are layers of committees and super committees, and the business is passed upwards stage by stage to a decision. When all the process has been gone through, the machine speaks, but what one gets at the end is not truth or wisdom or common sense: it is a White Paper. All that comes out of the machine is unreal and meaningless formulae expressed in official jargon and accompanied by fatuous grimaces.

Now let me tell the Committee, so far as I know the facts, the procedure by which an American admiral was appointed to the Supreme Command of the Atlantic. I have been looking into the workings of the machine, which, I hope, will interest the right hon Gentleman. Here let me say and let me emphasize that I have no doubt that Admiral Fechteler is a most capable and competent officer. Although he has no special experience of the Atlantic theatre, he is, I am sure, a naval officer of the highest quality. But so far as I have been able to ascertain, this is how the decision was taken by planning from the bottom.

The original proposal came at a meeting in Washington some time last year, and was made by the Canadian representative. So I ask the Minister of Defence, when he replies, to tell the Committee whether this was agreed or was, at least, a matter of consultation beforehand between the British and the Canadian Governments? If it was not, it would seem it ought to have been. All the other Powers present supported the proposal. The British representative, Vice-Admiral Schofield, who has been very vocal in the recent discussions, felt that the best he could do was to ask that the Supreme Commander's deputy should be British. Now I ask the Minister of Defence, did he have instructions to take this course? Surely on a matter of such high importance of this character, he should have had definite instructions from above. If he had none, he should, in my opinion, have said that the matter was too important to be decided without reference to higher authority, and asked for an adjournment. But all passed off very pleasantly with unanimous agreement. The matter then slumbered for several months while the machine was grinding away from day to day, until the decision leaked out from Copenhagen.

Let us look at some of these countries whose subordinate officers—I beg the pardon of the Committee for using that word—settled the matter. I may say that they are all countries for whom I have the strongest regard and from whom I have received many compliments and honours. But let me take four of them—Norway, Denmark, Belgium, Holland. Though we accept the statement that the American

Navy is doubly as strong as the British, the British Navy, even in its present phase, is more than twelve times as strong as all these four put together. Even if France be included, their combined strength is less than a quarter of ours.

These four Powers I am speaking of have between them one aircraft carrier, acquired from Britain since the war, and fifteen destroyers and sixteen frigates, many of which have been purchased from Great Britain. Yet the voting strength of each round the table was equal to ours, and also, of course, to the United States, whose navy is larger than everyone's. Everything went off smoothly, and the American representative, no doubt with a becoming blush, accepted the supreme command for his country. All this is happening far below the cognizance of statesmen, premiers, presidents and leading people—even, perhaps, Ministers of Defence—who manage our affairs. But it went on steadily up to the higher levels—the committees of greater status—until we reached the present situation.

Since the disclosure was made to Parliament the Government have become conscious that the policy to which they had been bound by the workings of the machine was neither sensible nor—what is, perhaps, for the moment more relevant to their preoccupations—popular. Why have we been waiting so long for the White Paper, and now have only an interim incomplete document? It is because His Majesty's Government suddenly became aware of what was going on and that it was bringing them into discredit, and they have tried to find some counterpoise to restore the balance and help them out of their scrape. Then the happy thought came: 'If we have given up the command of the Atlantic, let us try, as a sop to placate our people to keep or gain the commander-in-chiefship of the Mediterranean. That would make things more even.'

Though I have no definite information, I presume that most active discussions have been proceeding on the basis that as Britain has given up the Atlantic she must at least have the Mediterranean. But here again there is a great difficulty. This is the cause of the delay in our getting the full White Paper. The Mediterranean Powers, whose Governments have now been brought into the matter—not a mere committee of medium officials sitting round a table—want to have the Americans in command of the Mediterranean. There are almost as many powerful arguments in favour of the United States having the command in the Mediterranean as there are against them having the over-riding command in the Atlantic.

MR SHINWELL: At this stage I want to be quite clear about the statement the right hon Gentleman has just made. Do I understand him to say that Governments who are concerned in the Mediterranean zone have decided that there should be an American commander, or have suggested that there should be an American commander? If so, will the right hon Gentleman be good enough to let me have the evidence on this?

MR CHURCHILL: I will say what I have said and what I am going to say. I say that, since all this matter became public in discussions on the American command of the Atlantic, there has been a very great deal more attention paid to the discussions about the command in the Mediterranean; very much more.

MR SHINWELL *rose*——

MR CHURCHILL: The right hon Gentleman ought to keep something for his speech.

MR SHINWELL: The right hon Gentleman need be under no illusions. He will be surprised, and probably disagreeably surprised, at how much I have to say in replying to him. I want to put him right about the facts, because I think that is very desirable, and all I say to him now is that the discussions about the Mediterranean and the discussions about the whole command have been taking place simultaneously.

MR CHURCHILL: They may have been taking place simultaneously, but one ended before the other. That sometimes happens in horse racing. I am certainly not seeking to gain personal popularity by what I am going to say. On the contrary, I am saying only what I think is right and true, and should be considered and weighed by the Committee and the Government. I say that there are almost as many powerful arguments in favour of the United States having the command in the Mediterranean as there are against them having the overriding command in the Atlantic. Personally, if I had to choose I should prefer, on high military and national grounds, the United States having command in the Mediterranean. I am sorry to have to trouble the Committee with details, but it is better that the matter should be understood. A powerful fleet—and this will interest hon Gentlemen opposite below the Gangway—of American carriers can be and is being placed in the Mediterranean which, working in conjunction with the air bases America has obtained from France and in Tripoli, would bring a tremendous potential attack with the atomic bomb upon the most vulnerable parts of Russia, including the oilfields, in the event of war, and this fact constitutes an immense and precious deterrent against another war.

The United States can, if it chooses, have by far the most powerful fleet in the Mediterranean, and a fleet suited to the actual task which might have to be performed if the worst came to the worst. I think we should be ready and proud to be the hosts of our American allies and comrades at our famous and vital Mediterranean bases at Gibraltar, Malta and, presumably, Cyprus. I would much rather the British offensive atomic base in East Anglia were not the only major deterrent of this kind upon Communist aggression.

MR EMRYS HUGHES (South Ayrshire): Who is being aggressive now?

MR CHURCHILL: This is rather up the hon Gentleman's street. It is right to spread the risk of reprisals. We at home would be safer, and the United Nations and Atlantic Powers would be stronger. Therefore, I do not oppose the United States taking the command, if that is their wish, of the Mediterranean on the practical and strategic merits. Moreover, there are far-reaching political arguments. We are no longer strong enough ourselves to bear the whole political burden we have hitherto borne in the Mediterranean, or even to take the leading part in the diplomatic control of that theatre. But the United States and Britain together, aided by France—which in the Mediterranean, with her bases and her ships, makes a very different contribution to the common strength than is possible for her to do in the Atlantic—we three together would be in a most powerful position to deal with, say, the Egyptian problem and the whole question of the defence of the Suez Canal. We and the United States ought to act together there and in these matters.

I am always looking out for something to give the Government a good mark for, and I read the papers vigilantly every day, and I was very glad to see that about the Persian oil the Government are already working with the United States. That is right and wise. The same combination will enormously relieve our difficulties in Egypt, the Levant and throughout the Middle East. After all, the United States are now looking after Turkey, and have taken over from us the salvation of Greece. These countries would welcome the United States in the Mediterranean, and would gladly accord them the supreme command there.

What are the Government trying to do? Having let the question of the Atlantic command go largely by default they hope to put themselves right with the public—this is my guess—by claiming the Mediterranean. It is as if a man had put the wrong shoe on his right foot should say: 'I will put the other shoe on my left foot, and that will be a compromise which will make it all right.' Such absurdities have no part in the grim realities of warding off war or of war itself. I ask that this matter should be reconsidered from the beginning. I ask that the command of the Atlantic shall be agreeably divided between Great Britain and the United States on equal terms. In the war the line was eventually drawn at the 26th Meridian—quite a different thing from the 38th Parallel. But wherever the line is to be drawn, it would be easy to arrange for the taking over of the convoys and for their air defence; and the adjustments, sometimes almost daily, can be made quite easily, and can only be made, between the Admiralty and the Canadian and United States Navy Departments. If it is a question of large transfers of forces from one side to the other, that is really a matter first for a Combined Chiefs of Staff Committee, if they exist still, and in the ultimate issue for settlement between the Prime Minister and the President, who together control ninety per cent of all the effective air and naval forces involved in this whole business.

Now I come to the existing organization for the Atlantic Pact. The costly error was made when the Combined British and American Chiefs of Staff Committee was dissolved of sweeping this away, of breaking up this organization. It was a disaster. We speak the same language; we have many other ties. What a pity it was to let go that organization which served us so well, and which carried the direction of war between allies to the highest and most smooth-working efficiency ever reached in history.

The Prime Minister told us that he regretted the abolition of the Combined Chiefs of Staffs Committee. But why did he not put up a fight about it? Surely this was an occasion when he might have crossed the Atlantic and had a personal talk with the President on the top level. Keeping the Combined Chiefs of Staffs Commitee in existence need not have prevented a co-existent instrument with other Powers on it for the purpose of executing the Atlantic Pact. Half the misunderstandings which have been so dangerous to Anglo-American relations during the Korean War would, I believe, have been avoided had there been a regular and constant meeting, as there were in the bygone years, between our two Chiefs of Staffs Committees. We cannot afford in the dangers in which we now stand to make mistakes like this. By mismanaging these affairs the responsible Ministers may bring untold miseries upon the hard-working, helpless millions whose fate lies in their hands.

What organization have we got now to replace the contact between the President and the Prime Minister and the continued daily intercourse of the Combined Chiefs of Staffs Committee? We are told of a standing group of Powers under the Atlantic Pact. This group which deals with the forces deployed under that Pact, consists of three men—a French general, a British airman and an American vice-admiral. There is not a British sailor on it at all; not at the head of the fleets, nor in this higher organization. But surely the carrying of food and supplies from which Britain lives, carrying the armies of the New World to Europe, and maintaining them there across the broad oceans and through the narrow seas—surely that is a business in which sailors and merchant seamen and ships of all kinds, and naval skill and knowledge have their part. I hope that the House will carefully consider many of the arguments that I have ventured to put before them, and I hope that we shall not allow this matter to rest as a thing definitely settled. I hope myself that the mistakes that have been made will be recovered.

This White Paper, so long withheld, is mainly a repetition of the one we got over a year ago. It has the addition of the names of various officers appointed by General Eisenhower in his Continental Command. But it gives us no real information. It is only a painful exposure of the paralysis of Cabinet mentality. If the Minister of Defence is not able tonight to make a genuine contribution to our knowledge, I shall feel it my duty to move a nominal reduction of his salary as a protest against the manner in which these grave matters have so far been handled by him and by the Government as a whole.

# GRAND HABITATION OF THE PRIMROSE LEAGUE

A SPEECH AT THE ROYAL ALBERT HALL, LONDON
27 APRIL 1951

---

21 *April—Mr Bevan, Minister of Labour, resigns from the Government; this is followed on the 23rd by the resignation of Mr Harold Wilson, President of the Board of Trade. Mr Freeman, Parliamentary Secretary, Ministry of Supply, resigns on the 24th.*

22 *April—Communist forces in Korea launch an attack on a hundred-mile front, UN forces withdrawing. After a lull Communists resume offensive on 16 May.*

22–25 *April—Battle of Imjin River in Korea; gallant stand by The Gloucestershire Regiment.*

23 *April—A one-year supplementary Anglo-Argentine trade and financial agreement signed in Buenos Aires.*

26 *April—The oil commission in Persia resolves to effect nationalization of Persian oil immediately.*

27 *April—A United States-Danish agreement signed in Copenhagen for common defence of Greenland.*

---

[*27 April* 1951

We meet for our Annual Meeting this year in a grave hour for our country. I cannot recall any period in my long life when mismanagement and incompetence have brought us into greater danger. At home prices and taxes go up and up, abroad the influence of Britain goes down and down. In every quarter of the world we are regarded by our friends with anxiety, with wonder and pity; and by our enemies, including some of those countries we have helped most in the past, like Egypt and Persia, we are regarded or treated with hostility or even contempt. Not one of them is so weak that they cannot spare a kick or a taunt for Britain. It is hard to believe that we are the same nation that emerged from the last war respected and admired throughout the grand alliance for all the part we played, for a long time alone, in the defence of the cause of freedom. Six years of Socialist rule have brought us low.

Nevertheless we must not lose faith in our race and in our destiny. We are the same people, in the same islands, as we were in the great days we can all remember. Our spirit is unconquerable, our ingenuity and craftsmanship unsurpassed. Our latent resources are unmeasured. Our underlying unities are enduring. We have but to cast away by an effort of will the enfeebling tendencies and fallacies of Socialism and to free ourselves from restrictive Socialist rule to stand erect once more and take our place among the great Powers of the world. Never must we lose our faith and our courage, never must we fail in exertion and resolve.

We are all glad that the Prime Minister has left hospital and can turn from the jigsaw-puzzles of Cabinet shuffling to the urgent tasks which confront him. It is hard on any country when no one is looking after it. Mr Attlee combines a limited outlook with strong qualities of resistance. He now resumes the direction and leadership of that cluster of lion-hearted limpets—a new phenomenon in our natural history, almost a suggestion I could offer Mr Herbert Morrison for his fun fair—who are united by their desire to hold on to office at all costs to their own reputations and their country's fortunes, and to put off by every means in their power to the last possible moment any contact with our democratic electorate. This they do in the name not of principle or policy but of party loyalty enforced by party discipline carried to lengths not previously witnessed in our system of representative and Parliamentary Government.

But in the last week three Ministers resigned from this Government which itself stands on a minority in the country and hangs from day to day and night to night upon a thread in the House of Commons. I shall not occupy your time this afternoon in lengthy eulogies of these Ministers or explanations of their motives. The first might be deemed insincere; the second would certainly be laborious. But at any rate they have rendered a public service by exposing to Parliament the scandalous want of foresight in buying the raw materials upon which our vital rearmament programme depends. Frantic, belated efforts are now, we are assured, being made to repair the evil which resembles, though on a larger scale, and in a more dangerous sphere, the meat, the nuts, the eggs and other muddles with which we are already only too familiar. But for the resignations of these Ministers we should not have known about it until too late. We should have known no more about the raw material shortages than the Prime Minister knew about the appointment of the American admiral to the supreme command of the Atlantic. What is happening now in raw materials is typical of the way our affairs drift and bump and flop. Next week we shall bring the disclosures of the resigning Ministers to the full rigours of debate in the House of Commons.

Nowhere in the darkening scene has more harm been done during

Mr Attlee's tenure than in the loss of those intimate contacts between the British Prime Minister and the President of the United States which were so helpful and fruitful in the war. A wave of irritation is passing across the United States and the Isolationist forces there are glad to turn it upon Great Britain. The reproaches against General MacArthur—that great soldier and great statesman as his settlement of difficulties with Japan after the war have proved—in which Mr Shinwell, and even so staid a Minister as Mr Chuter Ede have indulged, enable those who do not like us in the United States to suggest that His Majesty's Government have had something to do with General MacArthur's dismissal. I cannot believe there is the slightest truth in this. Mr Truman is not only the President of the United States he is also Commander-in-Chief, and no one outside the great Republic, now bearing nineteen-twentieths of the whole weight of the war in Korea, has the slightest right to interfere between him and his officers. This great meeting here this afternoon should take the opportunity to pay their full tribute to our American friends and allies, for the sacrifices and exertions they have made, and are making, and are going to make, to save the world from Communist tyranny, and we should all of us bear in mind the well-known maxim 'United we stand, Divided we fall'.

And that applies with equal force to what is going on in our own islands now. We are rent by party struggles which are inevitably and deliberately provoked when a Government, which has no claim to rest upon the will and confidence of the people, continues to keep us month after month on the brink of an election and whose fear of the judgment of their own fellow-countryman is their only bond of union. I can assure you we shall do all in our power, by every constitutional means open to us, to bring this harmful suspense and uncertainty to a speedy end. Be sure you are ready for the call when it comes. Be sure that you lay aside every impediment and allow no class or privilege or vested interest to stand between you and your duty to the nation, and then all will be well and in the end all will be well for all.

# EXPORTS TO CHINA

A SPEECH TO THE HOUSE OF COMMONS
10 MAY 1951

---

28 *April—Dr Mossadeq appointed Persian Prime Minister.*

*General Election in Australia; Coalition majority reduced in House of Representatives but increased in Senate.*

2 *May—Germany admitted to the Council of Europe.*

3 *May—The Festival of Britain declared open by HM The King from the steps of St Paul's Cathedral.*

8 *May—TM The King and Queen of Denmark arrive in England on a state visit.*

---

[10 *May* 1951

I hope the Committee will forgive me if I try to look at this topic in its general setting. I am quite sure that justice cannot be done to it in any other way. In November 1949 I was in favour of the recognition of Communist China, provided that it was *de facto* and not *de jure*, or as it would probably be called among the old-school-tie-brigade of the party opposite, '*day yuri*', and provided that it could be brought about as a joint policy with the United States and the Dominions.

The United States had largely disinterested themselves in the civil war in China, and Chiang Kai-shek, who used to be paraded to me in those bygone days of the war as the champion of the new Asia, was being driven off the mainland. I could see no reason why, if we had diplomatic relations with Communist Russia, Communist Poland and other countries inside the Iron Curtain, we could not have them with China. Recognition does not mean approval. One has to recognize and deal with all sorts of things in this world as they come along. After all, vaccination is undoubtedly a definite recognition of smallpox. Certainly I think that it would be very foolish, in ordinary circumstances, not to keep necessary contacts with countries with whom one is not at war. However, a little later, the Government recognized Communist China, not only *de facto* but *de jure*, and they recognized it as an isolated act, without agreement with the United States or joint action with the Dominions. The date was oddly chosen. I am told that it was three days before the Colombo Conference of Commonwealth Foreign Secretaries. One would have thought that it was a matter that might

67

have been talked over there. The response of the Chinese Communists was very surly. They took all they could get from our recognition and gave nothing in return. They did not even recognize us. The United States were much offended by our isolated action, and that is how that part of the story ends.

Presently, the situation in the Far East was transformed and everything was sharpened by the Communist aggression in Korea, and was presently brought to a much more serious and intense position by the Chinese intervention. When the United Nations definitely passed the resolution, to which His Majesty's Government assented, branding China as an aggressor, we were left in an uncomfortable and illogical position of having diplomatic relations with a Chinese Government formally censured by the United Nations, and which was engaged in attacking United States soldiers—United Nations soldiers—and also our own small contingent in Korea. There is no doubt that the maintenance of our relationship with Red China had been and has been totally devoid of advantages to us or to the United Nations, and that it became a reproach against us in wide circles in America. This made a bad foundation between us for discussion with the United States about all the vexing questions of trading with the enemy—as the Chinese Communists had undoubtedly become. Of course, it is the first interest of Britain and of Europe, and also, I believe, of the United States, to make some kind of defence front against the at present overwhelming Soviet power on the European Continent, and all of us on both sides of the House saw good and cogent arguments for our not getting too deeply involved in Korea, still less in China.

We on this side, without taking academic views about the 38th Parallel, were most anxious that the United Nations Forces should not go beyond the waist or narrow part of the peninsula and should keep a broad no-man's-land between their own front and the Yalu River. It did not seem wise to broaden the front by another 200 or 300 miles by emerging from the narrow part of the Korean Peninsula into this much expanded area. As it was the policy of the United Nations and of the United States not to enter Chinese territory nor even to bomb beyond the frontier line, it seemed especially dangerous to advance close up to that frontier line. It is always dangerous in war to march or walk close up to a wall without being allowed to look over the other side and see what is going on there, and act against it if necessary. Therefore, personally, not having an opportunity of obtaining any technical information, I wanted to stop at the waist and have a no-man's-land. I think that there was pretty general agreement on that in the House. However, General MacArthur's forces became heavily involved on a much wider front far beyond the waist, and a series of heavy Chinese counter-attacks were delivered. War was in fact begun on a considerable scale between the United Nations and China without any formal declaration of war on either side; and that is the position that exists today with ever-intensifying gravity.

There is no doubt that the Chinese Communist Government is waging war at Russian instigation and with powerful Soviet aid in weapons and supplies against the troops of the United Nations. Our recognition and maintenance of diplomatic relations with China has undoubtedly been a cause of misunderstanding with the United States, and has made more difficult the discussion of our other joint problems with them in the Far East. I cannot believe that a policy of appeasement to Chinese Communist aggression will bring about peace with Red China. On the contrary, any form of weakness or indecision or division among the anti-Communist forces will only prolong the fighting and increase its scale. I have ventured to deal with these rather wider aspects this afternoon in order to place the matter objectively before the Committee.

I now wish to consider the position of the United States. I always watch the hon Gentlemen below the Gangway opposite, as that is where the weather comes from. I have an advantage over the Foreign Secretary in being able to keep them directly under my view, whereas if he were to keep his head turned it might well be thought that he was paying them undue attention. We cannot watch and listen to them without deriving the impression that their sympathies are, on the whole, more with Red China than with the United States. But Red China has been branded as an aggressor by the United Nations with the full assent of the present Socialist Government.

MR SYDNEY SILVERMAN (Nelson and Colne): Not with their full assent.

MR CHURCHILL: Even those Ministers who have resigned were members of the Government at the time that decision was taken. We now know that the Communists are killing United Nations soldiers, and our soldiers. We know that they have established a reign of terror in China, with horrible executions and mob butcheries and a merciless purge characteristic of Communist tyranny wherever it is applied, especially in the transitional stages, all over the world. We ought not, I say, to have any sympathies with Red China, and the more they are expressed and manifested in this House the more harm is done to our relations with the United States. After all, the United States are doing nineteen-twentieths of the work and suffering losses of fifty and sixty to one compared to us. We must try to understand their position.

We really cannot get through life either as individuals or as a State without trying to put ourselves in the position of others with whom we come in contact and have to deal. The United States have lost nearly 70,000 men, killed, wounded and missing. We know how we feel about the Gloucesters, and that should enable us to measure the feelings of people in the United States, in many cities, towns and villages there, when the news comes in of someone who has lost a dear one in the fighting overseas. Feelings are tense: very dangerous to distress or to disturb. We can measure these American feelings by our own. They also know that they are bearing virtually the whole weight of the Korean War.

Look also at all the money they have given to Europe. Look at the money they have lent or given to our country during the period of Socialist rule. I doubt whether we should have had the Utopia which we enjoy without their aid. Where should we all be without their assistance in Europe? Free Europe is quite incapable of defending itself, and must remain so for several years, whatever we do. These considerations must be kept in our minds when we discuss these matters of trade, which I consider minor matters, and the different points of friction between us and the United States. What would be our position in this island if Western Europe were overrun as it would be——

MR HAROLD DAVIES (Leek): If we went to war with China.

MR CHURCHILL: The hon Member really must learn to cultivate a sense of proportion in the matter. It is not a matter of whether there is a war with China or not but whether there is a rift between Britain and the United States or not. That is the thought that haunts me, and I hope and trust that it will be considered everywhere else. What would be our position, I say, if Europe were overrun, as it would be but for the immense American ascendancy in the atomic bomb, and the deterrent effect, not necessarily upon the Russians but upon the Communist Kremlin regime, of this tremendous weapon? The fact that we are bitterly divided and absorbed in party strife, and kept month after month——

MR ELLIS SMITH (Stoke-on-Trent, South): So is America.

MR CHURCHILL: Quite true, but they have at any rate a fixed date for their elections. To exist month by month in such an electioneering atmosphere as this may provide many topics to fill the public mind and what is left of the newspapers, but our external dangers do not diminish meanwhile; they grow continually. It is said that we are getting stronger, but to get stronger does not necessarily mean that we are getting safer. It is only when we are strong enough that safety is achieved; and the period of the most acute danger might well arise just before we were strong enough. I hope that may be pondered upon because it is a very potent and relevant factor.

Our great danger now is in pursuing a policy of girding at the United States and giving them the impression that they are left to do all the work, while we pull at their coat-tails and read them moral lessons in statecraft and about the love we all ought to have for China. I would plead in the very short time I beg leave to keep the House this afternoon—because our time is very limited—for a sense of proportion —[Hon Members: 'Hear, hear.']—yes, on the grounds of national safety and even of survival. I say that we must think not only of ourselves; we must think of our friends in Europe; of the Norwegians, the Danes, the Dutch, the Belgians, the French and others who lie still nearer to the Soviet Power with its mighty armies and satellite States. Their plight is even worse than ours. We at least have the Channel, although even that as a means of safety would, without air superiority, soon depart; and air superiority cannot be obtained by us without the fullest aid from the United States. Therefore I say that on every ground, national, European and international, we should allow no minor matters—even if we feel keenly about them—to stand in the way of the fullest, closest intimacy, accord and association with the United States.

I felt bound to raise these matters, these broader considerations, because we really cannot discuss the intimate and complicated matters which have brought about this debate without holding foremost in our minds all the time the overwhelming issues. If the Government so conducts our affairs that we become a cause of diminishing American help for Britain and for Europe, and stimulate the sentiment for isolation which has powerful exponents in the United States, they might well become primarily responsible, not only for our ruin, but for that of the whole of the free world. It is on this basis, and only on this basis, that I venture to examine the details, or some of the details, or some of the aspects of the exports to Communist China which are the cause of the debate—[Hon Members: 'Hear, hear.'] That is not, I hope, a reproach against me for having placed the matter in its proper setting.

These questions of raw materials and of trading with the enemy were brought prominently before us by the resignation of the three Ministers a fortnight ago. When the resigning Ministers threw the blame for raw material shortages in Britain upon the United States, the Americans immediately were greatly stimulated in making their counter-charge that we, while still recognizing the enemy and killing them by the thousand in the battles that were taking place, were making profits directly or indirectly out of commerce with them. This tangled question of the supplies of what are called strategic materials to Red China from Great Britain and the Commonwealth and our tropical Colonies is of course only part of the subject, much of which lies in spheres and forms, which are beyond our control. Red China is not the only place and Hong Kong is not the only channel.

Some months ago I complained of the export of high-grade war manufacture, and even machines and machine-tools, to Russia or to its satellites. The Government denied the charge, but took steps to stop it. Whether those steps have been successful I cannot pronounce, nor could we even in a much longer debate reach any definite conclusions here. But even on the direct point of strategic materials being sent by us to China, through Hong Kong or by other routes, it would be difficult this afternoon to reach plain and final conclusions. The statements made by the Minister of Defence, and after him by the Prime Minister, created, I am sure I am right in saying, general astonishment that these Ministers, whose responsibility in the matter is outstanding, were not better informed. It seemed typical of the way in which our affairs are conducted. It was refreshing on Monday to listen to what seemed at first to be a much more precise statement from the new President of the Board of Trade [Sir Hartley Shawcross]. Here at least there seemed to be evidence of the workings of a clear-cut mind which had been, in the last week or so, turned upon the problem, or upon his brief of the subject.

So far as the regions covered by the figures given by the right hon and learned Gentleman are concerned the general impression was that the scale of these transactions from the United Kingdom was small, and that there could be no ground for saying that the Chinese have received important assistance from the United Kingdom with the approval of His Majesty's Government. The exports from the United Kingdom are indeed petty, and the right hon and learned Gentleman the President of the Board of Trade was right in saying that it is wrong to suppose that they have been a factor of any significance in the Korean campaign.

We were surprised, however, that he confined his lengthy, well-drafted statement to the exports from the United Kingdom and only mentioned, by reference to the previous answer by the Under-Secretary of State for the Colonies, the exports of rubber from Malaya. This is the gravamen of the whole dispute. 'Exports of rubber from the Federated States of Malaya and Singapore to China,' said the Under-Secretary on 12 April, 'amounted in all to 77,000 tons in 1950, and are estimated to amount to 46,000 tons'—I am speaking in round numbers—'in the first quarter of 1951.' Up till 9 April therefore the

Government have taken no effective action in this matter and the exports in the first quarter of the present year show an immense and significant increase on what took place last year; 46,000 tons a quarter is—and I hope I am right in my arithmetic—184,000 tons a year—[HON MEMBERS: 'That is right.']—Is that right? Thank you very much. That is to say two-and-a-half times the annual rate of 1950. That is a very remarkable, substantial, significant advance at this time when matters are becoming more and more tense, serious and critical.

The right hon and learned Gentleman—I shall have to ascertain the right hon Gentleman's wish as to whether I continue to insert the complimentary and formal token 'learned', it will be just as he likes, but I am doing it for today, anyhow—the right hon and learned Gentleman ended his statement by saying that the Government had from 9 April announced their intention, and that of the Governments of the Federation of Malaya and Singapore, to control exports of rubber down to the estimated civilian requirements of China, namely, about 2,500 tons a month.

I raised the point of how the Government could be sure that these 2,500 tons a month would be solely devoted to civilian purposes, considering that in time of war any Government can commandeer for military purposes all civilian supplies. The right hon and learned Gentleman admitted that it was 'quite difficult'—that was his expression—to ensure that these limited rubber supplies were not being misapplied. Anyhow, on the Government's own figures, China has already had in the first quarter of this year, imports, approved formally and officially by us, of 45,000 tons; or half as much again as would be the full civilian Chinese ration, as calculated by the Government, for the whole year.

The question we have to consider today in this sphere, is whether it is worth while to go on nagging, and haggling, and higgling with the United States over a lot of details, and extremely complex details, and making little progress and creating ill will out of all proportion to any advantages gained by us. The United States have a valid complaint on the admitted fact that rubber is an indisputable strategic material. We ought not to be exporting any rubber to China at all, and we suggest on this side of the Committee to the Government, and to the Foreign Secretary, who has a direct responsibility in this matter, that as far as they have it in their power they should stop at once and completely all further export of rubber to China. If there is smuggling, we should do our best to prevent it, and we ought not ourselves to be in the position of agreeing that any rubber should be sent at the present time to Red China.

Surely this would be a simple and straightforward course? It is not so much for the actual facts that I am concerned, but for the consequences. To stop it abruptly and firmly and decisively would clear the air and it would make possible, and perhaps fruitful, the far more complicated discussions about the further steps that are necessary to control any trade which we and the Americans may have with China. It would be a step that everybody could understand, and it might well be the prelude to a whole-hearted agreement with the United States in this sphere, which causes offence and anger far beyond its actual military importance.

I hope we are not going to have another backbiting controversy with the United States about whether any goods are going from Japan into China with their consent.

HON MEMBERS: Oh.

MR HAROLD DAVIES rose——

MR CHURCHILL: Perhaps I am going to use the very argument of which the hon Gentleman is thinking. Anyhow, it is my show at the moment. It might be a very good debating point, if there were really no division between the two sides of the Committee on the matter, here this afternoon, or on some other occasion—a very good debating point—and it is a point which might well be used between Governments if we were bearing an equal burden with the United States— [HON MEMBERS: 'Oh.']—an equal burden in the war. But, in the present circumstances, is it really sensible——

MR POOLE (Birmingham, Perry Barr): Do not write down your own country all the time.

MR CHURCHILL: Will the hon Member yell it out again?

MR POOLE: I suggested that the right hon Gentleman should not so continuously write down his own country.

MR CHURCHILL: There is no better way of writing down your own country than to make boastful and untruthful statements about facts which are known to all. There is no doubt or question of the proportions of the troops who are involved or of the losses which are being suffered in the Korean War. The hon Member should not put out his hand like that; does he accept what I say? Really, the idea that we can uphold the prestige and standard of our country by adopting positions which are entirely divorced from actual and well-known facts is one of those which I think hon Members above the Gangway opposite should endeavour to rise above. I say it would be a great pity to get drawn into this discussion with the United States in detail at the present time and in the present atmosphere, irritating them about minor things, making ineffective repartees. That is not what we should do now when our life and future depend upon their aiding the Atlantic Powers in Europe. Neither let us be baffled by the local difficulties about Hong Kong. I have no doubt they can be solved by measures agreed upon with the United States. Together we have the command of the sea and of the air.

As to a direct attack by the Chinese upon Hong Kong, it must, of course, be resisted by force of arms. We have every sympathy with our fellow-subjects in Hong Kong, but the greatest disservice that we could do them would be to allow a rift to open between us and the United States as a result of our bowing to Communist threats and blackmail. Let me make this passing observation. Of course, it is always very dangerous, and never more so than at the present time, to predict anything that may happen in the future; but in my view, a Soviet attack will not arise because of an incident. An incident may be a pretext, but the moment will be fixed by the result of long, cold calculations, or miscalculations, and among the factors which will play a potent part, the season of the year including harvest time, will be extremely important. I do not, therefore, consider that the question of our doing our duty by Hong Kong should be overclouded by all the statements that may be made that this will bring on a general war. Nobody knows what will bring on a general war except those who have the supreme power in the Kremlin.

Our advice to the Government is to stop rubber entirely now and to reach an agreement with the United States on the general question of trade with China in a spirit which will make the United States feel that their cause is our cause, and that we mean at all costs to be good friends and allies. I read with emotion the testimony of General Marshall before the Senate Committee—[*Interruption.*] The right hon Gentleman had better take a back seat; well, he has done.

THE MINISTER OF DEFENCE [MR SHINWELL] *rose——*

MR CHURCHILL: It is quite right that the right hon Gentleman should take a back seat. He made a statement the other day about no appeasement and so on. I was glad to read it, but he had spoiled it all beforehand by the remark he made at a most disturbing moment in the United States that now, perhaps, things will go better in Korea, once General MacArthur had been dismissed. If anything——

MR SHINWELL *rose——*

HON MEMBERS: Withdraw.

MR CHURCHILL: Hon Members will not frighten me by their yelling. If anything could at that time have got about fifty million Americans furious with him, and with the Government for whom he spoke, it would have been to use language like that. I am very glad that he tried to undo the harm he did by making his speech against appeasement.

MR SHINWELL: The right hon Gentleman has just asserted that I declared that the dismissal of General MacArthur should be brought about because it would be of advantage to us. [HON MEMBERS: 'No.'] Let me tell the right hon Gentleman that the statement which he has just made, in which he alleges that I made that statement about General MacArthur, is utterly false, and I challenge the right hon Gentleman to produce the written evidence or withdraw. I challenge him in this House to produce the written evidence that I made a statement similar to what he has just said.

MR CHURCHILL: I understood, from what was reported in the Press——

MR SHINWELL: Which Press?

MR CHURCHILL:——that the right hon Gentleman said that perhaps things will now go better in Korea since General MacArthur had been removed.

MR SHINWELL: Let me tell the right hon Gentleman that I never made any such statement. I challenge him to produce that statement.

HON MEMBERS: Withdraw.

MR CHURCHILL: No, I would not think of withdrawing. I will produce the newspaper report on which I base myself. I have not got it in my notes at the moment, but I will get it. I thought it a most unfortunate statement.

MR SHINWELL: I never made that statement.

MR CHURCHILL: We shall be very glad to hear what was the statement which the right hon Gentleman actually made. It is always part of the tactics to throw the blame on to the Press, and so on. However, I will produce the Press reports which I read on the subject, and I think they were pretty widely noted. Of course, nobody wishes to accuse the Minister of Defence of crimes which he has not committed.

MR SHINWELL rose——

HON MEMBERS: Sit down.

MR SHINWELL: I shall not sit down. May I tell the right hon Gentleman that he has made a most false statement about me in this House, and that he has no right to make such statements about Ministers?

MR CHURCHILL: Do not be so nervous about it.

MR SHINWELL: I am not nervous about it. [Laughter.] You should be ashamed of yourself. The right hon Gentleman has done more harm to this country than anyone.

MR CHURCHILL: Very helpful, but it is not the right hon Gentleman who would have any right to teach me my conduct. However,

I am sorry to see him so infuriated. The French have a saying that 'it is only the truth that wounds'. I hope that is not the case, because no one would be more pleased than I to find him not guilty on this occasion.

May I now return to the few words I have still to say to the House. Our advice to the Government is to stop the export of rubber to China entirely now, and to reach a general agreement in the favourable atmosphere which this step would create in the United States. I read with emotion the testimony of General Marshall before the Senate Committee. This great world statesman has proved himself to be one of the leading figures in our life since the war. He has spoken with the utmost consideration for our point of view. In him, in General Omar Bradley and in General Eisenhower here in Europe are men in whose judgment on the world scene we may safely repose the fullest confidence. They are members or instruments——

AN HON MEMBER: What about the Admiral?

MR PATON (Norwich, North): What about Admiral Fechteler?

MR CHURCHILL: I try to give consideration to interruptions however irrelevant, and, sometimes, however foolish, but I really cannot be asked such a question as that. I have a great respect for Admiral Fechteler, but I do not think he was put in the right place, and it may be that my view on that will eventually prevail. These men are the members or instruments of President Truman's administration which have enabled him to take the valiant stand he has against the Communist menace, and to lead the great Republic to the rescue of the free world from mortal peril. It is the duty of His Majesty's Government so to act as to prove beyond all doubt or question that we are good and faithful comrades of the American democracy, and will stand with them, whatever may happen, as brothers in arms.

[*Later in the debate Mr Shinwell made the following intervention.*]

MR SHINWELL: With your permission, Sir Charles, and with that of the Committee, I should like to make a personal statement. In the course of the speech by the right hon Gentleman the Member for Woodford [Mr Churchill], I interrupted him because of some disagreement with what he said. My impression of what he said was that I am alleged to have said—the right hon Gentleman will correct me if I am wrong in that impression—something calculated to discredit General MacArthur. That was my impression. I resented it because I could not remind myself of anything that I had said which was derogatory to the General.

The right hon Gentleman was good enough to convey to me a report from *The Times* of 23 April. However, in the statement which the right hon Gentleman made, he appeared to have overlooked the context of the setting in which the speech was made and the matter with which I was dealing. Perhaps I may have the permission of the Committee to read a rather longer extract from *The New York Times* of 23 April. The heading of their report is 'Shinwell optimistic on outlook in Korea'. It states:

'Defence Minister Emanuel Shinwell said today that the removal of General of the Army Douglas MacArthur gave the United Nations and representatives of the Chinese Communist Government a new chance to negotiate peace in Korea.'

That was the subject with which I was dealing. The report continued:

'Addressing his constituents here, Mr Shinwell said:

' "It might be that, with the removal of General MacArthur from the Korean atmosphere, conditions may improve but we cannot tell. I am bound to say that I regret that the Peiping Government is not more responsive to the suggestions that have been made to negotiate peace in Korea.

' "I think that opportunity has been present for some considerable time, but here again is the opportunity for the United Nations representatives and the representatives of the Peiping Government to gather together to bring this Korean affair to an end." '

That was the statement I made and my submission is that there is nothing in that statement that was derogatory to General MacArthur. Certainly, there was nothing I said which seemed to imply that I was casting some doubt on the capacity of General MacArthur to conduct military operations, because that was not in my mind. I was dealing exclusively with the prospect of reopening negotiations with a view to promoting peace through United Nations in Korea. And *The Times* report, a somewhat shorter report, I should imagine conveys the same impression.

It may be that my impression of what the right hon Gentleman said to me, or about me, was wrong, and if so I ask that I should be forgiven for gaining a wrong impression. On the other hand, it may be that the right hon Gentleman, having seen the shorter report, thought I had said something which was calculated both to throw discredit on General MacArthur in the military sphere, and also to disturb our relations with the United States. That was indeed far from my mind.

[*Mr Churchill replied as follows.*]

I think it is a good thing that the right hon Gentleman has made this statement to the House, and has made it clear that he did not wish in any way to reflect on the military capacity of General MacArthur. I do not think I misquoted his actual words. I see that they were in the *Glasgow Herald* report:

'It may be with the removal of General MacArthur from the Korean atmosphere the situation there might improve, but we cannot tell.'
Then followed what he said about regretting that the Peiping Government were not more responsive. And the Press Association report is:

'It may be that with the removal of General MacArthur from Korea the atmosphere might improve, but we cannot tell.'

And in *The Times*, which was the report I had in mind, it said:

'It may be that with the removal of General MacArthur the situation would improve.'

What I said was that he had said that now, perhaps, things will go better in Korea, once General MacArthur had been dismissed—[HON MEMBERS: 'No.']—well, wait a minute. Then the right hon Gentleman got up and, I am bound to say, he did seem completely to misunderstand the words which had just come out of my mouth and the House had listened to, because he said that I had asserted that he had declared that the dismissal of General MacArthur should be brought about because it would be of advantage to us. I said nothing of the sort. I said absolutely nothing of the sort. I am sorry that he should not be able to follow the absolutely plain English of what I said. Then he was very angry and I repeated that he had said perhaps things will now go better in Korea since General MacArthur had been removed.

These are, I think, perfectly fair and straightforward quotations from what was published in the public Press. Then the right hon Gentleman said a lot of hard things—how I should be ashamed of myself, and all that. Well I am bound to say, on that, that I consider it is a very good thing he has made it clear—as it certainly was not clear to those who read the papers and who cannot have verbatim reports—that he was not referring to General MacArthur's military capacity; and what he meant by what he said was that he hoped better conditions for negotiations would be established now that General MacArthur was no longer on the spot, acting, as it were, in a political capacity.

If that was what he meant it is a good thing that that should be known in the United States; but I do not accept the slightest reproach for what I said in quoting him. I have given the fullest quotations both from what I said and what appeared in the Press where anyone could read it. I think that the remarks the right hon Gentleman has just made remove from my mind any unfavourable impression I might have derived from his anger and from his telling me that I ought to be ashamed of myself. I expunge them entirely from my mind, and I hope that any impression which may have got abroad in the United States and done harm through this misinterpretation of his words, will also be removed by what he said.

# SCOTTISH UNIONIST MEETING

A SPEECH AT THE ANNUAL CONFERENCE OF THE SCOTTISH UNIONIST
ASSOCIATION, GLASGOW
18 MAY 1951

It is a year almost to a day since we met at Edinburgh, and I wish indeed that I could tell you that our affairs have improved since then either at home or abroad. The Communist aggression in Korea was promptly and valiantly resisted by President Truman and the United States acting with the United Nations, of whom we are part, and under their authority fighting has been going on for nearly a year. It would not have been right for us to send more than a small force to Korea, but we may all be proud of the manner in which it has distinguished itself. The United States have borne nineteen-twentieths of the burden, and have suffered nearly 70,000 casualties. When we feel grief at our own losses, we ought to understand the keen feelings of the American people if they feel they are being reproached or hampered by weaker or less engaged allies.

The Americans are not only bearing the burden in the Far East but also are making heavy contributions in men, arms and money to the defence of Western Europe. Without their help there would be no hope of preventing the conquest and subjugation of all the free peoples of Europe by the immense Russian Communist armies and those of their satellite States which stand ready for action at any moment the order is given from Moscow. The presence of General Eisenhower in Europe at the head of such forces as the free peoples have so far been able to organize is a living pledge and symbol of the resolve of the American nation to use its measureless resources and its rapidly growing fleets and armies for the defence of civilization. Behind all this lies the dread and incalculable power which the United States possesses in the atomic bomb and it is this factor, fearful though it be, which alone gives us the hope of being able to form a front in Europe capable of deterring the Kremlin tyrants from further aggression there. Dark and tragic indeed is the picture which stares us in the face whenever we look up from our daily toil. The key to our safety and survival is of course our alliance and friendship with the United States.

I was shocked last week in the House of Commons to see how much anti-American feeling there was among the Left-wing Government supporters below the Gangway. They showed themselves definitely pro-Chinese, although it is the Chinese who are killing our men and the Americans who are helping us. This unhappy Government which itself rests on a minority vote at the last election and clings to office from day to day by a handful of votes, is hampered in dealing with our problems, even where it sees the light, by having at every stage to placate a section of its own followers and persuade or compel them by party discipline to come along with them in taking the necessary steps for the public safety. During all this last anxious and critical year abroad Mr Attlee's tactics have deliberately kept us in a state of party tension and protracted uncertainty at home. The General Election, he declares, will come at the moment which he chooses. Thus we are all compelled to be prepared from month to month and even from week to week. Prolonged electioneering is not good for Britain. We have already had fifteen months of election fever. We have this Government without the confidence of the country, trying to conduct all our grave and critical affairs, without a normal working majority in the House of Commons.

Parliamentary debate has become largely meaningless. The two great party machines grind up against each other in every village, every street, every town and city. Party strife is kept at its keenest point. This is a heavy cost to the ordinary life and daily business of the nation. Party interest and organization are magnified out of all proportion to national affairs. Everyone knows that the healthy, honest, clean thing to do would be for the Government to announce an early date for an appeal to the electorate. But the more it is plain that the Socialists have lost the confidence of the nation, the more tenaciously they cling to their offices. Mr Attlee bears an exceptional and by no means honourable responsibility for prolonging this hateful, costly uncertainty, and his party machine puts pressure upon the members of his party to toe the line, which has not been seen in modern British political history. Instead of trying to bring about or work towards a united nation, he does all he can to keep it bitterly divided by exploiting the narrow voting margin on which he lives, and placating his disreputable tail by acts of partisanship like steel nationalization, against which so large a majority was recorded at the General Election. I have borne a great deal of responsibility at one time or another in my life, but I am very glad never to have tried to lead this great country through its growing perils against the will of the British people and in fear of their verdict.

The performance of the administration is incompetent in an unprecedented degree. 'We are witnessing,' I said a few weeks ago in the House of Commons, 'a process of the gradual education of those who ought to know best and have the power, but who have to reach agreement by an endless series of compromises among themselves and with their military advisers.' Since then we have had striking proof of the divisions inside the Cabinet, and three Ministers—Mr Bevan, Mr Wilson and Mr Freeman—have resigned after stating their objections of one kind or another to the Government's defence programme and health policy. But while these Ministers have left the Government Mr Attlee still has to rely upon their votes and those of their friends to keep himself in office. What kind of defence policy and programme are we to expect if the Prime Minister has to carry with him at every step, men whose hearts are not convinced of the need for strong defence, and who have a deep-seated mistrust and jealousy of the United States, which they regard reproachfully as a successful exponent of the capitalist theory?

Sir Hartley Shawcross five years ago boasted: 'We are the masters now.' He has lately shown some signs of reformation and even talks about going back to the Bar. We shall place no obstacle in his path. A lesser figure, Mr Maurice Webb, the Minister of Food, has taken up his dictatorial style. We had a speech from him at Bradford on 6 May, in which he said: 'The Labour Party has got to understand that it is no longer a street-corner mob. It is the governing class of this country, and it has got to conduct itself like a ruling class. It has got to have the poise and self-assurance of the ruling class.'

I thought this was a revealing declaration. While I have always challenged the ridiculous claims that the Socialist Party have the credit for everything that has been done in Britain for the social progress of the British nation, I have never gone so far as to consider that they were until recently only a 'street-corner mob'. On the contrary I consider that the trade unionists, who are the backbone of all that commands respect in Socialist ranks, have, since their position was finally established by the Conservative Party seventy-five years ago, played an honourable and indeed indispensable part in the life of our country, and it is only Mr Webb's ignorance of our political history which leads him to use such an expression as 'street-corner mob' about the Labour Party. But the phrase to which I direct your attention is his claim that they are the governing class of this country and have to conduct themselves like 'a ruling class'.

We Unionists do not believe in class government or that any section of the community should set themselves up as a ruling class. We hold that everyone should have a fair chance to make the best of himself or herself under just laws and with representative government and parliamentary institutions should secure—to quote a definition of democracy I was taught many years ago,—'the association of us all through the leadership of the best'. The idea of setting up again in this country a ruling class, based on a political machine or rigorous party discipline or any other sectional device, is at once odious and obsolete. The Liberalism and the Tory democracy of the nineteenth century swept away these restrictive ideas. The French Revolution established, I trust for ever, the conception of 'la carrière ouverte aux talents'—the career open to talents.

It is indeed astonishing in the twentieth century to find a Socialist Minister, never heard of until he began to mismanage our food, claiming for a minority Government afraid to face their fellow-countrymen, that they are the ruling class. If this is their mood, the sooner they are subjected to the judgment of a free democracy the better.

We are often asked: 'Tell us exactly what you would do if you came into power. Please give us at once your whole constructive programme and the remedies which you would apply to all the evils which prey upon us at home and abroad.' I have no intention of attempting to solve the problems of Government without the power to act by deeds and not by words. We have no intention of bribing our way into office by all kinds of promises like the Socialists spouted forth in the 1945 election. A hard and difficult time lies before us, requiring not only patience and self-restraint, but a new effort and a broader theme.

Our first aim must be to preserve peace by helping the United States to marshal effectively the whole strength of the free and law-respecting nations. The core and life thrust of the world alliance of free peoples is of course the English-speaking world united by language, literature, history and tradition. The Empire and Commonwealth of Nations joined to the United States in fraternal association form a mass so vast and powerful that none would dare molest it, and with this central force we should have the power to sustain and build up a united Europe lifted for ever above the worn-out quarrels which have laid it in ruins. All this process is moving slowly but irresistibly forward, and in it lies the highest hope for the general reconciliation of self-tormented mankind. For our part we must do our best to revive and liberate the native energies and genius of the British race and to preserve and reassert the strength of our Empire and Commonwealth of Nations. We shall not seek to re-establish, like Mr Webb, a ruling class operating through a party caucus, but we shall try our utmost to undo the needless harm that has been done and to restore to all our fellow-countrymen the sense of pride and honour in our ancient land.

None of all the problems which faced Britain at home on the morrow of her victory six years ago compared in urgency with that of housing the people. None called for a more resolute effort by the Government of the day. House-building had perforce come to a standstill for six years of war; many homes had been destroyed by the enemy, and thousands which stood had been condemned as slums before the war started. Meanwhile the population had increased. That was the problem. In the wartime Coalition, of which I was the head, we estimated in 1943 that our long-term need after the war, if we were to give every family a separate home and replace slums and other unsuitable houses, would be at least 3,000,000 houses.

To have contrived the building of homes on such a scale would have been an achievement of which any Minister might have been proud. If the Government had given housing the proper priority they could have secured such a response from local authorities, the building industry and the public, that the problem could have been largely surmounted by now. Good housing is the first of the social services. Bad housing makes more disease than the best health service can cure. It undermines the efforts of our schools to produce worthy citizens. It prevents our people doing their best work in factory, field and office. That is why Conservative and Unionist Governments in the years before the war put slum-clearance at the head and centre of their drive to improve the social conditions of our country. Today those achievements are too often forgotten, but in the six years before 1939 we rehoused over 1,500,000 people who had lived in slums. But for the war the last of our slums would have disappeared seven or eight years ago.

Before the 1945 election the Socialist Party produced their statement of post-war policy, and called for 4,000,000 houses in the first ten years after the war—400,000 a year. Today, after nearly six years, they have built under 900,000 permanent houses, an average of only 150,000 a year. They are not even keeping pace with the growing waiting-lists. In Glasgow last month there were 100,000 on the waiting-list, and the Ministry allocation for 1951 is only 5,000 houses.

At Blackpool last October a gust of passion swept the annual conference of the National Union of Conservative and Unionist Associations when they debated the Government's housing failure. I said that I accepted their demand that the target should be 300,000 and added: 'No one can tell how the rearmament burden may strike our industry and finances, but however our fortunes may go and from whatever angle the pressures of life may come, the Tory Party puts homes for the people in the very forefront of all schemes for our development.' I repeat that now. 300,000 houses a year remains our aim. It is second only to national safety. We still believe that by giving builders freer initiative the rate of building can be increased and the rise in costs halted, even during the period of rearmament. No one can foresee the march of events. But we should try our best to reach again the rate of housebuilding achieved by the Chamberlain Government before the late war.

But now I come to the root of all our troubles at home—the ever-rising cost of living. The pound sterling buys only three-quarters of what it did when the Socialists took office after the war and is falling ever faster. Five shillings in the pound is now taken out of every wage-packet; out of every housewife's purse; it is cut off all family allowances and all the cash payments under the social security schemes, which all parties combined to bring forward during the war years. The increase which the Chancellor of the Exchequer boasts he is making in his Budget for the more elderly old-age pensioners will barely restore the cut which the financial policy of his predecessors took from them.

Socialist canvassers go from door to door saying that the Tories will reduce the social services. There is no threat to the social services today like the fate which threatens them if the fall in the value of money is not halted. It will not be a planned economy to fall less heavily on those who most need help, but a blind indiscriminate lopping off, and the worst victims will be the very poorest sections of our people. In the face of this danger the Socialist Government have no policy, only excuses. Their chief excuse is that the rise in the cost of living is the result of world rearmament since the fighting started in Korea. This is not true. We are only just beginning to experience in the shops the effects of the increases in the price of raw materials since last summer. The biggest cause of the rise in prices during the last eighteen months has been the devaluation of the pound in September 1949.

Four previous years of Socialist extravagance and mismanagement made devaluation inevitable. It raised the price of our dollar imports and cut the price of our exports by one-third. That means that we have as a nation to do twelve hours' work instead of eight to buy what we need from overseas, while we get paid only eight hours' reward for what we produce in twelve hours' work. No politician of any party could claim today that he has the formula to restore our money to what it was worth in 1945 when the Socialists took charge. Things have gone too far for that. It will take all our efforts to hold the value of the pound at whatever level the Socialists reduce it to before the country is able to dismiss them. In their six years of office they have spent some £23,000 million—£11 million a day. This year they are planning to spend an additional £1,300 million on defence without making any compensating economies in their other expenditure. I am quite sure that in the field of administration alone scores of millions of pounds a year could be saved by wise management. No economies would be popular, but they would be less hurtful than the calamity of unchecked inflation, which is what we face.

The Socialist Government are taking in taxation £1,000 million a year more than was deemed prudent at the height of the war. That is nearly 10s. a week more from every man, woman and child in the country. In addition there is the growing burden of the local rates, and the concealed taxation levied in the form of higher postal and telephone charges. In addition there are the increases imposed by our nationalized industries in their pretence of reducing and avoiding heavy losses, and the high and increasing charges for nationalized road and rail transport which fall with special severity on Scotland, where such long distances have to be covered.

You have very rightly been discussing the rehabilitation and development of the Highlands and Islands. A question you may well ask yourselves is—how much might not have been done in this direction, and in the improvement of our hill and marginal lands, if the Socialist Government had devoted to this purpose only a fraction of that £36½ million they frittered away on their Groundnuts Scheme in East Africa.

A Conservative Government would aim at keeping State expenditure within bounds. We believe that a healthy economy depends, as Mr Gladstone used to say, on money being allowed to fructify in the pockets of the people. For the production we need for the defence programme, for the export trade, and to maintain decent living standards at home, we look to the impulse of individual effort as well as a well-conceived State policy. We would encourage work and thrift. We shall call a halt to all further nationalization, and rely for increased production on the experience, skill and enterprise of our great industries. Wherever we can we shall restore freedom to those industries which the State has taken over. Iron and steel will become again a great free-enterprise industry, strengthened and aided as the TUC proposed, by a board representing workers, management and the Government. Where industries cannot be restored to the full freedom of competition we intend to do everything possible to lessen the unhealthy grip of Whitehall and revive local initiative and responsibility.

And here is where I come to Scotland. I have nothing new to say about the ancient and sacred relationship which joins us together in the United Kingdom. I predicted last year at Edinburgh that Scotland would not desert a friend in need. The fact that England, for the time being, is in eclipse and seems to foreign eyes to be declining, makes it all the more certain that Scotland will stand at her side. My faith in the free peoples of the British Isles and in Northern Ireland is strong. I do not believe that we are at the end of all our glories, and it is in the struggle to prevent such a catastrophe that all the sanity, wisdom and steadfast tenacity of the Scottish race must be engaged. We believe that together we can break this attempt to manage everything from Whitehall.

We are sure that Socialism has already proved its failure and that, as soon as the people have a chance to express their opinion, this foolish fallacy and aberration of a minority of our countrymen will receive a resounding rebuke at the hands of the electors. It would be wrong to attribute all the difficulties and dangers which are closing in upon us abroad to the Government. They would certainly have been very grave whatever party was in power. It is true and just, however, to say that they have been definitely increased and aggravated by the extraordinary lack of foresight and comprehension shown by a weak-minded and tottering administration, absorbed in its party affairs and setting their own retention of office, whether they have the confidence of the nation or not, above everything else. Let me give you a few examples.

Take the latest. On Monday of last week, when we saw how excited the Americans were getting about our trading with China—though it was no more than what they were doing themselves—we Conservatives asked that we should reach an agreement with them about an embargo on what are called 'strategic materials' going into China, and I requested that above all the import of rubber into China from Hong Kong and other British colonies should be stopped. On the Thursday the Government announced that they had done both these things. That was good, but why should it be left to the Opposition to point out the step, the need for which had been obvious for many months and which, if our affairs were conducted with ordinary foresight would have prevented a great deal of misunderstanding between us and our vital ally.

Another foolish blunder was made when an American admiral was given the supreme command of the Atlantic, although the bringing in of convoys to Europe and the feeding of this island can only be dealt with, as it was so successfully dealt with, from this side of the ocean and from this island with all its knowledge and experience during the two world wars. While the public outcry was going on about this, the Government have been seeking to gain the supreme command in the Mediterranean, to offset what they had given away in the Atlantic. But it would be in our interests that the United States should command in the Mediterranean. The closer they are associated with us and with France in the Mediterranean the better it will be for all our fortunes, there and in the Middle East. Two wrongs do not make a right, but that is exactly what the Government are trying to do. The best arrangement would I am sure be to have the passage of the convoys and of the trade across the Atlantic arranged as it was in the war, between the British and American Admiralties, and to welcome the Americans with their powerful fleets of aircraft carriers in the Mediterranean, as the leading Allied Power there. I have no doubt that if there were any guidance of our affairs from the top, and if intimate relations like we had in the war had been maintained between the Prime Minister and the President, all this could have been quite easily settled to the general advantage and satisfaction.

Since the Socialists obtained power in 1945, the prestige of Britain has fallen steadily. We have cast away our Oriental Empire with both our hands and at the cost of hundreds of thousands of Indian and Burmese lives. We have gained the hatred both of the Arabs and of the Jews. The Egyptians, in violation of all law and treaty, have closed the Suez Canal to the passage of oil-tankers. We have not only put up with this, but have continued to send arms, ships, aeroplanes, destroyers and all kinds of supplies to Egypt, although that Government is thoroughly unfriendly and demands our immediate evacuation of the Canal Zone. The Egyptian Government does not even have to pay for these weapons. All they do is to mark off the money involved on what are called the sterling balance accounts, which means the debt we are supposed to owe them for the supplies we bought in Egypt while we were defending them from being conquered by Germany and Italy.

The impression has got about the world that we have only to be kicked or threatened to clear out of any place. The Persians like the idea of nationalization of other peoples' property and, under the pressure of the terrorists in Teheran, they now propose to seize the Anglo-Persian oilfields, which have been discovered and developed by fifty years of British brains and capital. Iraq threatens the same policy of spoliation. Wherever you look you see our rights and interests disregarded. Albania murdered forty-four of our sailors by laying a mine trap for them, and refuses to pay the compensation awarded to us as the result of arbitration at The Hague, and the Argentine has planted her flag on British territory in the Antarctic as a prelude to their demand for the Falkland Islands.

All this and much else is happening within six years of the world war, in which for more than a year we sustained the cause of freedom alone and from which we emerged with complete victory and world-wide respect. Six years of Socialist rule have brought us low. Nevertheless, we must not lose faith in our destiny. We are the same people in the same island as we were in the great days we can all remember. Our spirit is unconquerable, our ingenuity and craftsmanship are unsurpassed, our latent resources are unmeasured, our underlying unities are enduring. We have but to cast away by an effort of the will the enfeebling tendencies and fetters of Socialist rule, and then we can stand erect once more and take our place among the Great Powers of the world. Never must we lose our faith and courage. Never must we fail in exertion and resolve.

Be sure you are ready for the call when it comes. Be sure you lay aside every impediment and allow no class or privilege or vested interest to stand between you and your duty to the nation.

# PORTRAIT OF LORD MORAN

---

22 *May—Agreement announced between Poland and Russia under which Poland cedes to Russia part of the Lublin area in exchange for part of Drogobych Province in the Ukraine.*

25 *May—United Nations forces in Korea advance on all fronts; 38th Parallel crossed on 26th.*

30 *May—General Election in Eire; Mr de Valera becomes Prime Minister on June 13.*

4 *June—HM The King ordered to rest; all public engagements cancelled.*

21 *June—Commonwealth Defence Ministers' Conference opened in London; agreement on defence of Middle East.*

23 *June—Mr Malik, the Russian delegate to the United Nations, broadcasts appeal for settlement of Korean War. On 29th General Ridgway offers talks on armistice.*

29 *June—An order in Council setting up a new Nigerian Constitution is promulgated by HM The King.*

1 *July—The Colombo Plan comes formally into effect.*

6 *July—Mr R. R. Stokes appointed Minister of Materials.*

8 *July—Italy proclaims end of state of war with Germany.*

9 *July—State of war between Great Britain and Germany officially ended.*

10 *July—Armistice talks in Korea opened at Kaesong; suspended by Communists on August 22, the talks are resumed at Panmunjom on October 24.*

---

[10 *July* 1951

First of all I must thank you for according me an Honorary Fellowship of the Royal College of Physicians. I also had the honour to be made a surgeon eight years ago, and now I can practise, in an honorary fashion, the arts of surgery and medicine. Unless there is a very marked shortage of capable men in both these professions, I shall not press myself upon you. No doubt in these difficult times it will be a comfort not only to the profession but to the nation at large that you have me in reserve.

I have not yet taken any final decision as to which of these beneficent branches I should give priority to (in case an emergency arises). Being temperamentally inclined to precision and a sharp edge, it might be thought that I should choose the surgeon's role. At any rate you can be sure of having something to show, and I have been told that this was the view of many young medical students. However, all comes out even at the end of the day, and I am assured that latterly an entirely new phase has come over the art of medicine. It has become much less a process of emphasizing or mitigating, or correcting tendencies, and making grave and luminous pronouncements upon them, than of taking hard and quick decisions. Science, progged on by the urge of the age, has presented to us in the last decade a wonderful bevy of new and highly attractive-medicinal personalities. We have M and B, penicillin, tetramycin, aureomycin and several others that I will not hazard my professional reputation in mentioning, still less in trying to place in order. And medical science has presented to you an ever-increasing growth of decisions as rapid and as refined as ever presented to the surgeon.

It is arguable whether the human race have been gainers by the march of science beyond the steam engine. Electricity opens a field of infinite conveniences to ever greater numbers, but they may well have to pay dearly for them. But anyhow in my thought I stop short of the internal combustion engine which has made the world so much smaller. Still more must we fear the consequences of entrusting to a human race so little different from their predecessors of the so-called barbarous ages such awful agencies as the atomic bomb. Give me the horse.

But in all this advance of science which we can no more resist or delay than we can stop the tides of destiny, there is one grand out-standing exception, the healing arts. All that cures or banishes disease, all that quenches human pain, and mitigates bodily infirmity, all those splendid names, the new arrivals which I have just mentioned to you, all these are welcome whatever view you may take of religion, philo-sophy or politics. Of course it may be said these discoveries only lengthen the span of human life, and then arises the delicate and difficult question, is that a good thing or not? It is a question which presents itself in a blunt form to the rising generation.

For my part I shall not attempt to pronounce because my impartiality might be doubted. I might be thought an interested party, and this brings me to my main and most agreeable task this evening, because, but for Lord Moran's wisdom and decision, I should probably not be here this evening discoursing jauntily to you all.

It is my duty to pay your tribute to Lord Moran and, when the time comes, to present him with the portrait which has been painted by Professor Pietro Annigoni. Well, I know Charles Moran I would say almost as well as he knows me. He was for nine years President of your illustrious College. His war record is magnificent. In the first World War he won the MC and was mentioned in many dispatches and has Italian decorations—all gained under the hard fire caused by the mistakes of our military experts in the first great struggle with which our generation has been afflicted. In the last war, Charles came with me wherever I went. That puts me in the position of the man who said one night, 'I think my companion here ought to have the VC because he has been everywhere I have been.' At any rate, we went for a good many long journeys by air at a time when the comforts of air travel had not been developed to the almost perfect state they have now. I do not think a great deal about travelling by air so long as you get there, and he will remember some awkward moments. I am deeply indebted to him. He was for twenty-five years Dean of St Mary's Hospital. He is a great figure in your life, for nine years head of the College, a man deeply versed in his profession and in all its most profound characteristics, a man who apart from his profession stands out as a leading figure in the public life of Britain. I must now mention Lady Moran, who sustained him as only a wife can, and I know all about that.

In the National Health Service, which you all enjoy so much, Lord Moran in my view did his duty in recognizing that he should lead the College in a policy of co-operation with the Government, with constructive criticism from time to time, and in spite of opposition from outside the College, and even perhaps sometimes within, he moved forward with this great body in dignified array. He left the College in your hands, Mr President—than whom no more worthy successor could be conceived—in a position of greater influence than it had held at any time in recent history. I am indebted to you for the kindness and receptiveness with which you have treated me tonight, and if I have digressed into the sphere of levity, I trust that you will consider that one of those minor symptoms, dwelling upon which would only complicate the ultimate diagnosis.

# WOODFORD CONSTITUENCY FETE

A SPEECH AT ROYAL WANSTEAD SCHOOL, WOODFORD
21 JULY 1951

---

*16 July—HM King Leopold of the Belgians abdicates in favour of his son
Prince Baudouin, who takes the oath and becomes King on the 17th.*
*20 July—HM King Abdullah of Jordan assassinated in Jerusalem.*

---

[*21 July* 1951

It is six years almost to a week since the Socialist Government came into
office and we entered upon that melancholy period of eclipse and
frustration which if it continues will lead to our decline and fall. What
a contrast between our position at the end of the war and that to which
we have been already reduced today. Not only were we victorious
after all the hard toils and struggles but we were more honoured,
respected and admired by friend and foe alike than we had ever been
before.

And where do we stand today in the eyes of the world? For the time
being we have lost our rank among the nations. There is hardly any
country in the world where it is not believed that you have only to
kick an Englishman hard enough to make him evacuate, bolt or clear
out. Countries we have defended from Nazi and Fascist violence,
countries we have rescued after they had been subjugated, countries
which had found us strong and steadfast comrades and allies, are
watching with astonishment a Britain which they think is in retreat or
in decline. Egypt, Persia, Albania, the Argentine and Chile compete
with each other in the insults and the humiliations they inflict upon
us—and what is the cause? It is the attempt to impose a doctrinaire
Socialism upon an island which has grown great and famous by free
enterprise and valour and which six years ago stood in honour though
not in size at the summit of the world. I say 'though not in size' because a vast larger world is growing up around us. But never forget
that fifty millions have come into being in Great Britain under the impulse and inspiration of former generations and now if our native genius
is cribbed, cabined and confined these fifty millions will be left physically stranded and gasping, like whales which swum upon the high
tide into a bay from which the waters have receded.

Almost every year we have some new crisis. Now this year we are

93

heading for another. The gap between our imports and exports during the first six months of this year was £550 million. The position is worsening and for the month of June alone the gap was nearly £150 million. The pound sterling which, when we came out of the Second World War, was worth 20s., has now in these six years fallen to 14s. 10d. What does that mean? Everybody's salaries, pensions, wages and savings have been reduced by more than a quarter. Think of all the thousands of millions that that means when translated into the life of a great people. Surely this is a tremendous fact. All the boastings of the welfare State have to be set against the fact that more than what they have given with one hand has been filched back by the other. More than what they have given by benefits and improvements has been taken back by the reduction in the value of the money we use.

'Oh!' they say, 'all this is due to Korea. If it had not been for Korea we should never have fallen into our present position.' This is an utter untruth. The main reason for the fall in the buying power of our money at home and still more abroad is not Korea but devaluation. But devaluation did not come by itself. It forced itself upon our Socialist 'Masters' as they call themselves by four years of grotesque, reckless squandering of our treasures and resources. They had got the control of the Government for their own party. No Government in our history has spent money to the vast extent and reckless manner as our present rulers. Apart from £2,000 million they have begged or borrowed from the United States and received from the Dominions, they have spent more than £11 million a day or £24,000 million in their six years. No community living in a world of nationalism and competition can possibly afford such frantic extravagances.

All this happened long before Korea or what is called 'rearmament'. Devaluation was the child of wild profuse expenditure, and the evils which we suffer today from what I have called 'the money cheat' are the inevitable progeny of that wanton way of living. The greatest national misfortune which we are now entering is the ever falling value of our money, or to put it the other way round, the ever increasing cost measured by work and thrift of everything we buy. Taxation is higher than in any country outside the Communist world. There they take all. There no one has anything except the salaries paid them by the privileged Communist aristocracy. British taxation is higher now than it was in the height of the late war—even when we stood alone and defied all comers.

Is not that an astonishing fact? Six years of Socialist Government have hit us harder in our finance and economics than Hitler was able to do. Look at the effects you face of devaluation abroad. We are an island with a population of fifty millions living on imports of food and raw materials, which we have to buy by our exertion, ingenuity and craftsmanship. We have to pay across the dollar exchange twelve hours of work, with hand or brain, to buy what we could before have got with eight hours. We are a hard-working people. We are second to none in ability or enterprise so far as we are allowed to use these gifts. We now have to give a third more of our life strength, energy and output of every kind and quality to get the same revivifying intake as we had before devaluation two years ago. 'Korea,' they say, but this is a shoddy excuse, utterly divorced from fact or truth.

'Rearmament,' they say, but it has hardly begun. No Government has ever had such generous provision for our national defence as has been made by Parliament with the full support of the Conservative Party during the Socialist reign. But when the Minister who called us 'vermin' and the Minister who said no one else but the organized workers of his party 'were worth a tinker's cuss' woke up to the fact that we were again in gravest peril, it was found that we were almost defenceless. So then there was a panic programme a year ago of £3,600 million of military expenditure in three years. And then the revised programme nine months ago—because they seem to have added up their figures wrong—by which £4,700 million are to be spent over these current three years. We have supported the steps that they took and done our utmost to meet the demands that they have made, but that does not mean that we condone the grievous social, political and administrative blunders they have committed or that we bear the responsibility for the plight into which we are now plunged.

The whole social programme of which the Government boast was devised in conception and detail by a National Government resting upon a House of Commons with a Conservative majority of one hundred over all parties. Only one single new idea has been contributed by the false guides who have led us far astray, who have robbed us of the fruits of our victory and mauled our daily life. Only one. You know the one I have in mind. NATIONALIZATION. What an awful flop! Show me the nationalized industry which has not become a burden on the public either as taxpayers or consumers or both. There is hardly an industry in which the employees are contented with changing the private employers with whom they could negotiate on equal terms through the trade unions for the hordes of all-powerful officials in Whitehall. And now our Socialist Utopians are getting fed back with their own tail in Persia and other countries, where we have in the past gathered or created valuable possessions. Others can play at that game too. It must be with many a prick of conscience that

Mr Attlee and Mr Morrison and the band of misguided careerist intellectuals they have collected around them regard the meagre and mouldy harvest of nationalization which they have bought for us so dearly both at home and abroad.

But they are incorrigible. Obstinacy at the national expense seems to them a virtue. Even at this moment of all others when they are confronted with failure, fallacy and exposure—as they well know—of their scheme of thought, they try to brazen it out by nationalizing, of all others, the steel industry which in enterprise, planning, organization and efficiency has raised itself, in spite of all deterrents, to a pinnacle in British production. Not one of them believes that the nationalizing of steel is good for our country at this moment. In fact in spite of their boasting they have been forced to admit that they cannot possibly manage the business themselves. They have recoiled from the consequences of their own arguments and at this moment the two Socialist millionaires, Mr Strauss, Minister of Supply, and Mr Hardie, head of the Socialist Steel Corporation, have had to confess by actions which speak louder than words, their utter inability to manage the business or deliver the goods. They have had to leave the whole working and conduct of the steel industry in the skilful, experienced hands of the Steel Federation from whom they tried to take it. They have learnt the lessons here at home which at present they are trying to teach Persia, that it is one thing to nationalize a vast industry and quite another to manage it so that it works and pays and provides the livelihood for all its wage-earners and a decent service for the community which depends upon it.

And now I come to the worst thing of all. We had a speech the other day from the Communist Horner in which he said: 'If a Tory Government is returned it is certain that there will be a national strike of the miners. . . . It is only responsibility and loyalty to the Labour Government that has caused the miners to pull their punches.' This speech, which is, of course, only a part of the Communist conspiracy to bring Britain under the whole of the Kremlin, would not have counted if it had only been the mouthings of a Moscow lackey. But there, sitting at his side, was a Minister of the Crown—Mr Griffiths. I give the Government credit for their hostility to Communism, though they are bringing it nearer by all they do. But fancy this Minister sitting there beside this Communist agent and not daring to open his mouth in protest or contradiction. And fancy that a week has elapsed without the Prime Minister or any other member of the Government disowning and denouncing the declaration which Mr Horner made. Let us see exactly what this declaration means. If the people of Britain should at any time be allowed to have a General Election, and if the will of the people expressed through the universal suffrage electorate should return a Conservative Government to power, Mr Horner says it is certain that there will be a national strike of the miners. This of course, if it happened, would paralyse the whole life and industry of our country.

Now I have always been a friend of the miners. Just over forty years ago I moved the Second Reading of the Mines Eight Hours Bill. I set up the system of mines inspectors drawn from the miners themselves which exists today as one of the main measures to ward off the perils of coal-mining. In 1925 as Chancellor of the Exchequer I provided £20 million to give a year for further negotiations to solve the difficulty in the mining industry and thus avoid a national or general strike. The only quarrel I have ever had with the miners was in the war when I had to forbid them from pouring out of the mines to join our armies in the field. Let them dismiss from their minds these malicious tales that a Conservative Government would be hostile to the mining community. I have always affirmed that those who work in these hard and dangerous conditions far from the light of the sun have the right to receive exceptional benefits from the nation which they serve.

But now the Communist Horner has stepped outside the sphere of industrial disputes, and threatens the whole British democracy, thirty million voters, with a national strike to bring the country down if they dare express their opinion and wishes at the polls. This is an insult to the will of the people which no free democracy could endure. The idea that one section, however worthy, in our island should claim the right to deny political liberties and rights to all the rest of us, is one which would never be tolerated and one which, in my belief, the miners themselves would be the first to repudiate.

But while these shameful menaces are uttered, the Socialist Government, intent on electioneering—and false electioneering as it will turn out to be—remains 'mum'. Attlee doodles, Morrison gapes and only Mr Bevan grins. Well, anyhow, we are going to have a General Election as soon as we can force these office-clingers to present themselves before their fellow countrymen. Then the people will have a chance to express their will. Great as are the difficulties of the time, ugly as the inheritance is which the Socialists will leave behind them, long as is the period of stable progressive government which will be required to remedy our misfortunes, and to rebuild our national power and fame, I have no doubt that it is the duty of all those who are here this evening and of every man and woman in the land, to prepare themselves fearlessly and faithfully for the splendid opportunity they will have of reviving the strength and renewing the glory of our island home.

# UNITED EUROPE

A SPEECH AT THE MANSION HOUSE, LONDON
23 JULY 1951

---

22 *July—General Craveiro Lopes elected President of Portugal unopposed.*
23 *July—Marshal Pétain dies, aged 95.*

---

[23 *July* 1951

In his memorable speech in London the other day, General Eisenhower made it clear that his task as Commander-in-Chief was made infinitely more difficult by the divergencies in Europe and the tangle of authorities with which he has to deal. Let us try to smooth his path and strengthen his hand.

How much we owe to the great Republic which has arrived at the summit of the world, only with the ambition to render service to others. We have here tonight, as a piece of good fortune, an outstanding American statesman, Mr Bernard M. Baruch. In the alliance of free peoples the USA provide the driving power and a large part of the resources. After helping to restore Europe's economy by the Marshall Plan, America has now created the North Atlantic defence system. We are particularly indebted to President Truman for sending to Europe to command our combined forces that great Commander and trusted friend of Europe—General Eisenhower. He has indeed undertaken an heroic mission. He has become deeply convinced of the need for closer European union. This was urged at Strasbourg in May. Now the British Government have at last accepted this view. Better late than never. But one ought not to be late in measures which, if taken promptly and unitedly, give the world its best chance of escaping another hideous catastrophe.

How clever the Soviets have been in preventing for so many months all progress with the German part of the plan by prolonging the futile discussions in Paris about the Agenda for the Conference of Foreign Ministers for which they asked. How foolish we have been in letting these many important months slip away. In the end no doubt the advice given at Strasbourg will be followed. But meanwhile one of the great deterrents on Communist aggression has been retarded. Take again the question of including Turkey and Greece in the European defence system. By staying out of the conference, we have had no say

98

in its decisions. It may well be that, as in the case of the Schuman Plan, the scheme which will emerge will contain features unpalatable to us. Still, without a European Army it will be almost impossible to get agreement upon German rearmament; and without a substantial German contribution there can be no effective system of Western Defence.

But look at the hideous delays which have occurred. It is more than a year since we passed our resolution at Strasbourg expressing the idea of a European Army in which France and Germany would play their parts. The main criticism has been that the European Army would cut across the organization of the Atlantic Force. This was, I think, the first reaction of the American Government, but there have lately been signs that they are looking upon the proposal for a European Army with increasing favour. They now see that it is the only basis on which France is willing to agree to German rearmament. And there also are disadvantages and even dangers to us in standing aloof. I trust, therefore, that a renewed attempt will be made to find some basis on which Britain can be associated in one form or another with the Schuman organization.

Then there is the proposal for a European Army. This has two aims. First, to create in Europe a permanent system of joint defence against outside aggression. The second is to make it as difficult as possible for the European nations at any time in the future to fight against one another. In the course of the negotiations the earlier proposals have been considerably modified, but the scheme still contains features which we do not like. I very much regret that the British Government did not accept the invitation to take part in these talks. I believe that if a British representative had been there, we might very likely have secured further modifications which would have made it possible for Britain to join in this scheme, either on the same footing as the others or as some kind of associate member. From the Continental standpoint the Schuman Plan is greatly weakened by the absence of Britain—the largest steel and coal-producing nation in Europe. The re-establishment of Franco-German relations has become something much more than a return to normality. There is being developed between them a close and active partnership such as was never dreamed of before. The most remarkable manifestation of this new spirit is the Schuman Plan, which, apart from its economic benefits, will make war between Frenchman and German more than ever difficult and improbable. However, we in this country could not accept the supra-national federal institutions envisaged originally in the Schuman Plan.

It was with a sense of deep comfort that I saw the representatives of the German Parliament take their seats in the European Assembly at Strasbourg. Our European Movement and the European idea for which it stands have undoubtedly played a large part in bringing nearer the reconciliation of these two foes whose quarrels through the centuries have wrought both them and all of us grievous injuries. The first notable forward step was the invitation to Germans to attend The Hague Congress convened by the European Movement in 1948. I well remember, at this unofficial but now historic conference, welcoming a distinguished delegation of Germans headed by Dr Adenauer, now the first Chancellor of the new German Republic.

The mainspring of all our efforts is the assembly at Strasbourg, where we sit together with the representatives of other European Parliaments under the vigilant eye of our President, M. Spaak. It is right that the seat of the Council of Europe should be situated in France. France is the keystone in the arch of European understanding which we seek to build. But the leadership required to unify Europe cannot be provided by one country alone. There can be no Europe unless it be based upon a solid foundation of trust and comradeship between the French and German peoples. Within the wider framework of the UNO a Council of Europe has been set up. A European Army is beginning to take shape, and a European Court of Human Rights is shortly to be established. In the economic field practical measures are being taken to reduce barriers and stimulate the flow of European trade. These are important and much-needed gains because the international situation has deteriorated, and the need for uniting and strengthening Europe has become ever more urgent.

I have long believed in the idea of a United Europe. In the turbulent year 1943 I said:

'Under a world institution representing the United Nations there should come into being a Council of Europe. We must try to make this Council of Europe into a really effective league with a High Court to adjust disputes and with armed forces, national or international or both, held ready to enforce its decisions and to prevent renewed aggression. This Council must eventually embrace the whole of Europe.'

Much of what I then hoped for is already beginning to come to pass. The cause of United Europe is growing in strength and resolve with every day that passes; there are forces at work in Britain which will enable our island and our Empire and Commonwealth to play their full part—and a leading part—in building the temple of peace and freedom upon foundations which none will dare assail.

# FOREIGN AFFAIRS (MIDDLE EAST)

A SPEECH TO THE HOUSE OF COMMONS
30 JULY 1951

---

*28 July—British and Commonwealth troops in Korea organized into the
1st Commonwealth Division.*

---

[*30 July* 1951

When the right hon Gentleman the Foreign Secretary [Mr Herbert
Morrison] asked me to forgo the opportunity of opening this debate,
I was encouraged to hope that he would have something to tell us.
I thought that he would be able to cast a light on some of these anxious
and serious problems which in more than one quarter press upon our
minds this afternoon. Instead, he has treated us to an able and agreeable
parade of bland truisms and platitudes which I fear must, in these busy
times, have caused him many long hours of toil and study.

I, also, will indulge in a somewhat general survey, though I shall
not go back so far as the collapse of the Ottoman Empire, which,
after all, took place at the end of the First and not of the Second
World War. The decline of our influence and power throughout the
Middle East is due to several causes. First, the loss of our Oriental
Empire and of the well-placed and formidable resources of the Imperial
armies in India. Second, it is due to the impression which has become
widespread throughout the Middle East that Great Britain has only to
be pressed sufficiently by one method or another to abandon her rights
and interests in that, or indeed any other, part of the world. A third
cause is the mistakes and miscalculations in policy which led to the
winding-up of our affairs in Palestine in such a way as to earn almost
in equal degree the hatred of the Arabs and the Jews. I was struck by
the fact that the right hon Gentleman should have confessed mistakes
which have been made in this matter. One failure, he said, we admit.
It has long been evident how disastrous was the course we followed
there, and all these put together, the loss of our power in the world,
and in that part of the world, the diminution of our resources, the mistakes which we have made, and the feeling that we are incapable of
putting up an effective resistance—most unjust assumptions I would
certainly say—all these have brought us to the melancholy and anxious
position in which we stand this afternoon.

The position is not necessarily irretrievable in its long-term aspects, but we certainly cannot restore it by ourselves alone. It can only be retrieved in any case at a lower level than before the Second World War, and it can only be retrieved, in my opinion, by the joint co-operative action of Britain and the United States, and, in the Mediterranean sphere, of France. [An HON MEMBER: 'And Turkey.'] And Turkey, I entirely agree with that.

It is for this reason that I have been most anxious to encourage the United States Navy to take a leading part in the Mediterranean, and that I welcome so strongly the support which they have given both to Greece and Turkey, and the keen attention they are at length—I might almost say, at last—giving to Persian and Iraqi affairs. The oil supplies from this part of the world have a value far above their commercial or financial importance, great though this be. The strategic aspect of the destination of the oil supplies and the immediate future of the Middle East countries is of immense importance, not only to Britain, but to the United States. It plays a part in their whole plan of creating ever-increasing deterrents, direct or indirect, to the spread of Communism, and thus to preserving the peace of the world by reaching conditions on which a lasting and friendly settlement may be made with Soviet Russia on the basis not of weakness and divided policy, but of strength, unity and well-conceived measures.

We may indeed, truly say that the events which are taking place in Egypt and Persia play an integral and, possibly, vital part in the whole purpose of the vast alliance, under the supreme authority of the United Nations Organization, to which we have all bound ourselves. The consequences of this alliance now present themselves to us in this country in a manner which dominates our domestic life, with our immense expenditure on rearmament and the reactions which that entails on the standards of life of all classes throughout Great Britain. The issues at stake in the Middle East are of capital importance to us at home and abroad, and to all our Allies.

Since the war stopped, I have always been anxious that the United States should become more interested in what is taking place in Persia and in Egypt. We admire and support the sacrifice and exertions they have made to resist aggression in Korea. Mortal injury would have fallen upon us all, upon the free democratic world, if we had been unable to serve, or unwilling to serve, the United Nations Organization in resisting armed aggression at any point. But in a material and geographical sense, Korea, after all, is a promontory jutting out into salt water, ruled by American sea-power under an air canopy controlled by, in the main, American air-forces. It is not a place from which things can spread in a physical way against the main interests of the United Nations. The moral and strategic importance of Persia and Egypt, on the other hand, and the relation of those countries to the Atlantic Pact system, profoundly affect American interests and the success of their world policy, in which Great Britain and the Dominions of the Commonwealth are all joined.

If, for instance, the Persian situation arising out of the oil dispute, and the wrongful treatment meted out to us by Persia, with the consequent prolonged paralysis of the Persian oilfields, were to lead to the regions from the Caspian Sea to the Persian Gulf being included in the satellite countries which are Kremlin-controlled today, the consequences would be far more deadly, not only to us, but to the United States than anything that could have arisen in Korea. Therefore I have done, speaking as an individual, whatever was in my power to impress upon leading American statesmen and citizens whom I have met and with whom I am in contact that their main interests are engaged in the Middle East at least as much as they are in any other part of the world outside their own country.

General Eisenhower's sphere of responsibility is also deeply affected by what happens in Persia and Iraq. Turkey is the right flank of any front that can be formed in Europe against Soviet aggression—should that occur, which I do not pre-judge—and the position of Turkey would be greatly endangered if the Soviet control covered all the regions immediately south of the Caspian Sea. The European situation is, therefore, directly involved in what takes place in Persia and Iraq. In surveying the general scene in the Middle East, our relations with Egypt, to which the right hon Gentleman devoted some of the closing passages in his speech, are of the first importance. During the war we preserved Egypt from the injury and pillage of Nazi-Fascist subjugation. I shall not speak of our loss of life, for that cannot be computed in material terms, but we spent vast sums of money in Egypt maintaining a local wartime prosperity there beyond that which any other country was enjoying in the whole world. Unhappily, that prosperity was shared almost exclusively by the rich and well-to-do classes, while the peasantry seemed to remain in very much the condition in which I saw them when I first went to Egypt as a young officer towards the end of the last century.

This point of view was confirmed and, indeed, emphasized by the Foreign Secretary in his speech. These rich, well-to-do classes who have so much control in Egypt are the very ones who are trying to keep a popularity with the masses of the people by ungratefully assailing us today. It was calculated at the end of the war that we owed more than

£400 million to Egypt. Most of it was for the local services and supplies we had purchased to maintain the armies which protected them. These are the notorious wartime sterling balances—I said wartime sterling balances, because more complicated forms of sterling balances have come into existence at later dates, but I am speaking of the wartime sterling balances, which are presented to us as British debts. The War Cabinet of the National Government had always reserved the right to present counter-claims against these debts for the services we rendered in saving Egypt from the horrors of war and conquest.

When, some weeks ago, I was referring to our immense volume of unrequited exports under the heading of sterling balances, the Chancellor of the Exchequer used extravagant language condemning anyone who could so violate, or talk of violating, contractual obligations as to refuse to pay or put in a counter-claim against these wartime debts. But his predecessor, the Minister of Local Government and Planning [Dr Dalton], used very different language, which I shall venture to quote to the House. This is what he said—it is a lengthy quotation, but I think hon Members ought to have it in their minds as it was spoken by so high an authority at the beginning of the Socialist reign:

'That vast accumulation of debt represents an unreal, unjust and unsupportable burden. If Lend-Lease and mutual aid had been applied among all the members of the Grand Alliance, as they were applied between the United States and the British Commonwealth, by far the greater part of these debts would never have been charged up against us. Sooner or later—and it would be better sooner than later—this mass must be very substantially scaled down. Britain is strong, but one side of her strength must be refusal to take on fantastic commitments, which are beyond her strength and beyond all limits of good sense and fair play. Nor could I, as the British Chancellor of the Exchequer, support financial arrangements which would mean that for years and generations to come this little island, which led the fight for freedom, would, through this peculiar wartime accountancy, carry a crushing load which even the defeated enemies of freedom—Germans, Japanese and the rest—would escape.'

Pretty good stuff, that. The Chancellor is not here—no doubt he has some other preoccupations—but I trust that this quotation may be brought to his attention by some of his colleagues on the Front Bench. It is of special importance because the Prime Minister—who, I understand, is to wind up the debate tonight—was asked on May 12, 1947, whether the Chancellor of the Exchequer's speech represented the views of the Government. The right hon Gentleman replied, with his usual laconic precision, 'Yes, sir.' Surely the Chancellor of the Exchequer should moderate his denunciations of a policy which his predecessor declared in such illuminating terms and which his chief endorsed without a qualification of any kind.

I hold that we should have presented counter-claims and that such a policy would have been supported by the United States. At the same time as we were being so strict, pedantic, meticulous and punctilious in paying Egypt, we were borrowing or accepting from the United States far larger sums of money which I doubt if we shall ever be able to pay back. It must be an odd state of mind in which the Chancellor of the Exchequer can go on begging and borrowing from one country in order to pride himself and preen himself and plume himself in cutting such a fine example of financial probity, dignity and decorum with another. It is said that one should be just before one is generous. In this case we ask the Americans to be generous in order that we may be just to the Egyptians and indeed, as I hold, unjust to our own people. I say that, because it was known at the time that the United States' object in lending to us, giving us these very large sums, by which the Government have maintained themselves so remarkably—which, as I think the right hon Gentleman said, have prevented unemployment rising to levels of millions in this country—the United States' motive in doing this was in order that the British people should be able to rebuild their own strength and stand securely on their own feet.

However, the payments of sterling balances continue on a large scale, and only the other day—I believe it was the day when the *Empire Roach* was attacked; but that was a mere coincidence, a pure accident, I am not making any serious point out of it—almost on that day another agreement for heavy payments was announced to the House. What form do these payments take? There is a destroyer of the Hunt class. HMS *Cottesmore* was her name. She, I understand has been traded to the Egyptian Government and her name has now been changed to the *Ibrahim el Awal*. [*Laughter*.]

MR H. MORRISON: They are laughing at the right hon Gentleman behind him.

MR CHURCHILL: I expect that the right hon Gentleman wishes that he had such cordial relations with his own back-benchers. It would have been strange for the Government to have sold a destroyer to any Power outside the Atlantic Pact at this time, when anti-submarine vessels are regarded as top priority in our shipbuilding programme. But to have given one to Egypt in the circumstance, and at this moment is, I think—I appeal to the ordinary unprejudiced common sense of the House—quite inexcusable.

And how will Egypt pay for it? They will not send us anything which will help our standard of life in this country; they will not send anything to us which will help us in our production of goods for export; not at all. All they will do is simply to scratch a few figures off their sterling balances account. I ask: Is this destoyer still in our shipyards or has she already been delivered? I am told that she is at present at Cowes—I may be misinformed. The Hunt class is a very valuable class of destroyer. Apparently we have not been able to afford to develop them for anti-U-boat purposes because of the money difficulties in which we are plunged. Here was one which we could have had for nothing. If it is not too late I say without any hesitation that she ought not to be handed over unless or until there has been a settlement of other matters.

There is another aspect which should be examined. After the brief war in which Israel, contrary to the expectations of His Majesty's Government——

Mr Crossman (Coventry, East): And of the Opposition.

Mr Churchill: Not at all. The hon Gentleman has been on all sides in this particular question. After the brief war in which Israel so conclusively demonstrated its fighting superiority over the much better armed Egyptian troops—perhaps the hon Gentleman would agree with that?

Mr Crossman: Armed by us.

Mr Churchill: All right. I think that was a very foolish thing to do, but it was done in the period of the war when, naturally, arms got loose in different directions.

But this is a question of this destroyer; it is a question of going on arming Egypt now, long after the war. I quarrel with the hon Gentleman on a great many things. I do not want to quarrel with him on any one of those points with regard to the innumerable facets of which we might occasionally get a gleam of agreement. After this war with Israel an armistice was arranged. In breach of this armistice the Egyptians have closed the Suez Canal. The Foreign Secretary—let me put hon Gentlemen at their ease—is entirely against the Egyptian closing of the Suez Canal, is he not?

Mr H. Morrison: Yes, sir, I am. But, unlike the right hon Gentleman, if I could come to an overall friendly agreement of good relations with Egypt, I would do so.

Mr Churchill: The question is whether the right hon Gentleman is adopting the right course or not. At any rate, the course which he has adopted, as I shall presently show and have to some extent shown, has certainly not led to the conclusion which the right hon Gentleman desires, and the closing phrases of his speech were instinct with an atmosphere of disappointment on this point. But an armistice was arranged after this war. In breach of the armistice the Suez Canal was closed to all passage of tankers to the Haifa refinery. Here was a property in which we had an important interest and which could have made our petrol position easier here at home. We have been putting up with this complete breach of the armistice, and utterly illegal blockade, as I contend—I do not think that the right hon Gentleman will challenge me—under the Suez Canal Convention—for more than two years.

And all through this time we have been releasing money—I am not talking about payments with Egypt; they were going on all the time—to Israel to buy oil that has to be brought all the way from South America. If one takes those things together—our treatment of Egypt, the misbehaviour of Egypt, our indemnifying of Israel; which I do not particularly quarrel with because it was our weakness that let them suffer through the Canal being blockaded—there one really has an example of British submissiveness to find an equal to which one would have to search the world very far. All the time we were sending valuable exports to Egypt for no return, including ships of war, aeroplanes and other munitions, while all they had to do, for their part, was to go on breaking the Suez Canal Convention, insulting us ever more bitterly every day, clamouring for the Sudan and extorting further sterling balances concessions from us in the various agreements which were made.

The extraordinary thing is to see the Foreign Secretary carrying out this policy and the Chancellor of the Exchequer carrying out what looks to be an entirely separate policy. It is not departmentalism, it is compartmentalism of a kind quite extraordinary. I have not seen its like before. I contend that no payments of sterling balances should, on any account, have been made to Egypt while they persisted in their illegal action in the Suez Canal. Fancy not bringing this strong point and leverage into the argument. There is the Prime Minister. I think it is a question to which he should address himself because he is not at the Foreign Office or the Exchequer; he sits over both. Fancy, I say, not bringing this into the general argument. Let the right hon Gentleman give us his reasons when he winds up the debate tonight.

Here is another fact. I do not know why we should have waited all this time for Israel to bring the breach of the armistice before the United Nations. Why could we not have done this two years ago, or supported Israel in doing it two years ago? Why could we not have refused all military exports and all payments on the ground of sterling balances until the matter was satisfactorily settled? That is an argument which I honestly think requires the attention of the Government. Although much can be brushed aside in our present course, nevertheless there are verities and sequences of causation which should be in the minds of hon Members of the House of Commons.

The right hon Gentleman is not directly responsible for much of this mistaken Egyptian policy. For more than a year we all watched with sorrow Mr Bevin's illness. It was evident that we were virtually without a Foreign Secretary——

THE PRIME MINISTER [MR ATTLEE]: That is quite untrue.

MR CHURCHILL: ——for a very long period. The Prime Minister is responsible for whatever happens, but I think it will be found that we were virtually without a Foreign Secretary during the whole of that period.

THE PRIME MINISTER *indicated dissent.*

MR CHURCHILL: The Prime Minister may hold a very different view, but he cannot dismiss an argument or even an assertion by muttering: 'Quite untrue, quite untrue.'

THE PRIME MINISTER: I was trying to correct the right hon Gentleman on a point of fact. It is quite true that my right hon Friend was ill, but he was an effective Foreign Minister throughout. It may well have shortened his life, but it is quite untrue to say that Mr Bevin ever let his hand go off the Foreign Office. Anybody in close contact with him knows that that is not in accordance with the facts.

MR CHURCHILL: That, of course, is a matter of opinion, but I adhere strongly to my statement. I fully admit that the Prime Minister had opportunities of closer study of what was actually taking place, but, anyhow, he is directly and personally responsible for allowing the Foreign Office to be without effective guidance during all this critical and, as it may well prove, costly time. We have now got a new deal. The curtain has risen on a new star. The right hon Gentleman is now at the Foreign Office. I have here a report of the speech delivered by him to the Durham miners a few days ago. I do not intend to inflame our debate or, indeed, to detain the House by reading it.

MR ELLIS SMITH (Stoke-on-Trent, South): Why not?

MR CHURCHILL: Because I do not wish to inflame or detain the House, I have already given those two reasons, and it did not require any 'why not' from the hon Gentleman. This, however, I must say. Viewed against the sombre background of the world scene it must be considered as one of the most lamentable utterances which a British Foreign Secretary or, indeed, the Foreign Minister of any important Power has ever made in recent times. It shows how far the right hon

Gentleman dwells below the level of events, and how little he understands their proportion in the discharge of the great office to which he has been appointed. It will certainly be viewed abroad as a measure of the contribution he is capable of making to foreign affairs, and of the spirit in which he approaches this grave and solemn task.

MR MORRISON: Will the right hon Gentleman be good enough, after condemning me so strongly and so sweepingly, to quote what is objected to?

MR CHURCHILL: It will certainly not make for the tranquillity of the House if I read it out. [HON MEMBERS: 'Read the lot.'] It will add considerably to the length of the proceedings. If the right hon Gentleman really wants it I will read it.

MR MORRISON: That is the sort of churlishness we are accustomed to. All I can say is that there is presumably in the speech something to which the right hon Gentleman takes strong exception. Will he read those parts of it to which he does take exception?

MR CHURCHILL: I really have no choice, but it will certainly add to the length of our proceedings and I expect it will give opportunities for cheering by partisans on both sides. I was hoping that we could keep this Foreign Office debate if not in uncontroversial at any rate in calm channels. Let me say this in advance. In judging what I am now about to read, the House, I am sure, will feel how much better it would have been if the right hon Gentleman had got Foreign Office officials to write for him his speeches to be delivered in the country and he had devoted some of the leisure made possible thereby to learning something about the great task he has undertaken. Here is what he said:

'But Mr Churchill had shown a sensible restraint, which, however, had not restrained the warlike fever of the Conservative back-benchers. A substantial body of Tory back-bench MPs and a number of Conservative newspapers are playing quite a vigorous party game in foreign affairs. It started way back in the days of Ernest Bevin and has, if anything, intensified in recent weeks. I make no personal complaint. I can take it.'

The right hon Gentleman must not be so touchy today.

'Indeed, I have naturally been a target of Tory attacks all my public life. And if some of the less distinguished chat paragraphists or London letter writers find their work easier by accepting cantankerous and untruthful copy from Tory quarters, well, have a heart! The weather has been warm and some folks find it tiring. Nevertheless, we have seen signs of dangerous Tory irresponsibility in Foreign Affairs. It is one of my duties as Foreign Secretary to stand up for the proper interests of our country. In doing so I rule out nothing that is legitimate.'

That is a very far-reaching assertion.

'But what I will not do is needlessly, precipitately and irresponsibly to take warlike courses.'

THE PARLIAMENTARY AND FINANCIAL SECRETARY TO THE ADMIRALTY [MR JAMES CALLAGHAN]: What is wrong with all that? It is very small beer.

MR CHURCHILL: The right hon Gentleman asked me to read it.

MR CALLAGHAN *rose——*

MR CHURCHILL: I expect the Foreign Secretary can look after himself, but will, no doubt, express his thanks to the hon Member for his chivalry in coming to his rescue.

'If you had seen and heard the semi-hysteria of back-bench Tory MPs in the last fortnight, if you have read the more excitable of the Conservative newspapers, then you will find it difficult not to come to the conclusion that, if they had had their way, we should have been involved in two wars in the last ten days.'

I say that was a falsehood, all the more shameful because all the facts were known to the right hon Gentleman. I could read more, but I have taken up enough time. I have been forced to take up the time of the House with it. Let me press this point. Here is the new Foreign Secretary, who shows to all the world that his main thought in life is to be a caucus boss and a bitter party electioneer. It is tragic indeed that at this time his distorted, twisted and malevolent mind should be the one to which our Foreign Affairs are confided.

Now I turn to Persia. The right hon Gentleman told us nothing new about Persia. [An HON MEMBER: 'Neither have you.'] The newspapers seem well informed, and I base myself on them. It is necessary for those on either side of the House to make their position clear. Judged by every standard, the conduct of the Persian Government has been outrageous, but this must not lead us to ignore what is fair and equitable in the Persian case. In February 1948, Sir Stafford Cripps appealed for dividend restraint—we seem to go round that circle still—the Anglo-Iranian Oil Company was earning about 150 per cent and paying 30 per cent. As payments by the company to Persia were in part proportional to the distributed profits, this had the effect of keeping down the amount received by the Persian Government, not on commercial merits, but because of the domestic policy of the British Government. All this was put before the House in June by my right hon Friend the Member for Warwick and Leamington [Mr Eden]. I must repeat what he said then:

'As they'—the Persian Government—'saw it, the company was earning 150 per cent or thereabouts but they were still paying 30 per cent. His Majesty's Government were getting a good rake-off, not as a shareholder but from taxation.'

It was quite clear from the moment this situation developed, and indeed before it, that new proposals must be made to the Persian Government. In 1949, negotiations between the Anglo-Iranian Oil Company and the Persian Government ended in a Supplemental Agreement, which was signed in 1949. Meanwhile, an agreement had been made in Saudi Arabia on a 50–50 basis by the American company which has been tactfully renamed 'Aramco'. Just watch that a little. It is as if we had changed the name of our company to 'Persanglo'. There is nothing like studying the customer.

The Supplemental Agreement of 1949—to quote the Foreign Secretary a few days ago—offered

'a more advantageous return for a ton of oil than was now enjoyed by any Middle Eastern Government'.

Nevertheless the agreement was not ratified by the Persian Government for eighteen months, and General Razmara, the Persian Prime Minister, who favoured it, was murdered on March 17. The fall of British prestige in the Near and Middle East, particularly as a result of Anglo-Egyptian relations, must be considered as the main reason why this beneficial measure was not accepted, as it deserved to be. It is also a reflection on the British Government that they were not more active or more effective in pressing this matter from here, during the long interval of eighteen months in 1950 and even before the end of 1949. Then was the time to send a British Minister of the Crown to the spot. Then was the time to try to form with the United States a properly-conceived joint or harmoniously co-ordinated policy; but the Foreign Office had fallen into the disarray to which I have referred, and which I believe was caused by the illness of Mr Bevin. It had not the acumen, at any rate, or the ability to enable the Department to benefit from the accumulated experience of the old Foreign and Political Department of the Government of India, whose personnel they had absorbed.

As usual, no foresight was shown and nothing constructive or effective was done. It may be said: 'How easy to be wise after the event,' but surely it is the business of the British Government to be wise before the event. In this case, the facts were obvious. The loss of India as a factor in these regions had effects plainly visible, not only on our prestige but on our power, which could only, and can only, be compensated by a closer association of British policy in Persia with that of the United States. The issue was of such great importance as to be well worth a visit by the Prime Minister to the United States at a time when the two countries were acting so closely together in matters like the Atlantic Pact and its development. This matter might well have been incidental to the important topics discussed; but, as we know, an interval of five years passed between his visit after taking office in 1945 and the hastily-resolved mission on which he went eight months ago. The truth is that the Government are so unequal to the enormous and complicated task and so oppressed by their own political preoccupations that they only live from hand to mouth and week to week, and seem to derive no benefit from the invaluable resources of special information and the opportunities of guiding and shaping events which, as an Executive, they enjoy.

I have before pointed out to the House the different characters of the responsibility borne by the Executive Government and the Parliamentary Opposition. This presents itself in the sharpest form where military operations are in question. It is not the duty of the Opposition to suggest or demand specific military operations. They do not know what are the forces available, nor what course of action the Government are pursuing. It has well been said—I think, by Lord Lansdowne, although I have not been able to verify this—that an Opposition may properly urge restraint upon a Government where military action is concerned, but ought to be very chary in demanding military action. [HON MEMBERS: 'Hear, hear.'] That is the course which I have followed. [HON MEMBERS: 'Oh!']

I say that if military action were to be taken, it would usually be unwise for the Executive Government themselves to describe it or to discuss it beforehand. For that reason, I and my colleagues thought that some private interchanges would be useful, and might help the Government and the general policy of the country, by avoiding undue Parliamentary interrogation and debate which otherwise was inevitable on a matter about which we would feel very strongly and which rouses so much justifiable anxiety. I may say here that there has been no question of any agreement between the representatives of the Opposition and those of His Majesty's Government at these private discussions. We have expressed our opinion. We have offered some suggestions. We have endeavoured to make the Government feel that a policy of firmness, exercised with prudence, would in this matter, as in other matters, be treated in a non-party spirit. On the other hand, there is one point, which I shall come to later, which we have made absolutely clear.

Our general attitude on this side of the House is not the same as that of the Prime Minister when he led his party into the Lobby against National Service less than four months before the late war. Then he was only asked to give the support of his party to measures which no one knew better than he were necessary and, indeed, overdue. If there is any urgent need which the Government feel for stronger military preparation, I can only remind them that they have always received our support in all major things that concern the national safety. But the giving and promising of our support to such measures of security and preparation is quite different from, and has no relation to, the urging upon the Executive of definite military operations. For these, the initiative and sole responsibility fall upon the Government of the day.

The situation in Persia is indeterminate. It follows from what I have already said that I attached great importance to the announcement that the President was sending Mr Averell Harriman to Persia. He is a man who has a complete grasp of the whole world scene and a man of the highest personal capacity. Naturally, he was not, in our view, going as a mediator, still less as an arbitrator. We rightly take our stand upon the judgment of The Hague Court. That was the attitude of His Majesty's Government. It is the prima facie duty of those who believe in the rule of law to sustain in every way they can judgments of this character and not to make compromises between them and some other solution. Mr Harriman does not necessarily represent British views. Nevertheless, I believe that the Harriman mission has been helpful and that it has improved, and not lessened, the hopes of eventual agreement. Mr Harriman's exertions have, at any rate, brought the prospects of a resumption of civilized conversations much nearer than they were before. We have been told nothing about this today, but at any rate I hope that what I have said will be found to be true.

If I may digress for a moment, it would seem that the Government have an advantage in their task in Persia in having so much in common with the Persian Government. They, like them, are holding on to office by the skin of their teeth and, like them, they are persevering in a policy of nationalization without the slightest regard for national interests. This can certainly form a basis for mutual sympathy and future understanding. We are now embarked upon a period of negotiations which may conceivably be protracted. The Government have been quite right to insist that the persecution and maltreatment of our personnel shall stop before sending a special envoy to Teheran. It does not follow that time is necessarily against us. The position in which the Persian Government have placed themselves so needlessly, and, as we all see, so heedlessly, has brought the whole process of producing and refining oil to a standstill. The tankers are dispersed on other business and cannot be replaced except as the result of an agreement. The markets to which Anglo-Persian oil was sent are almost entirely closed against them by agreements between the various oil companies. Finally, the Abadan refinery has been shut down. We, both British and Persians alike, suffer from the delay, but the Persians suffer more and run greater risks with each week it continues; and meanwhile their Government is standing between their people and the immense new benefits embodied in the Supplemental Agreement, or variants of it, and the further welcome and important promises of American aid in arms and money. This seems to me to be a situation calling, in an exceptional degree, for patience on the basis of firmness.

Obviously, if the House were not rising this week, we should have postponed this debate. As it is, we have no choice but to set forth our position upon essentials in plain terms. We do not mind if the Government consider it necessary to withdraw our oil personnel from the mountain oilfields into Abadan. It may be necessary or it may not, but it may well be that we could not easily protect them there from violence and murder in their scattered positions in the oilfields. If they are withdrawn—it is said in the papers that there are 300 or 400; it may be true or not, I do not know—to Abadan, they may quite well be the ones who would not be needed there and would be surplus to the essential staff. The matter is not one, in my opinion, which raises any important issue. We have, however, in all our discussions with the Government made it clear that the Conservative Party will oppose and censure by every means in their power the total evacuation of Abadan. [HON MEMBERS: 'Hear, hear.'] The refinery must continue to be occupied by a sufficient number of British Anglo-Persian personnel to make it possible for the installations to be maintained in an effective fashion and for the business to be progressively re-started whenever a settlement is reached. Every effort should be made to rally this nucleus of British personnel to the high opportunity they have of rendering distinguished service to their country. They must stay, and we must never agree to their being withdrawn. If violence is offered to them, we must not hesitate to intervene, if necessary by force, and give all the necessary protection to our fellow subjects. But this I must say in conclusion. If the Government so manage this affair as to lead in the end to the total evacuation of the British oil personnel from the Abadan refinery, it will be our duty to challenge them here and in the country by every means in our power. The issue between us—which I trust may not arise—is the total evacuation, in any circumstances which are at present foreseeable, of the Abadan refinery by the nucleus of British personnel.

We request that if this decision is taken, and if possible before it is taken, Parliament should be recalled in order that a clear issue may be presented. All the power lies in the hands of the Government. If they use their precarious and divided majority to cast away one of the major interests of the nation, and indeed injure, as I think and I have sought to show, the world cause, if they are found to have been guilty of such a course of action now that they are asking of all of us so many sacrifices to carry out the policy of rearmament, then I say the responsibility will lie upon them for this shameful disaster, and we are quite certain that in the long run justice will be done to them by the British people.

# RAF BENEVOLENT FUND

## A BROADCAST APPEAL
### 16 SEPTEMBER 1951

---

1 *August—Mr Morrison's article explaining British political values and foreign policies published in 'Pravda'.*

2 *August—Yugoslavia ends state of war with Germany.*

22 *August—The British delegation in Teheran break off negotiations with the Persians.*

31 *August—A Canberra jet bomber sets new record for an east-west Atlantic flight (4 hours 19 minutes).*

1 *September—The Pacific Security Pact between the United States, Australia and New Zealand signed at San Francisco.*

6 *September—The Emir Talal proclaimed King of Jordan.*

8 *September—Japanese peace treaty signed at San Francisco.*
*Japan and the United States also sign a security agreement.*

9 *September—Greek Elections; on 27 October a Coalition Government formed under General Plastiras.*

12 *September—General Marshall resigns as Secretary of Defence in the United States Government.*

---

*[16 September 1951*

'Never in the field of human conflict was so much owed by so many to so few.' With those words in 1940—our darkest and yet our finest hour—I reported to the House of Commons on the progress of the Battle of Britain, whose eleventh anniversary we now celebrate. I repeat my words tonight with pride and gratitude. They spring from our hearts as keenly at this moment as on the day I uttered them.

Time dims our memories of many events which, while they are happening, seem tremendous. But the fame of the pilots—a thin blue line indeed—who broke the aerial might of the enemy and saved their native land shines ever more brightly. Our debt is now not only to the few. As the Royal Air Force grew larger and larger and the hard years of war unrolled, many thousands of their comrades died so that our island might live, free and inviolate. By 1945, alas, as our casualty lists told the tale, the few had become the many. Had it not been for those young men whose daring and devotion cast a glittering shield between us and our foe, we should none of us be sitting at rest in our homes this Sunday evening, as members of an unconquered—and, as we believe, unconquerable—nation.

Let us all welcome this chance to pay a small measure of the debt we owe to the paladins of the Royal Air Force. And I will tell you one thing we can do, and do now. I am appealing to you tonight on behalf of the Royal Air Force Benevolent Fund. This fund exists solely to help members of the Royal Air Force—men and women—in time of need, and their families or dependants when they are in trouble. More than £2 million has been spent in this cause during the last three years. But the demands upon the fund are great. The rising cost of living presses heavily upon all, especially pensioners. During the last three years alone, the money which has had to be spent by the Royal Air Force Benevolent Fund has gone beyond the fund's ordinary income by nearly £600,000. A renewed effort must be made if the future is not to be overclouded.

My friends, I am certain that we are all together upon this and that we are all agreed upon our purpose. We all rejoice that there is a Royal Air Force Benevolent Fund to give help to the dependants of those undaunted men who lost their lives in the war or have died since, leaving their record behind them. This fine organization for which I now appeal, has fortunately up to the present always been able to give at least a measure of aid. It is our duty now to make sure that the fund will be able to go on helping, and will not fail as the survivors of the war grow old and feeble. Only thus can the fund maintain its claim and reputation that no genuine case of distress is ever turned away.

The Royal Air Force Benevolent Fund is part of the conscience of the British nation. A nation without a conscience is a nation without a soul. A nation without a soul is a nation that cannot live.

Please send whatever you can to: Winston Churchill, Royal Air Force Benevolent Fund, 1 Sloane Street, London, SW1.

I thank you all for listening to me. Good night.

# ELECTION ADDRESS

A SPEECH AT THE STADIUM, LIVERPOOL
2 OCTOBER 1951

---

19 *September—The Prime Minister announces in a broadcast speech that Parliament will be dissolved on October 5, that a General Election will be held on October 25, and that the new Parliament will meet on October 31.*

20 *September—The North Atlantic Council meeting in Ottawa agrees to admission of Greece and Turkey to NATO.*

23 *September—An operation on HM The King successfully carried out at Buckingham Palace.*

24 *September—The conference of Commonwealth Ministers on raw material problems opened in London.*

27 *September—HM The King signs a warrant authorizing the appointment of five Counsellors of State: appointment revoked on 10 December.*

*The refinery at Abadan comes completely under Persian control; most of the staff of the Anglo-Iranian Oil Company leave Abadan for Britain on 3 October.*

30 *September—Festival of Britain at South Bank closed.*

2 *October—Mr Bevan and his supporters secure first three places on National Executive of Labour Party.*

---

*[2 October 1951*

I come tonight to make my appeal to this great City of Liverpool in the most momentous election that I have ever seen. I have been many times on Merseyside, I was brought up politically in Lancashire and I have spoken in many other Lancashire cities, when party passions ran high at home or dangers threatened our country from abroad. It was all very vivid and exciting, but somehow or other I never had the same feeling—no, not even in the war—that I have now that the whole future of our country is hanging in the balance. Passions run deep rather than high. There are no spirited interchanges between political figures. The problems which surround us and are presented to us every day that passes are in so numerous an array, and so complicated, that they do not lend themselves to the ordinary bickerings and clatter of lively electioneering. A mood of deep anxiety, mingled with bewilderment, oppresses the nation. They have tried so hard and they have done so well, and yet at the end of it all there is a widespread sense that we have lost much of our strength and greatness, and that unless we are careful and resolute, and to a large extent united, we may lose more still. We have indeed reached a milestone in our national history, when everyone who cares about the life of Britain, with its fifty millions of people crowded in our small island, far more than we can win a living for, except by expression of our genius, must seek faithfully the path of duty and try to find the best way through, not for this party or that, but for us all.

In the main lines of foreign policy the Socialists have followed the course suggested to them by the Conservative Party. But they have done this so clumsily and tardily that much of what we might have gained, has been thrown away in the execution. They have joined the US in its effort to maintain the peace of the free world, but they have coupled this with so much ill-natured criticism of the Americans that they have lost a lot of the goodwill we had gained during the war years. On the Continent, outside the Iron Curtain, they have set back the cause of United Europe by making it only too clear that what they meant was a United Socialist Europe. Thus they and the other Socialist parties on the Continent have lost a great deal of their influence. The Government, after long delays, have adopted a more conciliatory policy to Western Germany, and now they seek German military assistance against the Soviet menace. But they kept up their demolitions of factories and trials of German generals so long after the war as to rob their present attitude of any sign of magnanimity; and magnanimity may be priceless in the advantages it may sometimes win for the victors. Thus they have lost in these six disastrous years much that Britain had gained and more that she might have gained for herself and for the Empire and Commonwealth by all our efforts and sacrifices during the war and after.

I did not intend to speak to you tonight about Persia. I understood until twenty-four hours ago that no final decision would be taken by the Government, pending the result of the belated appeal which they had made to the Security Council of the United Nations. But now they have given orders and made arrangements to withdraw and evacuate all the remaining British and Indian staffs from Abadan, and this is to happen tomorrow. This decision convicts Mr Attlee and the Lord Chancellor [Lord Jowett] of breaking the solemn undertakings they gave to Parliament before it rose early in August. Let me read them to you. In the House of Commons the Prime Minister said: 'There may have to be a withdrawal from the oil wells and there may have to be a withdrawal from some parts of Abadan, but our intention is not to evacuate entirely.'

In the House of Lords the next day the Lord Chancellor repeated the Prime Minister's assurance, and added that the Government 'accept all the implications that follow from that decision'. I do not remember any case where public men have broken their word so abruptly and without even an attempt at explanation. But the immediate issue is now settled. We have been ejected from the immense economic structure and organization built up over fifty years by British enterprise and management. We are markedly impoverished thereby. All this has been done in defiance of the ruling in our favour of The Hague Court. Mr Morrison, the Foreign Secretary, and his party associates no doubt hope to cover up their failure by saying that the Tories want war, while they are for peace at any price.

But this question of war or peace is not now a living issue. There is no question of using force. We have fled from the field even before the parleys were completed. Dr Mossadeq can hardly follow us over here. I don't know what would happen if he got loose in Downing Street, but that cannot happen, so the question of whether force should or should not be used to defend our rights or protect our people is settled. Dr Mossadeq has won a triumph, although at a heavy cost to his own people. He has penetrated the minds and measured accurately the will-power of the men he had to deal with in Whitehall. He knew that with all their cruisers, frigates, destroyers, tank-landing craft, troops and paratroops, sent at such great expense, and all their bold confident statements, they were only bluffing. They were only doing what the Prime Minister calls, 'rattling the sabre'. And the Persian Prime Minister shrewdly chose the moment of the election, knowing what they would be thinking about then. And so this chapter is finished. The Conservative Party accepts no responsibility for what has happened. Presently it will be my duty and that of my trusted friend and deputy, Mr Anthony Eden, to unfold and expose the melancholy story of inadvertence, incompetence, indecision and final collapse, which has for six months marked the policy of our Socialist rulers.

Had foresight, alertness and reasonable common sense been shown there need have been no danger of any serious conflict. But all this belongs to the past. We have now only to bear the loss and suffer the consequences. I now turn to our fortunes at home.

We have suffered seriously from six years of partisan rule and party strife. An attempt has been made to fasten upon the British people a doctrinaire system of society which is certainly foreign to our nature, and a form of economic life which is most injurious to our power to win our livelihood in the modern world. Whatever may be thought of the merits or demerits of the Socialist theory, there never was a time like these six years when the attempt to put it into force could produce more harm. We only survived the war because we were united. After the victory was won we had no less need of unity and comradeship than in the deadly days of the struggle, but the Socialist Party, who were returned in overwhelming strength at the Election of 1945, allowed themselves to use their power to force upon our varied society their strait-jacket system of State management and State control, although many of them did not believe in it and many more did not understand it. We hoped that the last Election eighteen months ago would put an end to these harassing and distressing conditions. Instead of that it only brought about a Parliamentary stalemate which resulted in futility of Government and harsh strife of factions.

Parliamentary democracy rests upon elections, but prolonged electioneering is not good for any country, least of all is it good for Britain in these years of world change and turmoil. For nearly two years we have suffered from electioneering fever. No doubt it takes two parties to make a quarrel and we certainly have done our duty in the Opposition, but I am dealing with facts which none will deny. A Government supported only by a minority of the electors, and split to the core from what we now see at Scarborough, dependent from day to day and night to night upon half-a-dozen members, a Government which, weak though it was, pursued its party aims with scrupulous and gigantic rigidity, could not possibly sustain our reputation or defend our rights amid all the new difficulties and perils which have fallen upon the free nations of the world. The result of these lamentable eighteen months of Socialist minority rule has been growing disunity at home and a continuous diminution of the respect in which Britain is held abroad. Our friends have been baffled and downcast by the way we seem to have fallen from the high rank we had won. Our enemies rejoice to see what they call 'the decline and fall of the British Empire'. You will have your opportunity in this fateful month to show that our enemies are wrong. But do not fail. The chance may not come again.

There is a conviction not confined to any one party that we cannot go on like this. What we need is a period of steady, stable administration by a broadly-based Government, wielding the national power and content to serve the nation's interest rather than give party satisfaction. What is required is a Government with the power to carry on a tolerant, non-partisan, non-doctrinaire system of policy for a considerable time. We need four or five years of calm, resolute policy and administration to enable us, after all we have been through, to regather our inherent strength and allow our native qualities and genius to shine forth and earn their reward.

This will be no vindictive triumph for Tories over Socialists, no dull exclusion of Liberal and independent forces, but rather a period of healing and revival. If this purpose is to be achieved there must be no subservience to class or privilege at home and no deflection from our known and agreed policy of acting with the other free democracies, with strength, patience and firmness; and we must do this in order to prevent a renewal in catastrophic form of the horrors of war. The only foundation is a Parliament, an enduring Parliament, which will cast its broad shield over our island and win it safety for itself and help it to get well after all it has gone through. I ask therefore for a substantial and solid majority to bring to an end this period of unavoidable but mischievous party strife, to let the nation get on with its work with the least possible political interference, and to promote the greatest measure of agreement among ourselves that is possible. So far as the Conservative Party is concerned, our whole effort will be directed towards national recovery, both at home and abroad, and we recognize that that cannot be done without a very considerable measure of good-will from the great majority of the people.

At this point I must turn aside from my main argument to a question regarding the armed forces. Unlike Mr Attlee, who led his party into the Lobby four months before the late war to vote against Mr Chamberlain's modest scheme of compulsory service, the Conservative Opposition have always supported the Socialist Government in all their changing plans of conscription. Nothing would have been more easy than for the Tory Party to gain votes at the expense of our political opponents by finding many good reasons to abandon compulsory service. We should have been ashamed to gain party advantage on terms which would weaken the whole structure of the free democracies of Europe and America. This did not prevent the Socialist Party agents at the last Election from spreading the rumour through all the garrisons at home and abroad, and especially in Malta from which I had scores of telegrams, that we intended to lengthen the period of National Service beyond eighteen months. I therefore gave this assurance at Leeds in February 1950:—the Conservative Party do not intend to take compulsory powers to lengthen the terms of National Service. However, our Socialist opponents, having got what they could by spreading the rumour, proceeded themselves to raise the period from eighteen months to two years, and that is what it is at present. It is in fact now higher than in France. In this Election, the one we are in now, they are trying to spread the same rumours by their whispering campaign. I can only repeat, and I am asked to do so for general information, the same statement which I made at Leeds in 1950, namely:

'The Conservative Party do not intend to take compulsory powers to lengthen the term of National Service.'

I have thought it necessary to diverge from my general argument, to make this position clear, because serving soldiers and their parents ought not to be left in doubt about it, and also the story is a good measure of the kind of tactics to which we are exposed, even on issues on which the Socialists depend on our support.

Let me make it clear that we do not intend to enter upon this electoral contest on the basis of Utopian promises. We shall not follow the bad example of the Socialist Party at the Election of 1945. It is evident that this Election has come upon us largely because the Prime Minister foresaw how dark and bleak were the winter months that lie ahead, and felt it good political tactics to cast the burden on to his opponents. It would be very unwise and also wrong for us who have no special or official knowledge of the exact state of affairs to make all kinds of promises for the immediate future. How can anyone suppose that the results of six years' government, warped by faction and class prejudice and hampered by quite unusual incompetence can be repaired by magic? Evils can be created much quicker than they can be cured. How easy to slide downhill! How toilsome to climb back uphill. Not only have we to face the present conditions, but the tide is still running and may even continue to run against us. Please remember that, and, this is important, bear witness: I have tonight, at the opening of our campaign, not concealed the hard and grim facts, and that we do not in any way underrate the difficulties with which a new Government will be faced. I do not promise or predict easy times. On the contrary, a new period of effort lies before us, and this effort will require the whole weight and drive of Britain behind it.

We must clear the obstacles from our path. The Socialist system of State trading has fostered recriminations between nations without ensuring delivery of the goods. State buying has provoked State selling. It has brought national feelings into what ought to be ordinary commercial dealings. Governments flourish their national flag at each other before they can even buy or sell a pig or a cow. State trading has given us bad quality in our imports of raw materials. The closing of commodity markets has lost us valuable foreign exchange. It has caused dislocation and uneconomic use of shipping. It has resulted in the housewife having to spend a lot more money on very little more meat. The 'invisible' international trade handled by British commodity merchants before the war amounted on the average to about £500 million a year. This represented control over the movement of a vast quantity of goods and the consequent use of British freight, of insurance on our market and financing through our banks. An expert merchant buying from abroad risks his own money on the experience of a lifetime. If he makes a mistake he suffers. If he makes too many mistakes he disappears. But a State official or employee has only to keep his office hours punctually and do his best and if anything goes wrong he can send in the bill to the Chancellor of the Exchequer. He is truly what is called 'disinterested' in the sense that he gains no advantage from wisdom and suffers no penalty for error. It is we who pay the penalty. In 1950 the Government agents did not buy because they hoped for a fall in prices, but this never happened. In consequence in 1951 stocks had to be increased in the middle of a startling boom. Also in 1951 the Socialist Food Minister agreed to buy Argentine meat for £128 a ton, when he could have got it for £120 a ton a month or two earlier. No penalty for him. It was only Britain that had to pay more for raw materials and meat than she need have done.

But look at cotton. When in 1946 the Socialists introduced the Centralized Buying Act, we were promised that their proposals would result in cheaper cotton, more stable prices, the end of speculation and more efficient buying. But what happened? In recent months the Raw Cotton Commission's prices to the spinner have more often been above the world price than below it. Lancashire has experienced severe fluctuations in the prices of most varieties of cotton. In the bad old days in the pre-war free market, the movement of a penny was regarded as being a considerable event. But now the mills of Lancashire have to face sudden jumps up or down of 6d. or 1s. a pound. An even worse fault in the State buying of cotton has been the failure to give to the spinner the same selection of the exact quality he requires that he used to get. This strikes a deadly blow at the Lancashire cotton industry, which cannot hold its pre-eminence except by quality. In addition to these hard facts—this is all the more true in view of what we must face in Japan—we have improvidently cast away the advantage of being the cotton market of the world. Our policy is to re-establish and reopen the Liverpool Cotton Exchange. But here again it is much easier to destroy than to rebuild. The resources of the market in men and capital have been scattered. They cannot be reassembled by a gesture. The Liverpool market was a world market, and once it was abolished by the Socialists other countries stepped in and many new arrangements were made. We should do everything in our power, if we become responsible, to retrieve the Liverpool Cotton

Exchange and bring it back to life. But time will be needed in this as in many other directions to undo the harm so wantonly done. There are few instances in this or any other country of a Government going out of its way to deprive one of its leading and key industries, at once of an invaluable piece of commercial mechanism and of a symbol of its primacy in world trade.

Let me give you another example of Socialist mentality and tactics. All parties know that it is of the highest importance to avoid what is called the wage-and-prices spiral. The present Chancellor of the Exchequer two months ago sought to freeze wage increases. To win the extreme section of the trade union leaders to this policy, he proposed that dividends should also be frozen. Observe that this was not done on the merits, but because much of the driving power of the Socialist movement is derived from jealousy and envy of others whom they think are more fortunate than themselves. Mr Gaitskell's declaration about the freezing of dividends caused a collapse of values on the London Stock Exchange. At least two hundred millions of our capital values vanished in an afternoon. So he was entitled to pride himself upon this example of soaking the rich, although it is a fact that the shareholders upon whom the bulk of the losses fell are not a handful of wealthy men, but masses of ordinary folk upon whose thrift or readiness to venture or invest their money our buoyancy and strength as a commercial country depends. His colleague Dr Dalton, a former Chancellor of the Exchequer, hastened to add insult to injury. 'My friend Gaitskell has thrown the Stock Exchange into complete disorder,' he said, 'that is good fun anyhow,' he said with one of those inevitable smiles which are only to be seen to be believed.

Six weeks later the Prime Minister obtained a Dissolution of Parliament from the Crown. October 25, a day which we must make memorable in our history, was fixed. Can you think it extraordinary that the investing public and those who handle their affairs in the Stock Exchange were encouraged by the hope and belief, which may not prove to be ill-founded, that Socialist rule may be ended? Values on the Stock Exchange recovered in a day about half what they had lost six weeks before. Instantly the Socialist Party managers rushed forward to proclaim that this partial recovery proved that the Conservative and Unionist Party were the tools of the speculators and gamblers in the City of London and to make the issue of the Election a vote between the working classes on the one hand, and the Stock Exchange on the other. Even the Prime Minister himself has lent support to this slander, by talking about 'A high old time, and high prices on the Stock Exchange' as being the result of a Conservative victory. But the day we are responsible we intend to form a Government which will be the servant of no vested interest any more than it will be the slave of party dogma. On the contrary we shall strive faithfully to administer the national trust without fear, favour or affection for the lasting benefit of all.

The present Chancellor of the Exchequer, Mr Gaitskell, speaking the other day about our decision to impose an Excess Profits Tax during the period of rearmament, which I announced in my manifesto on behalf of the party last week, called it a 'somersault'; he thus showed that he does not see the difference between taxation imposed for social justice and taxation imposed for party spite. His dividend limitations, as I said just now, had the avowed purpose to console the more bitter and violent elements in his party for the wage-freeze which is the Socialist policy by assuring them that he was hitting shareholders as well. It is a strange and un-Christian habit of mind which makes it easier to endure misfortunes because one sees that others are having them inflicted on them too. Between this ill-natured exhibition and the measure we have proposed there is this serious ethical gulf.

We seek a free enterprise society with minimum basic standards and competition above that. Subject to the well-established laws and customs, competition should be free. But if abnormal conditions are forced upon us by world events, and £5,000 million have to be devoted to armament production in all its complex aspects; if one set of producers are to be benefited by every kind of priority in materials and manpower, then surely it is right to consider special temporary arrangements to equate, or at least to mitigate, what is an unnatural element and phase in our affairs. Hence excess profits tax during this period is in accordance with social justice and would appeal to all true democracies. It has another aspect which is important. Considering the abuse to which we are subjected the fact that it has been accepted almost without a murmur by the Conservative Party shows how false is the tale that we are the servant of wealth or the Stock Exchange. We defend the rights of property. We recognize the many high qualities of our Stock Exchange which have often been considered a model to other countries, but a Conservative Government will view all institutions with a fair and level eye and do the best for the whole community, independent of any special interests.

The Chancellor of the Exchequer says, 'don't put the clock back'. But the danger that faces us today is not putting the clock back. The clock is running down. Everyone can feel it in their bones when they look at our position whether at home or abroad. No, what we need is a new impulse to wind up the clock and regulate it in an orderly and accurate manner so that it will tell the hours of a long day of recovery. To hear the Socialists talk you would suppose that there was nothing here before they came into office. Nothing was ever done by all the generations of which we are the heirs. All that we have that is worth having is due to the agitators and apostles of class warfare who came into office in 1945 and have lived upon, exploited and squandered the hard-won, long-stored treasures and glories of British history.

It was a fine legacy that they inherited when they took over in 1945. All our enemies had surrendered or were about to surrender. We stood at the pinnacle of worldly renown. All over the world our friends saluted us as the one solid, enduring champion of freedom, ready to stand alone, starting from the first day, and ending in full strength, on the last. But our vanquished foes, they also regarded us with a strange admiration. We alone had never hesitated to stake our life on freedom. We had never faltered in the year of darkest peril. We had given all we had freely and without stint from first to last.

Very different will be the inheritance which it may be our duty to take over from Mr Attlee and his friends in a few weeks' time. But we do not fear it. We have not lost faith in our race and in our destiny. We are the same people, in the same island, as we were in the great days we can all remember. Never shall we lose our faith and courage, and never shall we fail in exertion and resolve.

# PERSIAN CRISIS

A SPEECH AT LOUGHTON COUNTY HIGH SCHOOL
6 OCTOBER 1951

---

*4 October—Parliament prorogued.*
*6 October—Sir Henry Gurney, the British High Commissioner for Malaya,*
*killed by bandits.*

---

[6 *October* 1951

Mr Morrison has asked me whether in my judgment we should have gone to war with Persia or not. He had no right to ask this question. The responsibility is entirely that of the Socialist Government who alone had the power and should have had the knowledge. He is only asking the question in order to gain acceptance for the falsehood he and his associates—I can hardly call them his friends—are spreading about that the Conservative Party want another world war. I am quite sure that if a strong Conservative Government had been in power the Persian crisis would never have arisen in the way it did. It is only when the British Government is known to be weak and hesitant that these outrages are inflicted upon us and upon our rights and interests. I cannot believe there would have been any need for a war with Persia.

The Prime Minister has now explained that when he said he would not evacuate our oil staff from Abadan he meant he would not do so unless he was forced. His policy was that nothing would induce him to go unless he were pushed. If he were pushed nothing would induce him to stay. But this was not the interpretation which Parliament and indeed the whole world placed upon his words. And I am bound to say that after the private meetings I and my colleagues have had with him it was certainly not the impression I sustained.

When he saw he was being misunderstood by the whole country, Mr Attlee could easily have set the matter right. On the contrary, he allowed his Lord Chancellor, the next day, to repeat in the House of Lords what he had said, and to add the remarkable and decisive phrase: 'We accept all the implications that follow from that decision.' Of course he was hoping to deceive Dr Mossadeq. But Dr Mossadeq saw through his bluff. It was only the British people and the world in general who were taken in.

I repeat, no satisfactory explanation has been given by Mr Attlee of his and the Lord Chancellor's statements to Parliament when we separated in early August. I cannot recall any large matter of policy which has been so mishandled as this dispute with Persia. It arose out of the great decline of British prestige and authority in the Middle East which followed inevitably from the loss of India. But foresight would have enabled us to be much better informed than we were at the outset. For a long time we were virtually without a Foreign Secretary owing to Mr Bevin's ill-health. When the Persian Government decreed the nationalization of our oil industry we were quite right to go to The Hague Court. When The Hague Court had given its decision in our favour then was the time, nearly three months ago, to lay our case before the United Nations. But Mr Attlee and Mr Morrison have simply drifted until after every kind of humiliation, we have been ignominiously ejected a week before our appeal to UNO could even be considered.

Even at the last moment, after the mission of Mr Stokes, the Persian Government offered new discussions, and the answer from the Foreign Office was that they would not negotiate with Dr Mossadeq any more. How can this be reconciled with a definite resolve not in any circumstances to resist physical pressure of any kind? What we have been witnessing is not a policy either of resistance to violence or of negotiation. It is simply a case of Ministers drifting from day to day and week to week, unable to make up their minds, until now we have been confronted with a major loss and disaster.

The lamentable story shows that our influence in the United States, in spite of our close association with them and the great causes we have undertaken together to defend, has also fallen to a very low ebb. I cannot believe this would have happened with any other Government than this one. Of course, now it is known that we will not in any circumstances offer physical resistance to violence and aggression on a small scale in these Middle East countries, we must expect that Egypt will treat us more roughly still, and many other evils will come upon us in the near future unless the Ministers who have shown themselves to be utterly incapable are dismissed from power by the electors. Anyhow, the financial loss is most grave and affects the whole of our position in the present dollar crisis. Now that the Abadan refinery has passed out of our hands we have to buy oil in dollars instead of in sterling. This means that at least 300 million dollars have to be found every year by other forms of export and services. That is to say, that the working people of this country must make and export at a rate of one million dollars more, for every working day in a year. This is a dead loss, which will directly affect our purchasing power abroad and the cost of living at home.

Mr Bartholomew's newspaper, the *Daily Mirror*, coined a phrase the other day which is being used by the Socialist Party whom he supports. 'Whose finger,' they asked, 'do you want on the trigger, Attlee's or Churchill's?' I am sure we do not want any fingers upon any trigger. Least of all do we want a fumbling finger. I do not believe that a Third World War is inevitable. I even think that the danger of it is less than it was before the immense rearmament of the United States. But I must now tell you that in any case it will not be a British finger that will pull the trigger of a Third World War. It may be a Russian finger, or an American finger, or a United Nations Organization finger, but it cannot be a British finger. Although we should certainly be involved in a struggle between the Soviet Empire and the free world, the control and decision and the timing of that terrible event would not rest with us. Our influence in the world is not what it was in bygone days. I could wish indeed that it was greater because I am sure it would be used as it always has been used to the utmost to prevent a life-and-death struggle between the great nations.

# PARTY POLITICAL BROADCAST

## 8 OCTOBER 1951

---

*8 October—TRH Princess Elizabeth and the Duke of Edinburgh arrive in Canada.*

---

[*8 October* 1951

We have reached a moment when it is the duty of the British people to take a decision one way or the other about our political future. Nothing could be worse than no decision at all. We have lost a lot in the last two years by the party strife which belongs to electioneering times. We cannot go on like this with two party machines baying at each other in Parliament and grinding away all over the country in order to gain votes for one side or the other. We could not afford it for long even if the world were calm and quiet and if we were a self-supporting nation safer and more independent than we ever were before.

The uncertainty has got to come to an end at home if we are to play our part in the world and receive due consideration for our British point of view and, still more, if we are to keep a decent standard of life for our people and even keep them all alive. Remember, we have brought into being through the progress of Victorian times fifty million people in an island which only grows the food for thirty million and that all the rest has to be provided for by the goods and services we can render to other countries. There never was a community of fifty million people, standing at our high level of civilization, on such an insecure foundation. We have maintained ourselves there by the qualities of our race, by the soundness of our institutions, by the peaceful progress of our democracy, and by the very great lead which we had gained in former generations.

Thus we have been able to withstand and surmount all the shocks and strains of this terrible twentieth century with its two awful wars. We shall endanger our very existence if we go on consuming our strength in bitter party or class conflicts. We need a period of several years of solid stable administration by a Government not seeking to rub party dogmas into everybody else. It will take us all we can do to keep going at home and play our part, which is a great one, in maintaining the freedom and peace of the world.

Of course, everyone wants to win his own election fight and after the bitter wrangling of the last two years there is no prospect of a coalition except under actual mortal danger. Nevertheless, we need not magnify our differences. We have to make them more clear and not to make them more wide. After all, the whole policy of social reform, the Welfare State as it is now called, was the policy of the National wartime Government of which I was the head and which rested upon a Conservative and National Liberal majority in the House of Commons of 160.

At the height of the war, in the spring of 1943—in a broadcast longer even than I am making to you tonight, with the full agreement of the Cabinet of all parties, I unfolded what we called the Four Years Plan. This covered the Beveridge scheme of national compulsory contributory insurance for old age, accident, ill health and unemployment. It included what is called the Butler Education Act, the Hudson Agricultural Policy, the National Health Service, Family Allowances and other important schemes. But all of this was common policy. It was British policy, not party policy.

One of the chief boasts which the Socialists make is that they have cured unemployment. But in the National Government, before the end of the war, the principal leaders of the Socialist Party agreed with their Conservative colleagues in a report which was published and can be read today. It says:

'There will be no problem of general unemployment in the years immediately after the end of the war in Europe. The total manpower available will be insufficient to satisfy the total demands for goods and services.'

There was indeed no shortage of demand. There was, however, the danger of a shortage of materials. That difficulty was removed by the £2,000 million worth of gifts or loans from America and the Dominions which the Socialists have received. Mr Herbert Morrison admitted this fact when he said in Manchester in April:

'We should be facing big cuts in rations and a million or two people on the dole if our friends and allies in America had not come to our rescue.'

How, then, can these public men in high positions reconcile it with their reputation to claim the credit of full employment since the war as the monopoly of their party?

We were able to carry out some of our four years' plan during the war and what could not be done while it lasted occupied the Parliament which followed the victory. Our joint plans were mauled and marred by the plastering upon them of Socialist Party politics which added far more to the cost than was gained in benefits to the public. Fancy, for instance, knocking out the voluntary hospitals, excluding the friendly societies or showing spiteful and pedantic prejudice against the private builder! Nevertheless, it is true today that four-fifths of the social legislation since the war was the agreed policy of all parties when I was Prime Minister with a large Conservative majority. What has happened is that we have been mishandled for several years by a spendthrift and partisan administration obsessed by a false theory of life and economics. To continue like this would lead to ruin. But the British electors hold the remedy in the hollow of their hand. October 25! Just make a note of that date. While on this point let me remind and assure everyone that British elections are free. Everyone can vote as they choose with the certainty that the ballot is secret, and if they live in council houses or are on the long waiting lists to get houses, or even if they are State employees, they cannot be called to account for the way in which they use their vote any more than they can by the landlord or private employer.

There are of course two new features which have been introduced into our life by our masters of the last six years. First, the nationalization, subject to compensation, of a number of our leading industries and services, the whole amounting to about one-fifth of our production; and secondly, the maintenance of as many wartime controls and restrictions as possible in order to prepare for general Socialist state control.

Nationalization is now admitted to have been a failure. It has been very costly to the public. It has given a poorer service to the user or consumer and, except perhaps in the coalmines, it is not popular among the employees. This ill-starred experiment has caused immense injury both to our harassed finances and our creative energy. The Socialist Party, in their Election programme, do not even use the word 'nationalization'. They have a vague sentence which would enable them, if they got a majority, to strike at any industry or any firm which they did not like, and just to say it 'could fail', and either to take it over or make it bankrupt by starting a State-subsidized rival which could dump any of its losses on the taxpayer. That is what they now say. Such is the undignified exit of nationalization.

Now I come to their second contribution to our affairs, namely, the keeping on of the wartime controls and restrictions. This has hampered our recovery, fettered our enterprise and enormously added to the cost and apparatus of government. Here the difference between the two parties may thus be summed up. Our opponents say: 'The more controls and restrictions we have the nearer we approach the Socialist ideal.' The Conservatives say: 'The fewer we have the better for a vigorous and expanding Britain.'

The difference between our outlook and the Socialist outlook on life is the difference between the ladder and the queue. We are for the ladder. Let all try their best to climb. They are for the queue. Let each wait in his place till his turn comes. But, we ask: 'What happens if anyone slips out of his place in the queue?' 'Ah!' say the Socialists, 'our officials—and we have plenty of them—come and put him back in it, or perhaps put him lower down to teach the others.' And when they come back to us and say: 'We have told you what happens if anyone slips out of the queue, but what is your answer to what happens if anyone slips off the ladder?' Our reply is: 'We shall have a good net and the finest social ambulance service in the world.' This is of course only a snapshot of a large controversy.

But now, since the General Election of 1950, an additional heavy burden has come upon us. The Soviet aggression in Korea led to a fierce war on a considerable scale. This has started an immense additional process of rearmament against Communist Russia by all the free democracies of the world, with the United States doing and paying the bulk. We have supported the Socialist Government's proposals. At first we were told they amounted to £3,600 million, but later on, when they added the bill up again, they told us that it is nearly £5,000 million military expenditure spread over three years. This is a very heavy load for our island to bear. A Conservative Government would have the full right to examine in severe detail the way in which the money is being spent and what is the fighting-power and defensive security resulting from it. If anything like the groundnuts and Gambia egg muddles are being repeated in this vast field heavy sacrifices will be exacted from our hard-pressed people without enabling them to take their proper share in the world defence of freedom.

What are we rearming for? It is to prevent Communist Russia, its reluctant satellites and its ardent votaries spread about in many countries—some of them even here—from beating us all down to their dead level as they have done as much as they can to the people of every country they have occupied during and since the war. But rearmament is only half a policy. Unless you are armed and strong you cannot expect any mercy from the Communists; but if you are armed and strong you may make a bargain with them which might rid the world of the terror in which it now lies and relieve us all from much of the impoverishment and privations into which we shall otherwise certainly sink.

The Conservative and Liberal Parties and part of the Socialist Party support the policy of rearmament and the effective binding together of all the nations all over the world outside the Iron Curtain, not because we are seeking war, but because we believe it is the only method by which a reasonable and lasting settlement might be reached. I believe that if the British Empire and Commonwealth joined together in fraternal association with the United States and the growing power of Western Europe—including a reconciled France and Germany—worked together steadfastly, then the time will come, and may come sooner than is now expected, when a settlement may be reached which will give us peace for a long time. That is our hearts' desire.

I do not hold that we should rearm in order to fight. I hold that we should rearm in order to parley. I hope and believe that there may be a parley. You will remember how, at Edinburgh in the 1950 election, I said that there should be a meeting with Soviet Russia, not of subordinates but of heads of Governments in order to enable us at least to live peacefully together. You will remember, also, that this gesture, which I did not make without some knowledge of the personalities and forces involved, was curtly dismissed by the Socialist Government as an electioneering stunt. It might be that if such a meeting as I urged had taken place at that time the violent dangers of the Korean War and all that might spring out of it would not have come upon us.

But now we have a different situation. In a way it is more tense. We are actually at war. Blood is being shed and cannons fire. The murder on Saturday of our High Commissioner in Malaya, Sir Henry Gurney, reminds us how fiercely the struggle there burns on. On the other hand, the gigantic rearmament of the United States, their development of the atom bomb, the growth of British and of European defence and the unities which have sprung into being among the free democracies, including our old enemies in the war, give a foundation, ever growing in strength and solidity, upon which a fruitful and durable peace settlement might be made.

Britain has a great part to play in this if only she can regain the influence and the power she wielded during the war. She injures and weakens herself by her Parliamentary stalemate. She strikes herself cruel blows when she accepts humiliations such as we have suffered in the Persian Gulf. We have to face a great lowering of our reputation. The Persian outrage, in disregard of the decision of The Hague Court, has weakened the cause of peace all over the world. It is a grievous injury to the whole of the Western Allies in Europe or in the Atlantic Pact when Britain falls flat on her face as if she were a booby and a coward. But this is not the real Britain, it is only the grimace of an exhausted and divided administration, upon whose conduct the nation will soon be able to pronounce.

I have explained from time to time the Tory outlook upon our ever-changing British society. We feel that process of bringing larger numbers to an ever wider table ever more bountifully provided with the moral and material satisfactions of life is the true way to measure our national progress. Give everyone a better chance to rise and let the successful help to pick up and bring along those who do not succeed. We are resolved that this evolution shall be tireless and perennial.

If the electors choose to entrust to the Conservatives an effective measure of power for a considerable period I pledge my word that the party I have led so long through such historic years will not be the partisans of any hidebound doctrine but will try its best to make things good and continually improving for the nation as a whole. We stand for freedom and unceasing progress and this can only be achieved by valiant perseverance. On the other hand we make no promises of easier conditions in the immediate future. Too much harm has been done in these last six years for it to be repaired in a few months. Too much money has been spent for us to be able to avoid another financial crisis. It will take all our national strength to stop the downhill slide and get us back on the level, and after that we shall have to work up.

We ask to be judged by our performances and not by our promises. We do not promise to create a paradise—and certainly not a fool's paradise. We are seeking to build a lighthouse rather than to dress a shop window. All I will say is that we will do our best for all our fellow-countrymen without distinction of class or party. I cannot offer you any immediate relaxation of effort. On the contrary, we have not yet got through the danger zone at home or abroad. We must do our duty with courage and resolution. But there is a wise saying 'the trees do not grow up to the sky'.

If we can stave off a war for even five or ten years all sorts of things may happen. A new breeze may blow upon the troubled world. I repudiate the idea that a Third World War is inevitable. The main reason I remain in public life is my hope to ward it off and prevent it. The desire of mankind in this tragic twentieth century can be seen and felt. The human race is going through tormenting convulsions and there is a profound longing for some breathing space, for some pause in the frenzy. Why not make a change in this harassed island and get a steady stable Government, sure of its strength, fostering the expansion of our society, making sure of our defences, being faithful to our allies and to the common cause of law and freedom, but seeking as its final and supreme aim that all classes, all nations, friends and enemies alike, can dwell in peace within their habitations?

# ELECTION ADDRESS

A SPEECH AT WOODFORD

9 OCTOBER 1951

Obviously at this anxious time our first interest is to maintain the best and closest relations with the United States. Apart from the world-wide causes of freedom and peace in which the whole English-speaking world is solemnly engaged, what is happening in the Middle East and in the Mediterranean makes it all the more necessary for us to work in harmony and consultation. It is six months since I said in the House of Commons:

'We are no longer strong enough ourselves to bear the whole political burden we have hitherto borne in the Mediterranean, or even to take the leading part in the diplomatic control of that theatre. But the United States and Britain together, aided by France—we three together would be in a most powerful position to deal with, say, the Egyptian problem and the whole question of the defence of the Suez Canal.'

One gets quite tired of saying things which are first mocked at and then adopted, sometimes, alas, too late. I urged the Government to try to bring about a threefold combination of our diplomatic and other forces. On this basis I believe that much of the harm that has been done in Persia can still be recovered, and the evil developments with which the free world is threatened by disorder, aggression and the one-sided breaking of treaties, might well be solved in a peaceful but firm and honourable manner. This is only a part of the great world problem, but it is an important and crucial element in its solution. I was concerned to see that our influence with the United States has not so far brought us the support in the Persian dispute which it is their interest to give, as well as ours to gain.

The Prime Minister has been emphasizing in his election speeches the importance which he attaches to Anglo-American relations, and I daresay he has done his best. There is no doubt, however, that he has been hampered by the highly critical mood of his supporters below the Gangway in the House of Commons. Their prejudice against the United States has been painfully evident on numerous occasions. The result of the voting at Scarborough for the Executive Committee of the Labour Party has, however, placed Mr Bevan and his supporters and lieutenants at the head of the poll. This shows that the critical attitude of British Socialism towards the United States is not by any means limited to the group of members who have made themselves obnoxious in the House. On the contrary they have received support in the Labour Conference which shows only too clearly the anti-American current which is flowing among the Left wing masses. If the Socialists should be successful in this Election, Mr Bevan and his views would dominate or at least sway the Labour Government even if Mr Attlee or Mr Morrison succeeded in holding the nominal leadership. This is indeed a dangerous development.

It is vital to world peace and especially to our own safety that our relations with the United States should be continually growing stronger and that our influence with their Government, which wields such enormous power in the world today, should be restored and improved. The return of the Socialists to office, with Mr Bevan's following now proved to be so large, would increase not only British difficulties but also the dangers of a general war. A Conservative Government would, I am sure, be able to rebuild those relations of cordial and intimate comradeship and understanding with America which played so important a part in the war. Even I might be some help in this. For I have many friends in the great Republic and they have often listened to me, and I believe they would say that on the whole, the advice I have given during the last fifteen years has not always been wrong. But I have never accepted a position of subservience to the United States. They have welcomed me as the champion of the British point of view. They are a fair-minded people. They know a friend when they see one; and they have never resented the very blunt and plain things I found it necessary to say to them from time to time.

There can be no greater danger to world peace than for the Bevan movement and the momentum which it has in the Labour Party to become representative of Britain in American minds. The United States are in a very different position from our British island. They are a continent lapped by oceans. They are self-supporting, and far more than self-supporting. They are rapidly becoming the strongest military Power in the world. Some of the Socialists say: 'Well, let them go and fight Russia by themselves.' But Mr Attlee's Government, apart from binding us by solemn treaties like the Atlantic Pact, have given the United States in East Anglia their main atomic bombing base on this side of the Atlantic. This was a formidable step for any British Government to take. We supported it on our broad principle of sustaining national policy in defence and foreign affairs. If we were to lose our moral unity and contact with the United States and they felt themselves free to judge the world situation in isolation it might well be that we should run the gravest of perils without having our proper say in the course of events and without having the consideration which is our right.

A Bevan-coloured Government or even a Bevan-tinted Government or tainted (to change the metaphor excusably), might well lead to our still being left in the front-line of danger without our fair share of influence upon the course of events. I warn you solemnly that the mass growth of the Bevan movement inside the Socialist Party, which the Scarborough Conference revealed, may make the return of a Socialist Government a real blow to our hopes of escaping a Third World War. It would indeed be the irony of fate if the peace-at-any-price voters became the means of destroying our prospects of getting safely through the next two or three years of anxiety. It is certain that a vote for Bevanite Socialism is in fact, whatever its intention, a vote which increases the hazard of a world catastrophe. Let us make October 25 a day of liberation from fears, as well as from follies.

Mr Deakin, the trade union leader, has asked whether the Conservative Party contemplate legislation affecting the trade unions. He is a man for whom I have much respect because he holds the leadership of the largest trade union which exists and does not fear to take unpopular courses. I was much interested in his statement some months ago about the importance of preserving the 'differentials' in our complex industry. We certainly could never earn our living by world trade or even exist in this island without full recognition of all forms of exceptional individual contribution, whether by genius, contrivance, skill, industry or thrift. After compliments, as they say, let me now set Mr Deakin's mind at rest. The Conservative Party have no intention of initiating any legislation affecting trade unions, should we become responsible in the new Parliament. We hope to work with the trade unions in a loyal and friendly spirit, and if this is disturbed by party politics the fault will not be on our side.

There is of course the question of the political levy being exacted from Conservative and Liberal trade unionists, putting the onus on them to contract out. We do not think that this is fair. But the Conservative and Liberal membership of the trade unions is now so strong, and growing so steadily, that a wider spirit of tolerance has grown up and the question may well be left to commonsense and the British way of settling things. The trade unions obtained their charter and lawful foundation from the Conservative Party many years ago. We regard them as an essential factor, working for the stability and progress of the country. The trade unions will, I am sure, respect the verdict of the people as expressed constitutionally in a General Election. If we should be returned we shall consult with them and work with them on a non-party basis in a frank and friendly manner.

Take, for instance, the repeal of the nationalization of steel which we shall certainly carry out forthwith. There we shall adopt the kind of scheme which was recommended for many industries in the Trades Union Congress Report which owed so much of its wisdom to Mr Lincoln Evans. Of course, the trade union leaders and the Conservatives have recently gained another link. Both are insulted by Mr Bevan and his movement. We are vermin, they are stooges.

Fortified by this, let us try to get on with the job together. There is only one question which has to be considered at the present time, namely the closed shop. This has raised a legal issue between the present Socialist Government and the local authorities in Durham. In our view the Durham County Council was wrong to insist upon the closed shop principle for all its employees, and the Socialist Government were right in the attitude which they adopted with the assent of the trade union leaders themselves. Like other matters in this field, it may well be left to the working of commonsense and public opinion. There is, therefore, no issue open between us and the trade unions. Indeed we consider that by bringing to an end the policy of further nationalization we shall be leaving them free to exercise their long-established right and duty of collective bargaining between employers and labour without the State being involved except as a neutral mediator. I hope Mr Deakin will find that I have answered his question in a manner which is satisfactory.

# ELECTION ADDRESS

A RECORDED MESSAGE TO ULSTER
11 OCTOBER 1951

---

*11 October—A long-term meat agreement with Australia signed in London.*

---

[*11 October* 1951

I am grateful for this opportunity of sending a personal message to the people of loyal Ulster, for I recall with pride and thankfulness the great and essential part which they played in winning the last war. I have followed with interest your progress in recent years and your trading success in world markets, which have been a most valuable contribution to the economy of the United Kingdom.

In this General Election the Unionist Party is the only one which mentions that it is concerned with the constitutional position of Northern Ireland, and in our Policy Statement, *Britain—Strong and Free*, we reaffirm our determination that the present relationship of Ulster to the United Kingdom and the Empire shall never in the slightest degree be altered without the consent of the Parliament of Northern Ireland. This has ever been a fundamental principle of Unionist policy, this must continue, for your destiny is forever bound up with Britain and the British Commonwealth.

The people of Ulster can play a great part in the improvement of our standards of life at home and in the preservation of peace throughout the world by supporting all Unionist candidates at the polls on October 25. Make sure that that becomes a famous date in our history.

# CONSTITUENCY MEETING

The Prime Minister has been enlivening his tour throughout our land by making many attacks on me. I have not wished to be in personal controversy with him, especially when he is having such a bad time, but there is one statement in his speech at Leicester which I cannot overlook, and which is so remarkable that the general panorama of this Election would not be complete without it. Mr Attlee, speaking of the achievements of his Government, said that he was not satisfied with what had been done. Here are his words: 'How can we clear up in six years the mess of centuries?' 'The mess of centuries!' This is what the Prime Minister considers Britain and her Empire represented when in 1945 she emerged honoured and respected from one end of the world to the other by friend and foe alike after her most glorious victory for freedom. 'The mess of centuries'—that was all we were.

The remark is instructive because it reveals with painful clarity the Socialist point of view and sense of proportion. Nothing happened that was any good until they came into office. We may leave out the great struggles and achievements of the past—Magna Charta, the Bill of Rights, Parliamentary institutions, Constitutional Monarchy, the building of our Empire—all these were part of 'the mess of centuries'. Coming to more modern times, Gladstone and Disraeli must have been pygmies. Adam Smith, John Stuart Mill, Bright and Shaftesbury, and in our lifetime, Balfour, Asquith and Morley, all these no doubt were 'small fry'. But at last a giant and Titan appeared to clear up 'the mess of centuries'. Alas, he cries, he has only had six years to do it in. Naturally he was not able to accomplish his full mission. We have endured these six years. They have marked the greatest fall in the rank and stature of Britain in the world, which has occurred since the loss of the American colonies nearly two hundred years ago. Our Oriental Empire has been liquidated, our resources have been squandered, the pound sterling is only worth three-quarters of what it was when Mr Attlee took over from me, our influence among the nations is now less than it has ever been in any period since I remember. Now the Titan wants another term of office!

I have not replied to Mr Attlee before, but it would hardly be respectful of me to ignore all that he says about me. He charges me with putting party before the nation. This is ungrateful considering that the Conservative Party has supported him in every important measure that he has taken for national defence and safety. Last year when he proposed the great scheme of spending £4,700 million in three years upon rearmament, we immediately gave him our full support, although if we had suggested that such steps were necessary he and his friends would no doubt have called us warmongers. We also supported him in increasing the compulsory military service from eighteen months to two years, although at the Election of 1950 his party had tried to gain votes by accusing the Tories of this very intention. But what was the return we received from the Prime Minister for our aid in his rearmament scheme? Within a week of our giving him our full support he announced the intention to complete the nationalization of steel. This was a harsh act of partisanship which was bound to make the gulf between the parties wider. Now that we know what forces the Prime Minister had to contend with in his own Cabinet and party, and how he was being continually harried from behind and from inside by Mr Bevan and his crowd, we see the explanation of his conduct. In order to do what he knew was his duty to his country, he had to pay his way with these evil elements by creating fresh antagonism with the Tory Party, without whose support he would have fallen.

After all I suppose that it is a very complicated business to clear up 'the mess of centuries' and to have only six years to do it in. Let us look at our Conservative record on the charge of 'putting our party before our country'. Speaking in the House of Commons a year ago, I said:

'The Prime Minister the other day accused me of being party minded. . . . We are all party minded in the baffling and unhappy period between election decisions and between parties so sharply divided and evenly balanced. However, the nation may be assured that, whatever the conduct of the present Government and dominant party may be, the Conservative and, I believe, the Liberal Opposition will not, I am told, withdraw in any way the aid they have offered and given to all measures for the national defence. We shall do our utmost to encourage recruiting, and we shall be prepared to accept additional burdens wherever they are shown to be unavoidable.'

But let us look back on the conduct of Mr Attlee and his own friends in the years before the war. The Labour Party denounced the Baldwin Government for 'planning a vast and expensive rearmament programme which will only stimulate similar programmes elsewhere'. Mr Attlee said on 10 November 1935: 'The National Government is preparing a great programme of rearmament which will endanger the peace of the world.' Mr Morrison in the same month said: 'The Government leaders are all urging a policy of rearmament, and Mr Chamberlain is ready and anxious to spend millions of pounds on machines of destruction.' And again: 'Every vote for the Unionists would be a vote for an international race in arms and a vote for that was a vote for war.' Such was the language of the Socialist leaders in the years while Hitler's Germany was rearming night and day. But after all, actions speak louder than words, and the most remarkable event in the Prime Minister's conduct was his leading his party into the Lobby to vote against conscription on 27 April 1939, although this was four weeks after he and his party had welcomed the British guarantee to Poland against German aggression. And yet later on, when the war was raging, and after it was won, the Labour Party gained great credit by denouncing the Chamberlain Government as guilty men for not having made larger and more timely preparations. But that Mr Attlee, bearing this load upon his shoulders, should accuse the Conservative Party, on whose support as we now know he has lived in all matters of national importance, of setting party before country, deserves a prize for political impudence.

In their six years of office the Socialists have reduced the purchasing power of the pound by 5s. 6d. This is the consequence of vast and reckless expenditure and extravagance. It is the result of economic policies which have changed like the changing tints of autumn and of promises as thick as falling leaves. We must get back to honest money. Sound financial policies must restore confidence in the pound at home and abroad. This decline in the value of money represents a cut which falls most heavily on the shoulders least able to bear it—the elderly, and all in every class who live on fixed incomes; those who saved and who wish to save, those who draw benefits under our social insurance schemes. Take the one example of family allowances. Parliament fixed these at 5s. Today that 5s. is worth only 3s. 8d. Already the stream of small savings is fast drying up. This must not continue. Unless we can encourage thrift in all sections of the community our industries will never be able to obtain the capital and resources they require for new equipment to keep them abreast of our world competitors. If our industries are not kept modern and efficient, we cannot look for that increase in productivity on which our ability both to defend ourselves and keep ourselves alive depends. Socialist speakers are telling us that the rise of prices in this country is the result of Korea, rearmament and other world causes outside their control. This is not so. The chief cause of the rise of prices here has been the devaluation of the pound which four years of Socialist extravagance forced upon the Government in 1949. By that single act we had to pay more for the things we bought, and we got paid less for the things we sold. In the nine months between the devaluation of the pound and the outbreak of the Korean War, the wholesale price index rose by eleven per cent. It is that single fact which explains the increases in prices we found in the shops up to the middle of the summer of this year.

The second argument which Socialists put forward is that things are a lot better here than they are anywhere else. This again is a distortion of facts. If you compare today with 1947, when the worst of the wartime effects on economic life had been largely overcome, you will find that the cost-of-living has risen less in Norway, Denmark, Belgium, Italy, the United States and Switzerland than it has in Socialist Britain. One of the main contributions a Conservative Government will make to tackling the cost-of-living is to cut out extravagance where it is found. Some forms of Government expenditure are unnecessary. They must go. We must simplify the whole machine of administration. We will cut out all elements of waste and extravagance in every department, including the defence programme and the nationalized industries.

# ELECTION ADDRESS

A SPEECH AT THE TOWN HALL, HUDDERSFIELD
15 OCTOBER 1951

---

13 *October—Four-Power proposals for establishment of an Allied Middle East Command presented to Egypt. The British Government also present proposals for the future of the Sudan. Both proposals are rejected by Egypt on 15 October.*

---

[15 *October* 1951

The Conservatives in the Colne Valley have made a party sacrifice in not running a candidate of their own and in giving all their support to the Liberal candidate. Considering that nearly 16,000 electors voted Conservative at the last election, and about 10,000 Liberal, this must be considered a remarkable decision. It shows how deeply anxious the Conservatives in the Colne Valley are about the state of our country, and that they have come to the conclusion after much heart-searching that our safety, honour and progress as a nation depend upon the defeat of the Socialist Government. I admired this course of action because the crisis we have now reached is sharp enough to override the ordinary party differences which are a healthy part of our free constitutional political life. Indeed I was so much attracted by the far-reaching mental and moral vigour of the decision of the Conservative Association that I wished to come here myself to share in it.

My long experience of life has shown me that when any step is taken by a large body of people on national and patriotic grounds the great thing is not to do it grudgingly or half-heartedly. I said to my friends of the Conservative Association when they visited me in London:

'If you are going to make a sacrifice of your party claims, make sure you do it in style. That is the only way in which any advantage will be gained for the common cause.'

The Conservative Association have accordingly decided to do their utmost to return the Liberal candidate to Parliament without asking for any promises or for any conditions in return. The Liberal candidate for Colne Valley will have, I am sure, the fervent and ardent support of every true Tory patriot, not as the result of a political bargain or compromise, but because they feel that to rid the nation of its Socialist

146

incubus is a public duty at a moment so grave as this is in our national and international affairs.

I have been given a list of a dozen constituencies in which a Liberal candidate, without the faintest chance of getting elected himself, is doing what is most likely to get the Socialist in. Naturally, I am told this will make it very difficult to persuade all the Conservatives in the Colne Valley to vote for a Liberal candidate, and there are some who think that I ought not to have come here at all. I do so because the true guide of life is to do what is right. Both the Liberals and Conservatives who are unanimously opposed to Socialism and regard the return of the Socialists at this juncture as a very serious evil to our country, would be in the wrong if they fell away on party grounds from the main objective. I am sure that if the spirit which is running in this Constituency were to prevail, it could have nothing but advantage to the permanent good, both of the Liberal and Conservative Parties, and above all of our country.

Of course you cannot consider public and party questions apart from personalities. It happened that there descended upon the Colne Valley a bright figure in our public life. She came 'out of the blue'. In Mr Asquith's famous daughter you have one of the very best speakers, male or female, in this island at this time. She is also an absolutely unswerving exponent of the Liberal theme. She has never varied from her fidelity to her party, and there is no Liberal in the whole of Great Britain who can impugn or rival her record. Therefore there is no question of any Conservative or any Liberal in this Constituency departing by a jot from his principles or convictions. There is only that larger and higher feeling that in the anxious days through which we are passing, our respective party sentiments may find their fullest and most resolute expression by returning Lady Violet Bonham-Carter to Parliament by a resounding majority. As one who have lived his life in the House of Commons I feel interested in seeing fine speakers and strong personalities elected. The representation of Colne Valley will certainly not lack distinction if you return Lady Violet Bonham-Carter to Parliament.

That is all I have to say this evening about the party and political issues which come to so intense a focus in the Colne Valley. All over the country in this buoyant election, people are looking to the Colne Valley. I am sure the more the spirit which has prevailed here spreads, the fewer Liberal votes through the country will be wasted and the more surely a coherent and decisive verdict of the electors will be obtained against Socialism.

Let me mention to you some of the great issues on which

Conservative and Liberals are agreed, and which constitute the elements of the common cause vital to our national welfare. First, we proclaim that the State is the servant and not the master of the people. We reject altogether the Socialist conception of a division of society between officials and the common mass. We repudiate their policy of levelling down to a minimum uniformity, above which only politicians and their agents may rise. We stand for the increasingly higher expression of individual independence. We hold most strongly to the Declaration of Human Rights, as set forth by the United Nations at Geneva. It is worth noting that among all these United Nations we are the only great Power under Socialist rule. That is why Socialist policy has been in these past years increasingly out of step and out of harmony with, or lagging behind, the movement of thought among the free democracies of Europe and the modern world.

We then declare ourselves inveterately opposed to any further nationalization of industry. We intend to repeal the nationalization of steel. Further, we come to those large bodies of practical domestic reforms set forth in our booklet, *Britain Strong and Free*, and from a very slightly different angle, in Liberal election literature. No doubt there are other points upon which Liberals and Conservatives do not agree. But how small they are in scale and importance compared to the great body of fundamental principles and practical schemes of application on which both anti-Socialist parties are in accord, and which are now supported by a large majority of electors all over the country.

There is in fact a wide overlap of agreement, both in doctrine and in action, between those who have hitherto been brought up to regard themselves as political opponents. But now the times are very grave, and it is the duty of every man and woman who agrees upon so large a proportion of the main principles and practical steps, to make sure that these are not overwhelmed by the ignorant and obsolete doctrine of Socialism against which the British nation stands today in marked recoil. All I ask, and it is a modest demand, is that those who agree upon the fundamentals shall in our party conflicts try to help each other as much as they can and harm each other as little as they must. Let that climate of opinion and theme of conduct prevail and we should have cleared the path of progress of many of its pitfalls and barriers and perhaps have the power to rescue our native land from some of the perils and forms of degeneration by which it is oppressed.

More than forty years ago I sat myself in a Left-wing Government with a great majority, and I was one of their most prominent and controversial figures. The House of Commons returned in 1906 represented, in my view, more or less the same slice of the population, the people who elected it coming very largely from the same homes and from the same areas as does the Socialist majority today. But there was a great difference between those days of forty years ago and these days in which we are now living. The Liberal Government of 1906 was built around and upon those great principles of Liberalism which have since passed into the possession of every party except the Communists and are still spreading with irresistible appeal throughout the world. But now our opponents are not ranged around the great truths of Liberalism; they are ranged around the fallacy of Socialism, which is in principle contrary to human nature and which I believe can only be enforced upon nations in its entirety in the wholesale fashion of Communism.

We are now only at the beginning of the Socialist imposition. At present only 20 per cent of our industries are nationalized, and we have been living upon the other 80 per cent which the Government eye with so much disfavour and malice. The complete nationalization of all the means of production, distribution and exchange would make it impossible for this small island to support a large part of its population. There is indeed a great gulf of thought and conviction between us. It is more than a matter of thought; our actual survival is at stake. I look back with pride to the great measures of social reform—Unemployment Insurance, Labour Exchanges, Safety in the Coalmines, bringing Old Age Pensions down from seventy to sixty-five years of age, the Widows' and Orphans' Pensions—for which I have been responsible both as a Liberal and a Conservative Minister. I find comfort in the broad harmony of thought which prevails between the modern Tory democracy and the doctrines of the famous Liberal leaders of the past. I am sure that in accord with their speeches and writings, men like Asquith, Morley and Grey, whom I knew so well in my youth, would have regarded the establishment of a Socialist State and the enforcement of the collectivist theory as one of the worst evils that could befall Britain and her slowly-evolved, long-cherished way of life. All those who are resolved to strive for the restoration of Britain's greatness, for its tolerances and liberties and for its true progress, have this underlying sense of unity, which petty partisanship or outworn prejudices must never destroy.

You will have seen in the Conservative statement of policy, *Britain Strong and Free*, the detailed answers to many of the disputed and difficult questions of this anxious election. I hope, however, that you will keep foremost and paramount in your mind the intellectual and moral issue now to be decided for their future by the British electors.

The supreme question is, are we after our experience of the last six years to take another deep plunge into Socialism or regain the high road which all the rest of the English-speaking world are now treading, of free enterprise and opportunity for all, and of the strong helping the weak? It is better for the strong to help the weak than for the weak to hinder the strong. Basic standards of life and labour must be secured in our society and civilization, and on this foundation everyone should be free to use his or her gifts and qualities to the full. In this way alone can our fifty millions safeguard their food, their work and their homes.

But beware! For we may be at the parting of the ways. The wisdom of our ancestors for more than 300 years has sought the division of power in the Constitution. Crown, Lords and Commons have been checks and restraints upon one another. The limitation of the power of the Monarchy was the cause for which, as Liberals used to say, 'Hampden died in the field and Sidney on the scaffold.' The concentration of all power over the daily lives of ordinary men and women in what is called 'the State', exercised by what is virtually single-chamber government, is a reactionary step contrary to the whole trend of British history and to the message we have given to the world. The British race have always abhorred arbitrary and absolute government in every form. The great men who founded the American Constitution embodied this separation of authority in the strongest and most durable form. Not only did they divide executive, legislative and judicial functions, but also by instituting a federal system they preserved immense and sovereign rights to local communities, and by all these means they have preserved—often at some inconvenience—a system of law and liberty under which they have thrived and reached the leadership of the world. The Socialist conception of the all-powerful State entering into the smallest detail of the life and conduct of the individual and claiming to plan and shape his work and its rewards is odious and repellent to every friend of freedom. These absolute powers would make the group of politicians who obtained a majority of seats in Parliament the masters and not the servants of the people and would centralize all government in Whitehall. So far we are only at the first stage of this evil journey. But already enterprise, daring and initiative are crippled. Thrift is penalized by the heaviest taxation in the world. Regulations increasingly take the place of statutes passed by Parliament. There are many hundreds of new crimes unknown before the war, punishable by fines or imprisonment. And all this is avowedly only a step to complete Socialization.

'All men are created equal,' says the American Declaration of Independence. 'All men shall be kept equal,' say the British Socialist

Party. The only exceptions are no doubt to be the Ministers and the members of the Government and their associates. If this is already taking place before our eyes, when only one-fifth of our industries have been nationalized, and while we still retain our political rights and freedom, we can judge what will happen when the whole process is complete. The worship of an all-powerful State, beneath which the ordinary mass of citizens lie prostrate, is one of the most deadly and insidious delusions by which a free people as we still are can cast away rights and liberties, which for their own sake and the sake of their children, they ought to hold dearer than life itself.

The British nation now has to make one of the most momentous choices in its history. That choice is between two ways of life; between individual liberty and State domination; between the concentration of ownership in the hands of the State and the extension of a property-owning democracy; between a policy of increasing control and restriction, and a policy of liberating energy and ingenuity; between a policy of levelling down and a policy of finding opportunity for all to rise upwards from a basic standard. There is not a field in which the Socialists have acted during these six years in which they have not failed. In the domestic field we can see the cost-of-living; the disorder of our finances; the vast increases in the cost of Government. All that is apparent.

Abroad they have been false to the cause of United Europe by proclaiming that there should be no United Europe unless it is a Socialist United Europe. They have lost all their influence on the Continent. It was a wonderful thing, which really ought to be preserved as a model of what not to do, how they managed to excite equally the animosity of the Israelites and the Arabs in the Middle East. Towards the United States their attitude has been to take everything they can. Indeed they have been maintained upon the bounty of capitalist America, whilst at the same time trying to come the moral superior over them. Now is the time to break with these follies.

# ELECTION ADDRESS

A SPEECH AT ST JAMES'S BOXING HALL, NEWCASTLE UPON TYNE
16 OCTOBER 1951

---

16 *October—Liaqat Ali Khan, Pakistani Prime Minister, assassinated at Rawalpindi.*

---

[16 *October* 1951

I cannot recall any period in my long life when mismanagement and incompetence have brought us into greater danger. At home prices and taxes go up and up, abroad the influence of Britain goes down and down. In every quarter of the world we are regarded by our friends with anxiety and pity and by others, including some of those countries we have helped in the past, like Egypt and Persia, with hostility and contempt. Not one of them is so weak that they cannot spare a kick or a taunt for Britain. It is hard to believe that we are the same nation that emerged from the last War, respected and admired throughout the Grand Alliance for the part we played (for a long time, alone), in the defence of the cause of freedom. Six years of Socialist rule have not been good for us.

The Socialists started this Election on the basis that the party who could grovel best abroad would win most votes at home. We have yet to see whether that is true, whether it fully expresses the convictions of the British nation or whether it is the surest way to secure a lasting world peace. I do not myself believe that the British electors are thinking only of their material interests, seriously though these are affected. There is a deep-seated sense of pride in the greatness of Britain, and a widespread desire that our power shall be maintained and our reputation be restored.

Of all the countries in the world, none has given up more worldly and Imperial power and position than we have under Socialist rule. All our Oriental Empire has been given away, with the frightful slaughter of innocent and helpless people amounting to two or three times the total loss of lives suffered by the whole British Empire in the Second World War. Has that won us more respect in other parts of the East? For three years we have put up with the Egyptians, contrary to International Law, blocking the Suez Canal to the oil supplies for Israel and Europe. Did that pacify or placate them? No. On the contrary. When a great structure or organism like the British Empire seems to fall, for the time being, prostrate, every concession that is made is only an incitement to others to come and press upon it more. How is it that we who have given away and sacrificed more than any other country to this cry of anti-Imperialism, should also be the most hated? The French are holding on to their Empire and fighting for it against the Communists as we indeed are doing in Malaya. The Belgians hold firmly to the Congo, in the administration of which great reforms have been made. The Portuguese are holding on to Goa in India. But Britain, the greatest donor, who under Socialism has given everything away in all directions (except in Malaya), is the one who is denounced as the arch-tyrant and reactionary. It is an astonishing episode in world history. But after all it is only what you see in ordinary daily life, that if people are known to be ready to cast aside their rights and to give in and clear out, if their Government tries to undermine every argument by which their position may be maintained, to make a feature of it and glory in it, they will find lots of hungry wolves to come and eat up an easily-gotten prey.

In Egypt the Government in their latest proposals offer to hand over our historic position of defending the Suez Canal to a Five-Power combination of which Egypt would be one. Naturally I regret that this should be necessary, but having regard to our altered position in the world, I cannot say that it is wrong. It is six months since I said in the House of Commons:

'We are no longer strong enough ourselves to bear the whole political burden we have hitherto borne in the Mediterranean, or even to take the leading part in the diplomatic control of that theatre. But the United States and Britain together, aided by France —we three together would be in a most powerful position to deal with, say, the Egyptian problem and the whole question of the defence of the Suez Canal.'

I am very glad that Turkey has been added to the other Powers I mentioned. We now learn that Egypt has refused to accept this generous offer which would advance her sovereignty and which would at the same time secure her safety. We must all hope that the Socialist Government will adhere firmly to the position which they have taken up in conjunction with these important Allies and not let brave words be followed by ignominious deeds.

There is one other comment that may be made. Why have these proposals to bring America and France into the defence of the vital interests of the free world, in the Middle East, not been taken earlier? If at the time I offered my advice to Parliament the Government had accepted it a different reception might have been obtained from Egypt and it may well be that the Persian disaster would never have occurred. Owing, however, to the late Mr Bevin's ill-health there was practically no Foreign Secretary during the most critical months in the Middle East and when Mr Morrison succeeded him his mind was much distracted by the Festival of Britain and preparations for a General Election which were his specialities. The conduct of foreign affairs has therefore suffered all the evil consequences of delay and lack of attention. What is needed now is a period of stable and steady Government able to look ahead and foresee difficulties before they arise, and with time and authority at command to deal with them in the true national interest. In this way the greatest guarantee for the maintenance of world peace, so far as it rests with Britain to give it, will be secured.

Let me now come to our affairs at home and in Newcastle. This city of much renown both in peace and war has proved itself one of the key points in our national life. I remember my visits to you in the war and long before it. It is ten years since I last came to Newcastle and fifty years since I first came. I am very sorry that differences have broken out in the Conservative Association for North Newcastle. Naturally as Leader of the party I was kept informed of all that occurred and, while we do not interfere from the centre in constituency matters more than we can help, it was evident that this dispute should be examined by an impartial Committee of the National Union of Conservative Associations. This was done, and no one judging from a detached position could doubt that the report of the Committee should be our guide. Mr Gwilym Lloyd George is therefore the official and accepted candidate of the Conservative Party and he carries with him my warmest wishes not only for his own qualities but because he revives a name famous in the social history of Britain and also in our victory in the First World War. It is surprising that he should be opposed by an Independent Conservative candidate and I wish to make it plain that any Conservative who at this critical juncture in our history of our country allows personal or sectional motives to lead him to cast a vote which could only have the consequence of handing this famous seat over to the Socialists will have cause to reproach himself for having failed in his duty not only to his party but to his country.

I wonder if you have been following Mr Attlee's electioneering tours. I see that he complains that the Conservative Opposition have shown themselves party minded. But remember what happened when he proposed that £4,700 million rearmament programme. We gave him full support. We also supported him in his extension of compulsory service to two years, when he and his friends had tried to gain votes at the last Election by accusing us of wishing to do so. But what was the reception of our patriotic aid? Within forty-eight hours of the Conservative and Liberal Parties agreeing to support the Government's rearmament proposals just over a year ago, the Government announced that it was their intention to proceed at once with the nationalization of the steel industry. This was a double blow to the country. First it destroyed the prospects of national unity at a time of national danger and difficulty. Second, it struck at the smooth working of an industry whose position in the rearmament drive was fundamental. Here was an industry holding a prime place in our exports, an industry which has moved with the times and often led the way, one which for more than forty years had had no internal dispute between capital and labour, whose wage differences had been continually adjusted by the normal processes of collective bargaining, conducted by responsible trade unions, whose relations with the State and the users were agreeably regulated by the Steel Board. Here was an industry whose trade unions may be proud to have had at their head men like Mr Arthur Pugh, Mr John Brown, and a worthy successor, Mr Lincoln Evans. Let me, at this point, compliment you on all your candidates for Newcastle and Wallsend. They are all on our platform tonight. I do not wonder at all that Mr Alfred Edwards, your very able and distinguished candidate for Newcastle East, should, with his knowledge of the steel industry, have thought it his duty to leave the Socialist Party upon a major issue of this character.

Steel was an industry for whom the Trades Union Congress Report furnished an admirable guide for a working arrangement between employers and employed which, I understand, would give an acceptable basis for both sides. When you look out upon this troubled world and our anxious, embarrassed, bewildered country, you might easily say this was the brightest spot. Why should this then be chosen of all others for restrictive, hampering, convulsive regulation and change? When you think of all the evils that are rife and the muddles that are rampant, surely there were other reforms which might have claimed priority from the destructive zeal of Socialist doctrinaires and millionaires. Mr Attlee had long been reluctant to proceed with steel nationalization. Discussion of it has disturbed the Cabinet for two or three years. We may wonder whether it was the price he had to pay to keep Mr Bevan in his Cabinet, and to retain his support by the Left-wing of his party in Parliamentary and the country. It was a classic example of appeasement, and it obtained only the result of appeasement from weakness. Within six months Mr Bevan had left the Cabinet and the Left-wing was in revolt. Fortunately for the country there is now the chance to reverse this fateful and foolish decision about steel before it is too late. The organization of the industry and its individual firms still remain intact. The Socialists have not yet been able to go far enough or fast enough to undermine it. If we are returned to power we shall at once repeal the Iron and Steel Act. It is not too late for us to enable British steel to resume once again, under free enterprise, its high achievements of the past. We shall appoint a board representative of Government, management, labour and consumers, if need be with new powers, to supervise prices and development in the industry, as it did so successfully during the war and until it was wrecked by the Nationalization Act.

Steel leads me naturally to coal. The Conservative Party always had grave misgivings about the results of placing detailed responsibility for this basic industry on a national board located in London. Remote control of this kind is not the way in which to make the best use of our widespread coal resources. As the result of Conservative pressure on this point during the last five years the National Coal Board has recently been reconstituted so that it can concentrate more on questions of broad policy and general financial control. We welcome this development; but we must make sure that it is extended. If we are elected we shall propose the regrouping of collieries into districts of manageable size. Our aim is to see district boards which, while they would have to conform to national standards, would be free from day-to-day interference from the centre. Such boards would be able to inspire local enthusiasm and local loyalties. We intend to discuss all these matters with the miners. We do not want to have any discrimination against those areas where the pits are less modern or the coal is less easily won. But we do want to restore to the districts the sense of local pride they seem to have lost under Whitehall control. I believe that by giving the miners themselves more say in the working of the pits we should find an improvement in output. Let me make it clear that our proposals for reorganizing the industry will in no way affect the present machinery for wage fixing. A national minimum wage is now guaranteed for the industry and that system of negotiation must and will remain on a national basis.

Nationalization has disappeared from the Socialist election manifesto. In 1950, they were going to nationalize cement, sugar, water and the wholesale meat trade, semi-nationalize insurance, and possibly the chemical industry as well, besides proceeding with steel nationalization. The present manifesto is silent on these matters. This is not only because the Socialist Party has found out that nationalization is costly, but they see that it is unpopular. We should beware. Nationalization has been taken out of the shop window, but it is still under the counter. Their Scarborough manifesto says:

'We shall take over concerns which fail the nation and start new public enterprises wherever this will serve the national interest.'

This is asking for a blank cheque to enable them to nationalize anything they like, or dislike, if they get a majority. They would be able to strike at any industry or firm which they chose to say has 'failed'. They could either take it over, or make it bankrupt, by starting a State-subsidized rival, which would of course dump any of its losses on the taxpayer. We must not assume that the Socialists have abandoned their belief that the gentlemen in Whitehall know best—better than the housewife, better than the mother about what should be ordered for food and how the family should be brought up, and that we can prosper only if the bureaucrats plan our lives in minute detail. They have discovered that their theories are unpopular. The creation of the Socialist State has not been abandoned; it is only deferred until such time as their party can achieve a Parliamentary majority. Our aim and object is to get rid of the whole system of controls and restrictions as soon as possible. We recognize, of course, that while shortages persist some controls are inevitable, but we regard wartime controls in time of peace as a regrettable necessity. While they remain we should insist upon the closest scrutiny and review by Parliament. Post-war shortages must not be made the excuse for clamping a permanent system of control upon the free life of this great British community.

We are not going to try to get into office by offering bribes and promises of immediate material benefits to our people. The Socialists did that in 1945. We offer no smooth or easy path to the British nation now fighting for its life almost as it did in the war. We do not know what will be the facts with which we shall be confronted should we be returned to power. Certainly they have very gravely worsened in the last few months and we have found out much more about them only in the last few weeks. Nothing will induce me as your Leader at this Election to bid for office by competing with the Socialists in promises of Utopias round the corner, or of easy escape from the hard facts by which we are surrounded. It would be far better for us to lose the Election than to win it on false pretences. All I will promise the British electorate in your name, and the only pledge that I will give on behalf of the Conservative Party is that if the Government of Britain is entrusted to us at this crisis in her fate, we will do our best for all without fear or favour, without class or party bias, without rancour or spite but with the clear and faithful simplicity that we showed in the days of Dunkirk. We did not think then about party scores. We did not divide the men we rescued from the beaches into those we cared about and those for whom, to quote a Ministerial utterance, we did not 'care a tinker's cuss'. The rescuing ships that set out from Britain did not regard a large part of the wearied and hard-pressed army we were bringing back to safety, and as it proved in the end to victory— we did not regard them as 'lower than vermin'—we were all one then. However the voting may go in this part or that, in this district or the other, in the town or the country, our sole aim will be to act for all our fellow-countrymen and bring them out of the perils and privations by which they are now oppressed and surrounded. Above all, we shall go forward without fear and with unconquerable hope that our ancient and mighty people, who, as I believe and declare, saved the freedom of the world in the early stages of the war, are not confronted with any problem they cannot solve, or with any difficulty or danger they cannot overcome, if only they act with wisdom and courage and above all—if they act now.

# ELECTION ADDRESS

A SPEECH AT ST ANDREW'S HALL, GLASGOW
17 OCTOBER 1951

---

*17 October—The 16th British Parachute Brigade begin arriving by air in the Suez Canal Zone from Cyprus.*

---

[*17 October* 1951

Although we are in the midst of a General Election on which the fortunes of Scotland and Great Britain may turn for many years, I must address you first tonight upon Foreign Affairs. We have the curious situation of Mr Herbert Morrison, who last week was preaching peace-at-any-price because he thought that was the popular ticket, now declaring that we shall not retire from Egypt or the Sudan. In ordinary times, with any other Government than this, a statement of this kind would probably have been decisive, but when it is only a few weeks ago that the Prime Minister and the Lord Chancellor made similar statements about Abadan, the Egyptians and other countries may not attach the weight to this important statement which it deserves. The most serious thing is that no foreigner will trust what the Socialist Government say. Their words count no longer. The power of words to allay international quarrels has been deeply weakened by the ex-hibition Ministers have made of themselves over Abadan. Violence has broken out in Egypt. Blood has been shed and more may be shed. The Government are right to defend our interests in the Canal Zone and they will have full material support. There is, of course, no need for them to go to war with Egypt, any more than there was need for them to go to war with Persia. The weakness shown by Mr Attlee and Mr Morrison over Abadan is one of the main reasons why the Egyptian mob has got out of hand. Naturally, the Egyptian mob was encouraged by the humiliations which they saw us swallow when we fled from Abadan. A firm and resolute policy over Abadan would very likely not only have saved—without bloodshed—our vital interests there, but might actually have prevented the bloodshed that is now taking place in Egypt.

The sooner the present tottering British Ministers are replaced by a stable British Government with a strong majority and a long period of calm, steady rule before it the sooner will the dangers of violence and loss of life in the Middle East be diminished. I urged in the House of Commons six months ago that there should be a combined action by the United States, Britain and France in the Middle East. The Government have now adopted this plan, and they have very rightly added Turkey to our combination. If this policy had only been applied in good time or when I urged it, to Egypt and Persia and to the whole Middle East a lasting peace would have been established on the basis of law and respect for treaty and other obligations. But this cannot now be achieved by the present hesitating and crumbling administration which even when it does right and acts in accordance with our advice, always does so too late to prevent the very evils they fear most coming on top of them. Every patriotic Briton, no matter what party he belongs to, should use his vote on this occasion to make sure that whatever Government is returned has a solid and substantial majority. We cannot afford to go on as we have been doing for nearly two years in the equipoise of discordant factions. We cannot afford to consume our strength on what Mr Bevan calls 'the luxury of a quarrel'.

Seventy years ago, when Lord Randolph Churchill was invited to speak at Glasgow, he said that it seemed a presumptuous thing—these were his words—to come and preach to a lot of Scotsmen on home politics which they probably understood much better than he did; but he said he proposed to do so all the same. This evening I am going to follow in my father's footsteps. I could not have represented a Scottish constituency for so many years, or have surveyed for so many more the British political scene in all its variety and complexity without acquiring a keen sense of the tides of Scottish life and impulse. All our lives, whether Scottish, Welsh or English, whether as nations or as individuals, are being hobbled by the interferences and restrictions of Socialism. There are too many controls and restraints holding back the British effort and genius, too many orders and regulations made behind the back of Parliament and people, too many jobs local authorities or voluntary bodies used to do that the State now insists upon doing itself, too many things decided in London that really could be decided much better here in Scotland. This concentration of power in one place and in one set of party-biased hands is a process which runs counter to the whole liberal trend of British history across three centuries and to the message and guidance that the British people have always given to the world.

The Conservative and Unionist Party intend to halt and reverse this process. Our purpose is to give not less but more freedom to the individual, not less but more responsibility to the men on the spot. We do not accept the Socialist assertion and belief that the gentleman in

Whitehall knows best. Our motto and our philosophy has always been: 'Trust the people.' The Unionist Party has set out its proposals not only for releasing the energies of the whole British people, but for giving to Scotland special and new guarantees of her independent way of life. Should we now be entrusted with the power, a Unionist Government will carry out these policies faithfully and without delay. We propose to supplement our team of Scottish Ministers. We shall advise the creation of a new Minister of State for Scottish Affairs of Cabinet rank, to work in Scotland as Deputy to the Secretary of State. Confidence and a wider measure of responsibility will be restored to the county, burgh and district councils, and the Scottish universities will once again send their representatives to Parliament. In our overhaul and reorganization of the nationalized industries, we shall see that Scotland is no longer treated as though she were some province or appendage of England. We shall give all the aid that Government can give to further the prosperity of Scottish agriculture and industry and to develop, particularly by better communications, the distinctive life of the Highlands and Islands.

The principle on which the Socialists have drawn up their election policy is simple in the extreme. Everything that has gone well is due to their planning. Everything that has gone badly comes from world causes outside their control. All that is good in our island-life is due to them. All that is bad and wrong is due to the Tories. Even Conservative measures like the Butler Education Act or the Hudson Guaranteed Prices for Farmers are claimed by them. Full employment is due to them, but high prices are the result of world causes. Food shortage and other shortages are largely imaginary. High taxation they say is a blessing, and the housing performance would really be a great success if it were not for Tory attempts, to use their favourite word, to 'denigrate' it.

A year ago the Conservative Party set their target for housing at 300,000 new houses a year. Was this absurd? After all, before the war, under Mr Chamberlain's Government, without any fuss and hardly any subsidies, British enterprise and the local authorities were building 350,000 new houses a year. Now we are told that the best the Socialists can do is to aim at building 200,000 a year, and they have fallen below that. But since the war the need has increased in a tremendous degree. More than half-a-million dwellings were shattered by the enemy bombing. During the war years none of the ordinary repairs for wearing out and decay could be made. Slum clearance ceased. If ever there was an object upon which one would have expected any Government to concentrate after the victory it was houses. The Socialists recognized this in the 1945 Election, when Mr Bevan said we required a minimum of 4,000,000 new houses. The Socialist Party said this should be done in ten years, an annual rate of 400,000 houses a year. Mr Barnes, the Transport Minister, thought it could be done even quicker than that. That is what they *said*. Now we know what they did, or rather what they did not do. After six years not even a quarter of their ten-year programme has been achieved. When you think what misery, overcrowding and slums bring upon us, how fatal they are to family life, how they breed more illness than doctors can cure, this shocking failure of the Socialists is surely one which now presents itself to the verdict and to the sentence of the nation.

Now, of course, we are burdened by the immense rearmament programme which the Socialists have proposed and which we have accepted, subject of course to a searching examination of its character. We shall not hesitate to scrutinize the rearmament programme. We cannot afford to have that vast sphere infected by the groundnuts, Gambia egg stuff from which we have already suffered heavy losses. Next to the needs of rearmament we give the first priority to housing and we believe that by leaving party politics out of the problem and allowing enterprise and ingenuity to play their part under conditions of flexibility we shall, in spite of the rearmament priority, bring a substantial relief to the housing needs of the nation. You do not need a visitor from South of the Border to tell you that bad as the housing situation is in England and Wales, it is even worse in the towns and cities of Scotland. Mr Woodburn, when Secretary of State for Scotland, told us that overcrowding in Scotland is about six times worse than in England. Compared with the need, the record of 15,000 permanent houses, which is the total which has been built in Glasgow in six years under the restrictive policy of the Socialist Government in Whitehall, is a scandal. Surely we can do better than that. A Unionist Government will see that in the allocation of building resources Scotland's needs are given their full share.

After housing I come to what is in everybody's mind, the cost-of-living. In their six years of office the Socialists have reduced the purchasing power of the pound by 5s. 6d. This is the consequence of vast and reckless expenditure and extravagance. One of the main contributions a Conservative Government will make to tackling the cost-of-living is to cut out extravagance wherever it is found. We must simplify the whole machine of administration. We will cut out all elements of waste and extravagance in every department, including the defence programme and the nationalized industries. At home, let me make it clear that I am not making any promises of an immediate improvement. Do you think the Socialists would have gone to the country unless they had known that a worse time was coming upon us? Should we be returned we should not only have to deal with the situation as it is, but with what our predecessors have dissolved Parliament to avoid. It may well be we are just entering a grave financial crisis again affecting the whole value of our money at home in the sterling area and across the dollar exchange. All I can say is that the return to power of a British Government commanding the confidence of the leading Powers in the free world would give us our best chance of coping with the very grave difficulties which are descending upon us.

After housing and the cost-of-living let me come to unemployment. The Socialists claim that they have cured unemployment and they seek to make this a prime issue. Let us see how this matter stands. In 1944, when I was Prime Minister of a National Government resting upon a Conservative House of Commons with a majority over all parties of 160, I set up a Committee to inquire into the ways of preventing unemployment after the war. The principal members of the present Socialist Government and the principal members of the present Conservative Opposition were upon it; the Chairman was Lord Woolton. This document gives a most fresh, strong and ingenious view of what should be done on all occasions when a world slump threatens to affect the daily life of our island. It is published and can be read—and should be read; it expresses our policy today. The foreword to their report begins:

'The Government accept as one of their primary aims and responsibilities the maintenance of a high and stable level of employment after the war.'

It goes on:

'There will, however, be no problem of general unemployment in the years immediately after the end of the war in Europe. The total manpower available will be insufficient to satisfy the total demands for goods and services.'

This was the joint declaration of Socialist and Conservative Ministers, and of Sir Archibald Sinclair representing the Liberals, all serving side by side in a national administration, and with no conceivable motive except to find and tell the truth. They foresaw with remarkable accuracy the fact that in the years immediately after the war there would be no problem of general unemployment and they all declared jointly that one of the primary aims and responsibilities of the Government was the maintenance of a high and stable level of employment. This historic document, for the preparation of which no one was more responsible than the Chairman of the Committee, Lord Woolton, was approved by the War Cabinet and was presented to Parliament in May 1944. Now it is hard to believe that men like Mr Attlee and Mr Herbert Morrison can have the face to go about propagating the double falsehood, first, that it is they who have prevented unemployment after the war, and secondly, that their Conservative colleagues—now their opponents—would deliberately use mass unemployment as an economic weapon. I hope these statements which I have read to you, and the names of those who approved them in all three parties, will become known throughout the length and breadth of the country, in order that Socialist charges about the Conservative attitude towards unemployment may be refuted, and Socialist claims to have cured it with what they did in the last few years may be disproved out of their own mouths.

Leading Socialist Ministers have admitted that but for Aid from America we should have had very high unemployment in this country since the war. Mr Herbert Morrison, speaking in Manchester on 17 April 1948, said:

'We should be facing big cuts in rations and a million or two people on the dole if our friends and allies in America had not come to our rescue.'

Even Mr Aneurin Bevan had made the same admission; speaking at Scarborough on 18 May 1948, he said:

'If we did not have Marshall Aid unemployment in this country would at once be raised by 1,500,000.'

I wonder whether you have noticed that both Mr Herbert Morrison and Mr Gordon Walker—the Tshekedi gentleman—have been trying to set the trade unions against any other Government but their own and thus deter voters from using their votes freely as they think right. For this purpose they have mis-stated the facts about Conservative policy towards the trade unions. They have deliberately ignored my declaration of party policy made on October 9, three days before either of them spoke; and when corrected they have merely repeated their false allegations. I must therefore read to you again the statement which I made as Leader of the party and which will govern Conservative policy in the new Parliament.

'Mr Deakin, the trade union leader,' I said, 'has asked whether the Conservative Party contemplate legislation affecting the trade unions. ... The Conservative Party have no intention of initiating any legislation affecting trade unions should we become responsible in the new Parliament. We hope to work with the trade unions in a loyal and friendly spirit, and if this is disturbed by party politics the fault will not be on our side.' I am sure these eminent Ministers will not unwittingly fall into the Communist belief that if a lie is repeated often enough it is as good as the truth.

In spite of the party complexion which the trade unions have mistakenly, as I believe, assumed, there is a growing association of Tory democracy with the trade unions. After all it was Lord Beaconsfield and the Tory Party who gave British trade unionism its charter and collective bargaining coupled with the right to strike. I have urged that every Tory craftsman or wage-earner should of his own free will be a trade unionist, but I also think he should attend the meetings of the trade union and stand up for his ideas instead of letting only Socialists and Communists get control of what is, after all, an essentially British institution. Nationalization of industry is the doom of trade unionism. The trade union leaders in the nationalized industries, for many of whom I have much respect, are increasingly embarrassed by a dual and in some respects divergent loyalty. The trade unions are being attacked from both sides. The Communists intrigue and infiltrate from the bottom and the Socialist Government nationalizes and takes over the industries from the top. We no longer have the owners and the trade union leaders discussing matters together, with the State as an impartial arbitrator. We have the State in the nationalized industries as the owner and supreme power, and the trade union leaders more in the position of influential officials of the Government or party associates than as the single-minded servants of the members of the union. That is a very serious state of affairs. We hear much about unofficial strikes and many of them most wrongful and irresponsible and some at least are Communist inspired; but if the normal work of responsible trade union leaders is, to some extent, in abeyance because the industry has been nationalized, and the wage earners do not any longer have champions who are single-minded in their service, unofficial strikes are certain to recur.

If I were a craftsman or manual labourer (and I still hold my trade union certificate as a bricklayer), I would far rather work for a private employer who would go broke if he could not get on with his workmen over any long period of time, and in dealing with whom I should have the help of trusted union leaders, than deal with an all-powerful State. In all nationalized industries the worker loses the protection of his own chosen representatives. He is confronted with the mighty State of whom those representatives are already the agents, as in Russia they are the tools. And if there is a strike from which the State-owned industry loses money, they do not go to the bankruptcy court, they only send another bill to the Chancellor of the Exchequer and everybody has to take their share in paying it. The day we are responsible, the Government we intend to form, should we be returned, would be the servant of no vested interest any more than it would be the slave of party dogma. On the contrary we shall strive faithfully to administer the national trust without fear, favour or affection for the lasting benefit of all.

I do not know tonight the full extent of the harm which has been done to our finances, to our defences and to our standing in the world. I am grieved at what I see and hear; but it may well be there are worse facts not made public, and perhaps not even understood to our present rulers. Therefore we are not going to promise you smooth and easy times.

I have now dealt with the great choice we have to make in our domestic affairs. I have contradicted the falsehoods by which we are assailed. But I cannot end without looking beyond our island to the tremendous and terrible world that has grown up around us since our victory in the war. At Edinburgh, in the last General Election, I said:

'I cannot help coming back to this idea of another talk with Soviet Russia upon the highest level. The idea appeals to me of a supreme effort to bridge the gulf between the two worlds so that each can live their lives, if not in friendship, at least without the hatred of the cold war. At least I feel that Christian men and women should not close the door upon any hope of finding a new foundation for the life of the self-tormented human race.'

The Socialist Government dismissed all this by the scornful word: 'Stunt'.

What a reflection it would be upon our national dignity and moral elevation and indeed upon the whole status of British democracy, if at this time of choice, we found nothing to talk about but material issues and nice calculations about personal gain or loss! What a humiliation it would be if proud Britain in this fateful hour were found completely absorbed in party and domestic strife. Even on the material basis, a continuance of the present arms race can only cause increasing danger, increasing military expense and diminishing supplies to the homes. The only time when the people really have a chance to influence and in fact decide events is at a General Election. It is only by the agreement of the greatest Powers that security can be given to ordinary folk against an annihilating war. I cannot find it in my heart and conscience to close the door upon that hope. By its fruition alone can the United Nations discharge their supreme functions. I ask for a strong majority, one capable of giving both guidance and design and securing the necessary time to make great purposes effective. We do not seek for the power to enable one party to ride rough-shod over the other. Should we become responsible we shall govern on behalf of the entire British people, no matter to what party or class or part of the country they belong. We shall respect the sentiments of minorities in what is just and fair, no matter whether they vote for or against us. This is the true essence of democracy.

It is only by inspiring the nation with unity and common purpose, and by taking without fear or favour the necessary measures to restore our solvency and independence that we shall overcome the dangers and solve the problems that confront us. The British people have it in their hands to make or mar their future. An opportunity, which hardly comes once in a generation, may now be given to the Conservative and Unionist Party to serve the country. Working together in perfect unity, casting away every impediment, we may play our part in restoring the economic independence and well-being of our island, making it the centre not only of the brotherhood of our Empire and Commonwealth but of a higher unity of great and small nations who believe in progress through freedom.

# ELECTION ADDRESS

A SPEECH AT THE HOME PARK FOOTBALL GROUND, PLYMOUTH
23 OCTOBER 1951

---

*19 October—The Allied High Commission in West Germany announce
the transfer of control of foreign trade and constitutional matters to the
Federal Government.*

*United States of America end state of war with Germany.*

---

[*23 October* 1951]

I am always glad to come to the West Country and here we have the
candidates for Totnes, Tavistock, Bodmin, Sutton and, as you will
understand, last but not least to me, Devonport. The House of Commons will be the richer for the return or arrival of these capable,
earnest and patriotic members. Let us ram them all home with a run.
We can do it if we try.

The Prime Minister in his broadcast dilated upon the increase of
industrial production and improvements in national health that have
taken place in the six years since the war. 'The health of the nation is
better,' he says, 'than ever before. People are living longer. Many
fewer babies are dying than ever before.' He claims that the credit for
this is due to the action of his Government. But this is not true. The
advance in productivity and in physical conditions is not due to Socialism; it is science not Socialism that has the honour of whatever has
been achieved. Every day science is bestowing in an ever widening
flow upon mankind more material benefits than in any other period
ever known. All the machinery and electric power and improved
methods of production that are at work, are not the results of politics.
It was not the Socialist Party that discovered penicillin. M and B—
that marvellous healer—does not stand for Morrison and Bevan. It was
not the Socialists who made possible the tireless advance in medicine
and surgery. On the contrary it would be more true to say that the dose
we have had of Socialism has hampered and restricted the progress of
science, and reduced the benefits which the whole nation might have
gained from the tremendous conquest of natural forces which is now
being made all over the world, and which, if world peace can be maintained, and I believe it can be, may open to the whole human race an
age of prosperity beyond their brightest hopes. One-fifth of our indus-

tries have been nationalized. This is the part which is lagging behind. Our export trade by which we live, and the vast mass of our production which pays its way, is made by the other four-fifths on which Socialism has not yet laid its clumsy, partisan and rigid grip. The free enterprise four-fifths pays for the Socialists' errors and yet earns enough so far to keep us going by a narrow margin. The Socialists have no more right to claim the credit for the technical advance of this age of science than they have for maintaining employment. Both are the result of world causes, and £2,000 million in gifts and loans from the capitalist United States. A far richer harvest would have been reaped by our hard-working people if they had not been hampered by doctrinaire experiments, misguided planning and astonishing financial mismanagement and waste.

Of course everyone can say, especially at Election time, how much better we should have done it than the other chaps. But if the electors take a calm and sober view of how and where we stand this afternoon at home and in the world, surely there would be very few who would not feel that things would be much better in Persia and Egypt if Mr Eden had been at the Foreign Office for the last few years; and I think the housewives and the old age pensioners and others living on fixed incomes, might well feel the pressure upon them was a good deal less if Lord Woolton had been looking after our food supplies and if some check had been imposed upon the wild extravagances with which our limited finances have been dispersed.

The Conservatives and National Liberals come before the electors as a united party. In fact we are at once the least formally disciplined and the only united party. We seek to preserve the old dignity of a Member of the House of Commons which Edmund Burke asserted in his famous speech. For sixteen years my friend, Mr Eden, and I, whether in or out of office, have worked together in close accord and on all the great and changing issues of the foreign situation, whether before, during or since the war. We have measured the British position in relation alike to our allies and other countries with the same sense of values and the same guiding purpose. As I said at the Albert Hall a year ago: 'Mr Eden will carry on the torch of Tory democracy when other and older hands have let it fall.'

Mr Eden's recent visit to the United States was most helpful to our country. It did a lot to repair the damage to Anglo-American harmony which had been caused and is being caused by the constant attacks and criticisms of Mr Bevan and Mr Harold Wilson, the Dribergs, the Silvermans and the Foots—I hope that is grammar! Nothing could be worse for our country and nothing could be more injurious to the cause of world peace than for Mr Attlee to be returned, dependent upon a sham reconciliation between the main body of the Socialist Party and the powerful and turbulent Left-wing forces whom Mr Bevan represents, and who, as he says, are looking forward to the 'luxury of a quarrel'. The whole process of growing unity and confidence between us and the great Republic across the Atlantic Ocean would be weakened and our power to influence the course of American policy might be seriously impaired. I do not hesitate to say that such a situation would be prejudicial to the growing hopes of reaching a good working arrangement with Soviet Russia, by negotiation based upon the patient growing strength and living concord of the free world. This is not the time when we can afford either to weaken American comradeship or to lose our influence upon American thought based upon confidence and goodwill.

I must now refer to a personal issue. The Socialists somewhat shamefacedly, and the Communists brazenly, make the charge that I am a 'warmonger'. This is a cruel and ungrateful accusation. It is the opposite of the truth. If I remain in public life at this juncture it is because, rightly or wrongly, but sincerely, I believe that I may be able to make an important contribution to the prevention of a Third World War and to bringing nearer that lasting peace settlement which the masses of the people of every race and in every land fervently desire. I pray indeed that I may have this opportunity. It is the last prize I seek to win. I have been blessed with so much good fortune throughout my long life, and I am treated with so much kindness by my fellow countrymen far outside the ranks of party, and indeed also in the United States and in Europe, that all the daydreams of my youth have been surpassed. It is therefore with a single purpose and a strong sense of duty that I remain at my post as Leader of the Conservative Party through these baffling and anxious years. I applied the word 'ungrateful' a moment ago to the slander by which some of our opponents hope to gain advantage. I think it is the right word to use. It is quite true that at a very dark moment in our history I was called upon to take the lead for more than five years of awful war and that I did my best until victory was won. But that that should be made the ground, as Mr Shinwell suggests, for saying that I want to have a Third World War to show off my talents is mean and shabby. Trusting as I do to the sense of justice and fair play which inspires the British race, I am sure that these taunts and insults will recoil upon the heads of those who make them. We shall not have very much longer to wait before we shall see what the British answer is to all that.

Now I leave the personal question and am only sorry to have had to burden you with it. But the charge is also made that the expected return of a Conservative Government on Thursday next will increase the likelihood of a world war. This is also false and also ungrateful. Mr Attlee's Government in their six years of power, have taken many grave steps for national and international defence. They have introduced conscription in time of peace. They have taken part in a whole system of alliances to resist a possible aggression by Soviet Russia. They now call upon us to spend nearly £5,000 million in three years, on rearmament upon a vast scale. In all this the Conservative Party have given them their effective support. We now know what were the adverse forces at work inside the Socialist Party. They came into the light of day when Mr Bevan and his colleagues resigned and received such prominence by the election of Mr Bevan and his supporters to the head of the Socialist Executive at the Scarborough Conference. Is it not ungrateful as well as untruthful to turn on those upon whose aid the Government have depended, and accuse them of wishing to bring about another war?

But there is one particular instance to which I must draw your attention. Mr Attlee's Government agreed to the establishment of an enormous American air base in our Eastern Counties, which could have no other purpose than to bring home the threat of atomic war as a deterrent to Russian aggression. Again we supported them. I must, however, say that no more formidable step has been taken in time of peace by any Government that I can remember, nor one that would be more certain to put us in the front line should war come. Is it not disgraceful that they should accuse us of being war-minded because we have supported them in this as in other measures of defence on patriotic grounds? We can easily see what they would have done had the positions been reversed and we had been responsible for proposing such measures. We have only to look at Mr Attlee's and Mr Morrison's conduct before the last war in resisting every measure of rearmament and even in voting against conscription a few months before the outbreak. And then they spoke of Mr Chamberlain's Government as 'Guilty men!' We ought to be proud that our party record bears no such stain. But the fact that because we have acted fairly by them in these great matters of national safety and that they should now seek to make shameful capital out of our support reaches a lower level than anything so far recorded in the public life of modern times.

There is one subject with which I must deal though it is not in any way an issue at this Election. Several Socialist speakers have suggested that if I had been returned at the 1945 Election we should have been involved in war with the peoples of India. This is quite untrue. I and my Conservative colleagues were all pledged to the granting to India of Dominion status carrying with it the right to secede from the British Empire and Commonwealth. The only question open was how this transference of power was to be made. Mr Attlee so conducted the process that five hundred thousand innocent human beings were slaughtered in the Punjab alone and at least two or three hundred thousand more in other parts of the vast Indian peninsula. That is to say, three or four times as many lives were destroyed by violent and avoidable butchery in India as were lost by the whole British Empire in the Second World War. I am astonished that this should be treated as a mere incident in the progress of Oriental liberation and self-government. I am sure that it would have been possible to maintain law and order in India as we did in the face of the armed revolt of the Congress Party at the time of the attempted Japanese invasion without any serious difficulty or bloodshed; and that a Constituent Assembly far more representative of all the real forces of Indian life than the Congress Party could have shaped an Indian constitution and transferred the power to the new rulers of India in an orderly manner. This, of course, is arguable, but statements to the contrary are mere assertions. The vast human tragedy which occurred in the process of handing over is a fact for which I thank God I had no responsibility. I cannot leave this question without saying that what has been done in India is irrevocable. It can no more be reversed than we can bring back from the grave the myriads who have perished. The Conservative Party wishes the new India, Pakistan and Ceylon all success in their future. We shall show them all friendship and goodwill. But the burden which rests upon the Socialist Government for the frightful catastrophe of slaughter is one which only history can measure. As I said in the House of Commons some years ago, the Socialist Government's responsibility is not that of a criminal who throws a train off the line by sabotage, but rather that of a signalman who has pulled the levers in the wrong way or in the wrong order and thus caused the disaster.

While we demonstrate and argue among ourselves here at home events are moving all over the world. One must not suppose that resistance to lawless outrages contrary to treaty or other obligations by Powers morally and physically not in the first rank raise the issues of a world war. A Third World War could only come if the Soviet Government calculated or miscalculated their chances of an ultimate victory and fell upon us all in ferocious aggression. That is why I am hopeful about the future. If I were a Soviet Commissar in the Kremlin tonight looking at the scene from their point of view I think I should be inclined to have a friendly talk with the leaders of the free world and see if something could not be arranged which enabled us all to live together quietly for another generation. Who can look beyond that? However, I have not yet been chosen as a Soviet Commissar—nor for any other office that I can think of—there or here. But what I cannot understand is how any of the leaders of Soviet Russia or the United States or here in Britain or France or in United Europe or anywhere else, could possibly imagine that their interests could be bettered by having an unlimited series of frightful immeasurable explosions. For another world war would not be like the Crusades or the romantic struggles in former centuries we have read about. It would be nothing less than a massacre of human beings whether in uniform or out of uniform by the hideous forces of perverted science. Science, which now offers us a Golden Age with one hand, offers at the same time with the other hand the doom of all that we have built up inch by inch since the Stone Age.

My faith is in the high progressive destiny of man. I do not believe we are to be flung back into abysmal darkness by those fearsome discoveries which human genius has made. Let us make sure that they are our servants but not our masters. Let us hold fast to the three supreme purposes. The freedom of the individual man in an ordered society; a world organization to prevent bloody quarrels between nations by the rule of law; and for ourselves who have played so great a part in what I have called 'our finest hour', to keep our own fifty millions alive in a small island at the high level of progressive civilization which they have attained. Those are the three goals. To reach them we have first to regain our independence financially, economically and morally. If we are to play our part in the greater affairs of the free world, we have to gather around us our Empire and the States of the British Commonwealth, and bind them ever more closely together. We have to give our hand generously, wholeheartedly, to our Allies across the Atlantic Ocean, upon whose strength and wisdom the salvation of the world at this moment may well depend. Joined with them in fraternal association, drawn and held together by our common language and our joint inheritance of literature and custom, we may save ourselves and save the world.

We support the Government's belated policy of firmness in Egypt. If we become responsible we should go on with it firmly and resolutely. But if even six months ago they had taken the advice I gave in Parliament, and approached the problems of the Middle East on the three-Power or four-Power basis, as they have now at least done, how differently might all the Persian and Egyptian situations have been unravelled. We are no longer strong enough ourselves alone to protect the rule of law in these important regions. That was the reason why I thought we should much earlier have tried to bring the United States into our Middle Eastern problems. I have used every channel open to me to impress upon our American friends how much more important what is happening in the Middle East is to the cause of world peace even than the stern struggle which is still open on the promontory of Korea. I am sure that if even six months ago Britain, the United States and France, with Turkey by all means, had developed a united policy in regard to Persia, Iraq, Egypt, Palestine and Syria, none of the present unsolved embarrassments would have arisen. Without any question of world war for the free nations no needless loss and humiliation would have been inflicted upon John Bull. We recognize the difficulties and tangles of the Middle Eastern scene. No doubt the murder of the Persian Prime Minister was a disastrous surprise for the British Government, but a wider and more far-seeing view would have brought into action at an earlier stage these larger groupings which now all are working for and through which much better solutions for all, including the Persians and the Egyptians, might have been, and may still be, achieved.

We are now at the final stage in this fateful election. Whatever happens on Thursday, we must all hope that we get a stable, solid Government and get out of this exhausting and distracting electioneering atmosphere, where all the forces of two great party machines have to go on working in every street and in every village week after week, to try to range the British people in opposing ranks. This is indeed a crisis in our island story. Never before in peacetime did we have so much need to judge policy on the merits and act in the true interests of our country, and of its Empire and Commonwealth of Nations. To go on like we have for the last twenty months with a Government struggling to keep its head above water from day to day and thinking of its party chances and of an election at any moment, is to give all that is strong and noble and resurgent in Britain the heaviest load to carry and the hardest battle to win.

It is not my fault, nor indeed is it Mr Attlee's entirely, that we have had this prolonged period of uncertainty. He had a majority of seven at the last Election. The burden fell on him and on his party. It is indeed remarkable that under the conditions we have not fallen more. But we have only to go on indefinitely absorbed in our party quarrels to use up so much of our vitality and to be written down so much in world repute that our influence upon events may well become almost negligible. Terrible decisions that would immediately affect our whole lives may be taken by others at a time when we seem to count little more than many of the smaller states of Europe whom we liberated after the great struggle. We cannot afford to go on like this.

Here now is the main point I make to you, and indeed to all parties. Bear in mind that we ought to have a strong and stable Government resting on a majority that can uphold the responsibilities and burdens of Britain in the world for three or four years at least. The other point which I submit to you for your judgment and your vote is whether it is not time for a change? Ought there not to be an approach to world problems and home problems from a new angle, a new point of view? The Government is wearied and worn out. Its leading Ministers have borne nearly twelve years of stress. They have no message to give. Their principal figures, the late Mr Bevin and Sir Stafford Cripps, are no longer in the scene. Let me say how glad I am to see the recovery of health that Sir Stafford Cripps is making. And in this mood let me tell you how much I look forward to the time when this loud clatter and turmoil of party strife dies down for a spell and gives us a good, long, steady period in which the opposing parties may be able to see some of each other's virtues instead of harping on each other's faults. The British people are good all through. We face the same toils and perils. We share many of the same desires and anxieties. We are in many ways more truly one nation than can be found the wide world o'er. Let us rise to our full height above class and party interests, and guard with growing comradeship and brotherhood the land of hope and glory we all love so well.

# DEBATE ON THE ADDRESS

A SPEECH TO THE HOUSE OF COMMONS
6 NOVEMBER 1951

---

25 *October—General Election in Great Britain; state of parties (including delayed Barnsley election): Conservatives and Associates, 321; Labour, 295; Liberal, 6; Others, 3.*

26 *October—Mr Attlee tenders his resignation as Prime Minister to HM The King; Mr Churchill accepts invitation to form a Government.*

27 *October—The Egyptian Government abrogate the 1936 Treaty and the 1899 Condominium agreements and amend the Constitution, changing HM King Farouk's title to 'King of Egypt and the Sudan'.*
*A new post of Minister for Welsh Affairs established.*

30 *October—Mr Churchill announces cuts in Ministers' salaries.*

31 *October—The Kashmir Constituent Assembly holds its first meeting.*
*For first time since 1895 election of Speaker challenged; Mr W. S. Morrison elected.*

2 *November—Office of Minister of State, Scottish Office established: Earl of Home appointed.*

3 *November—The Festival Gardens and Fun Fair at Battersea Park closed.*

5 *November—HM The King confers the Order of Merit on Mr Clement Attlee.*

6 *November—New Parliament opened by Royal Commission.*
*General Assembly of United Nations meets in Paris.*

---

[*6 November 1951*

Before I enter upon the task of replying to the right hon Member for Walthamstow, West [Mr Attlee], I should like to congratulate him upon the honour he has received from the Crown of the Order of Merit. The news of this was especially gratifying to those who served so many years with him in the hard days of the war.

I join with the right hon Gentleman in the compliments he has paid to the speeches of the mover and seconder of the Address. We all thought they were admirable, and it is no mere repetition of a happy form of words which has led to these praises offered by the right hon Gentleman being accepted with goodwill by the House. Both hon

Gentlemen distinguished themselves, and one overcame the double ordeal of making a maiden speech in conditions of exceptional formality and importance.

The right hon Gentleman will excuse me if I say that he does not seem quite to have got clear of the General Election. A great deal of his speech was made up of very effective points and quips which gave a great deal of satisfaction to those behind him. We all understand his position: 'I am their leader, I must follow them.' A hard task lies before His Majesty's Government and grave responsibilities weigh upon the new Parliament. For two whole years our island has been distracted by party strife and electioneering. I do not see how this could have been avoided. Our Parliamentary institutions express themselves through party government, at any rate in times of peace. The nation is deeply and painfully divided, and the opposing forces are more or less evenly balanced. Naturally, neither side approves of what the other has done or said in the course of the conflict. We think on this side that the 'Warmonger' campaign did us great harm, and is probably answerable for the slender majority upon which His Majesty's Government must rest, with all its many Parliamentary disadvantages and uncertainties. We are, however, now in a position to answer this cruel and ungrateful charge not merely by words but by deeds. It may well be, therefore, that in due course of time it will recoil with compound interest upon the heads of those who profited by it.

We meet together here with an apparent gulf between us as great as I have known in fifty years of House of Commons life. What the nation needs is several years of quiet, steady administration, if only to allow Socialist legislation to reach its full fruition. What the House needs is a period of tolerant and constructive debating on the merits of the questions before us without nearly every speech on either side being distorted by the passions of one Election or the preparations for another. Whether we shall get this or not is, to say the least, doubtful. We ask no favours in the conduct of Parliamentary business. We believe ourselves capable of coping with whatever may confront us. Still, it would not be good for our country if, for instance, events so shaped themselves that a third General Election came upon us in, say, a year or eighteen months. Still worse for our country if that conflict, in its turn, led only to a continuance of an evenly matched struggle in the House and out of doors.

We must all be conscious of the realities of our position. Fifty million people are now crowded in our small island which produces food for only three-fifths of them, and has to earn the rest from over the seas by exporting manufactures for which we must also first import the raw material. No community of such a size, and standing at so high a level of civilization, has ever been economically so precariously poised. An ever larger and more formidable world is growing up around us. Very soon severe competition from Germany and Japan must be expected in our export markets. The problem of earning our independent livelihood stares us in the face. All our united strength will be needed to maintain our standards at home and our rank among the nations. If in these circumstances the electioneering atmosphere is to continue indefinitely, with the nation split in half in class and ideological strife, it will present a spectacle which the world will watch with wonder, and I believe, on the whole, with dismay.

My hope is that the instinct of self-preservation may grow steadily during this Parliament. Controversy there must be on some of the issues before us, but this will be but a small part of the work and interests we have in common. Although, while present conditions last, we all live in the shadow of another General Election, the Government will not fear to do unpopular things where these are found, in our opinion, to be indispensible to the general welfare. I trust, however, that British good sense may avoid an era of annual elections, narrow majorities, and fierce, bitter, exciting class and party war.

Do not let us forget, in reviewing our position as a community, that during the last six years immense financial help has been loaned or given to us by the United States and our Dominions. [*Interruption.*] Why should I say, 'Do not let us forget it?' It would be very foolish to forget it, for but for this help the true facts of our situation would have been brought brutally home to all classes and parties—and may be coming home now.

We have thought it right to make certain reductions in Ministerial salaries. They are not intended as a reproach upon the party opposite, but only as a signal which may be helpful for all. Realizing the gravity of the period upon which we have entered, I consider that this period of rearmament, when all the priorities of labour and materials are necessarily distorted and diverted from the normal peacetime flow, is one in which exceptional measures must be taken. The reductions are intended to mark the emergency character of the period upon which we have entered—into which we have been led by the leader of hon Gentlemen opposite. They are limited to the period of rearmament or three years, whichever ends the first.

Mr Percy Shurmer (Birmingham, Sparkbrook): How much did the right hon Gentleman sacrifice?

The Prime Minister: I am discussing it seriously. Hon Members will not gain anything by interrupting me, because I have had so much experience both of being interrupted and of interrupting. They are limited to this period of three years or to the rearmament period, and, therefore, will not affect conditions in future Parliaments or under a different Government. They are not intended as a reproach, but only as a signal for an abnormal period.

The Gracious Speech contains only one obviously controversial measure, the annulment—that is I understand, a term of art, but it may well be expressed by the more familiar word 'repeal'—the annulment of the nationalization of the iron and steel industry. The restoration of the university representation was one definite issue at both of the General Elections. On a strict interpretation of our mandate we should be entitled to make a change in university representation operative immediately, for that was the intention most clearly expressed; but, on reaching the moment of decision, I and my colleagues felt that for the Government to add to their majority in a Parliament already elected would create a questionable precedent. We should look a little like the London County Council—not that I should think of comparing University Members with so docile and trustworthy a band as those have proved to be. We therefore decided that it was better that any alteration of the franchise should follow the normal course of franchise measures and be operative only at the Dissolution.

I do not intend to repeat today the familiar arguments about the university seats. We have always felt that their abolition was harmful to the House. [*Interruption.*] It is possible to differ from a speaker without making verbal protests; we should have to make a great many if we followed that process out continuously. We have always felt that their abolition was harmful to the House. The House has benefited greatly by the contribution which the universities made. Moreover, we thought it unfair that a Government, exulting in its enormous majority of 1945, should depart from the agreement reached by all parties at the Speaker's Conference of 1943, in which matters were balanced fairly to agreement on both sides.

MR HERBERT MORRISON (Lewisham, South) *indicated dissent.*

THE PRIME MINISTER: The right hon Gentleman is shaking his head, but he will have to shake it a great deal to shake off his personal responsibility in this matter. This agreement was reached by all parties at the Speaker's Conference of 1943 under the Coalition Government. We have in no way departed from our intention to restore the university franchise, but the measure is no longer urgent and it will not become operative until the end of the Parliament.

Now, the repeal of the steel nationalization Act was a much larger and equally definite issue between parties at both Elections. In the first, the late Government commanded a majority of six in the House but were in a considerable minority in the country. In the second, we have a substantial majority for repeal in the country and, we believe, an effective majority in the House. I do not attempt today to argue again the rights and wrongs of the nationalization of steel. There will certainly be plenty of time for that. I did not think it was a wise measure or one conceived in the national interest. When in September 1950 the Leader of the Opposition, as Prime Minister, announced his immense rearmament programme and raised the period of National Service to two years in the Armed Forces, and when we gave him our support in those momentous decisions, I was very sorry indeed that he should have chosen that moment to retort upon us with his nakedly partisan measure. Had he not done so the great common task to which both parties had bound themselves might have led to wider understandings which, without any formal coalition or division of offices, would have prolonged the life of the late Parliament and restored a new sense of unity to our country amid all its difficulties. As the future years roll by, and as history is written—and I do not propose myself to write this part of it—it will be possible to judge whether things would have worked out better or worse for us all if some unity had been achieved at that moment. The denationalization of steel cannot be taken before Christmas. It will occupy us very fully, no doubt, next year.

We desire to bring this Session to an end as soon as the necessary business has been disposed of, and after providing full and customary opportunities for the discussion of the general situation. We hope that the House will adjourn early in December and will meet again in February, subject of course to the usual arrangements for recall in case of emergency. This period will give Ministers the opportunity which we need of acquainting ourselves with every detail of the administration, and of shaping with knowledge and study the many necessary measures which must be taken to secure our livelihood as a community and our safety as a nation. When we reassemble after Christmas we shall be able to speak—[*Interruption.*] I really think I might be treated with ordinary courtesy. This is quite unusual. I have not tried to go beyond the ordinary limits which are observed on these occasions. Hon Members, many of whom sat in the last Parliament, know quite well that nothing very much is gained by interrupting a speaker; it only prolongs the proceedings. When we reassemble after Christmas we shall be able to speak with much greater precision than is possible for men who have been six years away from official information, and for others, quite a number of whom have never held office before. We shall be able to make plans for dealing with our many cares and problems, which we have not been able to do in the ten busy days since we took office.

The King's Speech is no way limits the legislation which may be brought before Parliament if the public interest so requires. I am sure that it would not be wise for us to commit ourselves to complicated constructive proposals until we have had full and reasonable opportunity for studying the whole situation—[*Interruption.*] Well, in justice to hon Gentlemen opposite whose work can now be seen—until we have had full and reasonable opportunity for studying the whole situation, and for using the machinery of the Departments to aid us in framing and shaping policy. Time is required for thought and decision, and we shall not hesitate to submit to Parliament additional Measures not mentioned in the Gracious Speech if we consider at any time that this is necessary.

I might mention, however, that before we rise I shall require to have a day's debate on the defence position, on which I wish to give the House the fullest information possible. For this purpose I shall ask for a Secret Session. That is not because I shall tell the House State secrets which are not known to the General Staffs of Europe and America, but because I think that Members of Parliament should be equally well informed, and that it is better that we should talk these matters over among ourselves in the first instance without what we say becoming a matter of headlines and discussion all over the world.

The Debate on the Address will occupy the remainder of the present week, and will, it is hoped, be brought to a conclusion in the early part of next week. Under your guidance, Mr Speaker, we shall endeavour to arrange the debates, whether on Amendments or otherwise, to the general contentment of the House. The House is aware that my right hon Friend the Foreign Secretary is attending the opening in Paris of the General Assembly of the United Nations, but special arrangements will be made for a Foreign Affairs Debate on his return. That is additional to the days taken in the course of discussing the reply to the Gracious Speech. It will be necessary for the Government to take the full time of the House till the Adjournment for Christmas, and I now give notice that my right hon Friend the Leader of the House will make the necessary Motion tomorrow. When we meet again in the New Year, the Friday sittings will be devoted to Private Members' Bills and Motions, and there will then be no restriction upon the Bills under the Ten Minutes' Rule procedure.

Before I come to the most anxious and serious part of what I have to say this afternoon, I will deal with one or two criticisms that have been made about the formation of the Government. There are those which the Leader of the Opposition made when he asked me to define the exact relationship between supervising Ministers and the Ministers responsible to this House. He is very well familiar with it, because it was a process which continually operated during all the years of the Great War and was found very beneficial in many ways. But the rights and responsibilities of the Members of Parliament are in no way affected by the fact that these problems are studied in the larger bracket from a position of some detachment from the Departments which are grouped together. I believe very much in the policy of grouping Departments where it is possible, and that really is the designing principle upon which the Government was constructed.

The right hon Gentleman asked me whether I was not burdening myself too much by taking the Ministry of Defence as well as the office of Prime Minister. I am well aware of the burden of both these offices, but I did feel that I must, at any rate at the outset, master the situation in the sphere of defence and leave the future to be decided later on. That is what I propose to do. I do not feel that I shall have difficulty in discharging these two functions, at any rate until I am fully possessed of the actual situation in which we stand at the present time.

Then there is the question of whether the Minister of Education ought not to have a seat in the Cabinet. There is great importance in keeping the Cabinet small. It is now sixteen. There is not much difference between that and the eighteen which the right hon Gentleman had, but the fact that some Ministers holding important offices are not in the Cabinet does not deny them access. Any head of a great Department has only to ask the Prime Minister for him to be given every opportunity of presenting the case of the Department. Quite apart from this, the Minister of Education would always be summoned when anything directly or indirectly affecting education and its many concomitants were under discussion. I cannot think that that will form any great difficulty.

Then the right hon Gentleman turned to speaking about the other place. I gather he suggested that there were too many noble Lords in the Government. The right hon Gentleman not only employed noble Lords but even created them in considerable numbers. The position now is that there are eighteen Tory Lords as against sixteen Socialist Lords in the Government. If all our differences could be reduced to such modest proportions, how much better our fortunes would be.

There was also a complaint, so far confined to the newspapers, that the new representation we have given to the Principality of Wales should have been entrusted to a Scotsman. The reason why I placed it under the Home Secretary was because that is the Senior Secretaryship of State. I wonder whether it is a wise attitude for Welshmen to take, that their affairs can only be dealt with in the United Kingdom Parliament by one of their own race and nation. It seems to me that this principle might even be carried too far. Looking back upon the past—a long past—and even perhaps forward into the future, I should have thought that Welshmen might well expect a very much larger share in our affairs than a strict numerical computation of the population would warrant. Nevertheless, when one is trying to give pleasure it is always well to do it in the best possible way. We have therefore appointed an Under-Secretary under the Home Office who is a Welshman, and whose name is, I believe, quite well known throughout the Principality.

MR GEORGE THOMAS (Cardiff, West): Pronounce his name.

THE PRIME MINISTER: I will—Llewellyn. 'Mor o gan yw Cymru i gyd.' [All Wales is a sea of song.]

This additional Under-Secretaryship to the Home Office will require legislation, and we shall present a Bill to enable my hon Friend the Member for Cardiff, North [Mr Llewellyn] to take up his duties formally, and for the Home Secretary to be assisted by another Under-Secretary. The case will be so presented that the issue will be for or against the new Secretary specially charged with Welsh affairs. That, I think, is more likely to bring us all together than any other presentation of the case.

Now I come to the greatest matter that I have to bring before the House today—the financial and economic situation. The right hon Gentleman spoke in a jocular manner about making bricks without straw, but I quote that only to emphasize by contrast the seriousness of the position. We were confronted on taking over with a Treasury report setting forth the position as it stood at that date, ten days ago. I sent a copy of this to the Leader of the Opposition in order that he might know our starting point. It was certainly scratch. In overseas payments we are in a deficit crisis worse than 1949, and in many ways worse than even 1947. Confidence in sterling is impaired. In the present half-year, we are running into an external deficit at the rate of £700 million a year compared with an annual rate of surplus of about £350 million in the same period a year ago. That means a deterioration of more than £1,000 million a year.

The latest estimates show that in 1952, on present trends and policies and without making any allowance for further speculative losses, the United Kingdom would have a deficit on its general balance of overseas payments of between £500 million and £600 million, and the loss to the central gold and dollar reserves in the transactions of the sterling areas as a whole with the rest of the world might be appreciably more. These figures mean, in short, that we are buying much more than we can afford to pay for from current earnings, and this can only in time lead to national bankruptcy. The position has been made worse by the loss of confidence in sterling and by the additional strain of the loss of Persian oil supplies, to which the Leader of the Opposition has made reference in some of his speeches. Such was the statement presented to us within a few hours of our taking office, and it has taken first place in our minds and discussions since. We are convinced that it is necessary to present the facts plainly to the nation in order that they may realize where we stand. We do not believe that a full and frank statement of our position will aggravate the loss of confidence abroad which has been taking place. On the contrary, many of the facts are known in foreign and financial circles and are, in some cases, exaggerated by foreign speculation. We feel that a solemn resolve by Parliament and the British people to set their house in order without delay, and the measures necessary to give effect to that resolve, would act as a tonic to our credit all the world over. A full statement of the financial position and the remedial measures which, in the time we have had to consider these matters we consider imperative, will be made by my right hon Friend the Chancellor of the Exchequer at the opening of tomorrow's debate. I will not now elaborate the matter further.

We also find a bad position about coal supplies. Stocks of house coal are only half of what they were last year, and they are lower than they have ever been since the war. It is a tragedy that this great coal-producing country should have to import coal, and a comedy that at the same time we should be exporting coal with our limited shipping. I know that there are explanations for all this, but the resulting fact remains, and we cannot let our people suffer cold or our industries and rearmament be hampered if there is anything that we can do at this stage to prevent it. The failure to build up house coal stocks was evident during the summer, and it seems a pity that coal was not imported at that time to restore the position when import, although no doubt not easy, would have been less difficult than it is now across the winter Atlantic. In spite of this difficulty, the Government will do all they can to get more coal from abroad. It will not be possible in the time available to bring in enough for us to guarantee that there will not be hardship before the winter ends.

We have had to reduce the meat ration to 1s. 5d. worth a week. Our predecessors had already given notice that this would be necessary. [*Interruption.*] I am only reciting facts. It is a great pity to get into a state of mind in which we fear facts. They hoped that it would not fall lower during the winter and spring. My right hon Friend the Minister of Food, in consultation with Lord Woolton, felt it essential to reduce the ration to 1s. 5d. without delay. The meat supply is really worse than it was in wartime. In the period from April 1942 to 1945, the weekly ration averaged about 1s. 2d. That would be equal to about 1s. 9½d. to 1s. 10d. at our present prices. On the reverse calculation, the ration of 1s. 5d. of today's weekly ration would equal a ration of about 11d. at wartime prices.

The prospect of supplies in the first half of next year is far from ample, but we trust it will grow. The imports from the Southern Dominions and from foreign sources such as the Argentine, even if all are made good, could not relieve the anxiety. There can be no assurance that the 1s. 5d. level can be held. We hope to do so, but I cannot disguise from the House that there are many uncertainties. A serious shortage of meat cannot be overcome quickly. To regain a pre-war consumption we should need 600,000 tons more meat a year than we are getting. I cannot hold out any hope of that in the near future. We shall do our best, and my right hon Friend the Minister of Food will, I hope, deal with this matter later in the debate. So will the Lord President of the Council in another place.

I do not propose to deal at any length this afternoon with the foreign situation. When the Foreign Secretary has returned from the conferences in Paris he will make his report to the House in a special debate. We cannot accept the ill-treatment we have received about Persian oil supplies. His Majesty's Government are always ready to negotiate a settlement on the basis of a fair partnership for the actual benefit of those who live in the country which provides the oil, and for those who have created the wonderful industry and have the technical experience to extract the oil and to market it. We have so far suffered a great injustice and disaster, and we shall strive patiently and resolutely to repair the position as far as that is now possible.

In Egypt and the Sudan we are pursuing the policy adopted by the late Government and by the right hon Gentleman the Member for Lewisham, South [Mr Herbert Morrison], who was Foreign Secretary. We are resolved to maintain our rightful position in the Canal Zone in spite of the illegal and one-sided Egyptian action over the 1936 Treaty. We shall do our utmost to safeguard the Canal as an international highway, using, of course, no more force than is necessary. Here again I think that time, within certain limits, and restraint and forbearance—not so strictly limited—may give the best chance of the crisis being successfully surmounted.

But our great hope in foreign affairs is, of course, to bring about an abatement of what is called 'the cold war' by negotiation at the highest level from strength and not from weakness. Perhaps I may read again to the House, as I have already read to them, what I wrote to Mr Stalin and his colleagues in April 1945:

'There is not much comfort in looking into a future where you and the countries you dominate, plus the Communist parties in many other States are all drawn up on one side, and those who rally to the English-speaking nations and their associates, or Dominions are on the other. It is quite obvious that their quarrel would tear the world to pieces and that all of us leading men on either side who had anything to do with that would be shamed before history. Even embarking on a long period of suspicions, of abuse and counter-abuse and of opposing policies would be a disaster, hampering the great developments of world prosperity for the masses which are attainable only by our trinity.'

That was written more than six years ago, and, alas, all came to pass with horrible exactitude. I must explain that in speaking of our trinity I was, of course, referring to a period when France had not fully resumed her rightful place in the international sphere.

At Edinburgh, in February 1950, I appealed for a conference between the heads of States or Governments, and I and my right hon Friend the Foreign Secretary, who have acted in the closest, spontaneous accord in all these matters, still hold to the idea of a supreme effort to bridge the gulf between the two worlds, so that each can live its life, if not in friendship at least without the fear, the hatreds and the frightful waste of the 'cold war'. I must, however, today utter a word of caution. The realities which confront us are numerous, adverse and stubborn. We must be careful not to swing on a wave of emotion from despondency to over-confidence; but even if the differences between West and East are, for the time being, intractable, the creation of a new atmosphere and climate of thought, and of a revived relationship and sense of human comradeship, would, I believe, be an enormous gain to all the nations.

Never must we admit that a Third World War is inevitable. I heard some months ago of a foreign diplomatist who was asked: 'In which year do you think the danger of war will be the greatest?' He replied: 'Last year.' If that should prove true, as we pray it may, no one will deny their salute to the memory of Ernest Bevin, or their compliments to those who worked faithfully with him. Let us, in these supreme issues with party politics far beneath them, move forward together in our united fight as faithful servants of our common country, and as unwearying guardians of the peace and freedom of the world.

# LORD MAYOR'S BANQUET

A SPEECH AT GUILDHALL, LONDON
9 NOVEMBER 1951

---

*7 November—Reductions in imports announced by Chancellor of the Exchequer, Mr Butler; Bank Rate raised to 2½ per cent; Excess Profits Tax to become effective from 1 January 1952.*

*The United States, France and Britain submit disarmament proposals to Assembly of UN in Paris.*

*Sir Leslie Boyce installed as Lord Mayor of London.*

*9 November—United States casualties in Korea announced as 99,226, of which 15,002 were killed.*

---

[*9 November* 1951

Though I have very often in the last forty years or so been present at your famous Guildhall banquets to salute the new Lord Mayor, this is the first occasion when I have addressed this assembly here as Prime Minister. The explanation is convincing. When I should have come here as Prime Minister the Guildhall was blown up and before it was repaired I was blown out! I thought at the time they were both disasters. But now we are all here together in a union which I hope will bring good luck. I am sure we all wish the Lord Mayor a successful year of his arduous office. I share his regrets that we have no Member for the City of London in the House of Commons. It is an error to believe that the world began when any particular party or statesman got into office. It has all been going on quite a long time, and many movements and parties will rise and decline, and I trust many politicians will catch the fleeting glint of popular acclaim before the continuity of our island life is cut asunder or fades away. It is only by studying the past that we can foresee, however dimly, the future. I cannot help feeling the impact of these thoughts in this war-scarred Hall. Its battered monuments remind us of other struggles against the Continental tyrants of the past, in generations before the supreme ordeal of 1940 which we all endured and won together.

I am so glad my Lord Mayor that you have decided to replace the effigies of Gog and Magog. It was to me a painful blow when they were burnt to ashes by Hitler's bombs. They will look fine in the gallery up there. Indeed I think they are not only ancient but up-to-

187

date. It seems to me that they represent none too badly the present state of world politics. World politics, like the history of Gog and Magog, are very confused and much disputed. Still I think there is room for both of them. On the one side is Gog and on the other Magog. But be careful my Lord Mayor, when you put them back, to keep them from colliding with each other, for if that happens both Gog and Magog would be smashed to pieces and we should all have to begin all over again—and begin from the bottom of the pit.

Whatever are the differences between God and Magog, at any rate they are made out of the same materials. Let me tell you what the materials are: vast masses of warm-hearted, hard-working human beings wanting to do their best for their country and their neighbours, and longing to build their homes and bring up their children in peace, freedom and the hope of better times for the young when they grow up. That is all they ask of their rulers and governors and guides. That is the dear wish in the hearts of all the peoples of mankind. How easy it ought to be with modern science standing tiptoe ready to open the doors of a Golden Age, to grant them this humble modest desire. But then there come along all these tribes of nationalists, ideologues, revolutionaries, class warfare experts, and imperialists with their nasty regimentation of academic doctrinaires, striving night and day to work them all up against one another so that the homes instead of being built are bombed and the breadwinner is killed and the broken housewife left to pick the surviving children out of the ashes. There is the structure: that is the composition which Gog and Magog have in common and there is the fate which both will suffer if you, my Lord Mayor, and others concerned in our City affairs or those who deal with world affairs do not act with ordinary common sense and keep Gog and Magog from falling upon one another.

Somehow or other these ideas about Gog and Magog seem to have some suggestive relationship to the discussions which are taking place in Paris at the present time. But we must not let our thoughts be complicated by our imagery. So here I leave Gog and Magog, hoping I may have the chance to see them both in their proper places one of these days.

What is the world scene as presented to us today? Mighty forces armed with fearful weapons are baying at each other across a gulf which I have the feeling tonight neither wishes, and both fear to cross, but into which they may tumble or drag each other to their common ruin. On the one side stand all the armies and air forces of Soviet Russia and all their Communist satellites, agents and devotees in so many countries. On the other are what are called 'the Western

Democracies' with their far superior resources, at present only partly organized, gathering themselves together around the United States with its mastery of the atomic bomb. Now there is no doubt on which side we stand. Britain and the Commonwealth and Empire still centring upon our island, are woven by ever-growing ties of strength and comprehension of common need and self-preservation to the great Republic across the Atlantic Ocean.

The sacrifices and exertions which the United States are making to deter, and if possible prevent, Communist aggression from making further inroads upon the free world are the main foundation of peace. A tithe of the efforts now being made by America would have prevented the Second World War and would have probably led to the downfall of Hitler with scarcely any blood being shed except perhaps his own. I feel a deep gratitude towards our great American Ally. They have risen to the leadership of the world without any other ambition but to serve its highest causes faithfully. I am anxious that Britain should also play her full part, and I hope to see a revival of her former influence and initiative among the Allied Powers, and indeed with all Powers.

It must not be forgotten that under the late Government we took peculiar risks in providing the principal atomic base for the United States in East Anglia, and that in consequence we placed ourselves in the very forefront of Soviet antagonism. We have therefore every need and every right to seek and to receive the fullest consideration from Americans for our point of view, and I feel sure this will not be denied us.

In order to regain our position we must do our utmost to re-establish as quickly as possible our economic and financial solvency and independence. We were shocked and surprised by the situation with which we were confronted after accepting responsibility a fortnight ago. This resulted partly from world causes, but also partly from the prolonged electioneering atmosphere in which we have dwelt for nearly two years, and especially for the past two months. We have certainly been left a tangled web of commitments and shortages, the like of which I have never seen before, and I hope and pray we may be granted the wisdom and the strength to cope with them effectively. If these conditions of furious political warfare between the two halves of our party-divided Britain are to continue indefinitely, and we are all to live under the shadow of a third General Election, it will not be at all good for the main life interests of the British nation, or for her influence in world affairs. Nevertheless, whatever way things may go, we shall not fail to do our duty however unpopular that may be. It is not cheers that we seek to win or votes we are playing to catch, but respect and confidence. This cannot come from words alone, but only from action which proves itself by results. Results cannot be achieved by the wave of a wand. Time is needed for a new Administration to grasp and measure the facts which surround us in baffling and menacing array. More time is needed for the remedies we propose and will propose to produce their curative effects. Nothing would be easier than for this country, politically rent asunder as it is, to shake and chatter itself into bankruptcy and ruin. But under grave pressures in the past we have proved ourselves to be a wise and unconquerable people, and I am sure that we shall succeed. No doubt His Majesty's Government will make mistakes. We shall not hesitate to admit them. I made many in the war. It is, however, always a comfort in times of crisis to feel that you are treading the path of duty according to the lights that are granted you. Then one need not fear whatever may happen. It was in this spirit that we all came through our worst perils eleven years ago; and I have a good and buoyant hope that the great mass of the nation will give us its ungruding aid in all matters of truly national import. If this happens they may feel in two or three years' time that they have not been led on wrong courses and that Britain stands erect again, calm, resolute and independent, the faithful servant of peace, the valiant champion of freedom, and an honoured member of a united world instrument for preserving both.

# RETIREMENT OF MR SPEAKER CLIFTON BROWN

A SPEECH TO THE HOUSE OF COMMONS
15 NOVEMBER 1951

*11 November—General Peron re-elected President of Argentina.*

[*15 November* 1951

I beg to move:

'That the thanks of this House be given to Colonel the Right Honourable Douglas Clifton Brown for his distinguished services as Speaker for more than eight years; that he be assured that this House fully appreciates the zeal, ability and impartiality with which he has discharged the duties of his high office through a period of unusual labour, difficulty and anxiety, and the judgment and firmness with which he has maintained its privileges and dignity; and that his unremitting attention to the constantly increasing business of Parliament, and his uniform urbanity and kindness have earned for him the respect and esteem of this House.'

The late Speaker, Colonel Clifton Brown, succeeded Captain Fitzroy, who died at his post during the war. It was a hard test to succeed Captain Fitzroy who was, I think, much beloved and well regarded in every part of the House, but Colonel Clifton Brown did not prove unequal to this test. In the tumult and convulsion of the war, he sat in the Chair through the self-propelled missile and rocket bombardments which cost us 30,000 casualties in London. We can still look at the ruins of the Guards Chapel in which more than 100 people, including many notable officers, were killed in a flick when at a memorial service.

I remember that when we had to move again and met in the Church House, a Member asked me at Question Time why we had quitted our Chamber which was then in the House of Lords, and how somebody said: 'If the hon Member will walk 500 yards down Birdcage Walk he will see the reason.' This was one of those remarks that, so to speak, disposed of the issue for the moment in the House. It was also one of those many incidents with which Colonel Clifton Brown, as Speaker, was familiarized during the first part of his service in the Chair.

But the late Speaker had a more memorable and certainly a more agreeable experience than these wartime days. He conducted the move back into what is called the new House of Commons by very young people, but what I and some of the elders may fairly call the old House of Commons. The late Speaker went through all the birth-pangs of this building to which we are adapting ourselves by many trials and tests, but for which upon the whole there is a growing feeling of comfort and comprehension. This come-back was a great event in the Speakership of Colonel Clifton Brown. I am sure it was a joy to him to lead us all home again.

Let me speak of another sphere in which the late Speaker was distinguished. It was the strong, vibrant initiative and perseverance which he showed in strengthening the contacts and sense of brotherhood between the Parliaments of the Commonwealth in all parts of the globe. I remember the very remarkable gathering which he organized of all the Speakers of all the Parliaments of the British Commonwealth of Nations and Empire. Fifteen Speakers and thirteen other representatives of Commonwealth legislatures were assembled. That was a memorable gathering, because the Speaker represents and embodies the spirit of the House of Commons, and that spirit, which has transported itself to so many lands and climates and to countries far outside our sphere, is one of the gleaming and enduring glories of the British, and in a special way, if I may say so, of the English message to the world.

Besides all this, Colonel Clifton Brown had to look after the last Parliament for the twenty months of its existence. I do not wish to raise any form of controversy and it is far from my intention to disparage the late House of Commons. I will therefore content myself with saying that I did not feel it was the best, the happiest or the most useful of the dozen Parliaments in which I have been called upon to dwell for a while. But Mr Speaker had to do his best, which I think he did, to keep it up to the level and to hold the balance fairly between both parties. To have presided over a Parliament with a majority of six for the Government, sandwiched between two elections at the beginning and end of twenty months, and to hold his position of authority, dignity and responsibility was indeed an achievement of which any Speaker might be proud. In these hard party fights under democratic conditions, as in football matches and the like, there are moments when the umpire gets a very rough time. If you, Mr Speaker, in your tenure succeed to a more sedate period of office in which the quality of debate rises higher whilst passions cool, you will be more fortunate than your predecessor. But this will only enhance in the minds of Members of all parties the services rendered in very rough and tangled times by Colonel Clifton Brown.

# WELCOMING TRH PRINCESS ELIZABETH AND THE DUKE OF EDINBURGH HOME FROM CANADA

## A SPEECH AT GUILDHALL, LONDON
## 19 NOVEMBER 1951

---

*17 November—TRH Princess Elizabeth and the Duke of Edinburgh return to England after their visit to Canada and the United States.*
*Dr Chaim Weizmann re-elected President of Israel.*

---

[*19 November* 1951

I am proud to have the honour of proposing Your Royal Highness's health in the Guildhall on your return from your memorable visit to Canada and the United States. If all the tasks which fall to a Prime Minister were as agreeable and inspiring as this the competition for the office would be even less restrained than it is.

Madam, you and your husband left us in the days of deep anxiety for the safety of His Majesty the King, and everyone understood and realized your emotion on leaving your father's side at so critical a moment. But it was his wish that you should fulfil your mission to the great Dominion which rejoices in its partnership in the British Commonwealth and Empire and whose people were so eagerly looking forward to welcoming you both. There are no limits to the majestic future which lies before the mighty expanse of Canada with its virile, aspiring, cultured and generous-hearted people. Canada is the vital link in the English-speaking world and joins across the Atlantic Ocean the vast American democracy of the United States with our famous old island and the fifty millions who keep the flag flying here.

The symbol of the Crown and the preservation through the centuries of the British monarchy have rendered possible a sense of unity to which time and space have become the servants and not the masters. But all this evolution would not survive the changes of the modern world if it were not sustained and refreshed by the wonderful personal contributions made in recent generations by the occupants and heirs to the Throne. None have surpassed in brilliance and living force the mission which you and your husband have just discharged, and on the return from which we are gathered to salute you.

While you have been away we have been comforted by the steady improvement in His Majesty the King's health and his recovery of strength. But as we looked out on the stormy world and the tales of misfortune and misunderstanding in so many countries which fill our newspapers, it was a joy to the whole British nation to follow the progress of your journeyings through Canada and your visit to the United States. We all felt, with an instinct far above class and party disputations, the bright gleam which shone from a confused and sombre background, as the news of your devoted and tireless efforts came to us day by day; and the enthusiasm which your presence everywhere aroused made us feel the strength of our association and the splendour of our destiny. Madam, the whole nation is grateful to you for what you have done for us and to Providence for having endowed you with the gifts and personality which are not only precious to the British Commonwealth and Empire and its island home, but will play their part in cheering and in mellowing the forward march of human society all the world over.

# DEFENCE

A SPEECH TO THE HOUSE OF COMMONS
6 DECEMBER 1951

---

22 *November—The three Western Foreign Ministers and Dr Adenauer,*
*in Paris, approve draft general agreement on future status of Germany.*

24 *November—A ten-day airlift of 2,400 troops from Britain to Cyprus*
*begins.*

 3 *December—Dr Adenauer, the Chancellor of German Federal Republic,*
*arrives in London at invitation of Prime Minister and Foreign Secretary.*

---

[6 *December* 1951

Frankly, Mr Deputy-Speaker, looking around the galleries I am sorry
that I cannot spy any strangers today, for I think it would have been
more useful if we could have had a private talk about our common
affairs. But I must also recognize that there is no lack of topics on which
public statements can and should be made, and I will address myself
to these aspects. Let me, first of all, make my acknowledgments to the
late Government for several most important decisions about our defence
policy which they took during their six years of office and which form
the foundation on which we stand today. There was the establishment
of national compulsory service, now raised to two years, as a feature in
our island life, and this was a measure without which our national
safety could not probably have been preserved. The Atlantic Pact and
the creation of what, for short, we call NATO was a very great event
in which the Leader of the Opposition and the late Mr Bevin played a
distinguished part. The tremendous rearmament programme upon
which they and the former Minister of Defence led us has enabled us to
stand beyond question second only to the United States in our share
of the measures upon which our hopes of a lasting peace are based.

The Conservative Party, when in opposition, gave full and constructive support to the Government of the day in all these dominant
acts of national policy, and we hope we shall be able to compliment
our opponents, or most of them, in their turn on their steadfast perseverance in the courses on which they launched us. These policies do
not arise so much from the danger of war as from the importance of
the free world creating deterrents against aggression; so the theme
which His Majesty's Government will pursue and which I will illus-

195

trate this afternoon is the idea of deterrents rather than the idea of danger.

Looking back over the last few years, I cannot feel that the danger of a third war is so great now as it was at the time of the Berlin Air Lift crisis in 1948, when the Labour Government, acting in harmony with the United States, and with our full support, took great risks in a firm and resolute manner. Of course, no one can predict the future, but our feeling, on assuming responsibility, is that the deterrents have increased and that, as the deterrents have increased, the danger has become more unlikely; and we should be wise, as a House of Commons, to go on treading the same path in the immediate future with constancy, with hope and, I trust, with a broad measure of unity. That is at any rate the desire and intention of His Majesty's Government. In saying all this, I have no wish to minimize the important differences of method and execution which exist between us in the sphere of defence. They will have to be argued out by the usual Parliamentary process, but I should not like to dwell, as I must, on these differences—and they are neither few nor small—without setting things first of all in their broad framework of national agreement.

Sir, we must examine promptly but carefully the question of whether we are getting full value in fighting power for the immense sums of money and numbers of men provided for the three fighting Services. For the current year £420 million have been voted for the Army and over 450,000 men, soldiers, stand in uniform today. I recognize the severe strain that has been put upon the War Office by the crisis in Egypt and the Middle East, by Malaya, and by our share in the war in Korea, with its consequential reactions at Hong Kong. There is also the prime need to carry out our agreements under the North Atlantic Treaty for the reinforcement of our troops in Europe. We found, on taking office, that important increases were contemplated both in money and manpower in the coming year and in those that followed. Before presenting such proposals to the House, we must satisfy ourslves that every possible effort has been used so to organize our forces as to procure a true economy with its twin sister, efficiency. To say such things is to utter platitudes. To do them is to render public service. We must ask for a reasonable time to translate words into actions and in this, as in other matters, we seek to be judged by results.

In military matters, as well as in the economic and financial sphere, we are having a full, detailed statement prepared in every Department of the situation as we found it when we assumed office. In two or three years it will be possible to compare the new position with this record, and this may be of help to the House in forming its opinion of our performances, for good or for ill. There are many things, one knows, in which improvements can be made. There are, for instance, no less than 30,000 British troops awaiting orders to move or moving to and fro by land and sea in what is called the pipe-line of our communications. The cost of this movement alone is about £7 million a year. All this is partly due to our being forced to send National Service men to the Far East and Middle East, where their tour of duty is necessarily very short. It will be greatly to our advantage to have a higher proportion of young men volunteering for even three years in the Regular Army. To this end, a scheme has been introduced by the War Office whereby a man may volunteer for a short Regular engagement of three years in the Regular Army, and thus, by adding only one year to his National Service liability, gain the advantage of the higher Regular rate of pay. First indications make it hopeful that this new offer, which was already far advanced when we took over, may prove popular and fruitful.

The Navy Estimates for the current year amount to £278 million, including £30 million for new construction, modernization and conversion. This is an immense sum. It has also to be noted that nearly 10,000 civilians and 650 naval officers are employed in the Admiralty Departments compared with 4,000 in 1938, when the Navy was larger though, of course, much less complicated than it is at present. I would not pass from the Navy without saying that, as ever, it has played its full part under circumstances most difficult and trying in all the crises of what is called the 'cold war', whether in Korea or Malaya or the Middle East, and has always gained distinction.

The greatest source of concern in the Services is the slow progress made in developing the Royal Air Force, especially in the supply of the latest machines. To read the complaints that are made about the disappointments experienced in re-equipment, one would hardly believe that over £300 million is being spent this year. I must make it plain that what is being produced today is governed by decisions taken months ago, and in many cases, years ago. The whole system of supply and production is suffering from what might be described as acute indigestion. The sum of £4,700 million in three years as a plan represented an increased annual rate of expenditure on the Royal Air Force alone of nearly £100 million in the first year and much more in later years. It is scarcely surprising that at many points, in research as well as production, the aircraft programme is disjointed. We must not forget that the Soviet Air Force is formidable not only in numbers but in quality. The Korean War has proved how good the Russian jet fighter, the MiG15, is. We must strive to bring to our squadrons aircraft not only as good as but better than those to which they may be opposed. All this, as I have said, is a matter for active and earnest attention, and here again we must be judged by results.

Coming now to more controversial topics, I do not feel there ought to be any great differences between us about the European Army. We are, I believe, most of us agreed that there should be a European Army, and that Germany must take an honourable place in it. When I proposed this at Strasbourg eighteen months ago I said—perhaps I may be permitted to quote myself when I find it convenient—

'I am very glad that the Germans amid their own problems have come here to share our perils and augment our strength. They ought to have been here a year ago. A year has been wasted, but still it is not too late. There is no revival of Europe, no safety or freedom for any of us except in standing together united and unflinching. I ask this Assembly to assure our German friends that if they throw in their lot with us we shall hold their safety and freedom as sacred as our own.'

This assurance has now been formally given by the Allied Governments. I went on:

'There must be created, and in the shortest possible time, a real defensive front in Europe. Great Britain and the United States must send large forces to the Continent. France must again revive her famous army. We welcome our Italian comrades. All—Greece, Turkey, Holland, Belgium, Luxembourg, the Scandinavian States— must bear their share and do their best.'

We seem to have made good progress since then. General Eisenhower is in supreme command on the Continent. All the Powers mentioned have contributed, or are contributing, or are about to contribute, contingents, and many of their contingents are growing. The front is not covered yet. The potential aggressor has a vast superiority of numbers. Nevertheless, the gathering of our deterrents have been continued. As things have developed, my own ideas have always been as follows. There is the NATO Army. Inside the NATO Army there is the European Army, and inside the European Army there is the German Army. The European Army should be formed by all the European parties to NATO dedicating from their own national armies their quota of divisions to the army or armies now under General Eisenhower's command. At Strasbourg in 1950 the Germans did not press for a national army. On the contrary, they declared themselves ready to join a European Army without having a national army. Dr Adenauer has renewed to us this assurance, and that is still the German position and their preference—no national army. This is a very great and helpful fact which we must all take into consideration. The size and strength of any German army, whether contingent or otherwise, and its manufacture of weapons, would in any case have to be agreed between the Allied Powers concerned. There, in short, is the policy which I have always advocated and which I am very glad to find is steadily going forward.

Difficulties have, however, arisen about the texture of the European Army. Should it be an amalgam of the European nations divested of all national characteristics and traditions, or should it be composed of elements essentially national but woven together by alliance, common organization and unified command? On this point the discussions have at times assumed an almost metaphysical character, and the logic of Continental minds has produced a scheme for what is called the European Defence Community. That is, at least, an enlightened if not an inspiring title. The European Defence Force, which is to be a vital element in the defence of Western Europe, will be closely and effectively associated with the British Forces which constitute another element in the same defence system through their common allegiance to NATO. The European Defence Community has not yet taken its final shape. The Paris Conference has been sitting for nine months, and it is now on the point of producing its Report. I am sorry the late Government did not send a delegation to this Conference instead of only an observer. The technical discussions have proceeded smoothly and in great detail, and at last the far-reaching political issues which have been raised and which surround the military questions have been reached. We do not know how these will be settled, and we have had no voice or share in the long argument. As soon as the Conference reaches its final conclusions we shall consider the best way to establish the most effective form of association with the resultant organizations. In this way a European Army, containing a German contribution of agreed size and strength, will stand alongside the British and United States Armies in a common defensive front. That, after all, is what really matters to the life or death of the free world.

As far as Britain is concerned, we do not propose to merge in the European Army but we are already joined to it. Our troops are on the spot, and we shall do our utmost to make a worthy and effective contribution to the deterrents against aggression and to the causes of freedom and democracy which we seek to serve. These matters will, of course, require to be further discussed as the weeks pass by, and we shall probably know much more about what is the decision taken on the Continent than we can attempt to anticipate and imagine at this moment.

What I have called the most formidable step taken by the late Government was the establishment in July 1948 of the great and ever-growing American air base in East Anglia for using the atomic weapon against Soviet Russia should the Soviets become aggressors. As in the other great measures of national defence taken by the Labour Government, we supported this policy. I have on several occasions pointed out to the House the gravity of the late Government's decision and have quoted publicly the expression used in Soviet publications that our island had become an aircraft carrier. Certainly we must recognize that the step then taken by the right hon Gentleman the Leader of the Opposition places us in the front line should there be a Third World War. The measure adds to the deterrents against war, but it may throw the brunt on to us should war come. We shall not flinch from the duty which Britain has accepted, but we should never let the facts pass from our minds, as they must govern our actions.

MR SILVERMAN (Nelson and Colne) *rose*——

THE PRIME MINISTER: I was not making any attack on the hon Gentleman.

MR C. R. ATTLEE (Walthamstow, West): I am not quite sure exactly what the right hon Gentleman means. We certainly agreed to the stationing of American bombers in this country as part of Atlantic Defence, but it was never put forward specifically as a base for using the atomic bomb against Russia. We never suggested it.

THE PRIME MINISTER: That is the impression which, however mistakenly, they seem to have derived.

MR ATTLEE: The right hon Gentleman must be very careful about this. We have had conversations. The Americans have no illusions whatever as regards our position in this matter.

THE PRIME MINISTER: I am very well informed about it, and I have not said anything this afternoon that I have not frequently said in public before. I think it is absolutely necessary that the House should realize the serious effects to which the course of events and the policy of the party opposite, to which we have supported and shared, have brought us. It is no use going on blinking at the great underlying realities of the position.

MR SILVERMAN *rose*——

THE PRIME MINISTER: I really would like to be allowed to make my speech. The hon Gentleman is very skilled at interruptions of all kinds——

MR SILVERMAN: I do not intend to do anything like that.

THE PRIME MINISTER: Usually interruptions ought to be limited to questions where a misunderstanding has been created.

MR SILVERMAN: I think this is one.

THE PRIME MINISTER: All right.

MR SILVERMAN: I only want to ask the right hon Gentleman—and I shall quite understand it if he feels unable to answer—whether he could at this point answer the Question which stood on the Order Paper, addressed to him today, namely, whether the effect of this agreement for bombers on our shores would not have the result of removing from our control the question of whether we were to take part or not to take part in any war in which the United States happened to be involved. Does it not make us, therefore, a belligerent unless the agreement contains a provision for their removal at our request?

THE PRIME MINISTER: I thought the hon Gentleman was going to raise a point arising from the course of the debate, but it appears that he only wants to get a Question which he put on the Paper, and which was not reached today, answered by a different method. He will see the reply to the Question when it is circulated in the ordinary course.

This brings me to the strength of the forces we have in this country, as I found them on becoming responsible. Practically all our Regular formations have been sent to the Army in Europe or are engaged in distant theatres. The facts are, of course, already known to foreign countries, and the Communists have particular advantages in gathering information in many countries. I have spoken before of the danger of paratroop descents on a considerable scale, and everything I have learned since assuming office convinces me of the need to accumulate deterrents against this particular form of attack. For this reason we have taken the first steps to re-establish the network of the Home Guard units throughout the country, and we have already permitted the raising of a proportion of the Home Guard in the south-eastern part of England. The Royal Observer Corps is being strengthened, and we have decided to set up and begin the recruiting next year of a Royal Naval mine-watching organization.

Moreover, I have given directions that the numerous Regular military establishments in this country which contain a very large number of men—nearly 250,000—the training schools, depots and other units, should acquire an immediate combatant value. They must be armed and ready to defend themselves, and not only themselves, in an emergency. Arrangements are being made for their use away from their local centres, as far as other reasons and mobility permits. It is a mistake to keep so many thousands of our men in uniform without their playing a direct part in our safety. These measures are not particularly costly. The cost is the men, and here again we are in the field of deterrents. Our country should suggest to the mind of a potential paratrooper the back of a hedgehog rather than the paunch of a rabbit. We shall have next year to repeat the process adopted last year by our predecessors of calling up a proportion of the 'Z' reservists in order to enable a number of Territorial divisions, anti-aircraft and other specialist units to be assembled and exercised. The results were more valuable than I had expected from such a very short period of effective training. At any rate, there was the sense of assembly and incorporation in the regimental units.

Thanks to the National Service measures of the late Government we have a reserve of trained manhood, now beginning to flow from two years' service in the Army, of a quality and character superior to anything we have ever had before in time of peace. This enables us to raise our Territorial divisions on mobilization far more quickly and to a quality far in advance of anything that was previously possible in former periods. The reserve is only just beginning to come to us in strength, and we should indeed be failing in our duty if we did not take the necessary and consequential steps to secure full value in deterrent resources from the cost and sacrifice which two years' compulsory service involves. Growth and efficiency of the Territorial Army and its speedy mobilization in an emergency is essential to repair the inroads upon our strategic resources from which we suffer today. The House will no doubt wish to know more precisely the detailed conditions of the call-up. The Government proposes that the provisions of the Reserve and Auxiliary Forces (Training) Act, 1951, should be applied again in 1952, and the necessary Affirmative Resolution will be introduced immediately after the Recess.

Mr E. SHINWELL (Easington): Can the right hon Gentleman say for how long?

THE PRIME MINISTER: Just a little patience, and the right hon Gentleman's natural interest will be satisfied. In the case of the Army, this training will be on the same lines as it was this year, and it will involve the recall for fifteen days' training of up to 250,000 men, mainly 'Z' reservists. I agree I wish it could be longer than fifteen days. Another three or four working days would add greatly to the value of it, without any marked addition to the cost. But there is the effect that might be produced upon the permanent cadres of the Territorial volunteers, to whom we already owe so much. I did not appreciate that fact fully, but I do now and I have to consider it. I wish indeed that we could have a longer period for considering the cost involved, but I think it would be imprudent at this stage to run the risk of making the voluntary service which the Territorial Army bears so heavy a burden. The majority of the men will be trained in the units which they will attend in the event of an emergency, and the remainder, including up to 3,000 officers and certain specialists, will undergo particular courses of refresher training. The Royal Air Force will be calling up 5,500 men of their equivalent class 'G' reserve. The Royal Navy will continue the call-up of members of the Royal Fleet Reserves for service on a small scale.

Now I come to the other side. I have been dealing with the personnel aspects, and I come now to the other side of the rearmament plans, namely, the manufacture in this country of munitions and military supplies of all kinds. I found on taking over that, under the increased programme of £4,700 million, we were committed to an expenditure in the present year of up to £1,250 million, and, in 1952-53, on the basis of 1950 prices, which have since been exceeded, to a further £1,500 million.

We shall not, however, succeed in spending the £1,250 million this year, and some of the late Government's programme must necessarily roll forward into a future year. This point was, I believe, made by the right hon Gentleman the Member for Ebbw Vale [Mr Bevan] after his resignation. I do not reproach the late Government on this score. They tried their best to carry out what they had declared was necessary for our safety. I have never yet seen a munitions programme—and I have seen several—which did not lag behind the plans. This will, of course, be helpful to my right hon Friend the Chancellor of the Exchequer in his special problems.

We must, however, be careful to distinguish between reductions in expenditure which are due to bona fide economies, or to improved methods of using available forces, and those reductions which merely push payments forward to a later date. A very careful scrutiny is being made over the whole field of this immense new rearmament programme of the late Government in all its main aspects, and many of these items will be reviewed in the light of changing events. This process must be highly selective, so that we get first what we need most and in order that bottlenecks of any kind are eliminated. It is perfectly clear that, in the sphere of the material needs, the claims of the Royal Air Force must have first and special emphasis and priority. This will be made fully effective in any rearrangement of the programme upon which we may decide.

I have been trying to show——

MR ANEURIN BEVAN (Ebbw Vale): Will the right hon Gentleman give way? He has made an exceedingly important statement, the effect of which, as I understand it, is that it will not be found possible to spend the £4,700 million in the three years. [HON MEMBERS: 'No.']

That is the effect of his statement. [HON MEMBERS: 'No.'] It is really no use his trying to conceal this intention behind a mass of verbiage. If this first programme is not to be accomplished, then the second year's programme and the arrears of the first year's programme will not be carried out, unless the period is more than three years. Am I, therefore, to understand that the Government has abandoned the three-year period and has added some unknown period to the length of the rearmament programme?

THE PRIME MINISTER: As events develop, the right hon Gentleman will no doubt watch them with attention, and the discussions which, from time to time, he will have with his former colleagues will no doubt be both instructive and animated on both sides. [HON MEMBERS: 'Answer.'] I am not really wishing to embark on a debate with the right hon Gentleman. I was giving him an honourable mention in dispatches for having, by accident——

MR BEVAN rose——

MR DEPUTY-SPEAKER [COLONEL SIR CHARLES MACANDREW]: If the Prime Minister does not give way, hon and right hon Gentlemen must resume their seats.

THE PRIME MINISTER: I will give way in a moment. I was giving the right hon Gentleman an honourable mention for having, it appears by accident, perhaps not from the best of motives, happened to be right.

MR BEVAN: As the right hon Gentleman knows, when the statement on rearmament was made in the House of Commons by myself when Minister of Labour, I said, and the Prime Minister also said, that it may not be found possible, because of the shortage of raw materials and the lack of machine tools, to carry out the £4,700 million programme. The right hon Gentleman ought to try to be honest about this programme. Now, what period has he, in fact, substituted for the three years?

THE PRIME MINISTER: We shall get on as best we can. We shall do our best, but I should be wrong not to warn the House that there will be a lag, as there has been in all the munitions programmes which I have ever seen or with which I have been connected.

So far, I have been endeavouring to allay controversy and hasty feelings in every direction. I have, indeed, paid many compliments to the Front Bench opposite and some other quarters and so on, but now I come to two issues which are controversial in this House. Great Britain requires a pool of three million or four million rifles—that is what I am coming to—with the proportionate ammunition and supply arrangements. At the end of the war, we had over five million rifles;

we have got less than half of that now. The causes for this are being examined. The Army of a major Power must live under a large body of rifles, because exceptional needs cannot be foreseen and the wastage of rifles in war is very high. The only other large pools in the United Nations are the United States, Canada and France.

Our annual rate of rifle production is not large, nor is it easily expanded. In 1941, for instance, after two years of war and bombing, we had only managed to make about 200,000 rifles. The changeover from one pattern of rifle to another must, therefore, be a very lengthy process, which could not be even partially effective in under six or seven years. During this period, an additional burden would be placed on our resources of labour and materials, already so heavily strained, if there were two kinds of rifles in the British Forces. We cannot abandon the manufacture of one kind until we have enough to get on with of the other. A decision to rearm with the new rifle is one of high policy, involving the world situation and the position of our Allies. Standardization, not only of rifles, but of other weapons, must be regarded as a cardinal principle and aim among the Atlantic Powers. It can, of course, only be attained gradually. A marked departure from this principle in, say, small arms would prolong for many years the existing inconvenient differences of weapons, bore and ammunition. Every effort should therefore be made, in changes which can take place only so very slowly, to achieve agreement and convergence of thought on new types.

Now I come to the proposed new British ·280 rifle, which can only be rightly considered in the setting I have described. It may well be that we have now the best rifle and ammunition yet made. The hon Member for Aston [Mr Wyatt] urged me to go and see it for myself. I can assure him I followed his request, and I have had the opportunity of firing both the British and American weapons. I do not pose as a technical expert in these matters at all, but I will say that these are matters of technical dispute. Great credit in any case is due to the designers and all concerned with the creation of this weapon and also with the cartridge. I never argued against the quality of the rifle. We have at present 20 of these rifles, and if the re-tooling, etc., of our factories is carried out on the plans proposed by the late Government we could begin production in 1953, and by the end of 1954 we could be producing at the rate of about 100,000 a year. But the pool we should like to swin in would be over two million. This production would, at a time when we are so short of skilled labour, be additional, as I have just pointed out, to the indispensable maintenance of the .303 as the only weapon we can have in large numbers for a long time.

MR SHINWELL: As a point of elucidation, when the right hon

Gentleman refers to the ·303, does he mean the existing American rifle, or the proposed one?

THE PRIME MINISTER: I was speaking of the British ·303. The American is called a ·300. It is not exactly that, but it is called that. We cannot leave our pool and cease to replenish that pool until we have got something very considerable to go to. Therefore, we have to keep the two together. The Americans are also seeking a replacement for their present Garand rifle, of which they have a large pool. They also seek for an improvement in the cartridge, which again entails great changes in the design. But none of these changes will affect the military position substantially in the next three or four years. They are long-term projects, and a further effort should be made to secure their harmonious evolution among allies and thus prevent new rifts of organization being opened up in the common front, and especially between Britain and Canada, who, I hope, will move in unity in standardization. It is in the light of these considerations that a final decision should not be taken hastily. Indeed, I think it is our duty on both sides of the Atlantic to make new efforts to harmonize our long-term policy, and I propose to persevere in this and I trust that we may reach a good decision.

MR WOODROW WYATT (Birmingham, Aston): May I ask the right hon Gentleman whether, while this decision is being made, he is now going to stop the preparations which are being made to put the ·280 rifle into production or not, because if a final decision is made that we should go ahead with it, it is very important not to stop all the preparatory work now going on?

THE PRIME MINISTER: If the hon Gentleman had followed what I said he would have noted that I pointed out that production would not begin until the end of 1953 and that it would not reach 100,000 a year until the end of 1954. Obviously, a few months one way or another in trying to reach a general agreement would not be wasted. I do not propose at this moment to go forward with the re-tooling until we have had some further talks about it and to see more surely where we stand.

MR SHINWELL: Does not the right hon Gentleman realize that if we do not proceed to production of the new rifle and ammunition at a fairly early stage, we have either to rely on the existing British rifle and go on increasing production of it—a rifle which is now regarded as out of date—or accept the existing American pattern which is regarded by them as being out of date.

THE PRIME MINISTER: I was not thinking of accepting the existing American pattern at all, but we have to go on with our existing rifle until we reach a conclusion about a new rifle, which I hope may be reached with common agreement between all the Powers concerned. At any rate, I would not give that up for the sake of beginning two or three months earlier. I am not at all sure it is in our interest to embark single-handed on a lonely venture, even if that rifle is better than others put before us. At any rate, this is not a matter which can be said to be urgent as it will not affect our position for a good many years to come.

I now come to another controversial matter. I am not at present, as the House knows, convinced of the need for a Supreme Commander in the Atlantic. The question of the nationality of the commander is secondary once the need is proved. I should have thought that the method which was successful during our six years of struggle with the U-boats in the last war, with any improvements which experience may suggest, would have sufficed. The essence is that the British Admiralty should have complete control of direction of the reception end of transatlantic convoys and shipping. This ought to be managed by the First Sea Lord through his handling machine at Liverpool. The integrity of the management from hour to hour at the reception end is the key to the whole process by which any transatlantic or British armies can be landed or maintained in Western Europe. It is also the foundation of the process by which fifty million people in the British Isles have been kept alive in the teeth of the U-boat and the mining menace.

It is not a question of national pride, but a question of a good working arrangement on which victory and also life would in certain circumstances depend. As long as complete control of the approaches and reception end is exercised by the Admiralty from this small island, all the rest of the problems can be solved. But conflict or duality of control on the command level or between a supreme commander and the Admiralty might very well be injurious. The British Admiralty and the United States and Canadian naval chiefs should work together as they always did, and any question of transference of forces which could not be settled between the respective Admiralties could be adjusted, as they always were, at a higher level.

I am very glad that the United States should come as far east as they propose provided that the management of the reception end is un-impaired. It does not seem also—but this is a technical point—that the definition of coastal waters around Great Britain which has been agreed upon is satisfactory. The 100-fathom limit should be examined as an alternative. There should, moreover, of course, be no question of treating the Bay of Biscay differently from any other part of the approaches to this island or Western Europe. The problem must be solved as a whole, and I have no doubt it can be by further friendly discussions. It is certainly not solved now. I hope that we may reach some conclusions which will, without offending national pride on either side of the Atlantic, have the effect of enabling us to do the work, for which we have unequalled experience and expert knowledge, of bringing safely in to the Western shores the aid and supplies that come from across the Atlantic Ocean.

There are only one or two points to which I must refer. Statements have appeared in the Press suggesting that we contemplate widespread departures in the policy of manufacturing atomic bombs. Two years ago I commented unfavourably on the fact that the Socialist Government had not been able to make a specimen atomic bomb although they had been trying to do so for four years. When we came into office, we found that a great deal of work had been done, not only on making the crucial materials required for making atomic bombs, but in preparing to manufacture these weapons. I think the House ought to know about that. Considerable if slow progress has been made. The House will realize that this is not the moment to discuss the British research and manufacture of atomic bombs in detail. All that I will say is that we have taken over the very costly production of the Socialist Government. We have not decided on any important change in policy or principle. We hope, however, in this as in other matters, by different methods of organization and administration to effect some improvements, and there are certain aspects of this delicate subject which I hope we may clarify by discussions with the United States authorities.

Dull tragedy rolls forward in Malaya. The first thought of the Secretary of State for the Colonies on being appointed was to go to Malaya, the black spot in his Department. No decision can be taken until after his return. It is becoming painfully evident that there must be one mind with effective power over the administration in all its branches, including particularly the military and the police. Some brutal statistics may in the meanwhile be presented to the House. We have in Malaya over 25,000 British troops, over 10,000 Gurkhas and over 7,000 other soldiers. Added to this there are 60,000 local police in different stages of armament and many part-time auxiliaries. Thus the whole amounts to over 100,000 men employed in a most costly manner. The total expense of the Fighting Forces is nearly £50 million a year, quite apart from any other emergency expenses falling upon the Malayan Government. We are also suffering heavy loss in the restriction through terrorism of our tin-mines and rubber plantations. It is said that the bandits, or whatever they should be called, number 3,000 to 5,000, and I do not suppose that their maintenance cost is comparably at all heavy. Certainly it seems some improvement should be made in this theatre of tragedy and waste, but we had better wait before debating the subject until the Secretary of State comes home when we can weigh and measure the report which he will make.

I have nothing to add to the statements which have been made to the House about the position in Egypt and Korea. In Korea we all hope that the armstice negotiations will reach agreement and that this agreement will lead to a wider settlement in the country. In Egypt and the Suez Canal we stand by the Four-Power proposals for the organization of the defence of the Middle East and the safeguarding of the international waterway, and we hope eventually to associate the other countries in the area with the Four Powers in their joint task. In the meantime we shall do our duty in accordance with our treaty rights in the Canal Zone, and we hope for an increasing measure of aid from the Egyptian Government in preventing mob violence and other forms of lawless and murderous attack. We believe our forces in the Canal Zone, or within reach of it, are strong enough for any work they may have to do. We welcome the fact that good relations prevail between them and the Egyptian Army. Everyone would like to see a speedy and friendly settlement, but there are some problems in which time is a potent factor. We certainly propose to use it with patience as well as with firmness.

I have now covered, so far as I wish to at the moment, the immense variety of events in the world-wide scene which spreads around us. I have tried to do justice to those large issues in which we are in agreement with the policy pursued by the late Government. I have also tried to emphasize the urgent need of a complete and searching examination and review and, where necessary, the recasting of methods by which right decisions in major policy have been impaired by wrong methods or faulty execution. The process of examining the enormous expenditure on defence in all its forms in order while doing our duty to spend this money and spend the rest more effectively will continue without rest or pause until we meet again. I hope then, with the help of the Ministers responsible for the Service Departments, to be able to make a more precise and definite statement than it is possible for me to do after only six weeks' examination of this immense and tangled field.

# PARTY POLITICAL BROADCAST

## 22 DECEMBER 1951

---

15 *December—Decision announced to repay American and Canadian loan instalments on December 31.*

17 *December—Trading in foreign exchange renewed in London after twelve years.*

   *Mr Churchill and Mr Eden visit Paris for discussions with M. Pleven and M. Schuman.*

---

[*22 December* 1951

Tonight, my friends, it is my duty to tell you the broad truths of our national life and policy as they strike me on shouldering the burden again. I shall try to do so without regard to party propaganda and without seeking popularity at the public expense. I have but twenty minutes so I hope you will not reproach me for leaving out anything I have not time to say. The Conservative Party have now assumed control and bear responsibility for trying to make things better. During the eight weeks since I received His Majesty's Commission the new Government has been hard at work examining the state of the nation as we are now able to find it out. Six years of Socialist rule and the last two years of class warfare and party fighting have divided our strength and absorbed our energies. When we came in we found the country on the verge of insolvency. Our resources had been used up. The barrel had been scraped. There was nothing more that could be found without doing severe and unpopular things. That was why there was a General Election.

Let us look at the whole scene. It is quite certain that we cannot keep fifty millions alive in this island if they are divided half and half and electioneering against one another all the time. We have had more than two years of this electioneering. You cannot say it is the fault of one party or the other. It is the way in which our free and time-honoured constitution has worked in this crucial and it may be tragic period in our history. One thing is plain. It can't go on if we are to go on. It certainly can't go on if we are to hold our rank among the nations or even if we are to keep ourselves independent.

His Majesty's present Government intend, if we can, to bring elec-tioneering to a full stop. This is not the time for party brawling. Of course, we shall answer attacks made upon us and give back as good as we get. But we shall do what we believe is right and necessary for the country in its present crisis according to our convictions, without being dominated by the idea of winning or losing votes. We do not seek to be judged by promises but by results. We seek to be judged by deeds rather than by words. After six years we have a right to have a fair try, not for the sake of any class or party but to surmount the perils and problems which now beset us. To do this we require not only resolve and design but time, and we think that we have not only the right to claim time but the power to take it.

The difference between parties in this island are not so great as a foreigner might think by listening to our abuse of one another. There are underlying unities throughout the whole British nation. These unities are far greater than our differences. In this we are unlike many countries and after all it has pretty well soaked into the British nation that we all sink or swim together. Take the Social Services. These have been built up during the past hundred years by each succeeding Conservative, Liberal and latterly Socialist Government. Take foreign affairs and national defence. Nine-tenths of the British people agree on nine-tenths of what has been done and is being done and is going to go on being done.

I paid my tribute in the House of Commons to the work of the Labour Government in their resolute defiance of Communism, in their close association with the United States, in their establishment of national service and in their attempt to form a solid front in Western Europe against aggression. We respect the memory of Ernest Bevin for the work he did, and I am certain he could not have done his work without the help and guidance in some degree which the Conservative Party gave him.

But now we have got to face the fact which not merely the Government or the Tory Party or the Socialist Party but all of us have got in front of us tonight. If a train is running on the wrong lines downhill at sixty miles an hour it is no good trying to stop it by building a brick wall across the track. That would only mean that the wall was shattered, that the train was wrecked and the passengers mangled. First you have to put on the brakes. The Chancellor of the Exchequer has already done that and the train is coming under control and can be stopped. Then the engine has to be put into reverse. We have to go back along the line till we get to the junction. Then the signalman has to switch the points and the train has to be started again on the right line, which, I am telling you beforehand—please remember it—is uphill all the way. On an ordinary railway this might cause quite a long delay. In the vast complex evolution of modern life and government it will take several years. We require at least three years before anyone can judge fairly whether we have made things better or worse.

We hear much talk of our Election promises. Let me read you what I said as Leader of the Conservative Party the last time I spoke to you on 8 October at the beginning of the General Election. Here are my words:

'We make no promises of easier conditions in the immediate future. Too much harm has been done in these last six years for it to be repaired in a few months. Too much money has been spent for us to be able to avoid another financial crisis. It will take all our national strength to stop the downhill slide and get us back on the level, and after that we shall have to work up.'

Now, that is the warning I gave before you voted; and I have told you the same in other words tonight after you have voted.

Let me tell you what we found on taking over. First food. Our food supplies were slender. Our meat stocks were lower than they have ever been since 1941, during the crunch of the war and the U-boats. We shall be quite willing to take the blame if we fail, but let me make it clear that the price-rises and the cuts now being enforced are the legacy we received from those who during six years of peace have tried to buy the food for this island under wartime controls and through Government planners. They aimed at restriction. They got scarcity. It is not possible for us to recreate by a gesture the smooth-working trade process of food purchase that existed before the war. This can only be a gradual operation. We repudiate every scrap of responsibility for the state of things which has brought hardships upon the public this Christmas, and for other discomforts and shortages which may fall upon us in the coming months. It is only after a reasonable time has been allowed that the blame or credit for the quantity, quality and price of food and for the methods of distribution can fairly be placed upon us.

But the dominant problem is how to pay our way. In the year 1951 the United Kingdom has failed by over £500 million to earn the money to pay other countries for what we have bought from them. In the month of October before we took office, our gold and dollar reserves fell by about £115 million or at the rate of nearly £1,400 million a year. This was the result not only of our own over-spending, but also of the over-spending of other countries in the sterling area. Yet at that time, the total reserves were little over £1,000 million. Unless this rate of loss could be reduced, we were within a few months of national bankruptcy and having to choose between charity, if we could get it, and starvation. Of course, whoever had got in at the last

Election would have had to deal with this dire challenge not only to our standard of living, but to our life. I am sure that no British Government of either party would have failed to take very hard measures. The responsibility for meeting this crisis falls on us. We had no responsibility for bringing it about, but we are sure we can master it; and we shall not shrink from any measure, however unpopular, for which our duty calls. I must make it plain that if the late Government had called Parliament together at the end of August, and told them the facts, and if they had then taken even the emergency steps which we took in our first few days of office in November the sharpness of our crisis would have been definitely reduced.

The emergency measures which we have already taken are only part of the process of slowing down the train, and getting it under control. There is still more to be done before we can go forward on the right lines. When Parliament meets in January we shall be ready with a list of fresh proposals. Many of them will be unpleasant and I have no doubt that they will excite the loudest outcry from all those bitter politicians and writers who place party scores in front of national solvency. The nation must remember that these are the men—or the kind of men—who have brought us to our present pass. But we are resolved to do all that is necessary, first to clear the ground and then to rebuild on solid foundations the strength and prosperity of our people and our industries. It will be a long task. It will not be an easy one. But we shall persevere.

At the General Election much party capital was made by calling me 'a warmonger'. That was not true. Now that I am at the head of the Government I shall work ardently in harmony with our allies for peace. If war comes it will be because of world forces beyond British control. On the whole I do not think it will come. Whatever happens we shall stand up with all our strength in defence of the free world against Communist tyranny and aggression. We shall do our utmost to preserve the British Commonwealth and Empire as an independent factor in world affairs. We shall cherish the fraternal association of the English-speaking world. We shall work in true comradeship for and with United Europe. It may be that this land will have the honour of helping civilization climb the hill amid the toils of peace as we once did in the terrors of war.

What we have to face now is a peril of a different kind to 1940. We cannot go on spending as a nation or as individuals more than we can make and sell. We cannot go on counting upon American aid apart, that is to say, from the work of allied defence and rearmament, in order to make ourselves comfortable here at home. We cannot fail in our duty to what is called 'the sterling area', that great grouping of countries of whom we are the banker; we cannot fail by becoming a burden upon them. We must not plunge into further indebtedness to our Colonial Empire. All these are stern and grim facts which will not be changed by speeches or leading articles or canvassing or voting. There they are. Now we must meet them.

I have nothing to propose to you that is easy. A certain number of unpleasant things have been done already. They are only the beginning of what lies ahead. We are resolved to make this island solvent, able to earn its living and pay its way. Without this foundation not only do we lose our chance, and even our right to play our part in the defence of great causes, but we cannot keep our people alive. If we cannot earn our living by the intense exertions of our strength, our genius, our craftsmanship, our industry, there will be no time to emigrate the redundant millions for whom no food is grown at home; and we have no assurance that anyone else is going to keep the British Lion as a pet.

My friends, Mr Eden and I have just returned from France. We wanted our French friends to feel that we meant to be good friends and allies, and that we welcomed the measures which the French have taken to bringing Germany into the new European system and to end their age-long quarrel from which both these valiant races have suffered so much, and have brought so much suffering upon the rest of the world. You will remember that at Zurich in 1946 I appealed to France to take Germany by the hand and lead her back into the European family. I rejoice at the progress which has been made since then.

In a week we are to cross the Atlantic. I wish the United States and Canada too to have the feeling that we here are determined and also able to put our house in order and to play our full part throughout the international scene and that given the time we need we have the power to do so. I do not want to attach any exaggerated hope or importance to my visit to Washington. My wish and object is that we should reach a good understanding over the whole field so that we can work together easily and intimately at the different levels as we used to do. You must not expect the Americans to solve our domestic problems for us. In rearmament and in the North Atlantic Treaty Organization we have immense and intricate affairs in common, and I want to make sure that we can help each other as much as possible and in the best way.

My friends, my twenty minutes are finished, and I have only time to wish you from the bottom of my heart a happy Christmas in your homes, a Christmas inspired by hope—high hope—and unconquerable resolve for the New Year. Good night, and good luck to you all.

# CHATEAU LAURIER, OTTAWA

A SPEECH AT A BANQUET IN HONOUR OF MR CHURCHILL GIVEN BY THE
GOVERNMENT OF CANADA
14 JANUARY 1952

---

24 *December—Libya becomes an independent State.*

25 *December—The Anglo-Iranian Oil Company signs new agreement with Government of Iraq.*

31 *December—Mr Churchill, accompanied by Mr Eden, Lord Ismay and Lord Cherwell, leaves England for talks with Mr St Laurent and President Truman.*

> *The International Refugee Organization ends its official existence.*
>
> *The Economic Co-operation Administration which administered Marshall Aid since* 1948 *is wound up. Its staff and functions are transferred to Mutual Security Agency. During its existence the ECA allocated* 12½ *thousand million dollars for economic assistance in Europe.*

1 *January—In the New Year's Honours List Peerages are awarded to Sir John Anderson, Mr Robert Hudson, Mr Brendan Bracken and Sir Archibald Sinclair.*

7 *January—Defeat of French Government under M. Rene Pleven—new Government is formed under M. Faure.*

11 *January—Death in Paris of General de Lattre de Tassigny, French Commander-in-Chief and High Commissioner in Indo-China.*

---

[14 *January* 1952

I am indeed honoured that you should receive me with so much kindness. I came here first more than fifty years ago to give a lecture about the Boer War. A little later on I was Under-Secretary of State for the Colonies when Sir Wilfred Laurier came to England, and I saw a lot of that august Canadian statesman. He brought with him a young secretary named Mr Mackenzie King. I made a lifelong friendship with him and I shared my grief with all Canada, and indeed the free world, at his death after so many years of faithful and skilful service to the great causes which we uphold today.

The Prime Minister of Canada and his Cabinet have welcomed me and my colleagues, who are one-quarter of the British Cabinet, not only with Canadian hospitality but with that sense of true comrades facing difficulties together, which often makes it possible for these difficulties to be overcome. I am very glad to see here also my old friend, Mr George Drew, and I am truly sorry that I cannot now visit Toronto, where I have been invited to receive a Degree. Mr Drew is the Leader of the Opposition. Well, I have been a Leader of the Opposition too. In a free country one is always allowed to have an Opposition. In England we even pay the Leader of the Opposition a salary of £2,000 a year to make sure that the Government is kept up to the mark. I have no doubt Mr Attlee, whom you welcomed less than a year ago, will devote himself to his constitutional task with the zeal which, under totalitarian systems, might well lead him to Siberia or worse. However, we in the free nations have our own way of life, and are able to keep separate, except perhaps at Election times, those things which affect the life of the State from those which decide what party gets into office.

It is ten years almost to a week since I last came to see you in Ottawa. That was indeed a memorable occasion for me with all the burdens I had to bear. It was also an inspiring but formidable moment in the war. With the entry of the United States into the struggle, the pathway to victory seemed, and in fact was, open and sure. But I bore in my heart and conscience the knowledge, which I could not share with you, of immense, shattering disasters which were about to fall upon us throughout the East, as the inevitable consequence of the Japanese onslaught in vast regions where we were weak and ill-prepared to meet it. I knew and could feel beforehand, the heavy blows that must fall upon us, and the peril to Singapore, the Dutch East Indies, Burma and India itself. I had no feeling of self-reproach because between the fall of France in 1940 and Hitler's invasion of Russia in 1941, it had taken Britain and the British Empire fighting alone—every scrap of our life and strength—to keep the flag of freedom flying, until we were joined by mighty allies. But while I spoke to you gaily and confidently and was sure that final victory would be gained I felt like one about to come under the lash wielded by a strong and merciless arm.

I knew that many months must pass before the United States Navy could regain the control of the Pacific Ocean. We, with your gallant Canadian help, had to fight the Battle of the Atlantic against the U-boats, whose attack was ever-growing in strength and skill, and who were about to take their greatest toll along the American seaboard. An almost unbroken series of misfortunes and defeats lay before us, until the Battle of Alamein, won by your famous Governor-General and General Montgomery, and the concerted descent upon North-West Africa by General Eisenhower's Anglo-American Army, until these great events and great men turned the tide once and for all.

What is the scene which unfolds before us tonight? It is certainly not what we had hoped to find after all our enemies had surrendered unconditionally and the great world instrument of the United Nations had been set up to make sure that the wars were ended. It is certainly not that. Peace does not sit untroubled in her vineyard. The harvests of new and boundless wealth which science stands ready to pour into the hands of all peoples, and of none perhaps more than the people of Canada, must be used for exertions to ward off from us the dangers and the unimaginable horrors of another world war. At least this time I have no secrets to guard about the future. When I came last time I could not tell. Now I do not know. No one can predict with certainty what will happen.

All can see for themselves the strange clouds that move and gather on the horizons. But this time at any rate we are all united from the beginning. We all mean to stand by each other, here, in Canada, in the United States, in Britain, in Western Europe, all of us, are united to defend the cause of freedom with all our strength and by that strength we hope to preserve unbroken the peace which is our heart's desire.

I have spoken tonight a good deal about the past. Edmund Burke said: 'People will not look forward to posterity who never look backward to their ancestors.' The past is indeed the only guide to the future. But it is the future which dominates our minds. A great future is yours in Canada.

The two world wars of the terrible twentieth century have turned the economic balance of power from the Old World to the New. It is certain that Europe could not have survived without the moral and material help which has flowed across the ocean from Canada and the United States. Now we have the North Atlantic Treaty which owes much to Canadian statesmanship and to the personal initiative of Mr St Laurent. The treaty is the surest guarantee not only of the prevention of war but of victory, should our hopes be blasted.

So far this solemn compact has been regarded only in its military aspect, but now we all feel, especially since our visit to Washington, that it is broadening out into the conception of the North Atlantic community of free nations, acting together not only for defence but for the welfare and happiness and progress of all the peoples of the free world. For this we need to do all in our power to promote United Europe and the design of a European Army, including Germany. I have long been an advocate of both of these ideas. We shall do all in our power to help them to success. That does not mean that Great Britain will become a unit in a federated Europe, nor that her army, which is already in line upon the Continent and which will grow steadily, will be merged in such a way as to lose its identity. We stand with the United States, shoulder to shoulder with the European Army and its German elements, under the Supreme NATO Commander to face whatever aggression may fall upon us.

It was only ten weeks last Friday that I accepted His Majesty's Commission to form a Government in the United Kingdom. We have hardly yet had time to learn the full facts of our economic position. But what we saw at first sight convinced us of its gravity. By reducing our imports by £350 million and other measures we strove to arrest the evils which were advancing and descending upon us. We do not want to live on our friends and relations but to earn our own living and pay our own way so far as the comforts and standards of the British people are concerned. We gave all our strength to the last ounce during the war and we are resolved to conquer our problems now that it is over. The ordeal which lies before us will be hard and will not be short. We shall not shrink from any measures necessary to restore confidence and maintain solvency, however unpopular these measures may be.

Prime Minister, you have spoken about the Crown in terms which express our deepest feelings. No absolute rules can be laid down. But on the whole it is wise in human affairs and in the government of men, to separate pomp from power. Under the long-established constitutional monarchy of Britain and of the Commonwealth the King reigns but does not govern. If a great battle is lost Parliament and the people can turn out the Government. If a great battle is won crowds cheer His Majesty. Thus, while the ordinary struggles, turmoils and inevitable errors of healthy democratic government proceed, there is established upon an unchallenged pedestal the title deeds and the achievements of all the Realms, and every generation can make its contribution to the enduring treasure of our race and fame. You spoke, Mr Prime Minister, of the Crown as the symbol of our united life, and as the link between our vigorous communities spread about the surface of the globe. But perhaps you will allow me tonight to pass from the constitutional to the personal sphere. Besides the Crown there is the King. We have a truly beloved King. In constitutional duty he is faultless. In physical and moral courage he is an example to all his peoples. We are proud to pay him our tribute. This is no formal salute of loyalty, but the expression of our intense natural impulse. Here in Canada you have had what may be called a wonderful visit. HRH Princess Elizabeth and her husband have travelled the length and breadth of what you will not mind my styling 'The Great Dominion'. They have left behind them a long and lasting trail of confidence, encouragement and unity.

I claim here, in Ottawa, that tonight we make a valiant and, I believe, unconquerable assertion of the spirit of our combined identity and survival. We have surmounted all the perils and endured all the agonies of the past. We shall provide against and thus prevail over the dangers and problems of the future, withhold no sacrifice, grudge no toil, seek no sordid gain, fear no foe. All will be well. We have, I believe, within us the life-strength and guiding light by which the tormented world around us may find the harbour of safety, after a storm-beaten voyage.

This year will see the Eighty-fifth Anniversary of Canada's Confederation. A magnificent future awaits Canada, if only we can all get through the present hideous world muddle. When I first came here after the Boer War these mighty lands had but five million inhabitants. Now there are fourteen. When my grandchildren come here there may well be thirty. Upon the whole surface of the globe there is no more spacious and splendid domain open to the activity and genius of free men, with one hand clasped in enduring friendship with the United States, and the other spread across the ocean both to Britain and France. You have a sacred mission to discharge. That you will be worthy of it, I do not doubt. God bless you all.

# ADDRESS TO THE CONGRESS OF THE USA

A SPEECH AT WASHINGTON
17 JANUARY 1952

---

15-21 *January—Conference of Commonwealth Finance Ministers in London
under the chairmanship of Mr R. A. Butler.*

---

[17 *January* 1952

Mr President, Mr Speaker, Members of the Congress, this is the third time it has been my fortune to address the Congress of the United States upon our joint affairs. I am honoured indeed by these experiences which I believe are unique for one who is not an American citizen. It is also of great value to me, on again becoming the head of His Majesty's Government, to come over here and take counsel with many trusted friends and comrades of former anxious days. There is a lot for us to talk about together so that we can understand each other's difficulties, feelings and thoughts, and do our best for the common cause. Let us, therefore, survey the scene this afternoon with cool eyes undimmed by hate or passion, guided by righteous inspiration and not uncheered by hope.

I have not come here to ask you for money to make life more comfortable or easier for us in Britain. Our standards of life are our own business and we can only keep our self-respect and independence by looking after them ourselves. During the war we bore our share of the burden and fought from first to last, unconquered—and for a while alone—to the utmost limits of our resources. Your majestic obliteration of all you gave us under Lend-Lease will never be forgotten by this generation in Britain, or by history.

After the war—unwisely as I contended, and certainly contrary to American advice—we accepted as normal debts nearly £4,000 million sterling of claims by countries we had protected from invasion, or had otherwise aided, instead of making counter-claims which would at least have reduced the bill to reasonable proportions. The £1,000 million loan we borrowed from you in 1946, and which we are now repaying, was spent, not on ourselves, but mainly in helping others. In all, since the war, as the late Government affirmed, we have lent or given to European or Asian countries £1,300 million in the form of unrequited exports. This, added to the cost of turning over our industry from war to peace, and rebuilding homes shattered by bombardment was more than we could manage without an undue strain upon our life-energies for which we shall require both time and self-discipline to recover.

Why do I say all this? Not to compare our financial resources with yours—we have but a third your numbers, and much less than a third your wealth. Not to claim praise or rewards, but to convince you of our native and enduring strength, and that our true position is not to be judged by the present state of the dollar exchange or by sterling area finance. Our production is half as great again as it was before the war, our exports are up by two-thirds. Recovery, while being retarded, has been continuous, and we are determined that it shall go on.

As I said at Fulton in Missouri six years ago, under the auspices of President Truman, 'let no man underrate the abiding power of the British Commonwealth and Empire. Do not suppose we shall not come through these dark years of privation as we came through the glorious years of agony, or that a half century from now you will not see seventy or eighty millions of Britons spread about the world and united in defence of our traditions, our way of life and of the world causes which you and we espouse. If the population of the English-speaking Commonwealth be added to that of the United States, with all that such co-operation implies, in the air, on the sea and all over the globe, and in science, industry and moral force, there will be no quivering, precarious balance of power to offer its temptation to ambition or adventure'. I am very glad to be able to say the same to you here today.

It is upon this basis of recovery, in spite of burdens, that the formidable problem of the new rearmament has fallen upon us. It is the policy of the United States to help forward in many countries the process of rearmament. In this, we, who contribute ourselves two-thirds as much as the rest of Europe put together, require your aid if we are to realize in good time the very high level of military strength which the Labour Government boldly aimed at, and to which they committed us. It is for you to judge to what extent United States' interests are involved; whether you aid us much or little we shall continue to do our utmost in the common cause. But, Members of the Congress, our contribution will perforce be limited by our own physical resources, and thus the combined strength of our two countries, and also of the free world, will be somewhat less than it might be. That is why I have come here to ask, not for gold, but for steel; not for favours but equipment, and that is why many of our requests have been so well and so generously met.

At this point I will venture, if I may, to make a digression. After a lot of experience I have learned it is not a good thing to dabble in the internal politics of another country. It's hard enough to understand one's own. But I will tell you something about our British politics all the same. In our island we indulge from time to time in having Elections. I believe you sometimes have them over here. We have had a couple in twenty months, which is quite a lot, and quite enough for the time being. We now look forward to a steady period of administration in accordance with the mandates we have received. Like you we tend to work on the two-party system. The differences between parties on our side of the Atlantic, and perhaps elsewhere between British parties, are often less than they appear to outsiders. In modern Britain the dispute is between a form of Socialism which has hitherto respected political liberty, on the one hand, and on the other hand, free enterprise regulated by law and custom. These two systems of thought whose differences, I assure you, give plenty of room for argument between political opponents, fortunately overlap quite a lot in practice. Our complicated society would be deeply injured if we did not practise and develop what is called in the United States the bi-partisan habit of mind, which divides, so far as possible, what is done to make a party win and bear in their turn the responsibility of office, and what is done to make the nation live and serve high causes.

I hope here, Members of Congress, you will allow me to pay a tribute to the late Senator Vandenberg. I had the honour to meet him on several occasions. His final message in these anxious years gave a feeling that in this period of United States leadership and responsibility, all the great Americans should work together for all the things that matter most. That at least is the spirit which we shall try to maintain among British leaders in our own country. And that was the spirit which alone enabled us to survive the perils of the late war.

But now let me return to my theme of the many changes that have taken place since I was last here. There is a jocular saying: 'To improve is to change; to be perfect is to have changed often.' I had to use that once or twice in my long career. But if that were true everyone ought to be getting on very well. The changes that have happened since I last spoke to Congress are indeed astounding. It is hard to believe we are living in the same world. Former allies have become foes. Former foes have become allies. Conquered countries have been liberated. Liberated nations have been enslaved by Communism. Russia, eight years ago our brave ally, has cast away the admiration and goodwill her soldiers had gained for her by their valiant defence of their own country. It is not the fault of the Western Powers if an immense gulf has opened between us. It took a long succession of deliberate and unceasing works and acts of hostility to convince our peoples—as they are now convinced—that they have another tremendous danger to face and that they are now confronted with a new form of tyranny and aggression as dangerous and as hateful as that which we overthrew.

When I visited Washington during the war I used to be told that China would be one of the Big Four Powers among the nations, and most friendly to the United States. I was always a bit sceptical, and I think it is now generally admitted that this hopeful vision has not yet come true. But I am by no means sure that China will remain for generations in the Communist grip. The Chinese said of themselves several thousand years ago: 'China is a sea that salts all the waters that flow into it.' There's another Chinese saying about their country which is much more modern—it dates only from the fourth century. This is the saying: 'The tail of China is large and will not be wagged.' I like that one. The British democracy approves the principles of movable party heads and unwaggable national tails. It is due to the working of these important forces that I have the honour to be addressing you at this moment.

You have wisely been resolute, Members of the Congress, in confronting Chinese Communist aggression. We take our stand at your side. We are grateful to the United States for bearing nine-tenths, or more, of the burden in Korea which the United Nations have morally assumed. I am very glad that whatever diplomatic divergencies there may be from time to time about procedure you do not allow the Chinese anti-Communists on Formosa to be invaded and massacred from the mainland. We welcome your patience in the armistice negotiations and our two countries are agreed that if the truce we seek is reached, only to be broken, our response will be prompt, resolute and effective. What I have learnt over here convinces me that British and United States policy in the Far East will be marked by increasing harmony.

I can assure you that our British hearts go out in sympathy to the families of the hundred thousand Americans who have given their lives or shed their blood in Korea. We also suffer these pangs for the loss of our own men there, and not only there but in other parts of Asia also under the attack by the same enemy. Whatever course events in Korea may take in the near future, and to prophesy would be difficult—much too difficult for me to embark upon it—I am sure our soldiers, and your soldiers, have not made their sacrifice in vain. The cause of world law has found strong and invaluable defence, and the foundations of the world instrument for preserving peace, justice and freedom among the nations have been deepened and strengthened. They stand now, not on paper but on rock.

Moreover, the action which President Truman took in your name, and with your full support in his stroke against aggression in Korea, has produced consequences far beyond Korea; consequences which may well affect the destiny of mankind. The vast process of American rearmament in which the British Commonwealth and Empire and the growing power of United Europe will play their part to the utmost of their strength, this vast process has already altered the balance of the world and may well, if we all persevere steadfastly and loyally together, avert the danger of a Third World War, or the horror of defeat and subjugation should one come upon us. Mr President and Mr Speaker, I hope the mourning families throughout the great Republic will find some comfort and some pride in these thoughts.

Another extraordinary change has taken place in the Far East since I last addressed you. Peace has been made with Japan; there indeed I congratulate you upon the policy which in wise and skilful hands has brought the Japanese nation from the woe and shame of defeat in their wicked war back to that association with the Western democracies upon which the revival of their traditions, dignity and happiness can alone be regained and the stability of the Far East assured. In the anxious and confused expanses of South-East Asia there is another sphere where our aims and interests, and those of the French, who are fighting bravely at heavy cost to their strength in Europe, may find a fertile field for agreement on policy. I feel sure that the conversations we have had between our two Foreign Secretaries—between Mr Eden and Mr Acheson—men whose names and experience are outstanding throughout the world, will help to place the problems of South-East Asia in their right setting. It would not be helpful to the common cause, for our evils all spring from one centre, if an effective truce in Korea led only to a transference of Communist aggression to these other fields. Our problems will not be solved unless they are steadily viewed and acted upon as a whole in their integrity as a whole.

In the Middle East enormous changes have also taken place since I was last in power in my own country. When the war ended the Western nations were respected and predominant throughout these ancient lands, and there were quite a lot of people who had a good word to say about Great Britain. Today it is a sombre and confusing scene; yet there is still some sunshine as well as shadow. From the days of the Balfour Declaration I have desired that the Jews should have a national home, and I have worked for that end. I rejoice to pay my tribute here to the achievements of those who have founded the

Israelite State, who have defended themselves with tenacity, and who offer asylum to great numbers of Jewish refugees. I hope that with their aid they may convert deserts into gardens; but if they are to enjoy peace and prosperity they must strive to renew and preserve their friendly relations with the Arab world without which widespread misery might follow for all.

Britain's power to influence the fortunes of the Middle East and guard it from aggression is far less today, now that we have laid aside our Imperial responsibility for India and its armies. It is no longer for us alone to bear the whole burden of maintaining the freedom of the famous waterway of the Suez Canal. That has become an international rather than a national responsibility. I welcome the statesmanlike conception of the Four-Power approach to Egypt, announced by the late British Government, in which Britain, the United States, France and Turkey may share with Egypt in the protection of the world interests involved, among which Egypt's own interests are paramount.

Such a policy is urgent. Britain is maintaining over fifty thousand troops in the Suez Canal Zone, who again might be well employed elsewhere, not for national vainglory or self-seeking advantage, but in the common interest of all nations. We do not seek to be masters of Egypt; we are there only as the servants and guardians of the commerce of the world. It would enormously aid us in our task if even token forces of the other partners in the Four-Power proposal were stationed in the Canal Zone as a symbol of the unity of purpose which inspires us. And I believe it is no exaggeration to state that such token forces would probably bring into harmony all that movement by which the Four-Power policy may be made to play a decisive part by peaceful measures, and bring to an end the wide disorders of the Middle East in which, let me assure you, there lurk dangers not less great than those which the United States has stemmed in Korea.

Now I come to Europe where the greatest of all our problems and dangers lie. I have long worked for the cause of a United Europe, and even of a United States of Europe, which would enable that Continent, the source of so much of our culture, ancient and modern, and the parent of the New World, to resume and revive its former splendours. It is my sure hope and conviction that European unity will be achieved, and that it will not ultimately be limited only to the countries at present composing Western Europe. I said at Zurich in 1946 that France should take Germany by the hand and lead her back into the family of nations, and thus end a thousand-year quarrel which has torn Europe to pieces and finally plunged the whole world twice over into slaughter and havoc.

Real and rapid progress is being made towards European unity, and it is both the duty and the policy of both Great Britain and her Commonwealth, and of the United States, to do our utmost, all of us, to help and speed it. As a forerunner of United Europe there is the European Army, which could never achieve its necessary strength without the inclusion of Germany. If this necessary and urgent object is being achieved by the fusion of the forces of the Continental nations outside what I have called in former times, the Iron Curtain, that great operation deserves our fullest support. But, Members of Congress, fusion is not the only way in which the defence of Western Europe can be built. The system of a grand alliance such as has been created by the North Atlantic Treaty Organization is no bar to the fusion of as many of its members as wish for this closer unity. And the United States, British and Canadian troops will stand, indeed are already standing, shoulder to shoulder with their European comrades in defence of the civilization and freedom of the West. We stand together under General Eisenhower to defend the common cause from violent aggression.

What matters most is not the form of fusion, or melding—a word I learned over here—but the numbers of divisions, and of armoured divisions and the power of the air forces, and their weapons available for unified action under the Supreme Commander. We, in Britain, have denuded our island of military formations to an extent I have never seen before, and I cannot accept the slightest reproach from any quarter that we are not doing our full duty, because the British Commonwealth of Nations, spread all over the world, is not prepared to become a State or a group of States in any Continental federal system on either side of the Atlantic. The sooner strong enough forces can be assembled in Europe under united command the more effective will be the deterrents against a Third World War. The sooner, also, will our sense of security, and the fact of our security, be seen to reside in valiant, resolute and well-armed manhood, rather than in the awful secrets which science has wrested from nature. These are at present, it must be recognized—these secrets—the supreme deterrent against a Third World War, and the most effective guarantee of victory in it.

If I may say this, Members of Congress, be careful above all things, therefore, not to let go of the atomic weapon until you are sure, and more than sure, that other means of preserving peace are in your hands. It is my belief that by accumulating deterrents of all kinds against aggression we shall, in fact, ward off the fearful catastrophe, the fears of which darken the life and mar the progress of all the peoples of the globe. We must persevere steadfastly and faithfully in the task to which, under United States leadership, we have solemnly bound ourselves. Any weakening of our purpose, any disruption of our organization would bring about the very evils which we all dread, and from which we should all suffer, and from which many of us would perish.

We must not lose patience, and we must not lose hope. It may be that presently a new mood will reign behind the Iron Curtain. If so it will be easy for them to show it, but the democracies must be on their guard against being deceived by a false dawn. We seek or covet no one's territory; we plan no forestalling war; we trust and pray that all will come right. Even during these years of what is called the 'cold war', material production in every land is continually improving through the use of new machinery and better organization and the advance of peaceful science. But the great bound forward in progress and prosperity for which mankind is longing cannot come till the shadow of war has passed away. There are, however, historic compensations for the stresses which we suffer in the 'cold war'. Under the pressure and menace of Communist aggression the fraternal association of the United States with Britain and the British Commonwealth, and the new unity growing up in Europe—nowhere more hopeful than between France and Germany—all these harmonies are being brought forward, perhaps by several generations in the destiny of the world. If this proves true—and it has certainly proved true up to date—the architects in the Kremlin may be found to have built a different and a far better world structure than what they planned.

Members of the Congress, I have dwelt today repeatedly upon many of the changes that have happened throughout the world since you last invited me to address you here and I am sure you will agree that it is hardly possible to recognize the scene or believe it can truly have come to pass. But there is one thing which is exactly the same as when I was here last. Britain and the United States are working together and working for the same high cause. Bismarck once said that the supreme fact of the nineteenth century was that Britain and the United States spoke the same language. Let us make sure that the supreme fact of the twentieth century is that they tread the same path.

# ANGLO-AMERICAN CONVERSATIONS

A SPEECH TO THE HOUSE OF COMMONS
29 JANUARY 1952

24 *January—It is announced from Buckingham Palace that HM The King has approved the appointment of Mr Vincent Massey as Governor-General of Canada in succession to Field-Marshal Viscount Alexander.*

26 *January—Serious riots in Cairo. Sixty people are killed and extensive damage is caused to British and other foreign property.*

28 *January—It is announced that Field-Marshal Viscount Alexander has been appointed Minister for Defence and will take over that office from Mr Churchill on March 1.*

29 *January—Mr Butler announces in the House of Commons the second series of measures designed to overcome Britain's economic difficulties. The new measures are intended to save an additional £150 million annually in external expenditure (bringing total foreign exchange savings to £500 million).*

*[29 January 1952*

I should myself have thought that it would have been more for the convenience of the House not to delay the important debate on the financial and economic situation which must follow on yesterday's statement by the Chancellor of the Exchequer and I should myself have liked to present my whole case to the House in its proper setting during the course, or at the opening of, the debate we are to have on foreign affairs next week. However, in deference to the wishes expressed by the Opposition, to which it is always my desire to concede every possible point, I will try to clear up a few points about the recent American visit of myself, my right hon Friend and other Ministers in another place, and to deal with those points which, though not urgent, are the subject of misunderstanding or misrepresentation and have already figured upon the Order Paper of the House. I was led to cross the Atlantic by my conviction that, in view of all that is going on in all continents, it was important for His Majesty's new Government to establish intimate and easy relations and understandings with the President and the governing authorities of the United States. I also thought it important to try to give the impression to the American people that we rejoice in their effort to defend the cause of world freedom against

Communist aggression and penetration and that we will aid them in this purpose, which is also ours, with all our strength and goodwill.

My hon Friend the Member for Morecambe and Lonsdale [Sir I. Fraser] asked me a Question on the Order Paper today about the Joint Atlantic Command. I remain unconvinced of the need for the appointment of a supreme commander and I think that the method adopted in the last war afforded the most practical foundation for maintaining the traffic across the Atlantic in time of war. I was, however, confronted with the agreements which had been made and announced during the term of the late Government and with the fact that these agreements could not be altered except by discussions in the North Atlantic Treaty Organization. I felt it would be very unfortunate if a protracted argument arose between us and the United States in this wide audience, and I have therefore been forced to accept in principle the situation as it was left to me. The House will be aware, however, from the communique which was issued after my last meeting with President Truman on 18 January that I was able in my discussions in Washington to introduce into the Atlantic Command proposals certain alterations which will provide greater flexibility in the command of the whole Atlantic sphere and will also ensure that there is the fullest co-operation between the Commanders-in-Chief of the Eastern Atlantic and the Home Station, both of whom will be British officers. The Commander-in-Chief of the Home Station will be directly responsible to the Admiralty for the safe arrival and the dispatch of the convoys upon which our survival and the survival of any armies in Europe which the United States may have sent necessarily depend.

As an example of the greater degree of flexibility achieved in our discussions, I may say that it has been arranged that the new Supreme Commander will send instructions to his area commanders which will enable them to support adjoining commands in operations throughout the Atlantic and in British home waters without constant reference to himself. Further, His Majesty's Government, with the full agreement of the United States, are putting forward to the North Atlantic Treaty Organization an amendment to the existing command boundaries so as to extend our Home Command to the westward as far as the one-hundred-fathom line. The right hon Gentleman will remember that I mentioned that to him at the beginning of this controversy many months ago. The one-hundred-fathom line has many advantages; among others, it broadly corresponds to the limits within which moored mining is profitable and was a very well-known feature in all our affairs in the last war.

I can also state, subject to these amendments, that His Majesty's

Government are prepared, in the interests of NATO unity, to agree to the appointment within that organization of an American Supreme Commander and a British Deputy Supreme Commander. The choice of the officer whose name has been announced today, Admiral McCormick, is one which should ensure the highest confidence among all members of the North Atlantic Organization.

I now come to the question of the war in Korea, the prolongation of the truce negotiations there, with the possibility of their breakdown or breach after a settlement had been made, and the attitude we should adopt in that event towards the Chinese Communists whom we have recognized, but who have not entered into relations with us. As we all know on both sides of the House, we can recognize many people of whose conduct we do not entirely approve. In discussing these matters, we must first of all bear in mind always I think the fact, that the contribution by Britain and the British Commonwealth to the war in Korea is less than one-tenth of the forces employed; and while our losses, for which we grieve, have amounted in killed, wounded and missing, to nearly 3,000, similar American losses are over 105,000 or thirty-five to forty times as great. So there should be no party differences on the reasons why we are in this war. It was entered upon by the late Government with our full support, and it is authorized and sustained by the United Nations. I was most anxious, therefore, that we should make the United States Government feel that we meant to be their good comrades at the council board, as our Commonwealth Division and Naval and Air Forces have proved themselves to be in the field of action.

The House is aware that for six months negotiations for a truce have been going on between the United States and the Chinese Communist Government. We do not know whether the negotiations—[HON MEMBERS: 'The United Nations.']—what did I say?—[HON MEMBERS: 'The United States.']—between the United States on behalf of the United Nations—[HON MEMBERS: 'Hear, hear.']—we have a lot of things to quarrel about and we need not add to them—between the United Nations and the United States and the Chinese Government will be spun out indefinitely or whether a conclusion will be reached, or whether, after that conclusion has been reached, the Chinese Communists will break their engagement and take any advantages which might be open to them. Neither do we know whether a truce in Korea might not be reached only as a means of transferring Communist strength to the frontiers of French Indo-China or Malaya. This important aspect must be borne in mind. The whole hypothetical question of what should be done, should a truce be made only to be broken, had been discussed before we left for America between the United Kingdom and the United States and the other Governments who have fighting forces in the field. It was agreed that clearly a very serious situation would arise in such an event as a breach of the truce; and various contingencies had been examined without any definite or formal commitments being entered into.

No change was made in the situation while we were in the United States. In fact, the matter did not figure to any large extent in our discussions. I do not feel it would be an advantage to go into the details of the discussions which took place before we left upon our voyage, those discussions about what we should do, or should not do, in the event, first of a truce being reached, and secondly of it being broken. It is not wise, when a war is going on, to tell everything always to everybody, including the enemy. I suppose I may call them the enemy—they are shooting our soldiers—but including, shall we say, the other side. I think they may sometimes be left with something to guess about. I thought it better, therefore, when I was invited to address the American Congress—which I regarded as a very great honour for this House, and in which the Leader of the Opposition has also shared—to speak in general terms of the action we should take in the event of a breach of the truce, and I used the words, 'prompt, resolute and effective'. I do not believe they were bad words to use. Certainly, if one is dealing in general terms, they are better than 'tardy, timid and fatuous'. I certainly did not mean to suggest that the words, 'prompt, resolute and effective' represented any new designs or decisions arrived at during our visit——

MR JOHN PATON (Norwich, North): May I ask the right hon Gentleman—[*Interruption*]—this is very important——

THE PRIME MINISTER: They do not represent any new decisions arrived at during our visit.

MR PATON: Or before, in the preliminary conversations?

THE PRIME MINISTER: I said there had been discussions, but there had been no final or definite commitment, and that is the position now. But they do express frankly and fully the spirit in which we shall face our difficulties together.

I will now turn to some of the larger issues which are in the background of all thought upon the Korean campaign. At the outset, eighteen months ago, I was personally disquieted by seeing, as I told the House at the time, the attention and resources of the United States being diverted from the main danger in Europe to this far-distant peninsula in the China Seas. But we must recognize that the United Nations have gained authority by the fact that unprovoked aggression has been met by armed force, and that the rule of law which we seek to establish has not lacked either will-power or resources. This is of extreme importance. The ruin of the League of Nations, out of which so many disasters came, was because this will-power was lacking. It is also a fact that the stimulus of the fighting in Korea has developed to a degree otherwise impossible the rearmament of the free world, and, above all, of the United States. As I said to Congress, 'the balance of the world has been altered' by the decision of President Truman, with the approval of the United Nations, to make this bold American stroke against aggression, in support of which we have all followed.

At the same time, when the main dangers are so much nearer home, one does not want to see ourselves tied down or entangled in a war in Korea—still less in a war in China. That would indeed, as General Bradley so forcibly said, 'be the wrong war, in the wrong place, at the wrong time'.

MR SYDNEY SILVERMAN (Nelson and Colne): And on the wrong side.

HON MEMBERS: Traitor!

THE PRIME MINISTER: That, I think, is a very candid revelation by the hon Member that he thinks that we ought to be on the side of the Chinese Communists against the United Nations.

MR SILVERMAN: I do not raise a point of order, which might have been prompted by some of the remarks which have been made by some hon Members opposite—I do not think they are worth noticing—but I want to say to the right hon Gentleman that what I intended to convey was, that in any war in China, the issue of which would be whether the present Government should remain in power or whether Chiang Kai-shek should replace it, which would be the inevitable result of our taking part in those circumstances in a war in China now, it would not merely be the wrong enemy, the wrong war, the wrong time and the wrong place; it would also, in my opinion, be the wrong side.

THE PRIME MINISTER: I did not refer to General Chiang Kai-shek. I remember a time in the war when he was one of the great heroes and held to be the representative of the new Asia, and when he inspired marked enthusiasm in the hon Gentleman because of his strenuous efforts to separate India from the British Crown. But everyone has his day, and some days last longer than others. I am glad that the hon Gentleman has indicated that he was referring only to an inter-Chinese question, because I do not wish to burden him with any further responsibility than he already bears.

MR SILVERMAN: The right hon Gentleman will bear in mind that this whole question is complicated by the fact that the United States of

America still recognizes Chiang Kai-shek as the Government of China, whereas we do not, and that, therefore, if this country were in these circumstances to find itself involved in an extension of the war to China, it would be a war in which one of the issues, and perhaps in many ways the most important issue, would be whether the Government of China recognized by the Government of the United States or, the Government of China recognized by the Government of the United Kingdom would win. In such a war we should find ourselves ranged on the wrong side.

THE PRIME MINISTER: Of course, the hon Gentleman is to be complimented upon the assiduity and attention with which he studies the daily newspapers; and many other Members of the House do the same. But no issue has arisen as to the question of employing General Chiang Kai-shek on the continent. What I have said and repeat is that he and those who fought with him against the Communists and have taken refuge upon the island of Formosa should not be invaded and massacred there while the United Nations Forces possess such overwhelming naval superiority. I said 'the wrong war, in the wrong place, at the wrong time'. I entirely agree with those forcible remarks of General Omar Bradley. The facts are so serious that they ought not to be overlooked. There are, shall we say, the equivalent of ten divisions, including the most important part of the American Army and our one Commonwealth division in Korea, and we do not know how long they will have to stay there.

General Juin, the French General, said during his recent visit to the United States that but for the Communist attacks in Indo-China the French Army in Europe could be ten divisions stronger. If those were at home, it would presumably enable France to take a more confident view about the development of a German army, which is of the utmost importance to the problem. However, let us count the diminution of the French Army in Europe as ten divisions; that is certainly a moderate estimate. Then there are the British Forces which are spread about the Middle East and Far East resisting Communist menace or other forms of Communist-inspired disorder, in Hong Kong, in Malaya and to some extent in the Canal Zone of the Middle East. These amount to at least six divisions, far more costly in resources to maintain than if they were at home or in Europe.

This makes a numerical total of twenty-six divisions, but the equivalent in war power measured by divisions employed in Europe might well be thirty or even thirty-five. And all this is withdrawn from the European front, where the Atlantic Treaty Powers have so far only been able to deploy—that is a better word than concentrate—on this enormous front a very much smaller force. But for these pressures and assaults in the Far East, in South-East Asia and the Middle East, forces would exist to form a front in Europe against what are called the 176 Soviet divisions of which we have been given timely warning by the former Minister of Defence, an enormous force far superior to anything we have. I think those divisions are not numerically comparable to the United Nations divisions or the Atlantic Treaty divisions but they are far superior in total.

If we had fifty divisions deployed to protect the civilization of Europe, including Germany, at the present time, as we should have but for the ones which are detached all over the world, the Atlantic Treaty Powers would not be forced, as they are now, to rely so disproportionately on the immense and ever-growing American superiority in the atomic bomb, and there would be a chance of establishing a calmer atmosphere, and those conditions might well lead, if we were blessed by heaven, to at least a makeshift settlement lasting perhaps for a good many years. But the men in the Kremlin, who have many anxieties of their own to face, may at any rate at this moment compliment themselves not only on having subjugated or brought into their Communist grip half Europe and all China, but on having pegged down in far-distant areas around the globe a much greater force than the Atlantic Powers have so far been able to gather to defend the civilization of the West; and they may pride themselves on the fact that they have done all this without losing a single soldier in Russian uniform.

I leave this sombre spectacle, which I feel it is absolutely necessary to place before the House: actions and words cannot be judged except in relation to what is always the uppermost feeling in one's mind—anxiety. I leave this spectacle to return to the Korean front. I do not think we have gained security during this long period of haggling and wrangling which has gone on at Panmunjom. Apart from anything else, the Chinese Communist Government, whose troops were being slaughtered at the rate of about forty to one by the United Nations Forces, and who had a terrible mass of wounded and invalids flung back upon them far beyond their resources to handle, have, since the Soviet suggestion of a cease-fire and truce negotiations, re-established what is called their 'face'. That, I believe, is a technical term, a term of art which has great vogue in China, and they have since been bargaining all this time on equal terms with the representatives of the United Nations.

We still hope that an agreement will be reached. We still hope that, being reached, it will be kept. I think we have secured a better chance for the reaching of an agreement by making it plain that the United States and Britain are working together in true comradeship, and that in the event of a treacherous renewal of the war they will together take 'prompt, resolute and effective action'. We have improved the chances of a settlement and limited the risks of a spread by making this declaration instead of giving the impression that we were disunited and taking small points off one another. I am sure that the way to play into the hands of those who direct the Communist menace from the centre would be to magnify differences between Britain and the United States and that nothing would be more likely than that to lead to renewal on a larger scale of the local war in Korea. My own thoughts are never long absent from the European front and I was, therefore, very glad to have the opportunity in Washington of making it clear that the English-speaking world are acting together in true loyalty and unity and are resolved to bring the local events in the Far East into their proper relationship to our predominating danger in Europe.

Apart from the turmoil in the Far East and in South-East Asia, there are the troubles in the Middle East and Egypt. I have never had the feeling that we should make a bargain with the United States that if we worked smoothly with them in the Far East they should do the same for us in the Middle East. I think this should not be the subject of a bargain. Both cases should be dealt with on their merits, and both cases are pretty strong when looked at on their merits. It is certain that if Britain and the United States are known to be acting together, the difficulties will by that very fact be substantially reduced and the possibilities of peaceful arrangements will be greatly strengthened. It is certain also that the main interest of the Communist oligarchy in the Kremlin is to provoke or at least to suggest divergencies between us. That, I think, should not be overlooked even in our debates in this House. On the other hand, the fact of simultaneous or concerted action between us and the United States becoming apparent will be beneficial to both of us and even more beneficial to the free world as a whole.

No more hopeful course has yet been suggested for the Middle East than the approach to all its problems in the spirit of the Four-Power proposals. This was the policy of the late Government, for which they deserve the fullest credit, and we have given it immediate, cordial, sustained and determined support. Now that we no longer have available the former Imperial armies which existed in India, the burden of maintaining the control and security of the international waterway of the Suez Canal is one which must be more widely shared. It is upon an international basis that the most hopeful solution of our Middle Eastern difficulties will be reached, and I trust that all the Powers concerned will play their part, working together and sharing the burdens and responsibilities for the peace and security of the Middle East. It may be some time before that is achieved, but that should clearly be our aim and goal.

I have today been able only to deal with three points all relating to specific Questions which have been put on the Paper, but I think that they were the three points which were perhaps uppermost in the minds of hon Gentlemen. There are, of course, a number of other issues upon which the House should receive information. These I shall reserve for our debate next week, when Members will have the fullest opportunity of interrogating the Government upon any points of doubt or difference which may exist between us. I am very much obliged to the House for the patient hearing which they have given me, and I hope that we may now pass to the urgent and most important business of the day.

# A BROADCAST

---

1 *February—Conversations in Paris between Mr Eden and M. Robert Schuman preparatory to the NATO Conference at Lisbon.*
6 *February—Death at Sandringham of HM King George VI.*

---

[*7 February* 1952

My friends, when the death of the King was announced to us yesterday morning there struck a deep and solemn note in our lives which, as it resounded far and wide, stilled the clatter and traffic of twentieth-century life in many lands and made countless millions of human beings pause and look around them. A new sense of values took, for the time being, possession of human minds and mortal existence presented itself to so many at the same moment in its serenity and in its sorrow, in its splendour and in its pain, in its fortitude and in its suffering.

The King was greatly loved by all his peoples. He was respected as a man and as a prince far beyond the many realms over which he reigned. The simple dignity of his life, his manly virtues, his sense of duty alike as a ruler and a servant of the vast spheres and communities for which he bore responsibility—his gay charm and happy nature, his example as a husband and a father in his own family circle, his courage in peace or war—all these were aspects of his character which won the glint of admiration, now here, now there, from the innumerable eyes whose gaze falls upon the Throne.

We thought of him as a young naval lieutenant in the great Battle of Jutland. We thought of him, when calmly, without ambition, or want of self-confidence, he assumed the heavy burden of the Crown and succeeded his brother, whom he loved, and to whom he had rendered perfect loyalty. We thought of him so faithful in his study and discharge of State affairs, so strong in his devotion to the enduring honour of our country, so self-restrained in his judgments of men and affairs, so uplifted above the clash of party politics, yet so attentive to them; so wise and shrewd in judging between what matters and what does not. All this we saw and admired. His conduct on the Throne may well be a model and a guide to constitutional sovereigns throughout the world today, and also in future generations.

The last few months of King George's life, with all the pain and physical stresses that he endured—his life hanging by a thread from day to day—and he all the time cheerful and undaunted—stricken in body but quite undisturbed and even unaffected in spirit—these have made a profound and an enduring impression and should be a help to all. He was sustained not only by his natural buoyancy but by the sincerity of his Christian faith. During these last months the King walked with death, as if death were a companion, an acquaintance, whom he recognized and did not fear. In the end death came as a friend; and after a happy day of sunshine and sport, and after 'good night' to those who loved him best, he fell asleep as every man or woman who strives to fear God and nothing else in the world may hope to do.

The nearer one stood to him the more these facts were apparent. But the newspapers and photographs of modern times have made vast numbers of his subjects able to watch with emotion the last months of his pilgrimage. We all saw him approach his journey's end. In this period of mourning and meditation, amid our cares and toils, every home in all the realms joined together under the Crown, may draw comfort for tonight and strength for the future from his bearing and his fortitude.

There was another tie between King George and his people. It was not only sorrow and affliction that they shared. Dear to the hearts and the homes of the people is the joy and pride of a united family; with this all the troubles of the world can be borne and all its ordeals at least confronted. No family in these tumultuous years was happier, or loved one another more, than the Royal Family around the King.

My friends, I suppose no Minister saw so much of the King during the war as I did. I made certain he was kept informed of every secret matter; and the care and thoroughness with which he mastered the immense daily flow of State papers made a deep mark on my mind. Let me tell you another fact. On one of the days, when Buckingham Palace was bombed, the King had just returned from Windsor. One side of the courtyard was struck, and if the windows opposite out of which he and the Queen were looking had not been, by the mercy of God, open, they would both have been blinded by the broken glass instead of being only hurled back by the explosion. Amid all that was then going on—although I saw the King so often—I never heard of this episode till a long time after. Their Majesties never mentioned it, or thought it of more significance than a soldier in their armies would of a shell bursting near him. This seems to me to be a revealing trait in the Royal character.

There is no doubt that of all the institutions which have grown up among us over the centuries, or sprung into being in our lifetime, the constitutional monarchy is the most deeply founded and dearly cherished by the whole association of our peoples. In the present generation it has acquired a meaning incomparably more powerful than anyone had dreamed possible in former times. The Crown has become the mysterious link—indeed, I may say, the magic link— which unites our loosely bound but strongly interwoven Common- wealth of nations, States and races. Peoples who would never tolerate the assertions of a written constitution which implied any diminution of their independence, are the foremost to be proud of their loyalty to the Crown.

We have been greatly blessed amid our many anxieties, and in the mighty world that has grown up all around our small island—we have been greatly blessed that this new intangible, inexpressible but for practical purposes apparently, an all-powerful element of union should have leapt into being among us. How vital it is, not only to the future of the British Commonwealth and Empire, but I believe also to the cause of world freedom and peace which we serve, that the occupant of the Throne should be equal to the august and indefinable responsibilities which this supreme office requires. For fifteen years King George VI was king; never at any moment in all the perplexities at home and abroad, in public or in private, did he fail in his duties; well does he deserve the farewell salute of all his governments and peoples.

My friends, it is at this time that our compassion and sympathy go out to his Consort and widow. Their marriage was a love match with no idea of regal pomp or splendour. Indeed, there seemed to lie before them the arduous life of royal personages denied so many of the activities of ordinary folk and having to give so much in ceremonial public service. May I say, speaking with all freedom, that our hearts go out tonight to that valiant woman with famous blood of Scotland in her veins who sustained King George through all his toils and problems and brought up, with their charm and beauty, the two daughters who mourn their father today. May she be granted strength to bear her sorrow. To Queen Mary, his mother, another of whose sons is dead—the Duke of Kent having been killed on active service— there belongs the consolation of seeing how well the King did his duty and fulfilled her hopes, and of always knowing how much he cared for her.

Now I must leave the treasures of the past and turn to the future. Famous have been the reigns of our Queens. Some of the greatest periods in our history have unfolded under their sceptres. Now that we have the Second Queen Elizabeth, also ascending the Throne in her twenty-sixth year, our thoughts are carried back nearly 400 years to the magnificent figure who presided over, and in many ways embodied and inspired, the grandeur and genius of the Elizabethan Age. Queen Elizabeth the Second, like her predecessor, did not pass her childhood in any certain expectation of the Crown. But already we know her well, and we understand why her gifts, and those of her husband, the Duke of Edinburgh, have stirred the only part of our Commonwealth she has yet been able to visit. She has already been acclaimed as Queen of Canada: we make our claim, too, and others will come forward also; and tomorrow the proclamation of her sovereignty will command the loyalty of her native land and of all other parts of the British Commonwealth and Empire.

I, whose youth was passed in the august, unchallenged and tranquil glories of the Victorian Era, may well feel a thrill in invoking, once more, the prayer and the Anthem

GOD SAVE THE QUEEN

# MOTIONS FOR ADDRESSES OF SYMPATHY TO HM THE QUEEN, THE QUEEN MOTHER AND HM QUEEN MARY ON THE DEATH OF HM THE KING

## A SPEECH TO THE HOUSE OF COMMONS
### 11 FEBRUARY 1952

---

8 *February—HM Queen Elizabeth, having returned from Kenya, holds her first Privy Council.*

---

[11 *February* 1952

THE PRIME MINISTER [MR WINSTON CHURCHILL], at the Bar, acquainted the House that he had a Message from Her Majesty the Queen to this House, signed by Her Majesty's own hand. And he presented the same to the House, and it was read out by MR SPEAKER as followeth, all the Members of the House being uncovered:

'I know that the House of Commons mourns with me the untimely death of my dear Father. In spite of failing health he upheld to the end the ideal to which he pledged himself, of service to his Peoples and the preservation of Constitutional Government. He has set before me an example of selfless dedication which I am resolved, with God's help, faithfully to follow.

ELIZABETH REGINA.'

THE PRIME MINISTER: I have read with attention the speeches made on the demise of the Crown during the present century, beginning with the end of an epoch on the death of Queen Victoria. Mr Balfour, Mr Asquith and Mr Baldwin, as Prime Ministers or Leaders of the House, discharged the duty which falls on me today. I was a Member of the House on all those occasions and I shall follow, in what I say, the example of those eminent men. I have three Motions to propose which, though they will be put separately from the Chair, should be read all at once, and I shall confine what I have to say in support of them, in accordance with precedent, within the compass of a single speech.

First, there is the Address to the Queen. I beg to move:

'*That an humble Address be presented to Her Majesty to convey to Her Majesty the deep sympathy felt by this House in the great sorrow which she has sustained by the death of the late King, Her Majesty's Father, of blessed and glorious memory;*

'*To assure Her Majesty that His late Majesty's unsparing devotion to the Service of His Peoples and His inspiring example in the time of their greatest peril will always be held in affectionate and grateful remembrance by them;*

'*To express to Her Majesty our loyal devotion to Her Royal Person and our complete conviction that She will, with the Blessing of God, throughout Her Reign work to uphold the liberties and promote the happiness of all Her Peoples.*'

We shall also resolve as follows:

'*That a Message of condolence be sent to the Queen Mother tendering to Her the deep sympathy of this House in Her grief, which is shared by all its Members, and assuring Her of the sincere feelings of affection and respect towards Her Majesty which they will ever hold in their hearts.*'

Then there is the Motion for a message to Queen Mary:

'*That a Message of condolence be sent to Her Majesty Queen Mary tendering to Her the deep sympathy of this House in Her further affliction and assuring Her of the unalterable affection and regard in which Her Majesty is held by all its Members.*'

All the three Prime Ministers or Leaders of the House whom I have cited reviewed the history of the reign that had ended and paid their tribute to the former occupant of the Throne. The reign of Queen Victoria had lasted over sixty-three years. It is now nearly 115 years since she assumed the Crown. King Edward VII did not complete the tenth year of his reign; King George V reigned for twenty-five years, and our late lamented Sovereign for fifteen.

With the end of the Victorian Era we passed into what I feel we must call 'the terrible twentieth century'. Half of it is over and we have survived its fearful convulsions. We stand erect both as an island people and as the centre of a world-wide Commonwealth and Empire, after so much else in other lands has been shattered or fallen to the ground and been replaced by other forces and systems. When King Edward VII, so long familiar to his generation as Prince of Wales, passed away, both Mr Asquith and Mr Balfour dwelt upon his labours for the cause of peace in Europe, and many called him 'Edward the Peacemaker'. But only four years after his death we were plunged into war by forces utterly beyond our control.

King George V succeeded to a grim inheritance; first, to the fiercest party troubles I have ever seen and taken part in at home, and then to the First World War with its prodigious slaughter. Victory was gained, but the attempt to erect, in the League of Nations, a world instrument which would prevent another hideous conflict, failed. The people of the United States realize today how grievous was the cost to them, in life and treasure, of the isolationism which led them to withdraw from the League of Nations which President Wilson had conceived and which British minds had so largely helped to shape.

The death of King George V, in January 1936, was followed in less than a year by the abdication, on personal grounds, of King Edward VIII, and the Sovereign whose death we lament today then succeeded his brother. No British monarch in living memory had a harder time. It is true that the party and constitutional quarrels about the House of Lords and Ireland seemed more violent under King George V than those which we have had among ourselves since, but the greatest shocks fell upon our island in the reign of King George VI. His first three years were clouded by the fears of another world war, and the differences of opinion, and indeed bewilderment, which prevailed about how to avert it. But the war came and never, in our long history, were we exposed to greater perils of invasion and destruction than in that year when we stood all alone and kept the flag of freedom flying against what seemed, and might easily have proved to be, over-whelming power.

The late King lived through every minute of this struggle with a heart that never quavered and a spirit undaunted; but I, who saw him so often, knew how keenly, with all his full knowledge and under-standing of what was happening, he felt personally the ups and downs of this terrific struggle and how he longed to fight in it, arms in hand, himself. Thus passed six more years of his reign. Victory again crowned our martial struggles, but our island, more than any other country in the world, and for a longer period, had given all that was in it. We had victory with honour and with the respect of the world, victor and vanquished, friend and foe alike.

Alas, we found ourselves in great straits from the exertions which we had made, and then there came, in the midst of the ordeals of the aftermath and of the problems which lay about us, a new menace. The surmounting of one form of mortal peril seemed soon only to be succeeded by the shadow of another. The King felt—as the Leader of the Opposition, who was his first Minister for so long, knows well— the fresh anxieties which thronged up against us and the disappoint-ment that followed absolute triumph without lasting security or peace. Though deeply smitten by physical afflictions, he never lost his courage or faith that Great Britain, her Commonwealth and Empire, would in the end come through. Nor did he lose hope that another hateful war will be warded off, perhaps to no small extent by the wis-dom and experience of the many realms over which he ruled. As I have said, his was the hardest reign of modern times. He felt and shared the sufferings of his peoples as if they were his own. To the end he was sure we should not fail; to the end he hoped and prayed we might reach a period of calm and repose. We salute his memory because we all walked the stony, uphill road with him and he with us.

Let me now speak of his Consort, the Queen Mother, to whom our second Motion is dedicated. The thoughts of all of us go forth to her. It was with her aid that King George was able to surmount his trials. Let no one underrate what they were. To be lifted far above class and party strife or the daily excitements of internal politics, to be restrained within the strict limits of a constitutional Sovereign—in his case most faithfully upheld—and yet to feel that the fate and fortunes of the whole nation and of his realms were centred not only in his office but in his soul, that was the ordeal which he could not have endured without the strong, loving support of his devoted and untiring wife and Consort. To her we accord, on behalf of those we represent, all that human sympathy can bestow.

The third Motion is addressed to Queen Mary, who has now lost another of her sons, one killed on active service, the other worn down in public duty. May she find comfort in the regard and affection which flow to her from all who have watched and admired her through these long years when her example has inspired not only her family, but all the British people.

The House will observe in the Royal Proclamation the importance and significance assigned to the word 'Realm'. There was a time—and not so long ago—when the word 'Dominion' was greatly esteemed. But now, almost instinctively and certainly spontaneously, the many States, nations and races included in the British Commonwealth and Empire have found in the word 'Realm' the expression of their sense of unity, combined in most cases with a positive allegiance to the Crown or a proud and respectful association with it. Thus we go forward on our long and anxious journey, moving together in freedom and hope, spread across the oceans and under every sky and climate though we may be.

So far I have spoken of the past, but with the new reign we must all feel our contact with the future. A fair and youthful figure, Princess, wife and mother, is the heir to all our traditions and glories never greater than in her father's days, and to all our perplexities and dangers never greater in peacetime than now. She is also heir to all our united strength and loyalty. She comes to the Throne at a time when a tormented mankind stands uncertainly poised between world catastrophe and a golden age. That it should be a golden age of art and letters, we can only hope—science and machinery have their other tales to tell—but it is certain that if a true and lasting peace can be achieved, and if the nations will only let each other alone an immense and undreamed of prosperity with culture and leisure ever more widely spread can come, perhaps even easily and swiftly, to the masses of the people in every land. Let us hope and pray that the accession to our ancient Throne of Queen Elizabeth the Second may be the signal for such a brightening salvation of the human scene.

# FOREIGN AFFAIRS

### A SPEECH TO THE HOUSE OF COMMONS
### 26 FEBRUARY 1952

---

15 *February—Funeral of HM King George VI.*

17-19 *Discussion in London between Mr Eden, Mr Acheson, M. Schuman and Dr Adenauer on the forthcoming NATO Conference in Lisbon.*

20 *February—Ninth session of the North Atlantic Council meets in Lisbon.*

26 *February—Mr Churchill announces in the House of Commons that Lord Cohen will be succeeded as Chairman of the Royal Commission on Taxation by Lord Waverley.*

*Mr Churchill announces in the House of Commons that the Coronation Stone has been restored to its traditional place under the Coronation Chair in Westminster Abbey.*

---

[*26 February* 1952

When I learned the text of the Motion which has been put upon the Order Paper and saw that it took the unusual form of a personal Vote of Censure upon me I am bound to say that I did expect that some more serious attempt to frame and sustain charges would have been made than we have heard from the right hon Gentleman the Member for Lewisham, South [Mr H. Morrison]. I have hardly ever listened—from a skilled Parliamentarian—to such a weak, vague, wandering harangue which at no point touched the realities or which was so largely composed of quotations of all kinds, some of his own, and none selected with a view to proving or sustaining any effective case. I will in due course—I hope I shall not too long detain the House— deal with the attack which is made upon me today, but if I had to confine myself to those aspects of it which have been dealt on by the right hon Gentleman I am bound to say I should find myself very short of material with which to reply.

I wish, first of all, to draw the attention of the House to the agreement we reached in Washington about the atomic bomb. We reached an agreement about its not being used from the East Anglian base without British consent. This agreement states in a formal and public manner what had already been reached as a verbal understanding between the late Prime Minister and President Truman. We felt, however, that it would be an improvement if the position were made public and formal, and I expect that will be the general opinion. A much more important atomic development is now before us. I was not aware until I took office that not only had the Socialist Government made the atomic bomb as a matter of research, but that they had created at the expense of many scores of millions of pounds the important plant necessary for its regular production. This weapon will be tested in the course of the present year by agreement with the Australian Government at some suitable place in that continent.

This achievement is certainly a real advantage to us and when I informed the Americans in Washington of the position which had been reached quite a new atmosphere was created on this subject. I was interested to read in the newspapers on Monday week the following statement by Senator MacMahon, the author of the MacMahon Act of 1946 which, under extreme penalties, forbade all sharing of secrets with Great Britain or other countries:

'The achievement of an atomic explosion by Great Britain, when an accomplished fact, will contribute to the keeping of the peace because it will add to the free world's total deterring power. This event is likely to raise in still sharper focus the problem of atomic co-operation between ourselves and Great Britain. The British contributed heavily to our own wartime atomic project. But due to a series of unfortunate circumstances the nature of the agreements which made this contribution possible was not disclosed to me and my colleagues on the Senate special atomic energy committee at the time we framed the law in 1946. Now we may consider re-thinking the entire situation with all the facts in front of us.'

This is a very important declaration. We must now await the result of the experiment in Australia. While paying all credit to the late Government and their scientists for the action which they have taken I must, as an old Parliamentarian, express my surprise that a full and clear statement was not made of this policy to Parliament, especially in view of the immense sums of money which were voted by this House without their having any clear appreciation of what was being done. There was no reason why Parliament in time of peace should not have been made fully aware, not, of course, of the technical details, but of the large scale new departure in policy adopted on so grave a matter. The Conservative Opposition would certainly have supported the Government, as we did on so many other of their measures of defence, and their majority would no doubt have been overwhelming. Nevertheless, they preferred to conceal this vast operation and its finances from the scrutiny of the House, not even obtaining a vote on the principle involved, while, at the same time, with Machiavellian art, keeping open the advantage of accusing their opponents of being war-mongers.

MR C. R. ATTLEE (Walthamstow, West): I really cannot let those statements pass. We have carried on precisely the same policy on the advice of our experts and advisers with regard to the publicity of these atomic matters. I was ready at all times to see the right hon Gentleman, and I always understood that his closest confidant, Lord Cherwell, was fully informed of all these matters. I do not know why he had not told me about it, and as for the Americans not knowing what we were doing we were telling them every possible thing in order to get their co-operation.

THE PRIME MINISTER: The right hon Gentleman will no doubt have various opportunities of making full statements upon all this topic, but it does seem to me that some of the late Government's followers hardly relished their success in this sphere. I notice, indeed, a certain sense of disappointment with the statement that the achieve-ment which has been made could not be wholly attributed to us. Indeed, the right hon Gentleman the Leader of the Opposition is in the position of one who 'did good by stealth and blushed to find it fame'. Before the whole story passes from life into history he will have to do a good deal of blushing in the explanations which he will have to make to some of his followers.

This remarkable episode is a good prelude to the argument I shall now deploy in reply to the new move in the Socialist warmongering accusation, of which the right hon Gentleman's Motion is the latest expression. I am complimented by the fact that the official Opposition's Vote of Censure should concentrate its gravamen on me. It is not the first time I have incurred the wrath of the Socialist Party. [HON MEMBERS: 'Nor of the Tories.'] I remember that in March 1946, a Motion condemning a speech I made at Fulton was put on the Order Paper by just over 100 Socialist Members of Parliament, including seven who subsequently became Ministers. Here is the relevant part of the Motion:

'That this House considers that proposals for a military alliance between the British Commonwealth and the United States of America for the purpose of combating the spread of Communism, such as were put forward in a speech at Fulton, Missouri, by the right hon Gentleman the Member for Woodford, are calculated to do injury to the good relations between Great Britain, the United States and the USSR, and are inimical in the cause of world peace. . .'

That Motion was never debated. On the contrary, the policy which I outlined at Fulton five years ago has since been effectively adopted both by the United States and by the Socialist Party. Two years later, by the Brussels Pact, and in the following year by the North Atlantic Treaty, the whole substance and purpose of what I said was adopted and enforced by the Socialist Government, and today we all respect the foresight and wise courage of the late Mr Ernest Bevin in helping to bring those great changes about.

Now, today, the Opposition have adopted a position of protestation that there should be no war with China. We agree with them about the importance of avoiding such a war, but I seem to have a recollection that there was some trouble about the Chinese going into Korea, which began fifteen months ago, and that the Chinese Communists and their North Korean allies killed and wounded more than 100,000 Americans and nearly 3,000 of our own men, and that they lost themselves what has been estimated at over 1,250,000 killed and wounded. Even half that number would be quite a lot. One reads, too, in the papers every day about fighting that is going on even now with the Chinese. Apparently, however, according to the mentality of the Socialist Party, which only five months ago supported all this devastating struggle in Korea, nothing matters unless we call it 'war'. Apparently the important point is: What is it to be called? As long as it is not called 'war' the high condition of moral idealism of the Socialist movement is in no way impaired.

Hundreds of thousands of men may fall mangled and torn by bomb, bayonet, bullet or grenade; whole areas of Korea may be devasted in the advances and retreats of the opposing armies; 35,000 dead may be picked up in front of a single American division; our own men may have killed many times their number in deadly fighting; but, whatever happens, it must not be called 'war'. It is not the fact, but it is the name that counts. What a strange political philosophy. 'No war. Peace in our time'—that is what the Socialists said when they themselves were responsible, in conjunction with other nations, for using deadly modern weapons to share in the slaughter of a million or more Chinese and North Koreans. It is difficult to imagine such a process of self-delusion and mental obliquity.

But whatever has been going on in Korea in the last eighteen months is war, even though they choose to call it a 'collective police operation'; and it is a war entered upon by the Socialist Government, and waged by them, side by side with other members of the United Nations. Since we have been in office the truce negotiations, begun eight months ago, have continued, and the slaughter of the Chinese has abated. A comparative calm rests on the blood-soaked front, and the Socialist Party can turn their energies, I have no doubt with a measure of relief, from being warmongers to calling other people 'warmongers'.

I made it plain a month ago, in my first speech on my return from America, that I was opposed to action that would involve us or our Allies of the United Nations in a war in China. I drew the attention of the House to General Omar Bradley's statement which I will now quote exactly—[HON MEMBERS: 'Another quotation.']—for I was not quite accurate before. Verify your quotations is a good maxim. This is the quotation:

'We would be fighting the wrong nation in the wrong war and in the wrong place.'

MR CHRISTOPHER MAYHEW (Woolwich, East) *rose*——

THE PRIME MINISTER: We did not interrupt the right hon Gentleman the Member for Lewisham, South [Mr H. Morrison], who has just sat down, and I really must ask for an opportunity of unfolding my case. I must remind the House that I have never changed my opinion about the danger of our getting involved in China. When the Chinese first came into Korea, after the Russian-instigated attack by the North Koreans, I said in the House—[An HON MEMBER: 'Another quotation.'] What did the hon Gentleman say? Oh, I beg pardon. I thought it might have been an intelligent point. I said on 30 November 1950:

'The plan would evidently be to get the United States and the United Nations . . . involved as deeply as possible in China, and thus prevent the reinforcement of Europe and the building up of our defensive strength there to a point where it would be an effectual deterrent. It is one of the most well-known—almost hackneyed—strategical and tactical methods, to draw your opponent's resources to one part of the field and then, at the right moment, to strike in another. Military history shows countless examples of this and of variants of it. Surely, however, the United Nations should avoid by every means in their power becoming entangled inextricably in a war with China.'

I have never departed from those views in any way, either publicly or privately. I also endeavoured when I spoke here a month ago to show the danger which was arising in Europe by the dispersion of so many British, American and French divisions in Asia as a result of acts of aggression which the Soviet Government had promoted without losing a single soldier in Russian uniform. This made it clear that I disagree profoundly with the kind of statements, some of which have been read to us this afternoon, which have recently been made in the United States by various prominent Americans engaged in the impending Presidential Elections. I am not going to mention names. It is not for us to be drawn into American politics. Her Majesty's Government deal with the United States Government of the day, and with them our relations are very good indeed.

But let me now give the House some account of what happened about Korea under the late Government, and also since we have become responsible. The reason why I have to use guarded language instead of simple facts is that if military action, like, for instance, bombing, were referred to precisely, it would reveal what had been agreed and might therefore expose British and American airmen to extra danger. There is nothing I should like better than that all the relevant documents on this subject should be published. But that is not possible while fighting is going on or may be resumed on a large scale. I will give the House the fullest account I can at this present time. On several occasions in the last year the United States asked the British Government what military action they would agree to if certain things happened. Questions were addressed to the late Government and later to Her Majesty's present advisers. On the first occasion in May of last year, before the truce negotiations began, the right hon Gentleman the late Foreign Secretary replied to an inquiry that His Majesty's Government had decided that in the event of heavy air attacks from bases in China upon United Nations forces in Korea they would associate themselves with action not confined to Korea.

MR ANEURIN BEVAN (Ebbw Vale): On a point of order. Is the right hon Gentleman quoting directly from Cabinet papers? If he is, then I move that the papers be laid. If, as I understand, the right hon Gentleman is making references to discussions inside the previous Cabinet, then he is not in order in doing so. If he is quoting, then he must lay the papers, and I so move.

THE PRIME MINISTER: I am not quoting at all. I am carefully avoiding making any quotations on that account, but I am undoubtedly entitled in defence of our own position, which has been subjected to this shameful attack, to place the House in possession of the facts as far as that can be done.

MR SYDNEY SILVERMAN (Nelson and Colne): On a point of order. I understood the right hon Gentleman to say that some inquiry was addressed at some time by the American administration to the previous Government. Such an inquiry would presumably have been either in a document itself or, if the inquiry were made to the Cabinet, then in a document circulated to Ministers. Therefore, once the right hon Gentleman has referred to such an inquiry he has by implication referred to a document. That being so, I ask you, Mr Deputy-Speaker, whether the House is not entitled either to have the document laid before it or to have the statement withdrawn?

Mr Deputy-Speaker [Colonel Sir Charles MacAndrew]: The rule is that if a document is paraphrased, it does not require to be laid. If, on the other hand, it is quoted from, it must be laid unless it is against the public interest so to do.

Mr Silverman: Further to that point of order. Once a thing is paraphrased, the paraphrase may be a comment, but the right hon Gentleman did not do that. He referred to a specific question asked by one administration of another. That, Mr Deputy-Speaker, is not a paraphrase.

Mr Deputy-Speaker: I made the position perfectly clear. If a document is paraphrased it does not require to be laid. If it is quoted from, it should be laid unless it is against the public interest so to do.

Mr Bevan: If it is against the public interest so to do, it is against the public interest to make reference to it. May I respectfully submit to you, Mr Deputy-Speaker, that my first recollection of an action of this sort was when the right hon Gentleman made a quotation from a Cabinet document and was afterwards seriously chastised by the late Earl Lloyd George? It was on the occasion of the Stack assassination in Egypt, and the right hon Gentleman had to come down to the House of Commons and apologize for quoting without permission from a Cabinet document. In my submission all parties in the House in this case are seriously handicapped, because it should be to the interest of every party to see that there is no partisan disclosure of Cabinet papers unless the whole truth is made available. I ask you, Mr Deputy-Speaker, to accept my Motion that the papers be laid.

Mr Deputy-Speaker: All I can do is to quote briefly from the Manual the exact words which are probably better than those I gave in my own language. It says:

'If a Minister of the Crown quotes in the House a dispatch or other State paper which has not been presented to the House, he ought to lay it on the table. This rule is analogous to the rule observed in courts of law against quoting documents which are not produced in evidence. It cannot be applied to private documents or to documents which are alleged by the Minister to be of such a nature that their production would be inconsistent with the public interest.'

Mr Attlee: I certainly understood that the right hon Gentleman the Prime Minister was giving us the text of a dispatch. I think in that case and on all precedents that the whole of the document must be laid, and I submit that. I should like to know what we are having, whether this is some paraphrase or whether it is the actual dispatch because, after all, in fairness to the Government of the day, it is very easy to paraphrase things and to give them a twist. I should like to have the actual words.

MR SILVERMAN: Further to that point of order——

MR DEPUTY-SPEAKER: I can only deal with one point of order at a time. I was listening very carefully to what was said. I understood—and I was reinforced by the Prime Minister after the point of order was first raised—that he was paraphrasing and not quoting.

HON MEMBERS: No!

MR SILVERMAN: Further to that point of order. I respectfully submit that the Prime Minister did not say, and could not say, that he was paraphrasing. What he said, expressly, was that on 15 May 1950, a certain question—which he quoted to us—was addressed by the American Administration to Mr Ernest Bevin. By no possible twist of language can that be called a paraphrase. On the other point—as to whether it is in the public interest—I submit that the Prime Minister cannot possibly claim that it is not in the public interest to disclose it, because he has already disclosed it. Therefore, since this is not a paraphrase and it is not claimed to be in the public interest that it is not right to disclose it, I submit that the conditions of the Standing Order have been fully satisfied and the House is entitled to the papers. I beg leave to second the Motion which the right hon Gentleman moved.

MR DEPUTY-SPEAKER: It seems to me that that point is rather contradictory. If it has been quoted at all, it does not mean that it has all been quoted, and it may not be in the public interest to lay the paper before the House.

MR BEVAN: I understand from your quotation that the Manual makes no reference to a paraphrase.

MR DEPUTY-SPEAKER: Perhaps I have not read it very fully. If I quote from Erskine May I think the House may be satisfied. 'A Minister who summarizes'—I apologize to the hon Member if I have used the wrong word.

MR BEVAN: Then, in my submission, that puts my Motion entirely in order, because whether the right hon Gentleman was summarizing, paraphrasing or referring to, it was to a State paper that he was making reference. Indeed, he identified it, as my hon Friend has pointed out, by a date. In those circumstances, unless the right hon Gentleman shelters behind the question of public interest—and if he did he ought not to have been so cowardly as to have mentioned it. [*Interruption.*]

MR DEPUTY-SPEAKER: That Motion is not admissible in the middle of a speech.

HON MEMBERS: Oh!

THE PRIME MINISTER: I do not understand why there should be all this fear on the benches opposite.

MR GEORGE BROWN (Belper): We want it published.

THE PRIME MINISTER: I have already pointed out that the previous Administration committed themselves to action not confined to Korea. I am not making a quotation. I am stating a fact.

MR R. H. S. CROSSMAN (Coventry, East): Produce the document and prove it.

THE PRIME MINISTER: The United States Government did not give an unqualified agreement to the views of the late Administration because they did not think that their views provided sufficiently for cases of extreme military urgency. Subject to this, however, there was agreement, and I am entitled to inform Parliament of the fact. It was agreed between the United States Government and the late Socialist Administration that in certain circumstances and contingencies action would be taken not confined to Korea. Only they wished, quite properly in my opinion, that they should be consulted beforehand——

MR WILLIAM ROSS (Kilmarnock): Let us see it.

MR DEPUTY-SPEAKER: The right hon Member for Lewisham, South [Mr H. Morrison], had a perfectly quiet hearing and I think that the right hon Gentleman the Prime Minister might be allowed the same.

THE PRIME MINISTER: I am stating the facts perfectly clearly, as you will see when they are all set forward. They will show how very little ground there is for hon Gentlemen opposite making their slanderous accusations against us.

In September last year the Americans proposed that in the event of a breakdown of the armistice talks and the resumption of large-scale fighting in Korea, certain action should be taken of a more limited character. These proposals were accepted by the right hon Gentleman the Member for Lewisham, South, and they were endorsed by the then Prime Minister. Whereas in May the right of prior consultation had been required by the late Government in the specific instance, before our consent could be assumed, in the more limited proposals of September the Socialist Government did not insist upon this right. In both cases Her Majesty's Government consider that the decision of our predecessors was right and, in my view, in both cases it justifies the words which I used in the United States Congress, namely 'prompt, resolute and effective'.

MR H. MORRISON: I presume that the right hon Gentleman has got to the end of that part of his speech.

THE PRIME MINISTER: No, I have not. I was coming to the change of Government and what happened after that. If the right hon Gentleman wishes to say something now I shall gladly give way.

MR MORRISON: I was waiting until the right hon Gentleman had got to the end of his observations on the attitude of the late Government. I am not crying about it, because neither my right hon Friend the Leader of the Opposition nor I, nor any Members of the late Government, have anything to be ashamed of—but I am bound to say that I think it is unusual, doubtful in taste and constitutional propriety, for the Prime Minister to delve into the papers of his predecessors—as to the principle of which, and only the principle of which, there are well-known constitutional rules—and then come here, not with a fair statement of what took place, but with a partisan version, adjusted to his own constitutional ears and, when he is faced with a demand for papers, to hedge and evade, because of what he had done. As far as I am concerned—and I think I speak for my right hon Friend—I am quite willing for the papers to be fairly laid; but the right hon Gentleman is building up a precedent this afternoon for future administrations. There were long discussions with the United States about this and there is no analogy between what he is now discussing and what we were discussing earlier on. The whole point of the discussions to which he is now referring was what should be done in the case of our troops being attacked from the air from certain airfields. That is all. Obviously, from certain airfields, and it never went beyond that point—[HON MEMBERS: 'China.'] If hon Gentlemen opposite are quite incapable of listening, or are getting hysterical, I cannot help it.

MR DEPUTY-SPEAKER *rose*——

MR MORRISON: Certainly that was so——

MR DEPUTY-SPEAKER: I hope the right hon Gentleman will not wave to me to sit down when I stand up. [HON MEMBERS: 'Shame!'] I thought the right hon Gentleman waved to me to sit down when I stood up. If he did not, I beg his pardon, but I understood that he did. In any case, I rose to ask whether the right hon Member for Lewisham, South, was making a second speech.

MR MORRISON: I am in the hands of the Chair, but when a practice of this kind is introduced I think I have the right to deal with it. I was about to finish. If I was standing up while you were on your feet, Sir Charles, and if that was the point of your complaint, I apologize. Had I seen you stand up I should certainly have sat down at once. I finish by saying this. The discussions earlier on had very wide demands which were resisted——

MR JOHN MACLEOD (Ross and Cromarty): The right hon Gentleman has made one speech.

MR MORRISON: Hon Gentlemen opposite ought to be fair. It was confined later on to the point: 'What do you do if you are attacked from airfields over the border?'

CAPTAIN CHARLES WATERHOUSE (Leicester, South-East): From China?

MR MORRISON: Yes, that is right. In principle, one cannot stand by in that case and do nothing whatever about it, but there was insistence at our end that every effort should be made to see that there was consultation, because people can go a little bit off the rails in believing that something has happened when in fact something has not happened. Therefore, we required prior consultation. But that limited and direct military point about something happening in the field of military activities is a wholly different thing from this other argument in favour of widespread war and invasion.

MR S. SILVERMAN: On a point of order. I do really submit to you now, sir, that this position is becoming quite farcical without the papers. Here is a debate going on between the Prime Minister on one side and my right hon Friend on the other about the effect of certain communications made a long time ago, and about whether it is fair or unfair to make a comparison between those matters and the matters we are now discussing. In that dispute the rest of the House is completely lost. We do not know what the argument is about. The whole purpose of the Standing Order to which reference has been made was always to prevent the House from being put in the ridiculous position of having to listen to a debate between two of its Members about matters of which the rest of the House remained in ignorance. I say to you, sir, that it is quite impossible to continue this debate in this way without the House having access to the documents to which both right hon Gentlemen are referring.

MR DEPUTY-SPEAKER: I gave my Ruling perfectly clearly. I am of opinion that it was a summary which was made, and therefore the Prime Minister is quite in order.

MR SILVERMAN: How do you know it is a summary?

HON MEMBERS: Shame! Withdraw.

MR DEPUTY-SPEAKER: I did not say I knew. I said in my opinion it was, and I am quite entitled to my opinion.

MR SILVERMAN: With great respect to you, sir. You said that in your opinion this was a summary; and, indeed, it may well be so. What I am saying is that neither you nor any other Member of the House has any material whatever on which to form that or any other opinion.

MR DEPUTY-SPEAKER: Well, I have got my own opinion, and that is all I can go on in giving my ruling.

THE PRIME MINISTER: I do not know why there should be so much fear on the benches opposite.

MR CROSSMAN: Produce the papers.

THE PRIME MINISTER: It is a mere recital——

MR SILVERMAN: Is the right hon Gentleman afraid to produce the papers?

THE PRIME MINISTER: It is a mere recital——

MR A. C. MANUEL (Central Ayrshire): Is the right hon Gentleman afraid to produce the papers?

THE PRIME MINISTER: It is a mere recital of certain facts——

MR JAMES HUDSON (Ealing, North): On a point of order. Is the right hon Gentleman in order in stating that there is fear on the part of my right hon Friends when they have stated that they are willing to have published the documents about which the question has been raised? Has the right hon Gentleman the right, under your guidance, to make provocative remarks of that kind ascribing fear when he is not willing himself to have those documents examined?

MR DEPUTY-SPEAKER: If I could do anything to stop provocative remarks I certainly would, but I am afraid that they are in order.

THE PRIME MINISTER: We now come in the narrative which I am giving Parliament to the change of Government in this country. The General Election took place and Her Majesty's present advisers became responsible. The question was put to us by the United States: What would happen if a truce were agreed upon and then treacherously broken by the Chinese, greatly to the loss and disadvantage of the United Nations' armies, and if heavy fighting were resumed on a large scale? This involves one hypothesis on top of another, and on the whole it does not seem very likely to happen, especially if, as we hope, peace negotiations follow the present truce. Nevertheless, when allies or members of a common body like the United Nations are working together, the one who bears nine-tenths of the burden may well ask the others what they would do in certain circumstances, and Her Majesty's present Government agreed that it would be prudent to make clear that serious consequences would follow the breach of the terms of an agreed truce.

As I have already said today, and as I pointed out when I spoke a month ago, it is not possible, while military operations are going on, to state either positively or negatively exactly what those consequences might be. But let me make it clear that we conformed, in principle, to the policy of our predecessors. Indeed, in some respects it might be said that we did not commit ourselves even as far as they had done. Nevertheless, the action to which we agreed, like that of the Socialist Government before us, fully justified the description which I gave to Congress of being 'prompt, resolute and effective'. The dispatch in which our policy was set forth was approved by the Cabinet in December, and various communications were sent to other members of the Commonwealth. All this happened before my right hon Friend the Foreign Secretary and I set out for Washington. It is a fact that we did not discuss the matter further at any conferences in Washington with our American colleagues. They did not raise it, and we had received no answer to our reply. It is absolutely true therefore to say, as in the words of the Opposition Motion, that we adhered to the policy followed by the late Administration with regard to the Korean conflict and the relations between Great Britain and China. It is not true to say that I in any way departed from this position. There is no truth in the suggestion that any secret or private arrangements were made or any change of policy agreed upon, formally or informally, actual or implied, by me or my right hon friend the Foreign Secretary on these issues during our visit to the United States.

Having told the House these facts, some of which evidently surprised them, let me come to the address which I was invited to deliver to the Congress of the United States. I am very glad that the House wished to have this document circulated to them and that it should have been examined with so much attention. I cherish the hope that it will be found, as time passes, not to have been injurious to British and American relations which are, of course, all-important to our survival here at home and to the part we can play in averting a Third World War. It is the design and intense desire of the Soviet Union and its satellites and all its associates and fellow-travellers in many lands to drive a wedge between the British and American democracies and everything which tends to consolidate the mighty forces of the English-speaking world, upon which the hopes of United Europe also depend. Anything that secures that unity must be considered a service not only to freedom but to peace.

I must ask the indulgence of the House—if there is any of it left at the end of this statement, when, as I hope, some of the excitement has worn off as we go along—to let me present the background in my mind to what I said to Congress, for which I have been criticized by the official spokesman of the Opposition, the late Foreign Secretary. It was certainly no easy task, in the present circumstances of bitterness here at home and during election year in the United States, to choose the points on which to dwell. In July last, when I was a private person, a delegation of the American Senate, which had been sent round many countries, came to London, and during their visit they asked to see me, and I received them in my home. I was impressed by the fact that this powerful body was greatly disturbed by the anti-American feeling which they thought existed in the House of Commons. So I said to them: 'Do not be misled. The anti-American elements in Parliament are only a quarter of the Labour Party, and the Labour Party is only a half of the House. Therefore, you may say that one-eighth at the outside give vent to anti-American sentiments. The Labour Party as a whole, and the Government of the day, supported by the Conservative Party in this matter, are whole-heartedly friendly to the United States, and recognize and are grateful for the part they are playing in the world and of the help they have given to us.'

This was the message which I tried to give to Congress when I spoke, and in so doing I felt I was speaking—I hoped I was speaking—for the great majority of the present Parliament. Today, however, I must say that the attitude of a fraction of the late House of Commons and apparently of a larger proportion of the present House of Commons and the mood and temper which this Vote of Censure which the right hon Gentleman has moved personally upon me implies, can be made use of throughout the United States by Isolationist forces and by the anti-British elements which form a powerful minority throughout the great Republic. I say to those former Ministers whose records lie behind them and who have put their names to this Motion: Beware lest in petty manoeuvres about the leadership of the Socialist Party you do not injure causes to which you have pledged your honour and all our fortunes.

I had no wish or need to proclaim any new policy to Congress because, so far as policy is concerned, in Korea and China, we were only following in accordance with our own convictions the policy entered into and long pursued by our predecessors. But I hoped by my visit to the United States, first to establish an intimacy and an atmosphere of goodwill in the high circles that rule in Washington which would make it much easier in the future to deal with problems as they arise. I also felt a keen sympathy with the American people in their losses, and in having so many of their men serving so far away from home. I hoped also to give the Congress and people of the United States something of a glow and sense of our abiding friendship for them, and of our gratitude to them for all they have done for us, and for the causes which we also are resolved to serve with all our strength. On the whole I cannot feel, in spite of this party challenge, that I have failed in what I sought to do.

MRS BARBARA CASTLE (Blackburn, East) *rose*——

MR DEPUTY-SPEAKER: If the right hon Gentleman does not give way, the hon Lady must resume her seat.

MRS CASTLE: On a point of order.

MR DEPUTY-SPEAKER: Is it a point of order? If not, the hon Lady must resume her seat.

THE PRIME MINISTER: If the hon Member desires to ask if I have misstated anything or to correct me in any way, I should make an exception in her case because she always conforms to such a high level of courtesy.

MRS CASTLE: I would like to thank the right hon Gentleman and to ask him in all seriousness if, as he says, he made no new commitment additional to the one made by the late Government he can tell us why it has been widely reported in the United States responsible Press that there has been a change of policy in relation to Korea as a result of the right hon Gentleman's visit to the United States.

THE PRIME MINISTER: I am afraid that it is very difficult always to follow with complete accuracy all the movements represented in our own Press here at home, and I really cannot undertake to have a similar mastery of the mighty Press of the United States. But what I have stated here is a fact—that I made no new commitment in this field of foreign affairs of any sort or kind.

However, there are a few points of detail in this meticulous heresy hunt on which I will touch. The right hon Gentleman the Leader of the Opposition complained in his speech the last time we debated this matter that I had used the word 'United States' more often than I had used the words 'United Nations'. Surely, when speaking to the American Congress, whose troops have contributed nine-tenths of the fighting power and whose casualties are twenty times as great as all the other members of the United Nations put together, it would not be unnatural that I should speak of them and of their sacrifices. But technically I have a right to speak of the United States as a prime factor, because it is their commander who, under the United Nations, is the head of the Unified Command provided by the United States Government over all the forces employed. It only shows the limited and lopsided character of the Socialist trend of thought that they should complain that I did not deny the United States, in their own Assembly, the honour which belongs to them of being the supreme agent and chosen leader of the world instrument against Communist aggression.

The Leader of the Opposition admitted the other day that he agreed with what I had said to Congress about Formosa. This is what I said:

'I am very glad that, whatever diplomatic divergencies there may be from time to time about the procedure, you'——

that is, Congress—

'do not allow the Chinese anti-Communists on Formosa to be invaded and massacred from the mainland.'

It is the only thing that one could say about Formosa which could be agreed on both sides of this House and on both sides of the Congress of the United States, and, indeed, on both sides of the Atlantic Ocean. I thought it was rather a good selection—almost a bull's-eye. The fact that I selected it was, by implication, adverse to other statements which could be made on the subject and was, I believe, so understood and accepted by the great majority of my audience on that occasion.

Finally, I have been accused of speaking with two voices on different sides of the Atlantic. That is not true. I speak with the same voice, I can assure hon Members—the one to which they are having the opportunity of listening today. Wherever I speak, everything that I say on these occasions will no doubt be immediately reported or broadcast in the fullest manner on both sides of the Ocean. I am not conscious of the slightest change of thought or conviction on these important issues, and I do not retract a word that I have used on either occasion, here or on the other side, on our foreign outlook and policy.

Let me then sum up. First, there is no change in our policy towards the United States, towards the United Nations or towards the war in Korea. Secondly, on the circumstances which might justify action not confined to Korea, we have only followed and conformed to the policy for which the late Government were responsible and for which no two men were more personally responsible than the right hon Gentleman the Leader of the Opposition and the right hon Gentleman who has just spoken to us and who has thought it compatible with his personal candour and public behaviour to move this Motion. Thirdly, I believe that on both sides of the Atlantic we are convinced, as I have argued since the beginning of these troubles, that nothing could be more foolish than for the armies of the United States or the United Nations to become engulfed in the vast areas of China, and also that few adventures could be less successful or fruitful than for Generalissimo Chiang Kai-shek to plunge on to the mainland. Fourthly, if the truce is made only to be broken, a very grave situation will arise in which we must act as good comrades to our American and other United Nation friends and as a loyal member of the United Nations Organization. In this case, our action, like that contemplated by our predecessors, will be 'prompt, resolute and effective'.

Finally, the prospects of a truce being reached and respected in Korea will depend to a large extent upon the unity between Great Britain and the United States being proved to be not only unbreakable but growing stronger, and the attempts of all who seek to weaken or divide us being repulsed and condemned as they will be tonight by the House of Commons.

# DEFENCE

A SPEECH TO THE HOUSE OF COMMONS
5 MARCH 1952

---

22 *February—It is announced that Mr Steven Hardie has resigned from his
position of Chairman of the State-owned Iron and Steel Corporation.*
1 *March—Resignation of Egyptian Prime Minister, Aly Maher Pasha.
A new Government is formed by Ahmed Hilaly Pasha.
Heligoland is formally returned to German control.*

---

[*5 March* 1952

I beg to move: 'That this House approves the Statement on Defence,
1952 (Command Paper No. 8475).'

Although I feel that it will be in the general convenience that I
should make this statement, I can no longer speak as Minister of
Defence. On the day when I accepted the late King's Commission to
form a Government, I proposed the appointment of Lord Alexander
to this office, and His Majesty was greatly attracted by the proposal.
It was necessary, however, to obtain the assent of the Canadian
Government and to enable them to make all necessary arrangements
in due course. I had foreseen this delay, even if Lord Alexander were
willing to accept so onerous a task. In the meanwhile, I welcomed the
opportunity of surveying again this scene, which six years ago I knew
quite well, and noting the many changes which had taken place in the
interval. I will now, sir, on handing over these duties, commend this
White Paper, which has been circulated for some days, to the attention
of the House.

I must, however, put on record certain reserves which are necessary.
It takes a long time, and much Departmental work, as right hon Gentlemen opposite know, to prepare documents of this kind, and, for reasons
which the House will understand, we had to hasten its presentation
to Parliament. Meanwhile, events move constantly forward. Even the
present Service Estimates and the White Paper now before us must
be subject to unceasing scrutiny to eliminate all waste and, of course,
production may be affected by the non-delivery of machine tools and
by the shortage of dollar purchasing power.

I shall not occupy the House at any length with the Amendment
which I have heard that the Ministers mainly responsible in the late

Parliament for the conduct of our armaments—conduct good or bad—have placed on the Paper. We said something like this about them last year and we shall certainly not be offended by any opinion they may form of us. Our opinion, however, was based upon several years' experience of their methods. Theirs can only be a guess, and I trust will not be a hope. While we criticized the mistakes they made from time to time, and above all their repeated changes—vacillations, I think, was the word that was used—in the periods of compulsory National Service—now up, now down, now up again—we always gave them support in all necessary measures for national security. They always knew they had us with them if it ever came to a vote against their own tail. I do not suggest that we were with them yesterday morning. But this must have been a great help to any Government carrying on the business of the nation, especially as they were able at the same time to accuse us of seeking war and armament expansion whenever an Election came along. I hope that the Division which, I understand, we are to have tonight will not mean that the Socialist Party intend to revert to their pre-war practice of voting against necessary measures of defence, as they did against conscription before the war, and that they will at any rate consider themselves as bound to give general support to measures for which they themselves were originally responsible.

I will now endeavour to give some general account of the British defence position as I leave it. When I spoke to the House on defence at the beginning of December, I mentioned that there would certainly be a lag in carrying out the £4,700 million programme to which the late Government had given their support, and which they had increased from their original £3,600 million programme introduced earlier in the same year. This has manifested itself in a shortfall in 1951-52 of £120 million, as is shown in the White Paper. After the £3,600 million programme was proposed by the Socialist Government, they accepted an interim offer of 112 million dollars of aid from the United States of America in respect of machine tools. They had, indeed, stipulated for much larger help and relied on securing it in due course through the so-called 'burden-sharing exercise' then agreed in principle with the Americans. We are to receive this 112 million dollars progressively as machine tools are delivered, and delivery is only just beginning, but we hope it will be completed in about fifteen months' time.

Meanwhile the £4,700 million programme on which we are now engaged has not received aid on a scale in keeping with the defence burden undertaken by the late Prime Minister or with our needs. Following the recent studies of the Temporary Council Committee—

the 'three wise men', as they are sometimes called—the United States Government have allotted to us a sum of $300 million, none of which has yet been received. There is no question of reproaches on either side, but the fact remains, as I have foreshadowed, that the re-armament programme is much more likely to be carried out in four years than in three. Had it been carried out in three years as originally planned, the cost through the rise in prices would have been not less than £5,200 million. Of course, spread over a longer time the impact is less severe, but the total will be larger because of the added cost of the longer maintenance.

I should, however, be misleading the House if I led it to suppose that the delay which has taken place is due only to a shortfall in earnings by contractors for various reasons. We have pursued a def-inite policy of giving a somewhat higher measure of priority to materials needed for exports. The grave financial crisis under which we are labouring supplies more than sufficient explanation for this decision. We depend upon exports to purchase the imports of food and raw materials without which we can neither re-arm nor live as a solvent economic society. The expenditure set forth in the White Paper on Defence, and the Estimates of the three Service Departments which will shortly be brought before the House, represent the utmost that we can do during the present year; and it is certainly much more than any other country in the free world, except the United States of America, has attempted.

I am not suggesting that it is sufficient for our safety in the event of war, and I rely on the rapidly growing and already overwhelming power of the United States in the atomic bomb to provide the deter-rents against an act of aggression during the period of forming a defensive front in Western Europe. I hope and I believe that this will deter; but, of course, I cannot make promises or prophecies, or give guarantees. I accept responsibility only for doing all that was possible, having regard to the state of our defences and economic position when, after an interval of more than six years, the Conservative Party re-sumed office nineteen weeks ago.

My first impression on looking round the scene at home in Novem-ber as Minister of Defence was a sense of extreme nakedness such as I had never felt before in peace or war—almost as though I was living in a nudist colony. When the 6th Armoured and the 3rd Infantry Divions had left the country in pursuance of orders given or policies decided upon in the days of the late Administration, we had not a single Regular combat formation in the country; and although a sea-borne invasion does not seem likely in view of our and Allied naval power in surface ships, I thought it right to take what precautions were possible against paratroop descents, and I spoke, as the House may remember, about the importance of our showing the back of a hedgehog rather than the paunch of a rabbit to any unfriendly eye that might contemplate our island from above.

There were at that time a quarter of a million—249,000 was the exact figure—of officers and men in depots and training centres of many kinds. Most of these men, though uniformed British soldiers, had little combatant organization or value. They were engaged in preparing and maintaining the considerable Forces which had been spread about the world, in Europe, Asia and Africa. I considered it imperative to impart a combatant value to this potentially powerful body of British soldiers costing at least £400 a year each. Rapid progress has been made with this policy. All these men are now supplied with rifles and machine-guns and with ammunition, and they are organized into effective fighting groups which now comprise 502 mobile columns. These Forces are not, indeed, of the efficiency of the units on the Continent and overseas. Nor do they need to be. They are capable of giving a good account of themselves and of imposing a considerable deterrent upon any airborne adventure by being able to kill or capture the ones who land. The process has been greatly strengthened by the sailors ashore and the Air Force ground men, who also make important contributions. I am told by the weekly reports for which I called that morale is high, and that all ranks understand and have welcomed the reality and importance of their new duties, and that they like to feel that they are guarding their homes and their fellow-countrymen, as well as learning or teaching.

About two months ago, on the same line of thought, we started registration for the Home Guard. Since then 30,000 men have registered. This result is solid as far as it goes, but we still need many more volunteers. It may well be that many who have not joined have felt that the likelihood of war has somewhat receded, and they think they can make up their minds later on. They must be careful not to leave it too late. If war should come, it will be with violent speed and suddenness, and here at home, with almost all our Regular Army overseas, we must rely to an unusual extent on the Home Guard. Enough resolute men must be armed and ready to aid all the other forms of protection against raids, descents and sabotage. Although I had felt unable at first sight to provide the Home Guard with uniforms, and even with greatcoats or boots, I decided upon consideration to draw upon our mobilization reserves to the extent necessary to clothe at least the first 50,000. My successor may do better later on. I have directed the War Office to place, as speedily as possible, all orders for which their Estimates provide in the coming year with the clothing trade, in which a certain amount of unemployment and under-employment, especially in Northern Ireland, had begun to appear.

Thirdly, we have been able, by a severe combing of the tail—not the tail I mentioned just now, but nevertheless a very desirable and necessary process—to produce seven more Regular second battalions of famous regiments which had been imprudently disbanded. I would not use the word 'imprudently' if I had not long studied all the economic advantages of the Cardwell system, with a battalion abroad and a battalion at home, and an inter-flow of reserves and reinforcements between them. These battalions now raised, in one of which the hon Member for Ayrshire, South [Mr Emrys Hughes], took so much interest—the Black, what was it?

MR EMRYS HUGHES (Ayrshire, South): The Black Watch.

THE PRIME MINISTER: I thought it was the 'Black Welsh'. These will become effective units, and during the present autumn will give us at least a couple of Regular brigade groups to work with the numerous mobile columns I have already mentioned, and to go to any point of special danger in this island.

The expense involved in these changes is not great, and the gain in defensive and deterrent power resulting from them is out of all proportion to their cost in money. I hope the House will greet these measures with approval in that limited sphere of our dangers to which they are necessarily restricted. There is no doubt—honour where honour is due—that the Socialist policy of compulsory National Service in time of peace will enable Britain to create a much better and stronger Army than was ever possible before. Right hon Gentlemen opposite need not look too unhappy about it. We supported the late Government in this important decision, including their last step of raising the term of service to two years. Of course, the fruits of such a system only mature gradually. The yearly production of more than 100,000 well-trained reservists, representing the highest physical qualities of British manhood, will not only give us reserves for the Regular Army on mobilization of fine quality, but will also provide for the creation of a Territorial Army which, when mobilized, will be far superior in efficiency and readiness at the outbreak of war to anything that was previously possible.

The disturbed condition of the world compels us to maintain outside Europe the equivalent of nearly six Regular divisions, as well as the equivalent of five divisions, including three armoured divisions, which we now have on the Continent. As soon as a sufficiency of modernized equipment can be provided we shall have available for service abroad or at home a total of twenty-two divisions which are of a much more complex character than anything known in the late war, and a considerable proportion of which will be armoured. In the Centurion tank we have what many good judges believe to be the best tank now in service, and one which is in keen demand in Commonwealth and friendly countries. Not only is it of high military value, but it may also in time become a useful dollar-earning export. The plants which are being developed to make the Centurion tank will readily adapt themselves to the improved patterns which are on the way.

Before Christmas I spoke of the very heavy burden which distant foreign service throws upon our military organization, and of the 30,000 men always in the pipe-line back and forth. A very real and important economy in the true sense would be introduced into our military system if we could increase the number of men serving for three or four years with the Colours. There is no question of our prolonging the compulsory term of military service, as was industriously suggested at the General Election by those who were enjoying our support in their military policy.

MR HERBERT MORRISON (Lewisham, South): Who suggested it?

THE PRIME MINISTER: We have, however, started an active voluntary recruitment——

MR MORRISON: Who said it?

THE PRIME MINISTER: I hope hon Gentlemen opposite will not say this has not all been made clear to them.

MR MORRISON: Who said it? The right hon Gentleman, in telling his tale, has made an allegation. I am asking him who said this, and when?

THE PRIME MINISTER: We are very glad to see the right hon Gentleman on his feet again. Much of the difficulty—[HON MEMBERS: 'Answer.']—much of the difficulty we are suffering from——

MR MORRISON: Who said it?

THE PRIME MINISTER: Much of the difficulty—[HON MEMBERS: 'Answer.'] I have only a little time. Much of the difficulty we are suffering from——

HON MEMBERS: Answer.

MR SPEAKER: Order. If hon Gentlemen require an answer they must keep silent for it.

THE PRIME MINISTER: Much of the difficulty we suffer from on these occasions is that the leading men avoid making the charges, but a whispering campaign is started throughout the lower ranks and even the lowest ranks, which is a greater advantage to the statesmen who sit on the Front Bench opposite.

Mr A. C. Manuel (Ayrshire, Central): Down in the mud again.

Mr R. T. Paget (Northampton) *rose*——

The Prime Minister: I do not wish to be drawn into an altercation with the hon and learned Gentleman because it may not be generally known that his grandfather was the author of a very famous book to which I have always paid the most careful attention and in which he clears one of my forebears of a lot of disagreeable charges. Everyone knows the kind of campaign which was run, suggesting that we intended to increase the length of National Service. [*Interruption.*] I am so glad to be able to excite a sense of shame. [*Interruption.*] We really must get back to the laborious administrative details to which I had hoped to confine myself. [Hon Members: 'Tell the truth.'] Let me remind the House that we are not on any account going to increase the compulsory term. We have, however, started an active voluntary recruitment.

Mr E. Shinwell (Easington): We started it.

The Prime Minister: I am delighted to share any credit which can be found with the right hon Gentleman, but I must always be careful not to pay him too many compliments because his friends below the Gangway call that fulsome, and he himself might easily ask me some rude questions to put himself 'on side'.

Mr Shinwell: I am not going to ask the right hon Gentleman any rude questions. [Hon Members: 'Hear, hear.'] All that I am seeking to do is to ask him to give us the facts about this new measure for voluntary recruitment. I interjected to say that the right hon Gentleman's Government did not start this. It was, in fact, started by the late Government. The right hon Gentleman may make a song and dance about it, but I ask him just to tell the truth.

The Prime Minister: I have no desire to state anything but what is the truth. [Hon Members: 'Oh.'] Nor do I intend to. I say we have, however, started—we, the British nation, have, however, started—an active voluntary recruitment with incentives in pay for short Regular engagements of three or four years, particularly designed to attract National Service men and those about to be called up. This is making good progress. In the Air Force about 43,000 young men have taken these engagements in the past two years. In the three months—the right hon Gentlemen talked about telling the truth and he may have a bit of it—since the Army opened a similar engagement, we have gained about 1,000 from serving National Service men, and over 8,000 from civil life.

Mr Sydney Silverman (Nelson and Colne): Unemployment has been rising the whole time.

THE PRIME MINISTER: I thought that the right hon Gentleman was going to claim all the credit for this. Now the hon Gentleman comes in to take it away from him. The latter are young men who would otherwise have been called up for National Service in the near future. They were not expecting to be unemployed. They were expecting to be called up by conscription in the near future. Instead of being called up, they take on this long service and have beneficial pay. This is a most helpful development in our Army organization, and really, one might say, worth its weight in gold when one thinks of the cost of moving men to and fro from here to Hong Kong. That is all I am going to say about the Army this afternoon.

When the Navy Estimates are introduced tomorrow, the First Lord will give a full account of the naval position. Vote A at 147,000 is about the same as when I introduced the Navy Estimates of 1914. When I then introduced them it was 146,000. When I returned to the Admiralty at the beginning of the Second World War, Vote A was at 129,000. The growth of the Naval Air Arm more than accounts for the increase since 1939. As in the past, Vote A comprises mainly long-service men with valuable, important high-class reserves—that great background and foundation of hereditary seamen, generations going back to generations, gathered round our great seaports and towns, furnishing us with a magnificent supply of youth, sustained by the tradition of their fathers.

The volume of new construction is, of course, less in tonnage than in 1914, and much less than in 1939. But whereas a ton of new construction for, let us say, destroyers—that very vital element—cost in 1914 £150 a ton and in 1939 £325 a ton, the present new construction, with all the improvements and apparatus vital to modern efficiency, and with all the decline in the purchasing power of money, costs £700 a ton—that is to say, nearly five times as much. The whole maintenance and organization of the Royal Navy has also become vastly more complex and expensive than in former times. I am by no means satisfied with the progress so far made in pruning and purging. Nevertheless, the enormous increase in complexity is a dominating factor— I admit that. There is, of course, no potentially hostile surface battle fleet afloat. The Russians have three old battleships, about twenty cruisers, and a considerable annual building programme; but all the surface navies which exist on the waters of the world are comprised and are being woven together in the North Atlantic Treaty Organization. As large vessels take a long time to build, it is not likely that this situation will be altered in, let us say, the next five years.

None the less, the Royal Navy has three main threats to meet, each of which, if successful, would affect our survival in this island. I will state them in their order of gravity as they affect us—the mine; the U-boat—for that is what I call potentially hostile submarines, distinguishing between a wicked weapon used for wrong purposes and the honourable use of the submarine in the ordinary course of naval business; it is a good thing to separate them—[*Interruption.*]—I thought that would appeal to the hon Member for Nelson and Colne [Mr S. Silverman]—and the threat from the air, ever-growing in its shore-based power. It is upon improving and augmenting our resources to withstand these threats that our new construction and research of all kinds is in fact concentrated. Anti-mine and anti-U-boat measure absorb the overwhelming proportion of our new construction and material development. They also dominate our training, which includes constant anti-U-boat and mine-sweeping exercises. Here we also welcome the new shore mine-watching forces now being raised from men in civilian rig, who may well be as valuable to the Royal Navy and to the life of the island as are sailors afloat.

The House, I feel, may be assured that when the new frigates and mine-sweepers come into service they will be a proof of the perennial British ability to produce novel designs of high performance. From all that I have been able to learn and understand as a member of the Institution of Naval Architects—[*Laughter.*]—honorary, of course; I have made a few suggestions from time to time—I think the constructive Department of the Admiralty are entitled to take pride in their inventiveness and modernity. The difficulty is not only design or quality in these spheres of anti-U-boat and anti-mine warfare. It is numbers that count, and every improvement, however necessary, in speed or apparatus is the enemy of numbers. I think that progress is being made on right lines in what are necessarily reconciliations of opposing needs. I spoke just now about the threat from the air. This threat, of course, cuts both ways, and the important fleet of aircraft carriers which already exists and is developing, as well as the expanding range of shore-based aircraft, are vital factors in coping with mining and U-boat attack.

However, do not let anyone suppose that the problems have been solved or that these two dangers—the mines and the U-boat—present themselves in a less fateful form to us, or less important to the United States, than at the beginning of the Second World War. On the contrary, the dangers are greater, and the means of coping with them by rapid improvizations of civilian craft, like yachts and trawlers, are no longer effective against the new fast U-boat types, of which, however, the Soviets have, happily, at present only a few. Our aircraft carrier fleet is also a powerful defence. The newest aircraft carrier has just now come into service.

MR EMRYS HUGHES: What did it cost?

THE PRIME MINISTER: It bears the name of the *Eagle*, descended from her original namesake, commissioned in the first Elizabethan era.

MR EMRYS HUGHES: What did it cost?

THE PRIME MINISTER: I shall be revealing no technical secrets if I say that the design and construction of the new *Eagle* are of a very different kind from those of her ancestor, for fashions have changed in all sorts of ways in this as in other spheres. The expense is no doubt very much greater.

MR EMRYS HUGHES: It cost £15 million.

THE PRIME MINISTER: Why make these attacks upon the Front Bench opposite? Surely the hon Member for Ayrshire, South, might leave to the Government the necessary task of defending themselves against the Opposition instead of making this flank attack upon his right hon Friend who formerly represented the Admiralty in this House. To spend £15 million on an aircraft carrier—good gracious; fancy if the Tories had done a thing like that!

I now come to the third great Service. It is our air power which causes me the most anxiety. Deliveries of modern aircraft are seriously behind the original programme, which, in consequence, has had to be revised. As the result, the Air Force, though maintaining its size, is not being re-equipped with modern machines as rapidly as it should be. Our greatest need is for modern aircraft in the squadrons. For example, we have no swept-back wing fighters in service, such as the American F86 and the Russian MiG15. It is true, as the Leader of the Opposition said in our debate last December, that it is not unnatural in this competition of types for one nation temporarily to outstep its rivals. It is rather unfortunate, however, if war should come at a moment when the enemy has a great advantage in modernity. It is not a good arrangement to have the highest class of air pilots and all the personal staffs required and for them to have only second-best weapons to fight with.

MR S. SILVERMAN: Will the right hon Gentleman give way?

THE PRIME MINISTER: No, sir. I prefer to deal with this in my own way. The problem of when to change from existing production to an improved type is not a new one. It has occurred in all countries during the increasingly rapid improvement of weapons in the last hundred years. It has never occurred with the same significance as in the air forces, which must always be to some extent in a state of flux. I recognize the difficulty of the position, but the late Government, who are so critical in their anticipations of our ability, certainly did not produce good solutions. Here, as in other spheres, our inheritance leaves much to be desired. It is now that decisions taken soon after the war press upon us. If, indeed, all that was then forecast had come to pass, our problems would be simpler, but the appearance of the MiG15 in Russian squadrons in 1949, which the Russians now have in great numbers, marked a considerable advance in aeronautical design. This has falsified many predictions.

The ordering of new types off the drawing-board, with all the risks that attend such decisions, can help in part but cannot itself fill the gap, which is too large for safety. This gap now faces us as a consequence of estimates which events have now disproved. We are making great efforts to advance the production of the new Hawker fighter and also of the Swift, another first-class aeroplane designed to fill the same day-interceptor role. These types are much newer than the Soviet MiG15, but I must make it clear that we shall not have in the Service in the near future, or, indeed, for some time, anything like adequate numbers of these superior modern fighters. It will require intense exertions to build up production to the necessary level, and also to gain and to keep a lead in design.

I have directed that super-priority should be given to the production of the latest and best types of fighter aircraft. This does not mean that everything else is to be knocked about in their exclusive interest. The assertion of priorities, without the necessary refinements of application, might well be most injurious to production as a whole. I have seen undue assertion of priorities do harm in both world wars. The whole subject is far better understood now than it was even during the last war, and in this light I affirm that the first need of our defence is the re-arming of the Royal Air Force with weapons worthy of their daring and skill. The expansion of the number of aircraft in the front line of the Royal Air Force, or the improvement in their quality, must not mean an equal increase in its overall manpower. A longer period of training is, however, now necessary, not only for pilots and navigators but for some of the technical ground trades. The training organization of the Royal Air Force to produce in good time the necessary men is advancing. The response to the new trade structure, which was introduced a year ago and designed to offer a career with proper opportunities of advancement, has so far met with a most promising response. I am sure that the right hon and learned Member for Rowley Regis and Tipton [Mr A. Henderson], whose father I knew so well, will be very gratified, as he was responsible for that.

As I said in reply to a Question a few days ago, the other Commonwealth countries are kept informed of the defence plans of the United

Kingdom and are consulted whenever any of our commitments are likely to be of particular concern to them. Canada is, of course, a member of the North Atlantic Treaty Organization. But we must make sure that our contacts grow ever closer. The House will welcome the announcement made recently by the Canadian Minister of National Defence that, as part of the North Atlantic system of mutual help, we are to receive in due course from Canada a number of high-class fighter aircraft. F86 is the label given to them. The frames will be made in Canada, the engines in America and the Royal Air Force will fly them. These aircraft will be a welcome addition to our strength at home and in Europe—[*Interruption.*]—I think I said that the negotiations were begun under the right hon and learned Gentleman the Member for Rowley Regis and Tipton.

MR ARTHUR HENDERSON (Rowley Regis and Tipton): And they were completed, if I may say so.

THE PRIME MINISTER: May I not share with him in this event? It is far from me to wish to grasp any credit from anyone. Not even the late Foreign Secretary will say that I wish to rob him of any claim of his share in foreign affairs.

The Prime Minister of Australia has today announced to the Australian Parliament at Canberra that his Government have decided to send a fighter wing to the Middle East to operate with the Royal Air Force in that area. The wing will consist of two squadrons of the Royal Australian Air Force and should be ready to leave Australia for the Middle East next June. The actual station of the wing in the area will be decided later on. One possibility is Cyprus. I know that I shall be expressing the views of all parties in the House when I say that we warmly welcome this further practical contribution by Australia to the defence of the free world and of the interests of the British Commonwealth. We shall be very glad to have these Australian squadrons working with us in the task of defending the Middle East against external aggression should any occur.

I have not attempted this afternoon to deal either with the general problem of European defence or the still wider issues represented by what I think we have got sufficiently habituated to call NATO. We shall have a debate at the end of the month when the fruitful outcome of the Lisbon Conference and other questions larger than those comprised in the White Paper can be discussed. But I should like before I sit down, if the House will permit me, to repeat in substance what I said before upon the reason why I do not believe that war is imminent or inevitable, and why I believe that we have more time, if we use it wisely, and more hope of warding off that frightful catastrophe from our struggling, ill-informed, bewildered and almost helpless human race.

I am glad to find that the words I used two years ago in this House still express my thoughts. This is what I said:

'There never was a time when the deterrents against war were so strong. If penalties of the most drastic kind can prevent in our civil life crime or folly, then we certainly have them here on a gigantic scale in the affairs of nations. . . . The penalties have grown to an extent undreamed of; and at the same time, many of the old incentives which were the cause of the beginning of so many wars, or features in their beginning, have lost their significance. The desire for glory, booty, territory, dynastic or national aggrandisement; hopes of a speedy and splendid victory with all its excitement—and they are all temptations from which even those who only fight for righteous causes are not always exempt—are now superseded by a preliminary stage of measureless agony from which neither side could at present protect itself.

'Another world war would begin by both sides suffering as the first step what they dread most. Western Europe would be overrun and Communized. . . . On the other hand, at the same time, Soviet cities, airfields, oilfields and railway junctions would be annihilated; with possible complete disruption of Kremlin control over the enormous populations who are ruled from Moscow. Those fearful cataclysms would be simultaneous, and neither side could at present, or for several years to come, prevent them. Moralists may find it a melancholy thought that peace can find no nobler foundations than mutual terror. But for my part, I shall be content if these foundations are solid, because they will give us the extra time and the new breathing space for the supreme effort which has to be made for a world settlement.'

That is what I said two years ago, that is what I am not ashamed to repeat here now.

I thank the House for its courtesy and kindness to me. The interruptions which have occurred will not be deprived of the plea that they were unprovoked, for we have our own system of public business and of discussing our affairs across the Floor of the House while dealing with grave matters. In conclusion, the House will realize that I cannot claim that the estimates and schemes presented in the White Paper go as far as the proposals of the Socialist Government. This is partly due to physical causes, which invariably delay large rearmament programmes, but it is also due to the present Cabinet's decisions to increase the emphasis on exports at the expense of the speed of the rearmament programme.

The motives which inspired the Leader of the Opposition, the former Minister of Defence, and the Service Ministers of those days, to embark upon this great scheme of rearmament, are creditable to their military zeal, but it was a scheme loosely and hastily framed and declared, and only five months intervened between the £3,600 million plan and its being superseded by that of £4,700 million. Moreover, they did not take sufficient account of the serious financial situation into which they were moving and of which we are today the anxious legatees. It is a curious commentary on British politics that it should fall to a Conservative Government in the face of dire financial stress to have to reduce or slow down the military defence programme and expenditure on which the Socialist Government had embarked and to which they had committed the nation. We must, however, be governed by realities, and while trying our utmost to carry out the programme we must not mislead the country into expectations beyond what its life energies can fulfil.

# DEATH OF SIR STAFFORD CRIPPS

A SPEECH TO THE HOUSE OF COMMONS
23 APRIL 1952

---

8 *March—Following the defeat in the French Chamber of M. Faure, M. Antoine Pinay forms a new Government.*

11 *March—Mr Butler, Chancellor of the Exchequer, introduces the Budget. Victory for General Eisenhower in the New Hampshire Republican Primaries.*

13 *March—General Eisenhower wins Minnesota Republican Primaries.*

22 *March—Death of Mr D. S. Senanayake, Prime Minister of Ceylon.*

29 *March—President Truman announces that he will not be a candidate for the Democratic Nomination at the Presidential Elections in November.*

1 *April—United States State Department repudiates the statement made in Tokyo by Mr Dan Kimball, Secretary of the Navy, that the United States would 'stand on the side-lines and cheer' if the Chinese Nationalists attacked the Communist-held mainland from Formosa.*

11 *April—It is announced from the White House that General Eisenhower has asked to be relieved of his post as Supreme Commander Allied Powers in Europe by approximately June 1 and placed on the inactive list after his return to the USA. Mr Lovett, with the approval of the President, agrees to this request.*

*It is announced that General Matthew Ridgway, Supreme Commander Allied Powers in Japan, will succeed General Eisenhower.*

*It is announced at Clarence House that HM The Queen has 'declared her will and pleasure that she and her children shall be styled and known as the House and Family of Windsor, and that their descendants, other than female descendants who marry, and their descendants, shall bear the name of Windsor'.*

12 *April—Mr Holland, Prime Minister of New Zealand, announces that his Government has decided to dispatch the Vampire Fighter Squadron of the Royal New Zealand Air Force to the Middle East in September.*

21 *April—Death in Zürich of Sir Stafford Cripps, aged 62.*

---

[23 *April* 1952

Since we met here yesterday we have learned of the death of a states-man of national pre-eminence who had long served with distinction in the House of Commons, and it is in accordance with recent precedents that I should attempt to pay some tribute, necessarily brief and inadequate, to his memory. Stafford Cripps was a man of force and fire. His intellectual and moral passions were so strong that they not only inspired but not seldom dominated his actions. They were strengthened and also governed by the working of a powerful, lucid intelligence and by a deep and lively Christian faith. He strode through life with a remarkable indifference to material satisfaction or worldly advantages. There are few members in any part of the House who have not differed violently from him at this time or that, and yet there is none who did not regard him with respect and with admiration, not only for his abilities but for his character.

His friends—and they were many, among whom I am proud to take my place—were conscious, in addition to his public gifts, of the charm of his personality and of the wit and gaiety with which he enlivened not only the mellow hours, but also the hard discharge of laborious business in anxious or perilous times. In all his complicated political career he was the soul of honour and his courage was proof against every test which the terrible years through which we have passed could bring.

Having sat with him in the wartime Cabinet, which he joined in 1942 and of which he was always a member—or, as we called it in those days, a constant attender—I can testify to the immense value of his contributions to our discussions. There was no topic I can remember —no doubt right hon Gentlemen opposite have longer experiences of their own—on which he did not throw a clarifying light and to which he did not often bring a convenient and apt solution. Most of us have in our memories the distinction with which he filled the great office of the Exchequer and how easily he explained and interpreted the problems of finance. We all could not always agree with his policy, but everyone was grateful for its exposition.

As a master of words and dialectic both in the law and Parliament, he had also a most practical and organizing side to this nature. During the First World War he managed a small arms factory, and its excellence and efficiency were brought to my notice when I was Minister of Munitions. It was this that prompted me to offer him the most complex business of the Ministry of Aircraft Production in the Second World War, after he ceased to lead this House, and I have very little doubt that his conduct of it was not only most helpful to our interests but highly congenial to his nature. His was a mind that fastened itself as easily upon small as upon great things, and to him detail was not a burden but, often, almost a relief.

One of the most recent precedents for the intervention I am making today was when the House paid its tribute to Oliver Stanley, who, like Stafford Cripps, was in our own time a member for Bristol. Both had qualities which will long be cherished in that famous city, where they were so well known.

It is not for me in these few words to attempt to epitomize the place which Stafford Cripps will bear in the history of our life and times, or of his contribution to their political philosophy; but that, as a man, he had few equals in ability or virtue will be generally affirmed by his contemporaries, and that he brought an unfailing flow of courage, honour and faith to bear upon our toils and torments will be attested by all who knew him and, most of all, by those who knew him best.

Our hearts go out to the noble woman, his devoted wife, who through these long months of agony, mocked by false dawns, has been his greatest comfort on earth. To her we express profound sympathy, and we trust that she may find some solace in the fact that Stafford's memory shines so brightly among us all.

# GRAND HABITATION OF THE PRIMROSE LEAGUE

A SPEECH AT THE ROYAL ALBERT HALL, LONDON
25 APRIL 1952

It is a great pleasure for me to preside once again at your annual celebration and to do so this time as head of a Conservative and National-Liberal Government. [*Cheers.*] I am glad to hear that the work of the Primrose League is proceeding successfully throughout the country. There never was a time when this was more important or when the great causes for which we stand were more in need of steadfast and ardent support. Now, when we are passing through a period of effort and sacrifice, is the time for the utmost energies of the Primrose League to be exerted.

Her Majesty's Government is trying its best to undo the harm of six years of Socialist rule which have brought us to the verge of national bankruptcy and left to us a hard task to get back to the high road, stony and uphill though it may be, by which alone we can recover our position in the world and revive the moral and economic strength of our island society. Mr Attlee would not have had the General Election when he did but for the fact that he knew he would leave his successors a burden which he himself feared to bear. We have accepted the responsibility, not for what has been done in the past, not for what strikes over into the present from the past, but for doing out utmost to put things right even though, as we all know, the process must be long, painful and in many ways unpopular.

The steps we have taken so far have already brought a definite improvement in our international position. Mr Eden's conduct of foreign affairs and Mr Butler's courageous and comprehensive Budget have won universal recognition abroad among our friends and widespread agreement at home. Time must be required for the severe cuts we had to make in our consumption and expenditure to bring about their full results. It is my belief that in three or four years we shall be able to present to our fellow-countrymen a situation in which world peace will be more secure and British solvency firmly re-established. More than that, it is our faith, based upon resolve, that there will be a sense of improvement in conditions here at home which will be apparent throughout all classes of our fellow-countrymen.

Meanwhile, we are confronted in Parliament by an Opposition, which regardless of the reproach that falls upon them for the plight into which they have brought the nation during their long reign of power, seeks only to gain party advantage by opposing the necessary steps we are forced to take to remedy the evils that they largely, and even sometimes consciously created. We shall not be turned from our course by their clamour or obstruction. They are themselves most bitterly divided on the main issues of the day and the struggle for the leadership of their party is going on. They try to heal or conceal these differences as much as possible by spitting out their spite upon us. I cannot remember a time—and my experience is a very long one—when public difficulty and party strife have both risen to such heights together.

Very often a common sense of the dangers of the country has caused an abatement of party strife, but in this case we still seem to be living in an electioneering atmosphere, and it is only by long, steady, faithful and skilful administration that we shall get into the cooler and calmer atmosphere—so necessary to enable our country, by natural fruition, to attain its highest expression. Here let me say how much we owe to the Conservative Members of the House of Commons—and I see here my friend Sir Ian Fraser—who, by their regular attendances on all occasions, especially at long night sittings, have enabled us to maintain an average majority double that which we gained at the polls. I hope that you will carry this impression away with you to your homes and constituencies. Conservative organizations throughout the country should recognize the services which their Members are rendering, and the great severity which Parliamentary life has for the time being assumed.

It does not follow, however, that these harsh conditions will rule indefinitely. Once it is realized and proved that threats and bullyings do not deter us from our national duty, that we care nothing for abuse, except from people we respect, that the Government are proceeding upon a large design which unfolds itself step by step, and has to be proved, not by mere assertion but by results, to be serving the national interest, a more agreeable temper may prevail in the House of Commons. This, however, is only a hope of mine, based upon the saying that trees do not grow up to the sky. Anyhow, whatever happens, we are not afraid to face it. We are not asking for any favours; we shall do our duty not for any party or class or interest in the nation, but for the country as a whole. We shall do our duty without fear or favour and we are confident that so long as we maintain that attitude and are seen by the nation to be doing so, we shall be suffered to carry out our difficult task.

Among the Members of the House of Commons, or the Government, who do their hardest work, none stands out with more distinction than my friend the Home Secretary. In the arduous discharge of his duties (both national and party) he is second to none. On Monday he will explain to the House of Commons the measures which we have taken, and are going to enforce, to protect the travelling public and Londoners from the needless series of annoyances and deprivations which the Socialists—by their legislation—have cast upon them. We wish him good luck in this task. I only regret that ill-health will not enable Mr Maclay, the Minister of Transport, to introduce the Motion we have placed upon the Order Paper of the House of Commons. But in the Home Secretary we have a Cabinet Minister who knows every aspect of this story, not only of what has been made public, but what lies ahead in the near future, and we shall await with the greatest interest his opening of the debate on Monday. We are very fortunate in having him with us here today, and it is with confident anticipation that I now call upon him to address you.

# THE CONSERVATIVES' FIRST SIX MONTHS

A PARTY POLITICAL BROADCAST
3 MAY 1952

---

28 *April—Japanese Peace Treaty comes officially into force.*
    *Mr Churchill announces that instead of Lord Waverley, Lord Radcliffe will succeed Lord Cohen as Chairman of the Royal Commission on Taxation.*

---

[3 *May* 1952

At the Cup Final this afternoon I couldn't help taking a great deal of interest in the work of the goalkeepers. There seemed to be something —or several things—in common with their job as with that of Prime Minister. I only hope that as Prime Minister I may do as well as both the goalkeepers did this afternoon.

My theme, my friends, tonight, may be called 'The First Six Months'. It is in fact almost exactly six months since the Conservative Party became responsible for managing British affairs. But our first six months cannot be judged apart from the background of the previous six years. Mr Attlee's Government had a hard time in their last two years of office. They had to live between General Elections with a majority of only six. They were able to pursue a firm foreign policy of resistance to aggression abroad, and to set on foot a very large re-armament programme at home, because, and only because, they could count, for these purposes, on the support of a Conservative Opposition nearly as strong as they were themselves.

But the results of their six-year record of extravagance and waste, of over-spending and of living upon American money had brought us all within sight of a dead stop. National insolvency was what stared us in the face when we took over. The Socialist fault is two-fold: first, that when they saw and felt what was happening they did not take any of the necessary measures to preserve our solvency because these would lose them votes; and secondly, that having been defeated, they are trying to make all the party capital they can out of the difficulties they left their successors, which they themselves had been unable to face.

We knew well at the General Election that hard trials and problems would await us if we won. For this reason, speaking with the authority of Leader of the Conservative Party, I gave a solemn warning in my broadcast of October 8, a fortnight before the polls, while the Election fight was in full vigour, and this is what I said:

'We make no promises of easier conditions in the immediate future. Too much harm has been done in these last six years for it to be repaired in a few months. Too much money has been spent for us to be able to avoid another financial crisis. It will take all our national strength to avoid the downhill slide and after that we shall still have to work up.'

That is what I said, before the votes were counted. It is from that starting-point that I claim that our first six months should be judged. I must admit that when we took office we found things much worse than we knew or expected. At the time of the General Election we were spending abroad at the rate of £800,000,000 a year more than we were earning: and if hard and decisive action had not been taken, there and then, when we came into power, by the new Chancellor of the Exchequer, Mr Butler, and followed throughout what is called the Sterling area, its whole reserve and our whole reserve of gold and dollar securities would have been exhausted by the end of this summer. For an island of fifty million people, which grows only enough food for thirty million, and has to buy its raw materials wherewith to earn its living from all over the world, that would have been a shocking disaster, causing far more privation and hardship than all the cuts we have made or are likely to make in imports.

These, my friends, have already been severe. We have cut no less than £600 million from our purchases abroad, and other unpleasant remedies like raising the bank rate have been taken. The full effect of these acts of national self-denial and self-restraint has not yet been felt. The medicine is bitter, and the taste lingers; while the cure, on the other hand, has only just begun. If I tell you some favourable facts I hope you will not exaggerate them or think that we are out of our troubles. On the contrary, we cannot yet claim that we are paying our way in our foreign purchases.

There is, however, an improvement. We are not eating up our limited resources so fast. Here are some figures. The average monthly loss of our reserves for the last three months of 1951 was $311 million. In January it was $299 million. In February $266 million; in March only $71 million. So much for the first quarter of 1952. The April figure will be better still and the pace at which we were going downhill has greatly slackened. If our present progress continues, and is not upset by world misfortunes, we ought, before the end of the year, to be paying our way. After all, that is only what every household—every man and woman in the land—has to do, to preserve their self-respect and independence. Another favourable sign is that the reputation of the pound sterling abroad has improved. The devaluation from which we suffered in 1949 was a heavy blow. It meant that we had to send out more exports for less imports. We trust, up to the present at any rate, so far, that we have saved the country from a repetition of this.

Up to this moment I have been talking only about our buying power abroad. If we lose that we should be like a swimmer who cannot keep his head above water long enough to get a new breath. (No fun at all!) But the same kind of evils happen here inside the country when prices and wages and profits continue to chase each other up in a fantastic spiral. That simply means that the money we earn buys less and less. We have not, so far, overtaken this evil and peril. We are swimming against the stream trying to keep level with a bush on the bank. We shall persevere faithfully to the utmost of our strength, but a truly national effort is needed to make headway.

It was my hope, when I became responsible, that just as we in Opposition had supported what was done in the national interest in foreign policy and defence by the Labour Government, so they would help in matters at home which were national rather than party. For this reason, after taking office, I wanted to get out of the electioneering atmosphere and make sure that our whole national strength was available for the matters of survival with which we are confronted.

We are in the strange position that, although four-fifths of each of the great parties agree about four-fifths of the things that ought to be done at home and abroad, and although if the worst happened we should all sink or swim together, we seem to be getting ever more bitterly divided as partisans, and Mr Attlee even talks of another General Election. I cannot think of anything worse for any country, and this country above all other countries, than to have a General Election every year, and for us all to dwell in constant violent party strife, trying to set one half of the people against the other, bidding against each other for votes, and with no Government capable of doing the unpopular things that have to be done. Even in quiet and easy times it would be a very poor service to true democracy. Now, in our crisis and peril, it would be lunacy.

The date of a General Election does not, however, rest with Mr Attlee, or with the Leader of the Opposition whoever he may be, or may be going to be. We have the will, and I believe we have the power, to continue for another three or four years of steady, calm and resolute Government at home and abroad, making our mistakes—

who does not?—but devoting our life-effort to what we believe is the national interest; and we ask to be judged by results and by deeds rather than by words, and for a fair time to bring them about.

In our general policy, we are trying our best to encourage effort and enterprise and to evoke the creative genius of the British race. We think it is a good thing to 'set the people free' as much as possible in our complicated modern society—to set them free from the trammels of State control and of bureaucratic management. Of course, everything cannot be done at once, or even in six months. But quite a lot has been done already. And more will be apparent as the months unfold.

Next month the burden of PAYE will be lifted off the shoulders of another two million of our people and sixteen million in all benefit from tax relief. The harder they work the more they will benefit. But with incentives to the strong there must also march compassion for the weak and poor. The addition which will be made in the autumn to old age and all other insurance benefits will be a real relief if the cost-of-living can be controlled. We pledged ourselves that we would undo, as far as was possible, the harm and waste arising from the nationalization of steel and of road transport. Transport is more urgent than steel. Steel is being managed by the same competent hands which in later years have made it the foremost factor in our export industries. Our Bill is already drafted, and will be presented to Parliament this year. But it is in the reform of our transport system that I believe the most fertile hope of a genuine economic and social improvement is possible. The action we have taken on fares has shown our resolve to keep State industries under proper control and to protect the ordinary public from the rigid workings of the official machine.

In other fields, some minor fields, some larger, we have promptly accepted the recommendations of the Cotton Import Committee that spinners should be allowed the choice of buying their cotton from private sources. All the trade in timber is now in private hands. We have done our best to throw off some of the more irksome and needless restraints that have been laid upon the nation in these past years. We thought that you had carried your identity cards about long enough. We did not see why boys and girls should not take the General Certificate examination at the age their teachers thought they could pass it.

But it is over housing that the most definite advance has taken place. We in the Conservative Party have always held and always promised that housing should have first place in our social programme. We have given it first place. And already there are welcome results. The figures for the first three months of this year announced yesterday by Mr

Macmillan, the Minister of Housing, are certainly heartening to us all. They will bring hope to thousands on the waiting lists. They should provide encouragement to the fine efforts of the building industry. And—may I say?—they have given keen pleasure to us in the Government and our supporters as we push our way through the tangles of the times, and the ill-will of those who created many of the difficulties. In the first quarter of this new year, nearly 10,000 more houses were completed, nearly 30,000 more houses were building; and more than 15,000 more houses were begun than in the same period of last year. Nor are the houses all of one type. There are both more for letting and more for sale; more council houses and more privately built houses. Notice please, my friends, the word 'more'; that is our watchword in housing: 300,000 a year we proclaimed as our target. There is a bull's-eye we mean to hit. Of course, all our hopes of making things better at home depend upon keeping the peace. The fear of another world war casts its dark shadow upon every land on both sides of 'the Iron Curtain' that divides mankind. I have the feeling that this fear is becoming universal and that it is sinking deeper into all human hearts, and from that I draw the hope that all will in the end come right. If the shadow were lifted, an age of prosperity would dawn upon the masses of every race and nation. We have anxious years to endure, but I cannot believe that the danger of world war is as great as it was a year ago, or that the last six months have not seen an improvement. If that proves true, no one, I assure you, will rejoice more than those who in this country were so wickedly accused by their political opponents of seeking war when the present Parliament was being chosen. The wise and skilful conduct of our foreign affairs by Mr Eden, the increasing defensive strength of the free countries, and their growing intimacy have made things safer.

Our cause is sacred: peace and freedom. The way for us in Britain to serve this cause is plain. There are linked together the three circles I have often described. First, the British Empire and Commonwealth of Nations growing in moral and physical strength. Secondly, the irrevocable association of the English-speaking world around the great Republic of the United States. Thirdly, the safety and revival of Europe in her ancient fame and long-sought unity. In all these circles we in this hard pressed but unvanquished island have a vital part to play, and if we can bear the weight we may win the crown of honour.

# TRANSPORT (GOVERNMENT POLICY)

A SPEECH TO THE HOUSE OF COMMONS
21 MAY 1952

---

6 *May—Dr Rajemdra Prasad is re-elected President of India after the first Presidential elections held under the Indian Constitution.*

7 *May—Brigadier-General Francis T. Dodd is seized by Communist prisoners of war on Koje Island and is held as a hostage for four days.*

*The French Cabinet decide to confer the rank of Marshal of France on General Juin and posthumously on General Leclerc.*

8 *May—Municipal Elections. Conservatives lose 420 seats, Labour gain 641.*

*A Draft Treaty setting up the European Defence Community is initialled at the Quai d'Orsay by France, Western Germany, Italy, Belgium, Netherlands and Yugoslavia.*

9 *May—Conclusion of tripartite talks in London on Trieste between representatives of British, French and United States Governments.*

11 *May—The Canberra jet bomber flies from Lyneham, Wiltshire, to Melbourne, Australia, in the record time of 23 hours 5 minutes.*

---

[21 *May* 1952

I am sure that the House welcomed the tone and spirit of the speech which the hon Member for Bradford, East [Mr McLeavy], has just delivered. I should like to assure him that nothing is nearer to our wishes than to consult the Trades Union Congress, and particularly the important union that he mentioned, upon matters of this kind which have so close a contact with immediate affairs. The course we are taking will give plenty of opportunity for such consultation. If the answer was only a formal one in December last, it was because these matters were in a state of flux and consideration, and because the Government must at least make up their own mind and see clearly what their main line of advance must be before they go hawking their ideas around in all quarters. But the course that we are taking now will give ample opportunity. That is why we have brought out this White Paper—good or bad. It is brought out now in plenty of time to enable opinions to be collected and expressed from all quarters, friendly and unfriendly. The White Paper is, I think, a guide rather than a rule. It expresses our aims and policies, but it is capable of being influenced and affected by public opinion and by the consultations we shall have.

The right hon Gentleman the Member for Lewisham, South [Mr H. Morrison], also complained that the Transport Commission have not been consulted fully beforehand. Considering how much they were affected by our declared intention to denationalize road haulage—an intention declared so plainly that, if we had not acted upon it, we should have been taunted from that side of the House with going back on our promises—it was not, in the circumstances, really quite possible to consult with these appointees of the late Government about all the details of altering the legislation on which they depended and which they were administering. We have looked at it from a different angle, but, now that the facts are known and our policy has been brought forward in the White Paper, we shall, of course, welcome consultations with Lord Hurcomb and his colleagues, and I trust that they will continue to give us of their assistance in arriving at the best solution possible.

The right hon Member for Lewisham, South, is a curious mixture of geniality and venom. The geniality, I may say after a great many years of experience, is natural to himself. The venom has to be adopted in order to keep on sides with the forces below the Gangway. Some parts of his speech were unexpectedly moderate, but, obviously, he had thought it necessary to prepare the way, as I often see hon Gentlemen doing, in putting himself on good terms below the Gangway by saying a number of things in which I know he does not believe and of which I am sure he is ashamed. The right hon Gentleman accused me of being cowardly in asking my right hon Friend to open the debate. Does he believe that I am really afraid of opening a debate? Why would I be afraid? I can assure the right hon Gentleman that the spectacle of a number of middle-aged gentlemen who are my political opponents being in a state of uproar and fury is really quite exhilarating to me. I have not had fifty years' actual service in this House without having got used to the rough-and-tumble of debate.

It was not out of cowardice that I ran away from this position, but because I have great faith in the ability of my right hon Friend, although he has had such a very short time in this office, to present this extensive case in a masterly form to the House. I, who can speak when I want to or need to, would, I think, have been taking an unfair advantage if I had, as it were, usurped the best place in the debate, and left the Minister, who will fight this matter from the start to the finish, without the opportunity of putting his own stamp on the story and of gaining, as he has done, the confidence and respect of those who now see him in this new office.

There is another thing which the right hon Gentleman said which I thought was rather unworthy of him, and that was when he said that we did not know and we did not care what happened to the 80,000 workers employed. I should have thought that, apart from all questions of philanthropy and good comradeship, decent humanity and even self-interest would have actuated a Government in that matter, but we shall, in fact, embody in our action the exact clauses— Sections 98, 101 and 102—of the Socialist Government's Act of 1947, which deal with compensation and pensions. Nobody ever dreamed that any contrary course would be adopted.

The right hon Gentleman went on to use a really insulting taunt. He said that we were under some sort of obligation to the Road Haulage Executive. We are under no such obligation of any kind; not at all. They have never even been consulted in the matter. It is quite true that they had an agitation in the country, and that some of us agree with what they said, but our association with them is entirely non-existent in any form at all, and in no way compares with the close association in so many ways of the party opposite with the Co-operators, without whose influential counsel I doubt very much whether 'C' licences would ever have existed at all.

I have been drawn into this question on which I speak tonight because it transcends ordinary Departmental measures, and is a part of the main policy of Her Majesty's Government. It illustrates more clearly than almost any other example the fallacy of doctrinaire nationalization, as opposed to the fertility of regulated private enterprise. Therefore, it really represents, as was complained of by the Liberals, the doctrinaire division, the great division in principle, between the two principal parties in the State and the two sides of the House. I should like to say that no step has been taken by me without the approval of the Cabinet. The decision to intervene on the suddenly announced increased transport charges—the increase of fares—was the result of a five-hour Cabinet meeting on this subject on the Thursday before Easter, when the full legal rights of the Government of the day were examined, set forth and explained to us by the Law Officers and the Lord Chancellor. The Cabinet left the drafting of the communique and the timing of its issue and publication to me. That was the extent of my personal action, though I had and have very strong opinions upon what should be done.

Leaving these current issues, let me say that we felt it our duty, in accordance with the public pledges that we had given, to reverse the legislation of the previous Government about road haulage. This was not in a spirit of mere contrariness. We are convinced that a very considerable and needless injury was done to the national economy by the compulsory acquisition by the State of a section, only numerically a small section, of road transport, and we are sure that the arrangements which we propose to make will be a real help to public convenience, and consequently, to general recovery in these critical years.

This White Paper—I quite agree that I am not its author, and I dare say, in some ways, it has the defects which attach to a document which has been many times considered and in which many minds and many hands have played their part in arriving at the complete agreement—and the Bill which is being founded upon it have been the result of prolonged Cabinet study, beginning as soon as the Government was formed in November last. The Ministry of Transport, under the ex-Minister, whose loss through ill-health we greatly regret, worked in the closest harmony with Lord Leathers whose long proved practical business efficiency was of so much service to us in the war.

I have seen it suggested that this White Paper was a hurriedly produced document. In fact, it has been before the Cabinet for several months, and this is the fifth edition. [*Interruption.*] We are stating our opinion in good faith and sincerity against all hon and right hon Members have to say on the other side. When we became aware that the denationalization of road transport was even more urgent in the public interest than that of steel, we decided to lay this White Paper before Parliament, in order to carry the House with us and to do just what I have said, to profit by the movement of opinion on this intricate subject without in any way weakening our main purpose. The draftsmen have long been engaged upon the Bill, and we propose that it should be brought before the House in July. Meanwhile, we shall carefully reflect on well-grounded criticism and, of course, consult the Transport Commission, as I have already stated in reply to the hon Member for Bradford, East.

It has been suggested that there was no need to sell back to private enterprise the nationalized road haulage vehicles. It is no doubt true that the simple raising of the mileage of the 'A' and 'B' licences from twenty-five to even as little as forty miles would expose the Road Haulage Executive to destructive competition, plunging them into a growing deficit, affecting, in its turn, the British Transport Commission as a whole. The twenty-five-mile limit is the radius. Therefore, it is really fifty miles, and to lift that to sixty or even to forty would be to make an enormous difference, and it is quite clear that if we had taken that course it would have produced a much less smooth and speedy method than the one we propose in the White Paper and which we intend to embody in the Bill.

The Amendment dwells, first, upon the 'properly integrated' transport system which it alleges we are seeking to destroy. This is no true description of the present system of operating the road and rail services under the Transport Commission. The Railway Executive and the Road Haulage Executive are operated as separate entities, and the road undertaking can be quite easily disposed of separately. A transport system, whether 'properly integrated' or not, exists to serve the community, and must be judged not by its quality of integration, but by the quality of its service to the public.

The 1947 Act is not a 'properly integrated' system. It has not led to a more speedy or efficient service or to one more ready to adapt itself to the varied and often urgent practical requirements of trade and industry. That is the position in which we found ourselves. But we need not exaggerate the magnitude of the actual physical step we are taking. Some figures, with which I agree, were mentioned by the right hon Gentleman. Altogether, there are nearly a million vehicles on the roads which are involved. Of these numbers only about a twentieth part have been nationalized—41,000, and then there are the 14,000 which rest with the railway companies, but I am speaking of the 41,000—and all the rest are run by private enterprise under 'A', 'B' and 'C' licences.

We propose to transfer back that twentieth part from the State to the private user, or, if you like, to the general public. That is our intention. Our hope and our belief is that the liberation of this small though important part of our road transport will enable goods and services to be interchanged over the whole area of road transport in an easier, more flexible and more convenient manner than at present, and in our struggle to earn our livelihood and thus win survival in the modern world this is a factor which cannot be set aside.

It would be a wrong thing to complicate, hamper and often frustrate the whole organization and flow of road tansport just for the sake of allowing one section of it—albeit important long-distance—to remain under State management at the cost of imposing a vast mass of restrictions on all the rest. This is the case which we submit to the House and which will be argued out by all the processes of Parliamentary discussion when the Bill is in due course presented to the House. We believe, rightly or wrong but sincerely, that a thoroughly bad arrangement is going forward now. Take, for instance, the 'C' licences. 41,000 road vehicles, apart from the 14,000 of the railways, are nationalized and are run by the State for general purposes. Under

'C' licences alone over 800,000 are run by private people carrying their own goods without limit of distance, but allowed to carry only their own goods, so that the late Government, as I said, did not dare to abolish this right or privilege.

It is, of course, often a wasteful process to run an enormous number of vehicles which are restricted in this way. Many of them only carry half their full load on many journeys and many more, nay a vast majority, come back empty. Think of the petrol, and tyres, the wear-and-tear of the vehicles; the labour lost in driving them; the resultant overcrowding of the roads. This is a point which is not novel. It has often been made in debates in the House, and most frequently by Members of the party opposite. Socialist Members who have spoken in that sense must face fairly and squarely the reason for what is being done and what has happened.

Industrialists with their mind properly on costs—profit if you will—would not have taken the expensive course of operating under 'C' licences if they could have got from nationalized long-distance transport the facilities which industry and production need and are well entitled to expect. When the late Government, for reasons which I have described, exempted the 'C' licences and nationalized 41,000 important long-distance vehicles and restricted to a twenty-five-mile radius the 110,000 free haulage vehicles operating under 'A' and 'B' licences, they condemned the overwhelming proportion of our road transport to what everyone can see is a thoroughly wasteful misuse of our hard-pressed resources. It is indeed remarkable that the consequence of the Government nationalizing so small a section of the road vehicles has been to double the 'C' licences. Before the war there were fewer than 400,000, mostly short-distance delivery vans; now there are over 800,000. In the last four years nearly half the owners of the road transport have sought to escape becoming dependent upon the Government, and have chosen instead to put up with these obviously unsound economic conditions under which 'C' licence-holders work, like going often with half loads and many returning quite empty.

Is this a party question? I do not think it is, because many misgivings were felt on that side of the House and we feel them here. Can we really afford to hamper ourselves in this extraordinary manner? Think of it. 400,000, or 350,000, more road vehicles working only for private ownership—not private enterprise, because enterprise is crippled—rather than undergo the inconveniences of an inferior service in an economic sense offered by the State. What is the use of talking about a 'properly integrated system' of transport, when the great change which has so far resulted has been this enormous increase of between 350,000 and 400,000 'C' licence road vehicles? No one ought to be content with a thing like that going on. There is an argument— I think it is a bad argument; nevertheless, it is a classic Socialist argument—for forcing every load to be carried by the method chosen by the State.

There is an argument—which I am venturing to present this evening —for setting free this small section under State control and allowing it to be merged in a general harmonious system of regulated private enterprise. Surely, today, although we differ on the remedy, we might agree we are now having the worst of both worlds. I will make allowance for the fact that the scheme of the party opposite has not reached its full conclusion. But let us just look at these 41,000 vehicles under the Road Haulage Executive. (I am coming to the railway aspect presently). I must apologize for detaining the House and I will curtail my remarks as much as possible, but I feel we owe it to Parliament and the nation to show that what we do is out of no mere mood of partisanship or desire to undo what was done but because we firmly believe that we can produce by the process of liberation a beneficial accretion to our national wealth.

The 41,000 vehicles are about, as I have said, a twentieth of the road transport in question today. They are an eighth part only of those which have sprung into being under 'C' licences while the nationalized 41,000 vehicles were being taken over. It was pretty hard on people who had for many years run small but efficient businesses—the man driving the van and the wife keeping the accounts—that often happens —when their vehicles were acquired under the 1947 Act. True, they were paid a large sum—£30 million—for the goodwill they had built up. [An HON MEMBER: 'A fair price.'] I suppose at a fair price, the party opposite were responsible. Still, many of them bitterly resented the treatment they received, and a proportion of the smaller people took their share of the £30 million compensation and have now left the country for the Dominions and the Commonwealth.

The taking of these vehicles over was a harsh and unreasonable thing to do, even though the Socialist Government, in accordance with their hitherto correct principles of compensation, paid out this large sum of money. I say 'hitherto' because I shall have a word to say about that later. It pleased nobody except the politicians pursuing the theme of nationalization. Here was the variegated field of road transport, all of which had grown up naturally, responding from day to day to the laws of supply and demand, and corrected by the penalties constantly operative which befall private enterprise when it is unsuccessful. Here it was before us. This represented the end of a long process of 'the survival of the fittest'.

What have we now? We have the 800,000 private vehicles under specialized ownership which forbids them to touch any goods but their own. We have 50,000 under the 'A' licences and 60,000 under the 'B' licences, and against all this vast field of privately owned transport 41,000 nationalized vehicles to be managed by the Road Haulage Executive. Let us just see how they have managed their sphere. I make all allowances for their difficulties. The fact remains that the 41,000 nationalized road vehicles, apart altogether from those who drive them and keep them, and apart also from over 6,000 operating and maintenance clerical staff, require a headquarters and have set up a headquarters and administration staff of no fewer than 12,000 clerical and administration personnel. The exact figure I have been furnished with is 12,348.

I am told that the Road Haulage Executive staff of 12,000 which has sprung into being costs more than £6 million a year. I am told that is probably many times as much money as would be needed if these 41,000 vehicles were allowed once again to be merged in the general system of road transport. The whole of this vast apparatus has been brought into being to manage a twentieth of the road haulage vehicles of the country. This lies upon us as a deadweight and is an unnecessary burden upon our intimate communications which are a vital factor in our economic life. The question we have to ask is, why should this have been done, and, if it has been done, why should it go on?

Now we come to the railways. I have never been shocked by the idea of nationalizing the railways. In fact, I believe I proposed it on my own before almost all the Members of the House had even thought about going to Parliament. I am by no means sure I have been right. It is no part of my case that I am always right. Anyhow, we have to face the facts. The railways are and will remain nationalized, and the Tory Party will do their utmost to make them a great, living, lasting success in the vital, though limited, sphere that is open to them. If we wanted to do the most idiotic thing that we could conceive, it would be for our countrymen to divide themselves into two gangs, one lot backing road transport and the other backing rail, and trying to fight a political battle on that intimate and delicate, and in some respects tormented, front.

There is no development of road transport which can replace the services rendered by the railways. There are immense classes of traffic which only the railways can carry. There are important classes of non-remunerative traffic which must be carried. There are military needs—and I do not mean only definite military needs; this country cannot possibly get on in time of war by road transport alone, however great its development may be. There are military needs, as the right hon Member for Lewisham, South, said in a thoughtful passage of his speech the other day, which only the railways can fulfil.

We accept the nationalization of the railways. We do not mean to see them let down or maltreated in the vital and indispensible service they have given us. I do not look upon the railways—I rather echo the eloquent words of my right hon Friend the Minister of Transport and the harbour and port authorities connected with them—as a purely commercial business. I have a feeling that associates them with the defensive services of our island. Well do we remember how, in all their various ways, the railwaymen and their comrades stood by us in all the trials through which we made our way in the war. There are, no doubt, great opportunities for improving the administration of the railways. Decentralization, we hope, will yield fruits. Anyhow, it will bring about a revival of the old stimulus of competition—or disinterested competition, if you like. This, while not hampering the making of *Bradshaw* or the *ABC*, gave everyone employed a feeling of *esprit de corps*.

Then there is the levy on road transport of £4 million a year—not much to put upon the broad backs of liberated and free road transport; once set free, they will take it in their stride—but at least, the levy meets the actual purchase price of the goodwill and it will increase in the future only as new traffic is taken over from the railways. In this it offers them a solid security without hampering private enterprise road transport at all. Thus we believe that road and rail, Socialist and Tory, and even Liberals—although I fear they regard it as very essential to their position to find fault with whatever is done—might all live happily together in this field to the advantage of everyone.

I ventured to put these points before the House because I am anxious that hon Members should appreciate with how much care, zeal and earnestness we on this side of the House have worked to try to remedy the evil plight into which we have got, in a manner which will be conducive to the public advantage. But there is one grave issue to which I must refer before I conclude, and that is the threat to renationalize road haulage without paying fair compensation. The right hon Member for Lewisham, South, did not like the word 'threat'. He called it a public duty and an act of decency. I admit that he somewhat toned down the statements which we have recently heard from less responsible members of his party and, I think, from their party organ. Nevertheless, the words he has used today deserve very careful attention and must be most carefully studied.

Hitherto, British Socialist policy has been to nationalize what industries they thought fit and to pay reasonable compensation to the owners and shareholders. This is a matter of principle in which they differ from the Communist Party. That and the maintenance of political liberty are the two main points of difference. I should not like to see them weaken those barriers at all. To establish the principle of confiscation, even though it was preceded by a threat—I beg pardon, by an act of decency—would be a departure from what has hitherto been a fundamental practice, and it would undoubtedly affect the whole aspect of our laws. If persons acting in good faith under the full authority of the Crown and Parliament are to be dispossessed without compensation, or with inadequate or unfair compensation, a new era will open. Of course, one Parliament may change or reverse the legislation of another. That is what we are going to do when we reach the month of July. It is quite a different thing to violate the broad equities of legal or commercial transactions. It would not only affect our credit in many directions, but the constitutional authority of Parliament itself would be impugned.

Mr H. Morrison (Lewisham, South): The right hon Gentleman heard my speech. I said nothing to justify these observations. I said that we would pay compensation which, in all the circumstances of the case, would be fair, but that we must be fair to the community as well as to individuals, and that while we were against confiscation of private property we were equally against, and must protect the community against, the confiscation of public property. The right hon Gentleman's interpretation is not justified at all.

The Prime Minister: I am very glad to hear any reassurances of that kind, and I am willing to accept them for what they are worth. But we should certainly not be afraid to join issue with the party opposite on this ground. If the threat or 'act of public duty' were taken seriously it would, of course, affect the value of the national property which we propose to sell. That will not deter us from proceeding with our policy. It would mean, however, that the purchasers might get it very cheap because of this new element of risk, and that the State would be the loser, perhaps by a large sum. The responsibility will not rest with those who are pursuing a constitutional and Parliamentary course with the full right and authority of the House of Commons, but it will rest with those who, by an unprecedented and non-constitutional action, will be inflicting a serious injury upon the nation for the undoubted advantage of private individuals who will get national property very cheap. The more these sales are prejudiced by this kind of talk in which the right hon Gentleman and his party have been indulging, the more that evil will take place. It would seem, I should have thought, at any rate, only common prudence for the Opposition to wait and see what the situation and condition of the transport industry is before committing themselves, what may be long in advance, to steps hitherto accepted only by the Communist Party.

We believe that in less than the lifetime of this Parliament the benefits of a liberated road transport system, combined with the successful administration of the British Railways, may make it seem a very wrong and foolish thing to renationalize the road transport in a future Parliament. Thus the threat which is now made will be proved to have been vain and idle.

It might not, however, prevent it from having cost the State many millions of pounds and enabling individual purchasers to secure national property far below its value. I am sure that this has been carefully considered by the Leaders of the Opposition. I see evidences of it today, and the right hon Gentleman's eagerness to interrupt me to express his position is a sign of grace in the matter; but, nevertheless, much harm may already have been done. Never, however, in any circumstances would we be justified in surrendering in the teeth of such a challenge the undoubted rights of Parliament to legislate as it chooses.

To sum up, we believe in both road and rail transport. We believe that they should be helped by both parties to play their vital part in the internal economy of our hard-pressed society. We do not think that the levy on road transport will hamper its development and imperative expansion. We regard the temporary retention of the twenty-five-mile limit for certain classes of vehicles as no more than a lever and spur to the whole process of liberating road transport from its present tangle and restrictions. We have no intention either of cramping the full, natural expansion of road transport or of disinteresting ourselves in the future of the railways. We believe that a far better service will be available for the public as a result of the policy we are determined to pursue than what they would get if matters were simply allowed to drift.

# PRESS ASSOCIATION ANNUAL LUNCHEON

## A SPEECH AT THE SAVOY HOTEL, LONDON
## 11 JUNE 1952

---

26 *May—The War Office announces that General Sir John Harding, Commander-in-Chief British Army of the Rhine, will succeed General Sir William Slim as Chief of the Imperial General Staff on 1 November 1952.*

27 *May—Mr Lennox-Boyd, Minister of Transport, announces plans designed to enable independent operators to play a greater part in running scheduled air services.*

30 *May—General Eisenhower hands over his Command in Europe to General Ridgway.*

5 *June—In the Birthday Honours Peerages are conferred on Sir Basil Brooke, Prime Minister of Northern Ireland, and Sir Alfred Duff Cooper.*

---

[*11 June 1952*

The Press Association plays an important part in our national life by presenting from minute to minute the news about all kinds of things happening all over the world. You have two important guides in your difficult task: first, that your presentation should be factual and unbiased, and secondly, that it should preserve a true sense of proportion. Both these conditions have been observed in a high and increasing degree during the eighty-four years of your honourable service. It is because what you offer us is so valuable—indeed irreplaceable—that your responsibilities are heavy. Without your help the public would be uninformed; without your integrity they would be misled. You have also since the war had to exercise a discrimination never previously forced upon a National Press. As the world grows more complex and as time and space contract year by year, the news increases in volume and variety. But newsprint shrinks at least as fast. You have therefore to strike the balance between what people want to read and what you think they ought to know. Many will feel that you strike a fair balance, and I believe you will continue to resist temptations to diminish fact for the sake of sensation, or twist truth to serve partisanship.

Last week I watched the Trooping the Colour and our young Queen riding at the head of her Guards. I thought of the history of the past and the hopes of the future. Not only of the distant past—it is barely ten years since we upheld on our strong, unyielding shoulders the symbols, the honour and even perhaps the life of the free world. Certainly no one of British race could contemplate such a spectacle without pride. But no thinking man or woman could escape the terrible question: on what does it all stand? It does indeed seem hard that the traditions and triumphs of a thousand years should be challenged by the ebb and flow of markets and commercial and financial transactions in the swaying world which has sprung up and is growing ever larger around us, and that we have to watch from month to month the narrow margins upon which our solvency and consequently our reputation and influence depend. But fifty million islanders growing food for only thirty millions, and dependent for the rest upon their exertions, their skill and their genius, present a problem which has not been seen or at least recorded before. In all history there has never been a community so large, so complex, so sure of its way of life, posed at such dizzy eminence and on so precarious a foundation. Lands and nations whom we have defeated in war or rescued from subjugation are today more solidly sure of earning their living than we, who have imparted our message of Parliamentary institutions to the civilized world, and kept the flag of freedom flying in some of its darkest days.

Around us we see the streets so full of traffic and the shops so splendidly presented, and the people, cheerful, well-dressed, content with their system of Government, proud, as they have a right to be of their race and name. One wonders if they realize the treacherous trapdoor on which they stand. I would not say this to you if it was not your duty to expose any facts, however unpleasant, to them. Britain can take it.

To speak like this is not to cry despair. It is the Alert; but it is more than the Alert; it is the Alarm. We have never been beaten yet and now we fight not for vainglory or imperial pomp, but for survival as an independent, self-supporting nation. It has often been said we were approaching national bankruptcy in October last after our two years orgy of electioneering, and certainly the figures to prove it can all be produced. But any British Government, worthy of the name, called upon to bear the burden would have taken severe, unpopular measures of one kind or another to ward off the obvious and imminent peril. In wartime we were confronted with extreme decisions. There was nothing we would not have done for our life and cause. In time of peace happily we work under more limited conditions both in risks and in remedies. The dangers do not present themselves to the mass of the people in the same acute and violent manner as in the days when London was being bombed. Now the crisis is different in form, but as it seems to me, scarcely less fateful. Moreover there is this outstanding difference between the perils of war and of peace. In war we were united, now in peace we find ourselves torn apart by quarrels which bear no relation to our dangers, and, while we brawl along, our thought and action are distracted by a vast superficial process of reciprocal calumniation. We have to live our life from day to day and give back as good as we get, but I warn you that without an intense national realization of our position in all parties and by all classes, we shall find it very hard to reach that security without which all that we have achieved, all that we possess and all our glories may be cast away.

If I were not sure that the vital forces in our race, not only in this island, but throughout the British Empire and Commonwealth of Nations, have only to be aroused to conquer, I would not use these hard words. I use them to you because they may be a guide in the discharge of your responsible duties and also because, through your Agency, they may command the attention of our countrymen here and across the oceans. Thanks to the unpopular measures that have already been taken by the Chancellor of the Exchequer, we have reached in the last six months a position of equipoise. Our head is above water. It is not enough to float. We have to swim and we have to swim successfully against the stream. We are holding our own. That is a considerable return for the sacrifices which our people are having to make. But we cannot be satisfied with that. We must not only pay our way. We cannot be content to live from hand to mouth and from month to month in this world of change and turmoil. We must create, by long and steady systems of trade and exchange throughout our Empire and Commonwealth and throughout the wider world, reserves of strength and solvency which enable us to rise solid, steadfast and superior, above the waves of cosmopolitan speculation. Thus and thus alone can we stand firm and unbroken against all the winds that blow.

# UNITED NATIONS' POLICY IN THE FAR EAST

A SPEECH TO THE HOUSE OF COMMONS
1 JULY 1952

---

12 *June—The Chancellor of the Exchequer announces that since the end of
March Britain's Gold and Dollar Reserves have fallen by less than
£10 million, this decline in 2½ months comparing with losses of £227
million in the first three months of 1952 and £334 million in the last
quarter of 1951.*

18 *June—Mr Lester Pearson, Canadian Minister of External Affairs, states
that Canada will proceed independently with plans for the construction
of the St Lawrence Seaway and Power project, in view of the decision
of the United States Senate to postpone consideration of a Bill authorizing
United States co-operation on the project.*

23 *June—United Nations Air Forces carry out the heaviest attacks in the
Korean War on five important hydro-electric plants south of the Yalu
River.*

---

[1 *July* 1952

One would hardly have thought from the interesting and in many
ways excellent speech to which we have listened that a vote of censure
was being moved against Her Majesty's Government. Indeed, it seemed
to me that the whole emphasis and bias of the speech was directed
against the extremists in the right hon Gentleman's [Mr Noel-Baker's]
own party and was intended to teach them a lesson in the elementary
facts of the situation, and that what was left over of the censure by that
process, which was considerable, was directed, I regret to say, against
the United States. We, the Government of the day—whose fate and
fortune turn upon the issue of this evening's debate and Division—had
hardly a word of criticism directed against us. The only point, with
which I will deal fully, was that we ought to have been better informed.
Let us look into that in the course of our discussions. I was very much
interested in the right hon Gentleman's retrospect, which reminded
one of a great many things which are so easily forgotten in this bewilder-
ingly busy period. No one, I agree with him, can attempt to form a
true opinion about the question now before us without looking back.
I shall not attempt to go over all the ground he went over of the wartime decisions and so forth, but I think we should look back on the
recent sequence of events.

While the Communists were prospering in their aggression, as he reminded us, they brushed aside all proposals for a parley, and, in the three months from April to June, a great change took place. They suffered nearly 400,000 casualties against 50,000 suffered by the United Nations Forces, including those of South Korea. This was a great change and the Communist Government in China had what is called in that part of the world 'lost face'. Their demoralization was profound and widespread and that was no doubt why we had the Soviet proposal for an armistice of 23 June 1951.

The White Paper gives a very full account of all that has happened since—nearly a year's negotiations during which the Chinese Communists steadily recovered their 'face' by negotiating and arguing with the utmost—I almost said truculence, but let me use a neutral term—vigour with the United Nations. What they had lost in the field they recovered at the haggling table at Panmunjom. At the same time, as the House has already been told, they restored strength and order to their armies, doubled their size to nearly a million and made elaborate defensive works and lines of underground approach which would permit them to make an attack on a great scale. If we compare the position today with what it was a year ago, we can see how shrewd and how well-timed was the Russian request for an armistice and how heavy has been the cost to the American armies who are bearing nine-tenths of the burden and the brunt of the war in Korea. It is said that the United States Forces have had 32,000 casualties in the bickering on the front during these armistice negotiations. We ourselves have had 1,200. I was told that the armistice period had been costing the United States £4,500,000 a day and the British about £50,000 a day over and above the ordinary upkeep of their troops in both cases. That has been the rate of expenditure during the year of armistice and in the end we are about half as well off as we were in the beginning.

Anyone who attempts to read the details of the armistice negotiations in the White Paper may well be tempted to ask themselves in justice whether his own patience is equal to that of our negotiators. Certainly every possible concession has been made by the representatives of the United Nations to make an agreement with the Communists who were military pulp at the time they began the talks. The right hon Gentleman told us of a number of concessions which have been made. We have not been conscious of any desire on the part of the Chinese Communists and those who guide and direct them to come to a friendly conclusion. It was not likely that they would have such wishes when they were gaining so much at every dilatory step they took and with every month that passed.

The future which lies before us in this sphere is indefinite. This armistice negotiation is in itself only intended to lead up to a truce and the truce, if acted upon, is to lead to discussions about peace, which may be equally prolonged. All the time the immense expenditure of the United States will continue. I am not at this moment arguing the rights or wrongs of the world issue; I am only arguing that due consideration should be given—nothing I say here conflicts with the arguments of the right hon Gentleman—by the sympathizers with the Chinese Communists and by the British nation as a whole to the monumental patience, breaking all previous human records, which has been displayed by the American Government and people in discharging their duty to the United Nations. I defy anyone to show any other historical example which can equal it.

We in this country are all convinced that it would be a great mistake, with Europe in its present condition, for the United Nations or the United States, which is their champion, to be involved in a war with the Communist Government inside China. I have repeatedly emphasized the danger of such a development. But do not let us blind ourselves to the terrible cost that is being paid for their patience by the people of the United States. I think we ought to admire them for the restraint which they have practised, instead of trying to find fault with them on every occasion. There might easily come a time, especially during a Presidential election, when a very sharp reaction of emotion, even of anger, might sweep large sections of the American people, and when any candidate for the Presidency who gave full vent to it would gain a very considerable advantage.

We here have suffered our own losses, too, in this year of negotiation. Our casualties have been a twenty-fifth part of those of the United States, and in money a ninetieth part, but I think it is a very dangerous thing for this country—much though we mourn and regret these losses—making so comparatively small a contribution, although greater than any of the other United Nations members, to overpress its claims and complaints against those who are bearing almost the whole burden and who, as I have said, have shown patience beyond all compare. I can only hope that the American people will not suppose that the House of Commons is unfriendly to them or that we are simply naggers and fault-finders. They have their own political and election quarrels and understand the process full well, and I can assure them that the same sort of thing is going on over here in the Socialist Party, with its internal disputes about leadership and as they are experiencing themselves in America. Above all, I hope we shall not concern ourselves with American party-politics and that they will make all the necessary allowances for the struggles and rivalries going on on the benches opposite.

Let me come to the Motion of censure on the Paper. We have all watched with attention, mitigated by occasional fatigue, the twirls, twitchings and convulsions which are taking place on the Front Bench opposite, and it may well be that they will feel a sense of relief in putting their differences to the test of a Division in the House as well as those which, I understand, take place in other quarters. But there is a Motion of censure. As I said, nearly all of the speech of the right hon Gentleman dealt with the United States, their generals, speeches they have made and so on. We do not control the speeches which they make. But what does the complaint and censure against the Government amount to? It is that we have not sufficiently been considered by the United States, in spite of the visits that were paid to them by so many Ministers earlier in the year.

I have never denied the overwhelming contribution which the United States is making. Still, as the Foreign Secretary has said, we think that, as the second contributor to the United Nations campaign, although our contribution was so small, nevertheless we should have been consulted, or at least informed, before the bombing of the power stations in North Korea. Yet it cannot be disputed that these power stations were legitimate military targets. They supplied electric power to the military workshops and repair depots maintained by the enemy underground and in railway tunnels. They served also for the radar warning system operated by the enemy. That they were military targets cannot be disputed.

Some may ask why this particular moment was selected for the attack. According to the answer that I was given when I made that inquiry, air operations cannot be undertaken without reference to the weather conditions. Korea suffers from heavy monsoon rains in July and August, and it was necessary, if these attacks were to be made, and made successfully, that the operation should be carried out before the heavy cloudy weather set in. [*Interruption.*] I have been asked to give an explanation, and that is the information which I have been given.

One of the plants bombed lies on the frontier between Korea and Manchuria, and sends some of its output into Manchuria. This has certainly raised a matter of principle and was not, in my view, a decision of military routine. As we were not informed, we could not know. Therefore, although technically aimed at Her Majesty's Government, the censure of the official Opposition, as I said, really falls upon the United States. I am sorry that after the frank and generous statement made by Mr Dean Acheson in Westminster Hall last Thursday, such an attitude should prevail, even in responsible sections of the Opposition.

MR S. SILVERMAN (Nelson and Colne): On a point of order. The Prime Minister has made reference to a speech that was made outside here. [HON MEMBERS: 'No.'] He referred to a speech made in Westminster Hall. We all understood that that speech was made at a private meeting, and it was repeatedly said to be 'off the record'. It is very difficult if the Prime Minister refers to it and nobody else is able to refer to any other part of it. Ought it not to be excluded?

MR DEPUTY-SPEAKER [SIR CHARLES MACANDREW]: That is not a point of order for me.

THE PRIME MINISTER: May I say that——

MR JOHN PATON (Norwich, North): On a point of order. I wish to ask a related point of order, but not exactly the same one. I wish to ask you, Mr Deputy-Speaker, if it will be in order for Members on this side of the House, now that the Prime Minister has introduced this matter of a private meeting, to continue the discussion about what Mr Acheson said.

THE PRIME MINISTER: Might I inform hon Members that it is already on the tape. The whole report is already published in the United States.

MR DEPUTY-SPEAKER: No point of order arises, and I am not going to answer a hypothetical point of order.

THE PRIME MINISTER: As I say, I do not remember any occasion in international affairs when a more candid and manly course has been taken by a prominent public man. The meeting was 'off the record', but I obtained permission to give an account to the House, and I find that this account was released this morning in the United States by the State Department.

MR S. SILVERMAN rose——

THE PRIME MINISTER: The hon Gentleman is so busy finding fault that he is not able to keep himself abreast of the facts.

MR SILVERMAN rose——

THE PRIME MINISTER: I do not propose to give way, because I am going to read out——

MR SILVERMAN rose——

MR DEPUTY-SPEAKER: If the hon Gentleman really thinks that he has a point of order I will hear it.

MR SILVERMAN: If I had not thought that it was a point of order, I should not have attempted to raise it, Mr Deputy-Speaker. The point of order I wish to put to you is this: the right hon Gentleman has now referred to a document that we have all heard about, namely, the publication, in spite of our being told that it was 'off the record', of what purports to be a full account of the speech in Westminster Hall. There are many of us who do not accept it as a full record, and the point of order I want to put is this: in view of what the Prime Minister is now saying, will we on this side be in order in referring to those parts of Mr Dean Acheson's speech in Westminster Hall that do not appear in the report that was published?

MR DEPUTY-SPEAKER: I can only judge on a point of order when it arises. There has been no point of order at the moment.

THE PRIME MINISTER: I am bound to say, if I may make a diversion, that I do not think there is any practice of the House which is more a subject of abuse than this raising of points of order of an unreal or even fraudulent character.

MR S. SILVERMAN: On a point of order. I do not know, Mr Deputy-Speaker, whether you share the right hon Gentleman's contempt for the procedure of the House or his readiness to abuse his position in order to offer insults——

MR DEPUTY-SPEAKER: Order. I would ask for the point of order to be put in a more temperate way.

MR SILVERMAN: I am exceedingly grateful to you, Mr Deputy-Speaker, for reminding hon Members that points of order, or other things, might be put in a temperate way. I would ask whether the use of the word 'fraudulent' with reference to other Members of the House and their conduct in putting points of order is, in your view, in order, and whether the suggestion that you permit fraudulent points of order is not a quite unjustifiable attack upon the Chair.

MR DEPUTY-SPEAKER: I am in absolute agreement with the first comment. The points of order raised at the moment can certainly be described as fraudulent in my opinion.

MR ANEURIN BEVAN (Ebbw Vale): On a point of order. I should like to have your guidance, Mr Deputy-Speaker, in this matter. A very large number of Members of Parliament of all parties attended the meeting at Westminster Hall. We were given to understand that the whole thing was 'off the record' and that it was entirely private and could not be reported. I understand that a certain report has been made purporting to be a report of what occurred at that meeting. All of it, however, has not been reported and, as no shorthand notes were taken by any official persons at that meeting, so far as I know, are we, therefore, in a position to put any interpretation and to give any report we like about what we think happened at that meeting?

MR DEPUTY-SPEAKER: I cannot, of course, judge on what was said and what happened at the meeting, but those matters certainly do not arise as points of order.

MR BEVAN: May I respectfully submit that this is an extremely serious matter? It might be possible—I have never known this happen before—for very grave damage to be done to relations between two peoples if interpretations not supported by objective fact can be made purporting to be what the spokesman for foreign affairs in America said at a private meeting. What we want to know is are we free to do it? If so, then we must all take the consequences.

MR DEPUTY-SPEAKER: If a matter is serious it does not necessarily mean that it is a point of order.

MR S. SILVERMAN: In the hubbub of what has since occurred I am not quite sure whether I heard your answer to the point of order which I raised a little while ago, Mr Deputy-Speaker. The point of order that I put to you was whether the Prime Minister was entitled, within the rules of the House, to accuse another hon Member of having done something fraudulent. I did not hear the answer to that.

MR DEPUTY-SPEAKER: I do not think that the Prime Minister accused anyone of doing anything fraudulent—[*Interruption.*]—I should be grateful if I could have the courtesy of the House to allow me to finish my sentence. The Prime Minister did not refer to any hon Member as being fraudulent. He referred to the raising of fraudulent points of order. In my experience that has been happening frequently of recent years.

MR SILVERMAN: It is, of course, perfectly true that the right hon Gentleman had not the guts to say what he had to say about any individual Member by name, but he used the phrase about the fraudulent raising of points of order in a context which could only be related to the point of order which had just been raised. The point which I raised with you is whether, as reference to this speech had been made on one side, it would be in order when the time came for other Members to refer to other parts of that speech. I can see nothing fraudulent about that, and I should be sorry to see that anybody else can.

MR DEPUTY-SPEAKER: The word 'fraudulent' was not used in that context at all. The word 'fraudulent', as I understand it, was used against points of order which hon Members raise, when the Minister or the hon Member who is speaking refuses to give way, and think that the only way that they can get their word in is by raising a point of order. It happens time and again and, in my opinion, they are fraudulent points of order. I hope they will be stopped.

THE PRIME MINISTER: I should like, if I may, to read the version which has been published in Washington—the version which the hon Gentleman was not aware of.

MR S. SILVERMAN: I was.

THE PRIME MINISTER: One would not have thought so from what has been said; the version of what Mr Acheson said in Westminster Hall. It is open to hon Members to say so if they heard something different, but I hope that they will wait until the speech has been concluded, and then they can raise that point. This is what I am informed he has said. I am quoting him now:

'If I may digress for a moment I shall make some remarks about a matter which is one of controversy and which I would not speak about in England were it not for the fact that this is "off the record". I shall restrict my remarks to what I think it is my duty to say to you at this time. This is about the matter that you have been debating during the last two or three days.

'You would ask me, I am sure, if I did not say this, two questions, and I should like to reply very frankly to both of them. One question you would ask is: Shouldn't the British Government have been informed or consulted about the bombing? To that, my answer would be: Yes, it should have been; indeed, it was our intention to do it. It is only as the result of what in the United States is known as a "Snafu"*—

which word I have had to add to my vocabulary—

'that you were not consulted about it.

'I am sure that you are wholly inexperienced in England with Government errors. We, unfortunately, have had more familiarity with them, and due to the fact that one person was supposed to do something and thought that another person was supposed to do something, you were not consulted. Therefore, you should have been. We have no question about that.

'If you asked me whether you had an absolute right to be consulted, I should say no, but I don't want to argue about absolute right. What I want to say is that you are a partner of ours in this operation, and we wanted to consult you; we should have, and we recognize an error.'

There could not be a more full and generous statement than that, and the fact that it was said 'off the record', and that, afterwards, the speaker has waived all the secrecy which attended his remarks and made it public property, because he thought it in the public interest, only pays a higher tribute to his courage—[*Interruption.*] I would be hours if I am going to argue with everybody. Not that I mind it;

* Situation normal; all fouled up.

I do not at all, but I must consider a little the wishes of other hon Members who wish to speak.

I said that that is a complete answer—the statement I have just read—to the vote of censure which the Opposition have placed upon the Order Paper—a complete answer, certainly.

MR C. R. ATTLEE (Walthamstow, West) *rose*——

THE PRIME MINISTER: Not a point of order, I hope.

MR ATTLEE: I gather from the right hon Gentleman that the American Secretary of State thought this was a mistake, as we may understand, owing to one person having thought that the other had reported us the information, and the other had not done it. What the right hon Gentleman has not explained, and a point on which we should like an explanation is, why two Cabinet Ministers, who ought to be fully informed about operations, have themselves told us that when a major operation—something quite exceptional—came about, they never knew a word about it.

THE PRIME MINISTER: That is a point which I will come to in due course, but I am on one point at a time, and I say that a more complete answer to the vote of censure which the Opposition have placed upon the Order Paper could not have been given than was given, and given in the hearing of so many who are here, by the American Secretary of State.

Now, it has sometimes been said that we should meet force with force, but that is by no means always true. There are other and better methods often, but what is always true is that generosity should be met with generosity. It will, I am sure, be the true opinion of the House and of the country that Mr Acheson's statement, made to so many hon Members, should have ended this matter, so far as the past is concerned. [HON MEMBERS: 'No.'] If it had not been for an accident, as he said, we should have been informed and, therefore, where is the point of censure that our relations with them are such that we should not be informed upon this matter.

SEVERAL HON MEMBERS *rose*——

MR JAMES HUDSON (Ealing, North): He said that we have no right to be informed.

THE PRIME MINISTER: The former Minister of Defence said at the weekend that nothing like this breakdown in contact ever happened under the Socialist Government, or words to that effect. The most serious mistake that was made in the Korean campaign was the advance by General MacArthur, who has so many fine victories to his credit, not only beyond the 38th Parallel, but beyond the waist of the Korean Peninsula in November 1950. This involved an enormous scattering of our power and the lengthening of the front, and caused a most fateful setback to the operations of the United Nations. The Chinese were given a deadly opportunity to recover, of which they took full advantage. But nobody thought of moving a vote of censure on the Government of the day because they had not been consulted by the United Nations Supreme Commander.

So far, we have worked on the basis which we found on taking office. As for the future, the United States had expressed their willingness, as my right hon and learned Friend the Minister of State has told us, to receive a British Commonwealth military representative upon General Mark Clark's staff, and we have accepted this offer. The matter is not, however, as simple as it looks. I am trying to be perfectly candid with the House. Fifteen other nations are represented in the United Nations Army, and military operations can hardly be conducted in a babel of conflicting voices.

The question arises: to whom would the loyalty of a British representative be due? Would it be to the chief under whom he is serving, or to the country to which he belongs? If, for instance, he is told something of a secret character, is he to report it home, or is he merely to be permitted to express an opinion or give a warning, while keeping his information secret from us? The second course, I must express the opinion, would appear to be the right one, but it would not necessarily have prevented the bombing of the North Korean plants, nor would it have added to our information about it. I hope that the House will realize the difficulties involved in the various proposals that are made to strengthen the representation of the United Nations when one country is performing this vast preponderance of the toil. The right hon Gentleman the Member for Derby, South [Mr Noel-Baker], spoke of the situation in the previous war, and we all remember that which prevailed in North Africa in 1942-43. There, it is true, we had a political adviser to General Eisenhower—my right hon Friend the Minister for Housing and Town Planning—['No.'] Give it me again.

MR ATTLEE: Minister of Housing and Local Government.

THE PRIME MINISTER: I am much obliged to the right hon Gentleman; there is nothing like getting it accurate.

There was also an American adviser, Mr Murphy, but the forces were soon very evenly balanced, and, after that, we became nearly three times as strong and we still accepted General Eisenhower's command. I doubt very much whether a similar machinery could be set up in Korea. However, we have decided to accept the invitation courteously extended to us.

I must say I was surprised to read the bitter personal attack made upon Lord Alexander in the official newspaper of the Labour Party by the hon Member for Devonport [Mr Foot]. When General Mark Clark was appointed to succeed General Ridgway in Korea, I was very glad that one of his first thoughts was to invite his friend and former commander, General Alexander, to come out to see him. I was sure that nothing but good could come out of friendly talks between them. The idea was welcomed in most quarters. His journey acquired more formality by the decision to send my right hon and learned Friend the Minister of State along with him, but the mission, as it now became, in no way possessed the power to take decisions of policy. We wanted to be informed and to interchange our thoughts with our friends and allies. I must say I thought it was a hard ordeal for Field-Marshal Alexander to have to step out of an aeroplane on a dozen occasions and be surrounded by reporters asking any question that came into their heads and picking up any phrase of casual expression. This was a task which might well have tried a most hardened and practised politician. Even the right hon Member for Easington [Mr Shinwell], in spite of all his experience and tact, might have made a slip here and there. He spent the weekend explaining away some of his slips and creating new ones. I think that the House as a whole feels, as the Government do, that Field-Marshal Alexander discharged his difficult duties with the utmost tact and discretion.

On Monday we received a telegram from General Mark Clark in which he stated that he himself did not know that these plants were to be bombed while Field-Marshal Alexander was with him, and that if he had known he would certainly have told him. [*Laughter.*] I thought hon Members would like to know the facts. I had to be rather careful, because I was not quite sure what might or might not have passed, and therefore I walked as cautiously as I possibly could. But I am sure that this visit did nothing but good and that the friendly contacts which the Minister of Defence established, not only in Korea but also in Washington and at Ottawa, have been very helpful to our relations at this difficult time. Moreover, I personally feel comfort in having at the Cabinet table one whose eye in military matters I have learned to trust and whose judgment of values and of difficult events has so often shone in courage and in wisdom.

To come to the second question of the right hon Gentleman— prisoners of war. As he said, many difficulties have been settled at Panmunjom by concessions, mainly on the part of the United Nations, but in the early months of this year the exchange of prisoners, of which we held 132,000 and the Chinese Communists 12,000, became the crucial issue. There is a great deal about this in the White Paper, which I trust hon Members will have perused, and the facts disclosed should be shown in their true light. What is a prisoner of war? He is a man who has tried to kill you and, having failed to kill you, asks you not to kill him. Long before the Christian revelation, the world had found out by practice that mercy towards a beaten enemy was well worth while and that it was much easier to gain control over wide areas by taking prisoners than by making everyone fight to the death against you. Julius Caesar gained far more by his clemency than by his prowess. We therefore are much in favour of encouraging prisoners to surrender by giving them good treatment, and the United Nations' command have voluntarily accepted the principles of the Geneva Convention.

MR EMRYS HUGHES: Unconditional surrender.

THE PRIME MINISTER: That has absolutely nothing to do with it. It shows the confused mass of tangled irrelevancies and disjointed thoughts with which the hon Gentleman's head is filled, or almost filled. It would be most disastrous if we were to adopt the methods of the Soviet Government of keeping prisoners of war to be toiled to death as slaves. The recent Report by NATO on the 3,000,000 prisoners, most of whom have perished in Russian hands, will certainly be in many people's minds. I have no doubt that in the present 'cold war' struggle with the Communists, mercy and consideration towards prisoners of war is the wisest as well as the most honourable course we can pursue.

In April this year I noticed the lengths to which the Americans were going in their screening of prisoners in the camps over which they still had effective control. The questionnaires which were put to the prisoners, as the White Paper shows, were very severe. They were designed to persuade the prisoners, almost to coerce them, to choose to be sent back to Communist China or North Korea by warning them that their families might well be made to suffer and that the United Nations could offer them no future maintenance or employment. How can we be accused of wishing to prolong the truce negotiations? Their anxiety was visible, in every communication that we received from that quarter, to bring things to an end—and naturally, when you are paying so much and losing so much and gaining nothing out of it, naturally, there is a great desire to bring things to an end. One can easily go too far along such a road. When people say that they would rather commit suicide or would resist forcibly being sent back to the Communist zone, due consideration must be given to their wishes. Terrible things happened after the end of the Second World War about the repatriation of Russian prisoners. But, after all, we had been the ally of Russia, and many of these Russian prisoners had fought against their own country when it was in dire struggle. Moreover, the shape of the world was not defined as we can see it now.

But this I will say: that to force an anti-Communist prisoner of war, in spite of his threat to commit suicide, to go back to Communist China or North Korea would be inhumane and dishonourable. It would also be most short-sighted and unwise. Behind the Iron Curtain there are millions of people who long to escape the awful tyranny and terrorism under which they lie. We must be very careful that the gates of hope should not be closed upon them. We do not think that any prisoners of war in Korea in our hands should be forced to go back to the Communist area, especially now, after they have committed themselves, if they are still resolutely and sincerely resolved not to do so. I was very glad to see that this view, which I hold myself and with which my right hon Friend the Foreign Secretary was in full accord, was simultaneously and spontaneously expressed by the United States and that it has been approved by all parties in this House, including, in energetic and even eloquent terms, by the right hon Member for Derby, South [Mr Noel-Baker].

It is remarkable that the strongest refusal to go back to the Communist area was expressed by the Chinese: 16,000 out of 20,000 refused to go back. The American officers concerned saw very clearly how much this refusal would affect the truce negotiations. It would hit Communist China in its weakest point, namely, that so many of those who had lived there would want to get out of it and did not want to go back there. The Americans put pressure on these men to the fullest extent that decent humanity would permit, and still at the present moment upwards of 16,000 say they would rather die than return to their native land. That is a considerable fact in world history, and those who seek to discern the truth should let it sink into their consciousness. Who were these Chinese prisoners? We were assured that they were all volunteers—volunteers! They were not ordinary soldiers sent by their Government to perform some military task. No, they were the passionate volunteers, we were told, who, without involving the Chinese Government in the slightest responsibility, plunged forth to the rescue of South Korea from American aggression. That is what we were told. That has been the stuff, similar to that which is sucked up so avidly in various quarters in this country. That is the fiction on which we maintained our diplomatic representation. 16,000 out of 20,000 would rather die than go back. They must have undergone a very considerable conversion since they became prisoners of war; or perhaps the whole story of their being volunteers is wholly humbug from start to finish.

The Communist view is, of course, that they are being held back under duress, and have been coerced into changing their political convictions. No? I thought I would have got a cheer at this point. If this be so why cannot the offers we have made for a full screening by the Red Cross, or by any impartial or two-sided body that may be agreed, be accepted? That is the offer that has been made and has been rejected because the Chinese Communists and their Russian guides and puppet-pullers know quite well that they would not get the answer they want, and which to them is of the very first importance. I must say that this episode of the refusal of the great bulk of the Chinese prisoners to return to China, and the willingness of great numbers of them to take their own lives rather than do so, may be regarded as one of the most significant events of our time.

One practical question remains. Has harm been done to the truce negotiations by the bombing of the North Korean plants? It has been well said: 'Never prophesy unless you know.' There are some, like my hon Friend the Member for Lancaster [Mr F. Maclean], who contend that even good has been done. All that one can say at present is that so far no change in the existing unsatisfactory deadlock has occurred, but that the military security of the United Nations and United States Forces has been substantially increased by the destruction of plants that would have aided a heavy and formidable offensive against them.

There are other dangers that should be borne in mind. I read in this week's issue of the *New Statesman and Nation*, for instance, that

'Mr Truman should be told that unless, as Commander-in-Chief, he imposes his policy on his subordinates, and puts a stop to the provocative rearmament of Chiang Kai-shek on Formosa, Britain will withdraw her troops from Korea.'

MR EMRYS HUGHES: Hear, hear.

THE PRIME MINISTER: In my opinion, in the present electioneering atmosphere across the Atlantic there might well be Isolationists who would take such threats at their word and say: 'Let the British take their troops away and let us conduct the affair ourselves. We could easily replace their division with one of ours in Europe.' There are many Americans who think that China is more important than Europe. It certainly would be a great misfortune if that line of thought were to prevail. Indeed, it might easily lead to the ruin of the whole European structure of defence which is being built up with so much effort and sacrifice and would expose us all to mortal danger not only of war but of destruction. Everyone knows our main policy and that it is in full accord with the United States. At all costs avoid being sprawled about in China. That is and has always been our basic policy. That could not have been expressed more forcibly than by President Truman himself in his broadcast in April 1951.

I was, I think, the first in this House to suggest, in November 1949, recognition of the Chinese Communists. I thought at that time that the Americans had disinterested themselves in what had happened in China, and as we had great interests there and also on general grounds, I thought that it would be a good thing to have diplomatic representation. But if you recognize anyone it does not necessarily mean that you like him. We all, for instance, recognize the right hon Gentleman the Member for Ebbw Vale [Mr Bevan]. But it is just at the time when things are disagreeable between countries that you need diplomatic relations. But there is one thing which usually severs diplomatic relations, and that is the shedding of blood on a large scale by warlike action. It is remarkable that in spite of the fact that the Chinese have in no way responded to our diplomatic gesture and have, on the contrary, treated us with scorn and have shed the blood of our own soldiers and that of our allies, we should not only continue—our Government has continued the policy of the previous Government—to accord them diplomatic recognition; but, if we followed the advice of the party opposite, we would make it a major effort of policy to persuade the United States, with their twenty thousand dead, to do the same while the fighting is actually going on.

I have not endeavoured to answer the right hon Gentleman the Member for Derby, South [Mr Noel-Baker], because in the main I have only been preaching his theme by a parallel method. I can see hardly a point of difference between us, except that he has to do his best to move a vote of censure. We ask the House to cast this censure back upon those who have moved it. The attitude towards the United States of many of the Socialists below the Gangway is devoid alike of wisdom and of prudence. We denounce their wanton and reckless conduct, seeming to care nothing for the peace and freedom of the world and the safety of this island; and there is no one who cannot feel ashamed at the deference which has to be paid to them by their leaders on the Front Bench opposite.

# THE ECONOMIC POSITION

A SPEECH TO THE HOUSE OF COMMONS
30 JULY 1952

---

5 July—*It is announced in Bucharest that Madame Anna Pauker has been dismissed from the post of Foreign Minister.*

7 July—*The American liner 'United States' on her maiden voyage from New York to Le Havre and Southampton establishes a new speed record and wins the Blue Riband for the United States.*

12 July—*General Eisenhower is nominated on the first ballot as the Republican Presidential Candidate for the November Elections.*

15 July—*Mr William Draper, Head of the Mutual Security Programme, announces in Paris that the United States Armed Forces have placed orders in Europe worth nearly $700,000,000 for 'off-shore' purchases of military equipment in the year ended 30 July.*

23 July—*Coup d'état by General Neguib in Egypt.*

24 July—*The Prime Minister and the Minister of Labour receive the members of the TUC Economic Committee at 10 Downing Street to consider wages policy.*

26 July—*Governor Adlai Stevenson of Illinois is nominated in Chicago as Democratic Presidential Candidate for the forthcoming Elections in November.*

26 July—*Abdication of King Farouk.*

27 July—*Official opening of the 'V.I. Lenin Volga-Don Ship Canal'.*

28 July—*Field-Marshal Earl Alexander, Minister of Defence, announces that a British officer, Major-General S. N. Shoosmith, has been appointed Deputy Chief of Staff at the Headquarters of General Mark Clark, United Nations Supreme Commander in Korea.*

---

[30 July 1952

*Order read for resuming Adjourned Debate on Question* [29 July]:

'*That this House welcomes the determination of Her Majesty's Government to maintain the progress so far made towards improving the balance of overseas payments and to take such further measures as may be necessary for the economic security of the country.*'

*Question again proposed.*

There is no doubt that our financial and economic position has improved substantially in the first six months of this year as the result of the considerable measures taken since we became responsible. Nevertheless, at the beginning of June my right hon Friend the Chancellor of the Exchequer informed his colleagues that the margin of safety was not sufficient. He asked for a further effort to restore the balance between exports and imports by substantial economies, and he asked that these should be effective in the last six months of the present calendar year.

The Chancellor convinced us that a new and strenuous effort was necessary and urgent. Since then we have been engaged upon a severe scrutiny of our resources, unusual at this time of the year. The first objective was to find economies in imports and improvements in exports which would yield their results within the short period specified. This made the task particularly difficult because of the limited sphere of economies which come to hand in so short a time. This involved a midsummer overhaul of our expenditure in a good many fields. It was, however, a special and short-term study, and it is in no way a substitute for the detailed, long-term examination of the Estimates which usually begins in November and is the foundation of the Budget for the coming year; that is to say, the financial year 1953.

What we sought to achieve was a stronger protection of our gold and dollar reserves which at less than 1,700 million dollars, leave us too much at the mercy of unfavourable episodes outside these shores or in the immense sterling area of which we are the bankers. We are therefore now apprising the House and the world of a further tightening up and consolidation of our resources on a scale which, taken with all that has gone before, should not in any way be underrated.

I thought that the Chancellor's speech yesterday was somewhat ill-treated, both here and out of doors, considering the commanding position which he has made for himself in Parliament and the immense load he has had to bear. I have helped him all I could in those efforts to further economies and he has been successful to a remarkable degree. I am told of differences between us. I was not aware that any existed—[HON MEMBERS: 'Oh.']—but they are certainly nothing like the differences between a contented cat purring over a substantial meal—including a second helping—and the ravenous jaguar who, six weeks ago, was prowling round our spending Departments in search of prey. I think that if my right hon Friend found reasons for satisfaction yesterday, he may well justify himself by the very remarkable economies which he has effected by his influence and by his pertinacity at this period of the year.

Let me summarize shortly what he told us yesterday. Imports of unrationed foods will, in the second half of this year, amount to only three-quarters of what they were in the same period in 1951. That is a cut of 25 per cent. Imports of raw materials and manufactures will be even more drastically reduced. Pulp and paper imports, for example, will be less than half of what they were in the second half of 1951, and imports of manufactured goods will be reduced by 40 per cent. Exports of coal will be sharply increased in the remaining months of the year.

MR HUGH GAITSKELL (Leeds, South): I wonder whether the Prime Minister would clear up one point——

THE PRIME MINISTER: Today it is the desire that speeches should be kept as short as possible——

MR GAITSKELL: I do not want to interrupt the right hon Gentleman, but I should be obliged if he would tell us whether the import cuts which he has just mentioned constitute new decisions, adding further to the total of import cuts which the Chancellor announced in his Budget statement.

THE PRIME MINISTER: Well, I am giving the facts as I gathered them from the speech my right hon Friend made yesterday. [HON MEMBERS: 'Answer.'] Exports of coal, as I said, will be sharply— [HON MEMBERS: 'You do not know?'] I do not mind at all being interrupted. I think the habit of disorderliness which I have noticed on the benches opposite recently only shows what guilty consciences hon Members have. The aim at the end of the year—[HON MEMBERS: 'Answer.']—the aim at the end of this year—[HON MEMBERS: 'Answer.'] I will not answer a question if I do not choose. You distinguish yourselves by denying me a fair hearing. [HON MEMBERS: 'Answer.'] I could not have been making a simpler or plainer statement of what was said of our policy yesterday as announced by the Chancellor of the Exchequer.

By increased sales of military equipment we expect to earn another £10 million this year. All this was said yesterday, and then it was argued that no effective statement had been made. As a matter of fact— [Interruption.] I am not apparently allowed to adduce and define the statement to show that that assumption which has been so impatiently made by hon Gentlemen opposite is as devoid of foundation as many of their other dogmas. These measures to strengthen our reserves and to increase confidence in our resolve to maintain solvency must not be viewed by themselves alone. Apart from their beneficial effect upon the United Kingdom economy, they are the preliminary to the economic conference of the Commonwealth Prime Ministers which I announced to the House yesterday and which is to open here on 25 November. At this conference the whole position of the sterling area will be searchingly reviewed and we shall enter upon the discussions all the stronger for the action we are taking now.

Various questions were asked yesterday about the conference. It will be a meeting of Prime Ministers and, in accordance with custom, I shall preside. But I shall, of course, have the help of my colleagues who are directly concerned with the special matters under discussion. The preparations for this conference concern a number of Ministers, including particularly the Foreign Secretary, the Secretary of State for Commonwealth Relations, the Chancellor of the Exchequer and the President of the Board of Trade. These preparations, which are already in hand, are being supervised on my behalf by the Foreign Secretary in his capacity as Deputy Prime Minister.

The Chancellor of the Exchequer spoke yesterday mainly about the civil economy. It falls to me to speak more at length about defence. One of our greatest problems in the hard discussions which we have had has been that of finding means by which, despite our economic difficulties, we can still maintain a defence effort in accordance with our duties and our needs. We shall not weaken in our resolve to do our utmost in the defence of the free democracies. We reaffirm our determination to stand fast with the Commonwealth, with the United States and our other Allies, in resisting the encroachments of Communism. In particular, in the West, we are resolved to stand shoulder to shoulder with the United States and our Allies in Europe in resisting any aggression. But there can be no assurance of lasting military strength without a firm economic foundation, and no defence programme can stand without the economic resources to carry it through. The defence programmes must be kept within the limits of our economic strength. The right hon Gentleman the Member for Leeds, South [Mr Gaitskell], seemed to suggest that no review or revision of our armament scheme could be undertaken by us except in conjunction with all the other Allied Powers.

I trust indeed that we shall continue to set an example to the European States, and no doubt when the meetings of NATO take place in the autumn we shall all discuss together our common affairs and how we have got on. But to suggest, as the right hon Gentleman did, that we have no right to make necessary or even beneficial changes in our own military organization and expenditure without a general meeting of all the NATO Powers would be an abrogation of our rights and an alteration of our ordinary practice such as I have not hitherto seen in peace or war.

Let me now look back a little. Two years ago, after the outbreak of the war in Korea, the Socialist Government, with praiseworthy zeal but little study, announced a rearmament programme of £3,600 million to cover both new equipment and the maintenance of the

Forces, spread over three years. Five months later, for reasons which were not made clear at the time, they raised this figure to £4,700 million. Now, by the decline in the purchasing power of the pound, it would be about £5,400 million.

The original £4,700 million at the old prices was divided by the late Government in their three-year plan as follows: 1951, £1,250 million; 1952, £1,531 million; 1953, £1,694 million, making a total for the three years of £4,475 million, to which they added £225 million for civil defence and stock-piling, thus making up the total of £4,700 million. I pointed out, however, in December that it would not be possible to complete so vast a scheme in the period prescribed. There are the inevitable time-lags which may be put, in the first two years, at between 10 per cent and 20 per cent. In the first year, 1951, actual expenditure was only £1,132 million as compared with the programme figure of £1,250 million. In the current year, 1952, we expect, though this is nothing more than a very speculative estimate, to spend £1,462 million against the forecast of £1,531 million made by our predecessors. I thought that the House might like to have these figures in their minds.

Nevertheless, had we not made a considerable slowing down of the programme to which we had been committed, spreading it into the fourth year, the total bill for these three years would have been far above £4,700 million. Actually, on our present decisions and calculations, we and our predecessors, allowing for the price increase which has been continuous, will have spent in the three years a sum not far short of the £4,700 million originally proposed. But, through the time-lag and increased costs, there will be a short-fall in the results achieved in the first three years. Our resources are not expanding at the rate we need to enable us to recover in any period which can be foreseen the position which we held before the war. As a contribution to the immense new burden of the rearmament plan, we are receiving in this year, 1952, about £175 million from the United States; but this is quite different from the £400 million or £500 million a year enjoyed by the late Government before the arms programme was begun, in loans or gifts from the United States and, to a lesser extent, from Canada and the Commonwealth. It must never be forgotten that this foreign aid, on which the Socialist Government lived for its whole tenure of power, virtually made good the loss of foreign investments that we suffered at the beginning of the war. Now we are facing the increased burden without having either the one or the other. Now we are striving to repay the American loan with interest.

All these facts might well, I think, be taken into consideration by all fair-minded people friendly to Britain and her survival. If this cold war ordeal is to continue—and it certainly does not rest with us—we must organize our defences on lines which do not require a constantly expanding expenditure of money and materials over an indefinite period. Within those boundaries, very great improvements and economies, in the true sense of a higher fertility, will be possible, and it is to this that the Ministry of Defence, under Lord Alexander, whose knowledge in all these matters is of the greatest value to us, and the three great Service Departments, are now devoting their unremitting attention.

The original programme was conceived by the late Government in the mood of the crisis which came upon them when the Korean War began. Many of the resources and much of the equipment in hand at the end of the war had been improvidently dispersed or destroyed. Virtually no new equipment had been provided. For five years the Forces had lived on vanishing war stocks, and there was a heavy leeway to make up. Rearmament was such a violent reversal of the policy previously pursued that many errors in the programme were inevitable. Since we assumed office nine months ago, we have made a comprehensive review of defence policy and strategy, and we are now engaged in reshaping the original programme so as to bring it into accord with the results of our new assessment of the position.

There are two requirements to be met. First, we have to take account of the ceaseless technical developments which affect our preparations for a world war, should such a disaster come upon us. In the two years that have passed since the original programme was launched, some weapons, on which immense sums were to be spent, have become obsolescent, and new types and devices of a greatly improved character have come into view. These technical advances have resulted in changes of military tactics and, in turn, changes of emphasis as between the various sectors of the defence production programme. Immense strides have been made by the United States, not only in their stockpile of atomic weapons, but in the power of atomic weapons, and in the range and accuracy of their delivery. All this is reinforced by the advent of new aircraft which profoundly affect the tactics of air warfare and anti-air defence. Remarkable progress has also been made in our own development of guided missiles, or guided rockets, as was mentioned by the Minister of Supply the other day. On the other hand, the development, such as it may be, of the atomic weapon by Russia is a factor which, though unknowable, we must increasingly bear in mind. At sea, we have to be prepared to meet new and faster types of U-boat and novel methods of mining. All these developments change the picture of the likely course and character of a future war, and many consequential changes are enforced upon the scale and pattern of weapons and equipment required.

We must not think of a possible Third World War in terms of the first, or even the second, of these vast human catastrophes. The days of prolonged artillery bombardment, of immense and almost stationary armies, had vanished before the Second World War came. The expenditure on ammunition in the future may be far less than in the Second World War, and merely to proceed on the previous conventional lines would be to squander our military treasure and our strength. These developments have affected the views of our military experts on the character and course of any future struggle, and this process of change continues, and even accelerates, with the remorseless march of the science of human destruction.

The second requirement we may have to meet is the continuance of armed peace or cold war, as forecast by the right hon Gentleman the Member for Lewisham, South [Mr H. Morrison], for a prolonged period. The technical developments which I have just mentioned will not help us much in that. It is by more conventional armaments, mainly, in fact, by the infantry soldier serving in so many parts of the world, that we have to make our current contribution towards security against Communist encroachment. The need to maintain this kind of military strength in peace must be balanced against the other need to ensure that, if war comes, we shall be able to meet the first intense phase with all its new inventions. I do not doubt that, if the party opposite had continued in power, they would also have been impelled by these developments to review and recast their original scheme, which we supported.

To sum up this part of the argument, I would say that, allowing for the time-lag on the one hand, and the increase of costs on the other, we shall in four years have spent more on re-equipment than was proposed by the late Government for three. But the improvements in types of weapons will have enabled many practical economies and reductions to be made in the original programme with a positive increase in war power. Had that original programme been allowed to continue in its expanding course after the third year, the expenditure would have risen enormously beyond our power to bear. I will repeat, in a varied form, what I have said before—that a period of rearmament follows the rule: first year, nothing; the second, not much; the third year, more than you can pay for. With the great complexity of modern weapons, and particularly of aircraft, this rule must now be extended into the fourth and even the fifth year.

If we had followed up to its logical conclusion the defence programme which we found descending upon us when we took office, we should have been exposed in 1954 or 1955 to enormous increases in expenditure, unforeseen, so far as we know, at the time when the programme was originally launched, and utterly beyond our economic capacity to bear. Even if we had not been called upon at this time to make new efforts to stimulate exports and to reduce the investment programme and social expenditure at home, it would, in any event, have been necessary to grip the whole position in order to prevent the automatic growth of defence expenditure from rising in the third, fourth and fifth years far beyond the limits of our economic strength.

It must be remembered that the process of rearmament is a continuous one. Modern weapons take two or three years to make. Modern aircraft take four or even five years. It is wasteful to the highest degree to spend many months retooling factories for rearmament and moving labour for that purpose, and then, while the weapons are still good and current, to break them up and disperse the labour. Very good reasons must be shown in every case where contracts are modified or cancelled with heavy costs in compensation and ineffectual employment of skilled labour. It is the continuity of what we were committed to that I am drawing to the attention of the House. Therefore, although we are varying the programme, for the reasons which I have explained, it is still essentially the programme shaped and put forward by the late Government at a time when the right hon Member for Ebbw Vale [Mr Bevan] was one of its leading Members. Indeed, had he remained responsible, he, and others associated with him, would have had to make some of the changes which we are now making. But in view of the programme on which he helped to launch us, and the great mass of contracts already placed before he left office, he has every right to share the credit, as he shares the responsibility, for what was in the main a timely and patriotic decision.

So far I have been dwelling on finance. Money, however, is not the only limiting factor in rearmament. Steel and its companion products impose absolute limits, alike on our solvency and on our security. We are importing more than a million tons of steel and pig-iron this year, and prospects of an improvement in our outlook next year are not unfavourable. Perhaps that is an understatement. I hope so. If so, the understatement may be set against any errors in the opposite direction which I may be considered to make. The problem is how exactly the steel available after domestic needs are met should be allocated between defence services and exports, for without a sufficiency of exports, as the House knows and as I have so often said, a collapse of our economic and financial life would overwhelm us. It cannot be dogmatically stated that defence should have absolute priority over exports, or vice versa. Our supply of steel and various other metals is limited, and it would be equally foolish for the Government to lay it down that either armaments or exports should have an unlimited call on them at the expense of the other. Demands on these materials by those engaged in manufacturing goods for exports have to be carefully weighed one at a time—weighed carefully against our individual defence requirements—and we hope and believe that we can, with patience, strike a balance which will build up our defences without endangering our solvency.

What applies to steel applies also to the transfer of industrial capacity throughout the metal-using and engineering industries. This diversion of resources from defence to the export drive is just as necessary for our military strength as for our daily lives. Not to make it would be to plunge into bankruptcy. It seems, therefore, and it is true to say, that priority is given to exports over defence, but the sphere in which such transfers will be fruitful is a limited one, and there will still be left a very heavy quantity of steel for the defence programme. This process is going on now. Every case is being considered on its merits. I am not going to publish exact figures on these matters; we have no parallel information from Soviet sources. But I may say that, broadly speaking, the decisions we have reached after months of intensive labour will alter the pattern of defence production in a way which will limit its demands on the engineering industry, and in the coming years set free a valuable part of its capacity for the expansion of our civil exports.

Mr Aneurin Bevan (Ebbw Vale): How much?

The Prime Minister: I cannot possibly estimate how much.

Mr Bevan rose——

The Prime Minister: The right hon Gentleman is going to have an opportunity, I believe, of speaking later in the debate, so I hope he will allow me to complete my argument.

Mr Bevan: Perhaps the right hon Gentleman would give way.

The Prime Minister: Very well.

Mr Bevan: I asked the Chancellor yesterday whether he would give us the figure of the reduction, if any, in the arms programme, and the right hon Gentleman said he was leaving it to the Prime Minister to tell the House what he wanted to tell the House about defence today. Has the right hon Gentleman no figure in his mind at which priorities are to become exercisable? If the priorities for exports run ahead too far, at what figure will they be arrested for the defence programme?

The Prime Minister: Well, I have no intention whatever of trying to anticipate the study which will be given to these matters in their final form in the November examination.

MR HAROLD DAVIES (Leek): Have the Government not done anything? Nothing has been done.

THE PRIME MINISTER: After all, I am in possession of the House, and I am perfectly entitled to take that course.

MR DAVIES: We have had two speeches from the Government with nothing in them.

THE PRIME MINISTER: No doubt the hon Gentleman will later try to catch Mr Speaker's eye.

MR DAVIES: There was nothing in them about what we have been waiting for.

THE PRIME MINISTER: I have been endeavouring to show the general tendencies which are modifying and affecting our policy in rearmament, but I am certainly not in a position to say how these will affect the estimates of expenditure for next year, or even for the course of this year.

There is, however, one section of steel to be transferred from armaments to exports which will I am sure, interest the House, if only from its paradoxical character. I mean the export of armaments to friendly and allied countries. It may indeed seem odd, when we are straining to rearm that we should be willing to sell armaments to others. It was suggested yesterday that it would be better to starve the armaments plants and turn instead for all exports to civil production. I think the right hon Gentleman was one of those who raised that point. This would indeed be imprudent. Moreover, armaments are, in these uneasy days, best sellers; they find a ready and profitable market. But the savings and efficiency that come from mass production, and the advantage of having the plants kept at their full compass, with all that that means for reserve power in the plants and in the pipeline should war come, is so great that in this time of stringency we feel fully justified in making contracts with Canada, with the United States or with other countries for the supply of tanks and aeroplanes which will thus form a valuable addition to our high-grade exports, and at the same time enable our parent plants to develop their full strength.

MR PERCY SHURMER (Birmingham, Sparkbrook): They are obsolete.

THE PRIME MINISTER: The price we pay is, of course, that some weapons that we make in this time of need will go abroad, though care will be taken not to deprive our front line of its essential requirements. I feel keenly the responsibility of this decision, but I find myself in fullest agreement with the Minister of Defence, the Foreign Secretary and the Chancellor, with whom I have so long pondered upon these and similar matters. I feel myself in full agreement in believing that the export of a certain proportion of our munitions will be a feature in the growth of our munition plants, as well as an aid to our trade balance. Moreover, it will strengthen our friends and Allies throughout the Commonwealth and NATO.

We are now, as I have explained, approaching the third year where expansion of our armament programme is beginning to come into full swing, and when, if the process is not to get out of control, effectual limits must be assigned to its demands. It will be necessary for all three Fighting Services to divide their budgets between the maintenance of existing forces and new and improved equipment. At the Admiralty we have always considered maintenance and new construction as separate features. But this is less easy in the Army, where manpower has been in former times the outstanding factor. In the Air Force, which is a newcomer to the first place in our defence, the pressure of new types and superior inventions is intense.

The worst thing that happened to the Air Force since rearmament began was the failure to take the steps needed to accelerate the arrival of the newest and finest types of aircraft. This is now being remedied under, what I venture to call, super-priorities. For the sake of this, it will be necessary to reduce the maintenance charge in the existing Air Force by ceaseless economies in the overheads, or what perhaps may be called in this connection 'the under-foots'. The key figure of all Air Force administration is the number of men required to keep a fighting aeroplane and its pilot and crew in the air. In the late war this rose to 112. At present it is, according to Air Force figures, 113, but with the expansion of the Air Force it is planned to reduce it to 95. Of course, the new types of aircraft which are coming into service, and more so those that await us in the future, require many refinements of care both in the training of the crews and the maintenance of the machines. The rule must, however, be that every man on the strength of the Air Force must be judged by his contribution to our flying fighting strength. The provision and skilled use of the latest types must, above all things, remain at the head of the list. It might well be that the number of air personnel could be reduced without detriment by a system of what I have called in the past 'immediate reserves'. In the Navy, before the First World War, we created an 'immediate reserve' several thousand strong of highly-skilled men, sailors and mechanics, who were held ready to come up if called upon in a precautionary period, without, or in advance of, any general calling out of the reserves. This system still exists in the Navy and has been applied in the Army. It may prove a great help to the Royal Air Force at the present juncture.

In the Army the obvious way of reducing maintenance is to reduce numbers, and the question always arises where to strike the balance between a smaller number of men, fully trained and highly equipped, and a larger number at a lower level of training and equipment. The intake of men into the Army next year will be about 30,000 fewer than this year. The explanation of this is that a decrease is taking place in the number of Regular non-commissioned officers who train the new entry. These non-commissioned officers are departing to civil life, as they have a right to do, and the War Office do not feel that they can handle the full intake without some loss of efficiency. This misfortune will incidentally reduce the cost of maintenance. It will, however, have very little effect on the need for new equipment which is required for the existing trained formations.

MR F. J. BELLENGER (Bassetlaw): Are we to understand that the Regular Army content is to be reduced, or the National Service intake?

THE PRIME MINISTER: No; the National Service intake will be reduced.

LIEUT-COLONEL LIPTON (Lambeth, Brixton): How?

THE PRIME MINISTER: I am assured that there is no difficulty about that. I do not desire to go too much into detail on these matters.

MR ALFRED ROBENS (Blyth): As the National Service intake is to be reduced, does that mean that there is now to be a study of the deferment of call up?

THE PRIME MINISTER: That question ought to be put to the Secretary of State for War. I have answered five questions and I will answer no more questions at this juncture. [HON MEMBERS: 'Oh.'] Five is quite a lot. Even if the right hon Gentleman holds up his hand like a boy at school, I will not defer to his wishes.

MR ROBENS: May I pursue my point?

THE PRIME MINISTER: In the third year of rearmament, namely, 1953, a very heavy fertile crop of new equipment will be coming along. At this point may I say that I was astonished at the suggestion made by the late Minister of Defence, the right hon Member for Easington [Mr Shinwell], in a speech at Rugby on 12 July, that the period of compulsory National Service should be reduced from two years to eighteen months. It would hardly be possible to adopt a more improvident course. The fighting units of our Army today are almost all overseas; at least one-half are in the far-off foreign stations of the Middle East, Malaya and Korea, and in all of these there are rather more National Service men than Regulars.

The final six months of their two years' service is of the utmost value, since their efficiency as soldiers will by then have reached its peak. It is during these last six months that a man really begins to gain that degree of training and morale on which so much depends. Indeed, we are today relying on many of those fine young men to play their part in junior leadership, and many National Service junior officers and non-commissioned officers are to be found in our fighting units abroad. To reduce the period of service would aggravate in the most wasteful manner our movements problem. A very large number of men, over 30,000, would be permanently and completely out of action travelling to and fro in the pipeline. In the Middle East, for instance, the rate of reinforcement would rise from 24,000 a year, on the two years' system, to 35,000 a year on the eighteen months' system. In Korea it would rise from 5,500 a year to over 12,000. The saving in cash of about £17 million by the reduction of service would bring a loss of 58,000 men, which would grievously injure the Army structure built up at such heavy cost. Moreover, from the saving of £17 million on Estimates which are over £450 million, there would have to be deducted the cost of extra transport.

There is one further argument which should not be overlooked, and which the right hon Gentleman I think should not overlook.

Mr E. Shinwell (Easington): Is the right hon Gentleman arguing with me?

The Prime Minister: We have been pressing our friends on the Continent, in France and the Benelux countries, to raise their service to two years. Belgium has already adopted it. Such a step is absolutely necessary to the re-creation of the French Army, with its heavy burden of foreign service. If we were to step back now and reduce our service, it is certain that the hopes of NATO would fail.

How, then, should we without casting doubts upon our sincerity reduce our two years' period of service at this present critical juncture in the build-up of a Western defence organization? It is not long since the right hon Gentleman was himself pressing this view on the House. It was as recently as 30 May in the present year.

Mr Shinwell: Will the right hon Gentleman give way?

The Prime Minister: I will certainly give the right hon Gentleman time to get up when I have finished this point. I am taking a lot of trouble with him because I am most anxious that some of the good things that he has done shall not be entirely swept away from his credit account. As recently as 30 May, speaking in this House, he said:

'. . . there is not a high military authority in this country or associated with NATO or elsewhere who does not agree that, even if all the equipment were provided in the build-up of the Western defence organization, it will not serve our purpose in the event of aggression unless the period of National Service which we have imposed upon ourselves is accepted by the other countries.'

That is what the right hon Gentleman said on 30 May. Yet on 12 July—not six weeks later—he urged that our period of National Service should be reduced to eighteen months. What an example to set.

MR SHINWELL: I cannot do it just now for obvious reasons, but one of these days I will take trouble with the right hon Gentleman and explain to him exactly the reasons we decided upon a two years' period of National Service. Might I remind him that at the time we did so we said that this was a temporary measure? That is the first point. The second point is this. When he talks about the difficulty that would present itself in our cutting down the period of National Service, he should have regard to the fact that there are many existing commitments which will in due course be reduced. Let me give him one example and then I will sit down, because I do not want to argue with him at this stage. Just now we have nearly three divisions in the Middle East, far more than ever we had in peacetime before. One of these days we shall be able to reduce the number of divisions in the Middle East and then, as we have a vast number of trained reserves, we shall be able to reduce the period of National Service. Let the right hon Gentleman argue against that.

THE PRIME MINISTER: I am sorry that the right hon Gentleman should deprive himself of the consistency of his policy, because, as I have shown, up to 30 May he was strongly in favour of the maintenance of the two-year system—and the credit of introducing it is due to him—but now he turns to this new proposal—which I consider to be alike dangerous and unthrifty—for, I suppose, highly complicated reasons connected with the movement of opinion in the party opposite.

MR SHINWELL: Will the right hon Gentleman give way for one moment?

THE PRIME MINISTER: I cannot give way again.

MR SHINWELL: That is a shocking and disgraceful thing to say. The right hon Gentleman should be ashamed of himself.

MR DEPUTY-SPEAKER [SIR CHARLES MACANDREW]: Order.

MR SHINWELL: The right hon Gentleman has given way.

MR DEPUTY-SPEAKER: Order. The Prime Minister is sitting down because I am standing up. If the Prime Minister does not give way, right hon Gentlemen must remain in their seats.

MR SHINWELL: The right hon Gentleman ought not to have said that. It is disgraceful. He should be ashamed of himself.

THE PRIME MINISTER: The French have a saying that it is only the truth that wounds.

MR SHINWELL: It was a disgraceful thing to say. The Prime Minister does not give anybody any credit. I will deal with him next Monday.

THE PRIME MINISTER: Why not on Sunday evening? Yesterday, I was surprised to see the right hon Gentleman the Member for Leeds, South [Mr Hugh Gaitskell], standing so smiling and carefree at the Dispatch Box as if he had no responsibility for the shocking and shameful state to which our finances were reduced during his tenure of the Exchequer. When a Minister has in a single year brought his country from the best position it had held since the war to the verge of bankruptcy, and when he has left to his successors heart-tearing problems to face and solve, I wonder indeed that he should find nothing to do but mock and jeer at the efforts that others make to clear up the confusion and disorder that he left behind him. Indeed, I almost think it is a pity that he ever escaped from Winchester. Let me also say in answer to him and to that shining star of television, my hon Friend the Member for Aberdeenshire, East [Mr Boothby], whose rays were turned upon me last night— I very much regret not having heard his speech—that I do not take back a word I said in describing, not the immediate crisis, for that we are dealing with, but the general financial economic position of our country. My resolve is that the people should realize how different is their position from that of all other Western communities; fifty million of us here standing at a level of civilization not surpassed in the world, and yet barely able to earn our living and pay our way, and dependent for the food of two-fifths of our people on how we can do this in this vast swirling world.

Tragic it is indeed. [*Laughter.*] Why is there laughter? Surely it is not a party matter. [*Interruption.*] Hon Gentlemen opposite cannot get much by shouting me down. Tragic indeed is the spectacle of the might, majesty, dominion and power of the once magnificent and still considerable British Empire having to worry and wonder how we can pay our monthly bills. I fully admit I am tortured by this thought and by the processes which I see around me, and I will do everything in my power—[HON MEMBERS: 'Resign!']—to bring home to the mass of our race and nation the sense of peril and the need for grave and far-reaching exertions.

# ST BARNABAS SCHOOL

---

4 *August—First meeting of the Pacific Council in Honolulu. The United States is represented by Mr Dean Acheson, Australia by Mr R. G. Casey and New Zealand by Mr Clifton Webb. No British representative is invited to the meeting of the 'Anzus' Powers.*

11 *August—The two Houses of the Jordanian Parliament decide that King Talal is mentally unfit to rule, declare his reign at an end and proclaim his son, the Crown Prince Hussein, as King of Jordan. As King Hussein is only 17 years old, a Regency Council of three is appointed.*

15 *August—250 square miles of North Devon and West Somerset in the Lynton-Lynmouth area are completely flooded.*

20 *August—Marshal Stalin announces that the Communist Party of the USSR will hold its 19th Congress in Moscow on October 5.*

24 *August—Government of Kenya issue a statement that the continuance of a state of growing unrest and disregard for law and order will not be tolerated.*

30 *August—New Anglo-American proposals for the solution of the Anglo-Persian oil dispute are handed to Dr Mossadeq.*

2 *September—It is announced from Buckingham Palace that HM The Queen, on the recommendation of HM Ministers in Australia, has appointed Field-Marshal Sir William Slim as Governor-General of Australia in succession to Sir William McKell.*

6 *September—Thirty people killed and sixty-three injured when a de Havilland 110 prototype plane piloted by Mr John Derry, DFC, disintegrates during an air display at Farnborough.*

---

[6 *September* 1952

Parliament is having a holiday. That is a very good thing for the House of Commons. I have rarely seen it more jaded in the fifty years I have served there. Those who value the strength of our Parliamentary institutions will realize that nothing weakens them more than for the House of Commons to go on bickering and biting and barking, with only short intervals all the year round, with everybody tired of their scenes and nobody reading their Debates. For the House of Commons to keep its influence and authority with the nation, definite pauses are needed so that the Members can recover their physical and mental strength, and make good contacts with their constituents, while Ministers are able to take a more general view of their problems, and while the life, work and thought of the country can go forward in a calmer and quieter mood. I have therefore exerted myself to procure for Parliament a ten-weeks' break, from which they will return I trust with new health and strength, and better poised to discharge their duties.

There is another reason which I must not forget for Parliament having a holiday. We felt it would be a good thing for the Opposition to have a little leisure to think over their political position, and arrive at some more coherent form of thought, and consistent line of policy. Something better than class warfare is surely needed at a time when parties are so evenly balanced that it is really like setting one-half of the nation against the other. As I have said, four-fifths of both parties agree on four-fifths of what should be done and after all we all sink or swim together on our perilous voyage into the unknown future. It certainly was a fine thing to see the great trade unions pronounce so clearly upon the need of building up the defence of Britain as one of the United Nations of the free world, and I hope that our policy of keeping our rearmament within the bounds of national solvency will also commend itself to sensible men and women throughout the country. Wise statesmanship has also been shown at Margate on the vital question of wage restraint, so important to the success of our renewed export drive. The action of the TUC will do much to assist the Government in its all-out attack on the cost of living. In asking for wage restraint, I want to emphasize that we do not in any way wish to limit the earnings of any section of the working population. On the contrary, it is our aim to encourage the highest possible level of earnings in every industry, provided these swim upon increased output and efficiency.

British trade unionism is a national institution, representing much that is solid in our island character, and I have always urged Conservative wage-earners, of whom we have so many millions, to join their unions and take an active interest in their work. The increasing association of employees and wage earners with business and industry, through joint consultation, profit-sharing and varied forms of co-partnership, certainly opens paths we should not hesitate to tread.

There is also a larger reason why Parliament should have substantial periods of repose. The strength and character of a national civilization is not built up like a scaffolding or fitted together like a machine. Its growth is more like that of a plant or a tree. The British oak, on which for centuries our Navy depended, grows slowly and noiselessly without headlines or sensation and no one should ever cut one down without planting another. It is very much easier and quicker to cut down trees than to grow them. In cases where bad, oppressive laws warp the free development of human society much cutting down may be needed and sometimes the forest itself has to be cleared. Great work was done by the Liberal and Conservative Parties in the nineteenth century, but the twentieth century with its terrible events has brought us problems of a different order, not many of which can be solved merely by passing Acts of Parliament.

In order that the business of Parliament shall be properly planned, it is desirable that the principal Bills of the session should be introduced before Christmas, and this requires long months of preparation and drafting beforehand. As we did not become responsible till the end of October, and were hardly formed as a Government till the middle of November, it was not, in any case, possible to bring in the measures we announced in the King's Speech until much later in the session. We had also to face at the very outset of our task the grave financial crisis, with its imminent danger of national bankruptcy. It was the fear of having to cope with this which had forced our predecessors to have a General Election. I will presently speak to you about the measures we have taken to restore our solvency and build up our reserves. But they certainly dominated our thoughts and action during our first few months of power. The solemn event of the demise of the Crown involved a further suspension of normal Parliamentary business, and for these reasons it was not possible for us to pass into law this session the two principal measures to which we have pledged ourselves, namely, the denationalization of road transport and of the steel industry. The delay, however, has enabled both these complicated problems to be studied with deep attention, and both these measures will be introduced in the new session in November and will, I have no doubt, be passed into law before it ends next year.

I will first speak to you about the Transport Bill. This is a measure designed to restore vitality and flexibility to our road transport system, as well as to improve and strengthen the working of our national railways. It is not generally realized what a small part of our road transport has been taken over by the State. Only 41,000 lorries had been acquired, out of a total of over a million mercantile road vehicles. For this twenty-fifth part of our road transport an enormous centralized overhead organization has been set up at a very heavy cost and with far-reaching powers. I have no doubt that all the 12,000 officials, apart altogether from the ordinary management, did their best to manage the 41,000 vehicles.

I was, however, astonished to learn that over 800,000 vehicles are run under 'C' licences and still more that these 'C' licences have risen by 300,000 since the 1947 Act. Now what is a 'C' licence? It means that the lorry or vehicle can only be used to carry the goods of its owner. This means that a very considerable portion of our road transport wastes its strength in one way traffic, and consumes labour, petrol and machinery in processes which cannot be reconciled with sound economy and good housekeeping. It also means that the alternative service offered by the State vehicles did not attract this enormous number of users. Surely in times like these, when we have to do everything in our power to promote the vitality and efficiency of British industry, we cannot afford this waste. This startling increase in 'C' licences—which has not merely taken place in the small delivery van type of vehicle but also in the large types capable of carrying heavy loads—is the best indication of how dissatisfied traders are with the road services provided by the British Transport Commission. It is our belief that a vehicle in the hands of a private haulier, able to carry anyone's goods and allowed to cater in free competition for the public need, is a more flexible and efficient instrument than it can be in the hands of a vast, unwieldy, centralized public corporation, for whose sake other hauliers must be hampered and restricted. And by the cheaper rates which we hope to see being offered, we trust that the increase in these 'C' licensed vehicles will be halted.

Another part of our proposed measure liberates the railways from some of the ancient statutory fetters which prevent their competing, as they would wish, with road transport. Thus in both spheres—railway and road transport—we are setting free the capacity to provide cheaper transport. Of course a question like this has got to be debated by Parliament, but I am sure any responsible Government trying to expand the productive energies of our country would have been wrong to leave our road transport to suffer the unnatural direction and restriction to which it was being subjected for the sake of Socialist theory.

We do not think there will be any difficulty in transferring the 41,000 vehicles back to private ownership, thus making the interchange of goods between man and man throughout our island, more smooth, more easy and more fertile to the public welfare. That at any rate is what we are going to do. I claim that these measures, on which we shall concentrate next session are inspired solely by the resolve to make things go better for the advantage of all. I will go further. I claim that we have been actuated by no thought but to bring our country out of the troubles of peace as we did out of the perils of war.

We have also tried to increase the incentive to active and skilful labour. In Mr Butler's first Budget, two million wage-earners were exempted altogether from income tax, in order to produce more in the hard times through which we are passing. Another form of incentive is the possibility of having, and still more of owning, a home of your own where a family can live and grow and have its own front door, which none may pass except by invitation or with proper warrant. Insufficient and bad housing is a hindrance to production, and this is especially true in times of rearmament and change. More than that, it is destructive of happiness and morality and a reproach to a Christian nation. Some of our political opponents used to mock us because we have set before ourselves as our goal a rate of building 300,000 houses a year. We mean to reach our goal and we are already making steady progress towards it, under the skilful and broad-minded management of Mr Harold Macmillan, the first Cabinet Minister of Housing. He has been helped by his able Parliamentary Secretary, Mr Marples, and by his colleagues, Lord Swinton, the Minister of Materials, and Mr Eccles, the Minister of Works. All this is going forward well. The rigid ratio upon private building has been removed. Today local performance will decide the local programme. The more the local authorities build, the more they will be allowed to build. Builders and their men—including bricklayers—need have no fear they will work themselves out of their job. Measures have been taken to improve the supply of bricks, cement and tiles. New methods are being devised which, while maintaining essential standards, may enable us to build British homes with British materials and so, while increasing the number of houses, lessen the burden upon our imports from overseas. This will take time; but when you see how British genius shines in the design of aircraft, in which we have for the moment out-matched the world, we may be hopeful that in a year or two novel and beneficent improvements in housing may be achieved. Anyhow we are resolved to persevere. We have also a right to be encouraged that 19,000 more houses were built in the first half of this year than in the first half of 1951. This should surely be a matter for general rejoicing.

Finance is the worst of our problems. Ten months have passed since the Socialist Government recoiled from the consequences of their long administration and sought the refuge of a General Election. I must again remind you that before the poll I said in a broadcast:

'We make no promises of easier conditions in the immediate future. Too much harm has been done in these last six years for it to be repaired in a few months. Too much money has been spent for us to be able to avoid another financial crisis. It will take all our national strength to avoid the downhill slide, and after that we shall have to work up.'

When we took office I found that we were in a far worse plight than I had feared. We were spending abroad more than £800 millions a year beyond what we earned. Our gold and dollar reserves were draining away. To go on like that would be to plunge into national bankruptcy. That means we should have been unable to buy the food and raw materials from abroad in order to eat and work. It ought not to be forgotten that we took office in the shade of bankruptcy and that unless prompt measures had been taken we should have sunk into ruin and famine. How then do we stand as this summer draws to an end? We have not hesitated to do many unpopular things. Our imports have been drastically cut. The first steps to curtail and control departmental expenditures have already been taken. The rates of interest at which money can be borrowed have been raised. Intense efforts are being made to stimulate our exports, even to some extent at the cost of our rearmament.

Thus we may now forecast that we in this island will in the second half of this year, after taking credit for defence aid, be in general balance with the non-sterling world, and that the whole sterling area will be in balance with the rest of the world. Do not forget that, apart from the American contribution to our remarmament effort, we are now supporting ourselves. We have none of that American Loan and Marshall Aid—400 millions a year—which our predecessors enjoyed and used up so lavishly. We are not living on the United States; nor are we abusing them in spite of receiving their aid.

The Chancellor of the Exchequer has had a remarkable success in the first stage of restoring our world solvency. He has not feared to face a torrent of abuse, ill-deserved in itself, and especially shabby because of the guilty quarters from which it comes. I should be misleading you if I led you to suppose that greater efforts were not needed. We have got our head above water. Our future task is to swim up against the stream. Fifty millions in this island only grow the food for thirty. We can only buy for the other twenty by sending the things across the oceans which our Commonwealth and foreign customers need and desire. We must improve our balance of trade. We must strengthen our reserves of dollars and gold. That is what we are going on perseveringly to do. It is by results that we seek to be judged, and time will be needed for the results to be achieved.

We have had one heavy loss, which I think might have been avoided by courage and firmness. We have been robbed by violence of the Persian oil industry, which we created, and from which Persia derived such great benefit. I was happy to join President Truman in presenting new proposals to Dr Mossadeq for solving the deadlock resulting from our expulsion from Abadan. These are fair and reasonable proposals and were put forward upon the authority of the British and American Governments. I trust they will be given the attention which their constructive character and serious purpose should command. It is a good thing for all the world to see our two countries in agreement and working together. It quite reminds me of the great times not so long ago. We are all watching with keen interest the Presidential election in the United States. Democracy works by different methods in the great Republic from those we are accustomed to over here. But there are two things about which there is no doubt. The first is that the American system has produced two candidates for the Presidency who are in character and ability two of their finest men; and the second is that, whichever wins, the United States will not abandon the mission of leading the free nations in resistance to Communist aggression, and that the solid foundations of the English speaking world will grow broader and deeper and stronger, as the years roll by.

Then there is steel. This vital industry was nationalized by the Socialist Party last spring. But, apart from expropriating the shares of the previous owners, there was not time for any extensive damage to be done in the few months which intervened before the General Election. Fortunately we got into power in time to preserve the separate identity and independence of the great steel companies, whose world-wide reputations and trade connections constitute such important national assets. Thanks to the directions given by the Minister of Supply, Mr Duncan Sandys, immediately the Conservative Government came in, any undesirable interference by the State Corporation in the management of the companies was effectively prevented. By this action the position was held pending the introduction of a Bill. This will be presented to Parliament early in the new session in November.

Our detailed proposals were published last July in a White Paper, and have met with a most favourable reception from fair-minded people both inside and outside the industry. Unlike the Socialist Act of nationalization, our scheme for steel is not based upon political doctrine and theory. On the contrary, like all Conservative policies, it is founded upon practical needs and experience. The system of organization and supervision which we propose has been progressively evolved by the industry itself over the last twenty years. And in its general conception it follows closely the views expressed by the TUC in its well-known report on the public supervision of industry. In that report the TUC made it clear that they did not regard nationalization as being the only or necessarily the best method of securing for the State an effective say in industry. A more practical means of public control, they said, would

337

be a tripartite board of control on the lines of the former Iron and Steel Board, which was composed of representatives of employers, trade unions and consumers. That is precisely what our scheme sets out to do.

We feel entitled to ask that our proposals should be viewed against this background of common thought and experience. If they are examined in this spirit, we believe that, subject to improvements of detail, which we shall be glad to consider, our scheme will be found to offer the best basis for a lasting and workable solution to the problems which confront the steel industry. Meanwhile the industry has not been standing still. Its great companies under their experienced managements, have continued to make progress in output and efficiency. Our home production of steel this year is running at the rate of nearly half a million tons more than in 1951 and it is expected to increase by an even greater amount next year.

Our opponents say, 'If you want the country to work together, why do you bring in these controversial measures to undo the work of your predecessors?' It would not have been right to repeal either the Transport or the Steel Nationalization Acts merely to undo the work of our opponents, or to condemn a doctrine which we deem fallacious. In the case of Transport we are confronted with an evil position, detrimental to the interests of the general public and to the efficient running of our industrial life. We are sure that a definite easement and improvement will be achieved, from which the whole country and all classes will be the gainers. It is that object alone which makes us undertake this heavy labour. In the case of steel, the main step we are taking in reconciling State supervision and control with free enterprise is one which springs as much from the minds of trade unionists as from employers, and is really the culmination of a very long period of growth and progress in an industry which, for sixty years, has not been the cause of any serious trade dispute.

# CONSERVATIVE ANNUAL CONFERENCE

---

17 *September—The Foreign Secretary, Mr Eden, flies to Belgrade for discussions with Marshal Tito.*

26 *September—'Pravda' accuses Mr George E. Kennan, United States Ambassador to the Soviet Union, of 'malicious hostility'.*

29 *September—Annual Conference of the Labour Party at Morecambe. Mr Morrison and Dr Dalton lose their seats on the National Executive.*

30 *September—It is announced in the 'London Gazette' by Garter King of Arms that HM The Queen has by Royal Warrant dated 18 September ordained that the Duke of Edinburgh 'shall henceforth upon all occasions and in all meetings, except where otherwise provided by Act of Parliament, have, hold, and enjoy place, pre-eminince and precedence next to Her Majesty'.*

3 *October—Soviet Government declare Mr Kennan is 'persona non grata' and demand his immediate recall.*

3 *October—First British atomic bomb is detonated in the Monte Bello Islands.*

4 *October—It is announced that Sir Roger Makins, Deputy Under-Secretary of State at the Foreign Office, has been appointed Ambassador to the United States in succession to Sir Oliver Franks.*

9 *October—Annual Conference of the Conservative Party opens at Scarborough.*

---

[11 *October* 1952

Twelve years have passed since in the crisis of the war I was chosen Leader of the Conservative Party, as our chairman has reminded you, but this is the first time I have had the honour to address our Annual Conference as Prime Minister. I do so this afternoon with feelings of growing confidence and hope for our party and, what is far more important, for our country. I believe we may fairly claim that there is a definite improvement in British affairs at home, and also in our position in the world and that this has taken place since we became responsible. As has been made plain by the Ministers who have addressed you, we do not seek to be masters, but to serve supreme causes: the maintenance of world peace founded on strength, the unity of the British Empire

339

and Commonwealth, of which our island is still the heart, and the preservation of national solvency without which all our power and reputation would be cast away.

We have been in office for almost exactly a year. That is not a long time in which to change the course or the aspect of our complicated modern life. No doubt we have made mistakes, especially, it is said, in propaganda. I would rather make mistakes in propaganda than in action. Events are the final rulers and time is needed for them to make their pronouncements clear. Still, it would be best to have no mistakes at all. I do not speak this afternoon in any complacent mood. I can assure you we will try to do better. I wish indeed I could promise that we would solve all the problems that lie before us. We can only try our best for the interests of the nation as a whole. Although we live in a period of keen and even bitter party strife on narrow margins, the country split in twain, and although an intellectual and moral gulf separates us in doctrine from those who try to reduce us to a Socialist State—in spite of all that—we are an ancient and neighbourly race. There are an awful lot of British folk, and perhaps in Yorkshire I may even be allowed to say English folk, who think much the same way about an awful lot of things. I can assure you that we have no thought nor wish, nor indeed could we have any personal or party interest, but to bring about British recovery and be helpful to all our fellow-countrymen.

When we took office last October we were plunging into national bankruptcy at a rate of £800 millions a year. Large further inevitable increases in expense impended upon us. These could in many cases only be avoided by a wholesale scrapping of much of the costly effort already made. We therefore had to face the full impact of rearmament at a time when the £400 millions a year of American and Canadian aid from loan or gift, on which British Socialism had lived, came to the end. Thus we inherited the quadruple onrush of Social Services growing automatically, of rearmament getting into its full stride, of the end of the American bounty, and of rapidly approaching insolvency in our overseas payments. Here was the grievous and menacing combination which the Chancellor of the Exchequer has striven and is striving so manfully to conquer. And that is the task in which it is our duty to give him all possible aid and not flinch before abuse from those who are themselves directly responsible for the hazardous plight in which they left us. It is said reap where you have sown. That is a hard rule, a stern rule and we accept it. But we are not now reaping where *we* have sown, we are reaping where others have sown, where they have sown weeds as well as grain. We have to hold firmly to our duty, and stand resolutely together, persevere along right lines and then we shall be able to reap where we have sown ourselves, and by that we shall be ready to be judged.

We have two hard tasks before us. The first and the less difficult is to maintain and improve our position as a party in the House of Commons and in the confidence of the electors. We owe a debt to our Members of the House of Commons who, by their admirable attendance, often at serious sacrifice, have enabled us with an overall majority of only sixteen to average thirty in all the 230 divisions we have had since the new Parliament began. I hope the constituents of all these Members will make them feel how much they appreciate the effort and sacrifice which they have made, without which our business might indeed be in sorry confusion. And here we must not fail to pay a tribute to the excellent discharge of their strenuous task by the Chief Whip and his devoted colleagues. He has done a fine job. If we can maintain this high standard and also improve our propaganda and public relations service, as I hope we may, we shall have created that solid political foundation upon which our second and larger task—our national recovery—must stand.

Here indeed the problems tower menacing and inscrutable above us. The Socialist Government during their six years of power, spent every penny they could lay their hands upon, including, as I have said, over £2,000 millions or more borrowed or begged from the United States whom they now abuse, and from the Dominions. We have stood on our own feet, independent, apart from military aid for the common cause of the free world.

In the last year of the Socialist rule they committed us to an enormous three year programme of rearmament, first of £3,600 millions, increased a few months later—by what calculations I do not know—to £4,700 millions. On patriotic grounds and because of our loyalty to the cause of the free world and the United Nations the Conservative Opposition supported this well meant though loosely and hurriedly framed policy. Now in the first year the expense of a munitions programme is of course comparatively little. Plants have to be altered, factories re-tooled, and skilled labour trained or re-disposed.

But in the present year, 1952, and still more next year, what was started so lightheartedly on a finance already heavily strained by years of reckless extravagance and waste, in the third year, next year all this comes into fruition, requiring ever more expenditure and skilled manpower and eating ever more steel and other raw materials. That is what we have to face and the Socialist Party who knew quite well what they were leaving behind them should not be allowed to forget these facts. They tell us we have broken our promises. Well, that can only be proved by time. It would be more true to say that the Socialist predictions of the General Election have already in many cases been falsified. What was the first thing they promised us if a Conservative Government was elected? War. Churchill, the warmonger, would plunge us into war. Only a year ago that was what they were using. Well, it has not happened yet. On the contrary there is a general feeling in the world that on the whole the danger of world war has receded since we became responsible.

We politicians have all, I think, been honoured by the presence among us as a member of our party and as Minister of Defence of a great military commander, Field-Marshal Alexander, whose name will shine in history. I was struck by the pith of the point which he made when he said:

> 'Always remember that many of those who now say that re-armament is no longer necessary are the very same people who, during the General Election, put forward the idea that there would be another war if Mr Churchill became Prime Minister.'

I wonder what is the answer to that. Anyhow that Socialist slander and libel, and the whispering campaign, which may have cost us fifty seats, is as dead as a doornail. Our opponents have got to think of another lie for next time. And, as they are now realizing, really paying lies, upon which the whole Socialist Party can unitedly agree, are rather hard to find. Do not let us hurry them too much.

There was another Socialist prophecy which has been proved false. At the election the nation was threatened by the Socialist Party machine with mass strikes of a political character if they elected a Conservative Government according to their rights. This prediction has not come true. The trade union leaders (I shall have to refer to them later) have set an example to Socialist political agitators in the firmness with which they have denounced the idea of using the strike weapon to effect constitutional changes. Such a threat which the Communists and their fellow-travellers in or out of the House of Commons freely use would be a challenge to the whole life of Parliamentary democracy, as it has so slowly been built up among us, and all that has been built up across the centuries. The foundations of Parliamentary democracy would be overthrown by the use of the strike weapon for political and constitutional purposes.

But now let me come to a more concrete point you will have in your minds. I do remember last time I was with you two years ago the explosion of the feelings in our Party—'mob rule' the Socialists called it (they ought to know)—in favour of a target of 300,000 houses

342

a year. 'What an absurd proposal,' cried the Socialist organs. 'Do you really think that if Aneurin Bevan can only build 200,000 houses in a year there is any other statesman in the world who could surpass him?' I believe, or at least I have heard it said, that there is not nowadays the same unanimous agreement, even in his own party or in his own party within his own party, there is not the same unanimous agreement about his genius, or even about his character. Certainly I think that among the hundreds of thousands of young couples who seek a home, with its own front door, where they can rear a family of valiant Britons, there is more hope in Mr Harold Macmillan and his energetic lieutenant, Mr Marples, and other Ministers like Mr Eccles and Lord Swinton, who are all involved in this special team, there is more hope that they will achieve what we have in hand than there ever was in the ambitious demagogue who called one half of his fellow-countrymen 'vermin'.

I will, at that point, leave the Socialists and their predictions to stew in their own juice and turn to the field of constructive, positive action. It is our intention, when Parliament meets, to introduce and carry the repeal of both the Transport and Steel Nationalization Acts. We do not doubt that we shall be able to accomplish our purpose. Of course, as the oldest child of the House of Commons—or shall I say, the one who has spent the longest time in the cradle of parliamentary government—I do not take the view that every Bill must be rammed through Parliament exactly in the form that the Cabinet of the day thinks fit. I believe in parliamentary discussion and I hold strongly that the elected representatives of the people, and the House of Lords, in its relation established by the Parliament Act, should both share in the shaping of legislation. We are not like the Czar, or the Kaiser, or Hitler, or Lenin, or Stalin, or a lot of others of the same brand, who utter ukases or other decrees which cowed assemblies, elected by swindling and intimidation, have to endorse and swallow. We are not like that. Lots of people have a say in what happens here and I hope that may long be so. It is not necessarily a humiliation to a Government to defer to the House of Commons feelings and to genuine sense established in debates, provided that it does not sacrifice any moral principle or inflict injury or injustice on the public. Nevertheless, making all allowance for what I have said, I am confidently able to assure you that Road Transport and Steel will be de-nationalized before we are a year older, and that subject to the necessary State supervision they will continue in freedom indefinitely, before a Socialist administration has the power or thinks it worth while to disturb or assail them again. I put this plainly before you because in the last session the demise of the Crown and other difficulties made it impossible for us to carry these important measures; but we are resolved in every way that they should be on the Statute Book before the next Session of Parliament is over.

Now let us look at these two proposals, and the reasons for them. Why do we wish to repeal the Transport and Steel Nationalization Acts? I can assure you that it is not for party spite or out of mere contrariness. It is because we believe profoundly that a more flexible, fertile, virile and growing industry can be restored, serving for the interchange of goods and services between the British people and also, by this fact, aiding our export trade. If I were not convinced that this was true I would not pursue or advise my colleagues to pursue either measure. Rather than do what we had become convinced was unwise, I would not hesitate to ask release from the pledges we have given in opposition. Of course, it is better to be both right and consistent. But if you have to choose—you must choose to be right. I declare, therefore, that we are sure that the British people as a whole will have a better time and a better chance with steel as we propose it and with the reorganization and liberation of our transport, giving a chance to the nationalized railways, which we accept and which we mean to make the utmost success, and also for steel a better chance than under the present rigid regulations which were only made for the sake of party politics and for fallacious doctrine in which many of those who pronounced them have lost faith. That is why we go forward on our course.

Now take transport. Who can be satisfied with the confusion and restriction in which it now lies? The whole of our road transport system is obstructed and distorted for the sake of keeping nationalized 41,000 vehicles managed by an overhead staff of 12,000 officials. (Did I say 12,000? I beg Mr Morrison's pardon, I should have said 11,919. I accept his correction. I hope it will be a comfort to him. He must need some cheering up nowadays.) But the fact remains that for the sake of giving a national road monopoly to these 41,000 vehicles, thousands of small hauliers have had their livelihood taken from them, and those who have been allowed to retain their property are cramped within a twenty-five-mile radius. Yet so unsatisfactory is the service of the 41,000 vehicles, owned by the State, that what are called 'C' licences have gone up from 300,000 to over 800,000 since the Nationalization Act in spite of the fact that they are only allowed to carry their owner's goods, and often return half empty or quite empty.

Think of the waste involved in this. It is—I offer this to my political opponents—the quintessence of private ownership made uneconomic by law. More than that, there are not even 41,000 vehicles at work in the State monopoly. In the last year they have fallen off by 3,000 and yet for the sake of these remaining 38,000 vehicles all the others on the road or which would like to go on the road are to be held in one form of strait-jacket or another. Now this is one of the evils we set out to cure, and it is my firm hope that we may render the whole movement of traffic, the interchange of goods and services between one man and another in this island quite definitely more easy and elastic than what now prevails, and thus make a contribution, only one of many that is needed, to our productive efficiency, at this most critical time. So much for transport.

Then there is steel. If ever there was an industry which was unsuitable for nationalization, it was this vital business of steel production. The degrees of damage which nationalization can do vary from industry to industry. It is one thing to apply it to public services like railways, gas, electricity. But the harm to our economy is incomparably greater when nationalization is turned upon an industry like steel, whose products in the form of materials or manufactured goods, are exported in great quantities and have to hold their own against the keenest competition throughout the world. Unlike the Socialist Act of Nationalization, our scheme for steel is not based upon political doctrine and theory. On the contrary as all or at any rate most Conservative policies ought to be, it is founded upon practical needs and experience. The system of organization and supervision which we propose has been progressively evolved by the industry itself over the last twenty years. And in its general conception it follows closely the views expressed by the Trades Union Congress in its well-known report on the public supervision of industry. In that report the TUC made it clear that they did not regard nationalization as being the only or necessarily the best method of securing for the State an effective say in industry. A more practical form of supervision they said, would be through a tripartite board of control on the lines of the fomer Iron and Steel Board, which was composed of representatives of employers, trades unions and consumers. That is precisely what our scheme sets out to do. We feel entitled to ask that our proposals should be viewed in this setting of common thought and experience. If they are examined in this spirit, we believe that subject to improvements in detail which we shall be glad to consider, our scheme will be found to offer the best basis for a lasting and workable solution of the problems which confront the steel industry. And let me give this warning to our opponents, and to everyone. Any loss of efficiency or blunting of initiative in the steel industry may only too easily price our exports out of foreign markets and may strike a fatal blow at our engineering industries, upon whose overseas sales we, all of us, not Conservatives only—all parties—the whole country, rely to balance our external trade. Happily, as you may remember, we got into power just in the nick of time to save this great industry from disaster. Although the Socialists took over the shares of the steel companies, they did not have time, in the few months between nationalization and the change of government, to upset seriously the practical working of the industry.

One of the first acts of the Conservative Minister of Supply, Mr Duncan Sandys, was to direct the State Corporation not to interfere with the structure of the companies or their management without the Government's consent. This has effectively preserved the identity of the companies, famous throughout the globe as they are as symbols of British efficiency, and has maintained their experienced leadership. We have in fact by prompt action held the position pending de-nationalization. The Bill to de-nationalize steel will be presented to Parliament next month. Apart from criticisms of detail, our plan as set forth in the White Paper has been very favourably received, both inside and outside the steel industry, and we go forward with the encouragement that we have wide support among those who know the industry and desire its wellbeing. Meanwhile steel itself is not standing still. The foresight and enterprise of the companies enabled them to make plans at the end of the war to expand our pig-iron steel production. These schemes were set on foot long before nationalization, and in spite of its menace, are now bearing fruit. New blast furnaces and more pig-iron swell the output of our steel. We confidently expect that Britain's output of steel next year will beat the previous all-time record. And let nobody be misled by the humbug we shall no doubt hear that all this was the result of a few months' nationalization. It is, on the contrary, a vindication of years of preparation under free enterprise which was rescued only just in time by the expulsion of the Socialists from power.

I have not attended your Conference, though I have followed it with diligence. We had a striking speech yesterday from Mr Mawby, a trade unionist, who reminded us that Mr Pollitt, speaking in Moscow, had said that the trade unions in this country are going to be used as a political pawn in Soviet aggrandisement or words to that effect. Mr Mawby, you will remember, warned us against the danger of the unions becoming a tool of any party in our country. There is great force in what he says.

Two years ago at Blackpool I pointed out to the trade union leaders how much harder would be their task in dealing with a corporate Socialist State like Russia with its totalitarian structure than with present day employers who have to get on with their people in the long run or hand over their business to someone else. We owe a great deal to the trade unions. They are an institution in our land, an institution given its original Charter of Rights by the Conservative Party. I regret that many of them have been misled by what is the undoubted fallacy of Socialism and that they show an undue bias towards the Socialist Party. Would they not be wise to concentrate upon looking after the interests of their own members in all the processes of collective bargaining which on the whole work well? Everyone must, however, recognize the quality, character and courage of the trade union leaders. We do not agree with them on doctrine, as I have said, nor on the part they should play in domestic politics, but we respect them, and there is no doubt the country could not get on without them. And after all the Conservatives or Tories (I am certainly not afraid of that word Tory) have the matter in their own hands. Today at least one-third of the trade union members vote Conservative. Why should we stop there? All Conservative wage-earners should join their trade unions and attend the branch meetings as regularly as the Communists do. But I do not suggest that they should attend in order to try to capture the trade unions' political influence for our party, but in order that their force should primarily be concentrated upon the relations between employers and employed, and should in addition aid and explore those large issue of profit-sharing and co-partnership which may play so fruitful a part in our hard-pressed national life. We know they are our party opponents. But there is no aspect of our social policy that our successful, capable and tactful Minister of Labour, Sir Walter Monckton—or if need be I myself—would not readily discuss with responsible leaders of the TUC. I hope, therefore, that whatever fighting there may be will be conducted with the minimum of interference in the efficient earning of their daily bread by the entire mass of the British people.

You heard on Thursday last our Deputy Prime Minister, Mr. Eden set forth in weighty words the broad conceptions and purposes which we pursue in the vast sphere of foreign affairs in which his experience and world-wide repute are of great value to us all. In the main these conceptions are a continuance of the policy which, under the late Mr Bevin and with the loyal support of the Conservative Opposition, was followed during his long tenure of power. It will indeed be a pitiful exhibition if the leaders of the Labour Party desert the causes to which they committed the nation, just because they have ceased to be Ministers of the Crown. I do not believe myself that the bulk of them will do so, though a hard time no doubt lies before them. It may well be a case where virtue will have to be its own reward.

The foundation of our foreign policy is a true and honourable comradeship with the United States, in defence of the life of the free world against the immense aggression and ceaseless infiltration of Communist Imperialism. This has already since the war dominated half Europe and all China without the loss of a single soldier in Russian uniform, and at the present time, the oligarchy in the Kremlin, wielding autocratic power far exceeding that exercised by any Czar in the old and bygone days, controls armies in Europe at the present time far beyond any which we and our Allies have been able to gather together. We intend to persevere faithfully and resolutely in strengthening the ties of friendship and kinship which have brought us into such effective alliance with the great English-speaking Republic across the Atlantic Ocean. On this the future peace of the world and the survival of its freedom depend. This does not mean, as Mr Eden indicated to us, that we find ourselves always in complete agreement with our American allies or that we should hesitate to press our view on matters about which we differ. I certainly never hesitated during the war to put our case strongly to them, and very often succeeded in having our views accepted to what, in the end, was found to be advantageous to the common cause. But we shall certainly not fall into the snare laid for us by the Soviet Government and their Communist adherents and fellow-travellers here or in other countries, and allow any breach in the effective harmony of thought and action between Britain and the United States which is the mainstay of all we hold dear.

Most of us are watching from day to day the Presidential Election in the United States. Democracy works by different methods in the Great Republic from those to which we are accustomed over here. But there are two facts about which there is no doubt. The first is that the American system has produced two candidates for the Presidency who are, in character and ability, two of their finest men; and the second is that whichever of them wins, the United States will not abandon the mission of leading the free nations in resistance to Communist aggression and that the underlying unities of the English speaking world will grow broader, and deeper, and stronger as the years roll by. This has been a memorable meeting of the Conservative Party at Scarborough. It has come at a time of difficulty and strain, both at home and abroad. The sober realization of all our members that they must face the real facts of British life, grim though they be in many ways, and not fear passing gusts of unpopularity in the discharge of our duty to the nation as a whole—that resolution is outstanding in our minds. That has been the keynote of the Conference. It needs no background such as might well be found at Morecambe of what other parties have done to command the attention and respect of all who cherish the enduring strength of Britain. Her Majesty's Government are grateful to those who have sustained them by their confidence and loyalty, and we shall go forward on the uphill march with our willpower stimulated by the wish to be worthy of your respect.

I have used the word 'memorable' about our Conference. Let us also endow it with lasting effect. The Recruiting Campaign which Lord Woolton (whose absence we so much regret) has launched may well bring enduring reinforcement to our party's strength. Let us march forward with our sturdy lions, jaunty lions—yea, unconquerable lions—enrolling our members as we go. So many people believe in us and vote for us who remain silent between elections. We need the encouragement and help of their declared fellowship in our grand design to restore Britain to freedom and to reviving fame.

# PILGRIMS' DINNER TO GENERAL RIDGWAY

## A SPEECH AT THE SAVOY HOTEL
## 14 OCTOBER 1952

---

*13 October—Turkish Prime Minister, M. Adnan Menderes, and the Foreign Minister, Professor Fuat Koprulu, come to London for an official visit at the invitation of the British Government.*

---

[*14 October* 1952

We all regret the absence from our dinner this evening of Lord Halifax, whose career as British Ambassador to the United States added lustre to his long record of eminent service. Tonight we have a distinguished gathering at the Pilgrims' Dinner. You will note, by the way, that in this well-known and long-known island we have succeeded for nearly a thousand years in preventing any invaders from coming in. But you should also note—as pilgrims—that we have never prevented any from going out—not even in the *Mayflower*—and speaking as a Briton I must admit that some quite good ones have gone out. But now larger syntheses (if I may use the kind of learned jargon which is fashionable) are bringing together by forces, which are primarily moral and intellectual, all the individuals and all the nations who would die rather than submit to Communist rule. But there is no reason why the free world should die. On the contrary, it has only to remain united and progressive not only to survive, but to preserve its right to live in its own way without the need of another hideous catastrophe.

Here tonight we have two of our famous British Commanders, Alex and Monty. I am sure that in their separate spheres they are going to do all in their power to help our guest of the evening, General Ridgway, to carry out the enormous task which he has undertaken. General Ridgway had a predecessor. I am afraid that I might get into trouble if I told you his name. All I will say is that those who understand the work he did in Europe will ever remember it with thankfulness. We are fortunate indeed that General Ridgway has come to our aid in this critical period with his record in the war and in Korea as soldier and statesman.

We have also been forced to spare from the Cabinet Lord Ismay (his international status prevents my using his pet name) who is doing the same sort of thing for NATO as he did for me in the war—to make all things go as well as possible between the military and the politicians and to weave together many diverse elements into the harmonious structure of a machine capable of giving decisions for millions of men.

All down the ages many and varied, but not always wholly successful, have been the expedients which have been tried to bring the nations together in peace or war. It may be that NATO, our shield against war, can also unite us for peace. There are hopeful stirrings in Europe today, most of which find their inspiration directly or indirectly in the leadership which NATO has given. From small beginnings who can tell what blessings they may bring us? Come what will, at the present time it is in NATO that wise men in Europe and America will do well to place their trust as a benevolent combination of the free peoples for their defence against mortal danger.

Our policy, the policy of the English-speaking world, the policy of NATO, and of all who prefer Parliamentary democracy with its many defects—never concealed—to totalitarian rule wherever it comes from, our policy is by hard sacrifice and constant toil to increase the deterrents against an aggressor. I can assure you tonight that we shall do our utmost, short of going bankrupt, to increase these deterrents and also to convince the other side that we are planning no assault on them.

We all hate and fear war. Let me tell you why in my opinion, and it is only an opinion, not a prophecy, a third World War is unlikely to happen. It is because, among other reasons, it would be entirely different in certain vital aspects from any other war that has ever taken place. Both sides know that it would begin with horrors of a kind and on a scale never dreamed of before by human beings. It would begin by both sides in Europe suffering in this first stage exactly what they dread the most. It would also be different because the main decisions would probably come in the first month or even in the first week. The quarrel might continue for an indefinite period, but after the first month it would be a broken-backed war in which no great armies could be moved over long distances. The torments would fall in increasing measure upon the whole civilian population of the globe, and Governments dependent upon long distance communications by land would find they had lost their power to dominate events.

These are only a few of the grave facts which rule our destinies; but we can be sure that this proved and experienced General of the United States Army, whom we welcome here tonight as our guest of honour, will do his utmost for our common cause, and it is with sincere feelings of hope that I support our President in asking you to drink the health of our distinguished guests at these tables tonight, and first and foremost of General Ridgway.

# DEBATE ON THE ADDRESS

A SPEECH TO THE HOUSE OF COMMONS
4 NOVEMBER 1952

---

28 *October—Mr Oliver Lyttelton, Secretary of State for the Colonies, flies
to Nairobi to investigate the situation created by the Mau–Mau terrorists.*

---

[4 *November* 1952

I naturally join with the Leader of the Opposition in the compliments
which he has paid, in a long-established custom, to the hon Members
who have proposed and seconded the Address in reply to the Gracious
Speech. I am bound to say that I think they both gave us the feeling of
having lived fully up to the high standard observed on these occasions
and attained, almost without exception, by all three parties in any
period which my lengthy recollection can recall. I admit that I do not
go back so far as the reign of Queen Victoria in 1837, but at any rate
my hon and gallant Friend the Member for Berwick and East Lothian
[Major Anstruther-Gray] may comfort himself that his seconder
managed to get through his ordeal with distinction. Now we have
had a speech, as is customary on these occasions, from the Leader of the
Opposition, and I can only hope that the moderation and sobriety of
his statement will not expose him to any undue risk among his own
friends. I am sure I may offer him my congratulations on his being able
to address us from those benches as stroke and not, to quote the term
he has just used, from the tow-path.

The Gracious Speech refers in several important passages to foreign
affairs. I do not propose to deal with these today, except to say that in
the main we have hitherto preserved continuity in foreign policy, and
I do not know of any new marked disagreement which has arisen between the two main parties up to the present time. We shall all, no
doubt, have a clearer view of the whole situation after the result of
the election—I mean, of course, the one in the United States—is known.
It has now, I understand, been arranged that the debate on Thursday
will be devoted to the foreign situation and to defence, and my right
hon Friend the Foreign Secretary will take part in the debate before
he flies the next day to New York to attend the United Nations'
meeting. I shall, therefore, confine myself this afternoon to the tangles
and disputations of the domestic field. Let me, however, say from a
business point of view that the debate on the Address will occupy the

remainder of the present week and will, it is hoped, be brought to a conclusion in the early part of next week. Under your guidance, Mr Speaker, we shall endeavour to arrange the debate, whether on Amendments or otherwise, in accordance with the general wish of the House.

We propose that Private Members should enjoy their rights in respect of Bills and Motions in the same manner as last year, including the right to bring in Bills under the Ten Minutes' Rule. Perhaps I may now give notice that my right hon Friend the Leader of the House will tomorrow propose a Motion naming twenty Fridays on which Private Members' Bills and Motions will have precedence. It is proposed that the first of the Private Members' days should be Friday, 28 November.

No mention has been made in the Speech in regard to various features of legislation which are under consideration. As we move on we shall be able to see our way more clearly on the long pilgrimage through public business. We have made no mention in the Gracious Speech of legislation about the preservation of historic houses, for it has seemed best to confine the Speech to Measures of first importance, but we hope to proceed with a Measure on this subject when time permits. This would apply to some of the other topics to which the Leader of the Opposition has referred.

Compared with this time last year, almost to a day, the Parliamentary situation in the House of Commons gives a definite impression of greater stability. We no longer feel that we are dwelling in the advent of another General Election. Right hon Gentlemen opposite ought to cheer that; I am anxious to give as much reassurance as I possibly can. The strength and unity of the forces supporting Her Majesty's Government have been proved, and we do not doubt our ability to carry the legislation mentioned in the Gracious Speech, and in particular to pass into law the two important rectifying Measures of transport and steel.

MR E. SHINWELL (Easington): Wrecking Measures?

THE PRIME MINISTER: Rectifying Measures. Part of the process of cleansing the Statute Book is a definite element in any general scheme of rectification. We do not doubt, I say, our ability to carry these Measures, which were leading issues at the General Election, into law. Both these Bills will be presented to the House tomorrow.

One of the complaints made against us is that we ought not to introduce controversial legislation at a time like this, with such a small majority, especially in Coronation year. I wonder what would have been said by the right hon Gentleman—by the same mouths—if we had not introduced these two Bills. What a howl of broken pledges and broken promises would have gone up. It is quite true that we are keeping our promises, as hon Members opposite will find out. This is not the sole reason for proposing these Bills. Neither is it true that we are only giving expression to the ideological differences between the free enterprise system, to which we hold, and the foolish, as we deem it, system of socialism. These reasons, powerful and valid though they may be, would not give sufficient warrant in themselves for the effort we are making to repeal these Acts of nationalization. It is only because we believe on the merits that these changes are necessary and will be beneficial to the general and modern economy of our harassed island that we press them forward at the present time.

The story of steel nationalization since the war must be viewed in its completeness. This was an act of nationalization which the late Government, with all their power, considered with the greatest misgiving. We know very well the alternative solutions which many of their wisest leaders hankered after. On the other hand, it was evident that it was in the interest of the extreme elements of the right hon Gentleman's party to force steel nationalization on the Government and the country, because the frontiers of the steel industry are so undefined, so vaguely defined, that by nationalization they could break into many other fields and thus smudge at one stroke the whole page of British industry. I was looking for the former Minister of Supply, but he seems to be missing at the moment. I venture to quote what he said in moving the Second Reading of the Iron and Steel Bill in 1948. He said:

'This great reform removes from the private sector of our economy to the public, the industry which is the citadel of British capitalism.'

He is himself very well circumstanced to defend that citadel from every point of view. [HON MEMBERS: 'Cheap.'] We consider that the nationalization of the steel industry in the circumstances in which it was brought about was a wrongful and needless act of partisan politics. The fact that the final step to bring it into operation was taken at the time of our entry into the Korean War and of the Socialist rearmament policy may well excite curiosity as to whether it was part of a deal in the party to persuade the Left Wing to do their duty by the country.

We had a debate the other day upon this subject of steel, and the Minister of Supply explained in friendly terms why the new Measure for regulating steel ought not to be regarded with hostility by the Labour Party. The right hon Gentleman the Member for Lewisham, South [Mr H. Morrison], had to turn down his appeal. I am sure that was not due only to its consideration on the merits. It is an illustration of a fact, which will become more evident from day to day, that the leaders of the Front Bench opposite can only hold their position by giving renewed and repeated signs of their extremism, which in their hearts they abhor. We do not intend to vie with them in partisanship on this issue. The Bill which we are presenting to the House has the purpose of securing the widest opportunity for initiative and enterprise within the industry, coupled with the necessary measure of public supervision in the interests of the nation as a whole, on the lines of the Trades Union Congress report. We are all the more confident in the solution we propose in that it is based upon practical experience over many years and is the next logical step in the constitutional evolution of this primary basic industry.

We hope—hope springs eternal in the human breast, and so, I say, we hope—that whatever differences of political approach there may be, the Bill will at least be judged on both sides of the House by the one primary test, namely, how it will help the iron and steel industry to maintain and further develop its productivity. [HON MEMBERS: 'Hear, hear.'] All right, hon Gentlemen opposite take me at my word. I assure them that if they act up to that principle we will not fall behind it on this side of the House.

MR SHINWELL: Hon Members opposite should cheer up.

THE PRIME MINISTER: The right hon Gentleman should restrain his enthusiasm until he comes to speak on defence.

Now I come to transport. No one underrates the difficulties and complications which the present century has brought to every country in the constant adjusting and readjusting of road and rail transport. Since we rose for the Summer Recess, we have given long and continuous study to the many difficult questions that have been opened. When the Bill is published tomorrow, the changes that we have made will be seen. I am sure that prolonged discussion has been beneficial. Personally, Mr Speaker, I am always ready to learn, although I do not always like being taught, but I shall not attempt to foreshadow the proposals which will be brought before the House tomorrow. Today it will be sufficient and appropriate to deal with the obvious difficulties and confusion of the situation as we found it on taking office. Everyone must be conscious of the evils which exist and which we inherited— the restriction in one form or another of some nineteen-twentieths of our vehicles for the sake of 41,000 to be nationalized, the indefinite maintenance of the twenty-five miles limit, the growth of 'C' licences, which have risen by 339,000 to a total of 826,000 since the Transport Act became law on 1 January 1948. It is a very remarkable fact that people should prefer to be bound only to carry their own goods, with all the restrictions that that involves, rather than avail themselves of the advantages of nationalized transport.

The failure of the 41,000 vehicles, of which I believe only 35,000 are working at the present time, is certainly not due to any lack of sincerity or zeal on the part of those who operate them. They have tried sincerely to meet the public need, but the mere fact that this enormous expansion in other forms of restricted transport has come into play is surely one which Parliament might, without partisanship, gaze at in thought. We all live in one country, and there is no harm in thinking about a thing like that. Then there is the millstone round the neck of the railways—the terrible fact of the £300 million or something like that. [*Interruption.*] I am a very old supporter of the nationalization of the railways, and hon Members opposite must take me with my past and all, but I am bound to say that to hang this millstone round the neck of the nationalized railways was a very formidable event. [HON MEMBERS: 'What millstone?'] The £300 million on which interest has to be earned. I am well aware that the party opposite has always adhered to the principle of compensation. That was perfectly right, but in choosing the moment which involves this enormous burden, this permanent dead weight hanging round the necks of the railways, they took a very grievous step. It may undoubtedly be that, had they not done so, and had the railways not been nationalized, the shareholders would have had to go home and nurse their grievances and many of their losses. This is what happens under the capitalist system. Now there has been fixed round the necks of the railways, by law, this permanent burden of £300 million.

MR HERBERT MORRISON (Lewisham, South) *rose*——

THE PRIME MINISTER: I will give way in a minute. On top of all this——

MR MORRISON: What £300 million?

THE PRIME MINISTER: On top of all this—[*Interruption.*] I will not give way yet. [*Interruption.*] I shall certainly take my time. On top of all this is the number of restrictions on the railways' freedom in the matter of charges, dating from the days when, having swallowed the canals, they were really a monopoly.

MR MORRISON: In connection with compensation to the railways, the Prime Minister has referred to £300 million as a millstone. Will he be kind enough to say what he means by '£300 million' and to what it refers?

THE PRIME MINISTER: It was the price paid to the shareholders.

HON MEMBERS: No.

MR JAMES CALLAGHAN (Cardiff, South-East): Will the Prime Minister take it from me that the price paid to the shareholders was in the region of £1,100 million to £1,200 million and that the annual interest which is payable to the shareholders is between £30 million and £40 million?

THE PRIME MINISTER: I have not those figures in my notes, but to have to pay £30 million to £40 million a year constitutes a very heavy millstone tied round the necks of the British Railways.* [*Interruption*.] I was merely asking at that moment for a glass of water.

The Gracious Speech mentions a third important Measure relating to the Town and Country Planning Act, 1947. Again, I will not anticipate its provisions but will offer a few introductory remarks. I remember the old days, which were my young or younger days, when the taxation of land values and of unearned increments in land was a foremost principle and a lively element in the programme of the Radical Party to which I then belonged. But what is the situation which presents itself to us today? In those days we had the spectacle of valuable land being kept out of the market until the exact moment for its sale was reached, regardless of the fact that its increased value was due to the exertions of the surrounding community. Then we had the idea that, if those obstructions could be cleared out of the way, free enterprise would bound forward and small people would have a chance to get a home, or to improve their existing homes, and many other things besides. But here at the moment we have the exact opposite.

The problem which now confronts us directly and urgently is that of the £300 million established by the 1947 Act, and also the development charge. [*Interruption*.] Before hon Gentlemen opposite work themselves up into a rage, I would remind them that the 1947 Act was based upon the Report of the Uthwatt Committee of 1942, which was accepted in substance by the Coalition White Paper of 1944. So we are all in it together. I might remind hon Gentlemen opposite that we are all in quite a lot of things together. The White Paper proposed a once-for-all payment, not strictly speaking compensation, for loss of development value at 1939 prices. That is the origin of the £300 million to the landowners which is payable under the 1947 Act. The foundation of the 100 per cent development charge is, no doubt, the 80 per cent included in the Coalition Government White Paper. Any man, however modest his means—and a very great number of very small owners are involved in this—must pay this very heavy price in addition to the cost of building anything in times when everything is becoming more expensive, although at a definitely less rapid rate than was the case under the previous Administration.

* Mr Churchill intervened later in the debate to explain that through a mistake in his notes he had misled the House. The compensation to the former stockholders was £900,000,000 on which the annual interest was nearly £30,000,000.

The result of the development charge or betterment charge is that it has become a direct deterrent upon enterprise and production and has brought a lot of it to a standstill. We may ask ourselves, is that what we want now? If ever there was a subject which might be considered calmly and coolly without partisanship by both parties, who are both concerned in what has been done in the past and are also concerned in what emerges in the future, it is here in this Measure that will come before us this session. The logic of the Uthwatt Report may be impeccable, and both parties yielded to it and are involved, but in practice the result has been unhappy. To pay out £300 million next year, as the Act requires, would put money into the pocket of many who have no intention of ever exercising development rights and who suffered no loss. The ordinary small landowner also does not understand the theory that he must buy back potential development rights. The process is unenforceable except by the drastic use of compulsory powers. Before the end of the month the Government's full proposals on this subject will be presented to the House of Commons, and I trust that they may receive fair consideration in view of the association of both parties for over eight years in this extremely difficult situation.

I have dealt now with the three principal Measures, steel, transport and the one I have referred to dealing with the development charge under the Town and Country Planning Act. I do not want to keep the House too long. [Hon Members: 'Go on.'] Hon Members opposite are not getting so much out of it as they try to encourage themselves into thinking they are. I come to the position which we occupied a year ago. When we succeeded hon Gentlemen opposite a year ago we were moving into bankruptcy and economic ruin at a hideous pace. There is no doubt that any Government called upon to bear the burden would have had to take prompt and severe measures, many of which would have been unpopular, in order to avert the disaster which was imminent. Hence the General Election.

The right hon Gentleman the Leader of the Opposition the other day derided us for saying that we are doing our best. He said if that were true it was the strongest argument for turning us out. The justice and even the decency of such a remark can only be judged in relation to the facts. A year ago we were certainly in a crisis of the first magnitude. Our taxation, especially on wealth, was and still is the highest in the world. Our reserves drained by the war have been spent with lavish hands, and many schemes of social welfare have been set on foot which increase normally and almost irresistibly every year. The fall in the purchasing power of money, or in other words the rise in the cost of living, was increasing rapidly. [Hon Members: 'And still is.'] It is still increasing, but not so rapidly. On the top of all this was this new rearmament programme, which, in principle, we supported, and which had been launched and was getting into its stride. We had to face, on taking over, not only a gigantic expenditure, but many formidable increases which have not reached fruition but have become inevitable. No one pretends that we have yet mastered that problem. We have warded off imminent catastrophe by many painful measures, and we are strengthening our margin of safety. On the whole, no one can doubt our position is better, actually and relatively, than it was a year ago. We always said we could be saved, but that several years of resolute policy and steady administration would be needed. We should also remember that during the first five years of Socialist rule £2,000 million of sterling was received mainly from the United States of America in loans or gifts. At £400 million per annum this more than equalled the loss we suffered in the early part of the war in income from foreign investments. We have had none of this since we took office, except the earmarked payment to aid our rearmament programme. It ill becomes those who after six years of power, power unequalled by any Government in this country in time of peace, and who are responsible in no small measure for the evils and dangers by which we are surrounded, to mock us when we say we are doing our best.

As a result of the measures we took, the United Kingdom recovered so far that in the first half of this year we achieved a small surplus, even before counting the defence aid received from the United States. Further, as a result of the Conference of Commonwealth Finance Ministers held in January, the position of the sterling area as a whole has also improved, and we confidently expect it to balance with the outside world in this second half of 1952. Since the end of June the monthly figures of our gold and dollar reserves have also shown improvement. We must not judge, of course, by a single month's figures, but it is true that the October results published today are the best since April 1951. Hon and right hon Members opposite must not look gloomy when a thing like that comes along. They should rejoice as we rejoice, even though, as I have said, a single month's returns cannot be taken as a criterion. These encouraging results are merely signs that we are able to enjoy what the Chancellor of the Exchequer has rightly called a breathing space in our task of putting our overseas finances on to safer and sounder foundations. It is not enough merely to balance our accounts and so pay our way. We have debts to repay, and the future holds many risks and many unknowable factors. The only way to provide for all this is, of course, to expand our overseas trade by an all out effort to increase our exports. It will be the

Government's primary endeavour not only to keep this objective before the country, but to foster the conditions under which it can be most easily and swiftly achieved.

Naturally, we are disappointed at the decline in production, which the Leader of the Opposition also deplores. The shortage of steel has been having a restrictive effect, but the steel is coming along, and we are looking forward to an increase in our production of steel. The prospect for the textile and clothing industries appears to be improved, and we hope to see an increase in output and employment. Unemployment in those industries is already tending to fall, and elsewhere it remains very low. The total unemployment remains below 2 per cent of the vast number of persons employed. There are also signs of a more mobile state in our economy. One welcome sign is the flow of manpower to the mines. Another sign, equally welcome, in view of our need to divert exports to dollar markets, is the recent increase in our exports to Canada. Our economy has been able to adapt itself to the stresses and strains of outside influence, in spite of the fact that these adjustments take time. We believe that events will show, both externally in our trade balance and internally in our domestic production, that our policy has been justified. That more might have been done is a field in which there may be argument, but at any rate we have tried our best, and we have so far made definite and indisputable progress.

Her Majesty's Government attach the greatest importance to the Conference of Commonwealth Prime Ministers which will open in London at the end of this month. It has not been called, like so many others in recent years, to examine immediate steps for escaping from a crisis already upon us. Indeed, since the meeting of Commonwealth Finance Ministers in January, things appear to have improved. The object now is to try to chart a course to a more secure future in which recurring crises will not occur. That is the end which we all seek, and as a means to that end we shall survey the economic and financial problems which are common to all our several countries, and shall consider any possible steps which will strengthen Sterling and help us to move towards the goal, accepted by the Commonwealth Finance Ministers, of a world in which trade will be free to move unhampered by the controls and arrangements which at present restrict it. The Government look forward keenly to welcoming our Commonwealth colleagues in London—not the Government only, but all parties—and to discussing with them these issues, which are of such great importance to every citizen of every country and to the Commonwealth as a whole, and to the great part which the British Commonwealth of Nations has yet to play in the wider world outside.

# LORD MAYOR'S BANQUET

A SPEECH AT GUILDHALL
10 NOVEMBER 1952

---

4 *November—HM The Queen opens Parliament in State.*

4 *November—The Conservative candidate is elected in the High Wycombe by-election with an increased majority.*

4 *November—General Eisenhower is elected President of the United States, carrying 39 of the 48 States.*

6 *November—Publication of the text of the Government's Iron and Steel Bill.*

9 *November—Death of Dr Chaim Weizmann, first President of Israel, at Rehovoth.*

---

[10 *November* 1952

MY LORD MAYOR, Your Excellencies, My Lords, Ladies and Gentlemen: When I came to your Banquet a year ago our Government had only just been formed and we had to face with a slender, and it might well have been a precarious, majority not only the partisanship of our opponents, but a task, the full magnitude of which was becoming every day more plain. We were moving into bankruptcy at an alarming rate. Only prompt, vigorous and unpopular action could gain us the breathing space necessary to place our affairs upon a sound foundation. By severe exertions we have gained the breathing space, but it will require several years of sober and persevering government to restore our financial and economic strength, without which our nation cannot play an effectual part, during this twentieth century of storm and tumult and terrible wars, in the vast world which has grown up around us.

I should not wish tonight to exaggerate our achievements. I am content with the modest plea that we have tried our best with no other aim but the common interest of the whole people. We are still only at the beginning of our task, and it may well be that disappointments and set-backs will afflict us. They will not, however, conquer us. We are encouraged by the fact that both at home and abroad there is a feeling that our position has definitely improved; that we are recovering our strength; that danger of a Third World War seems to have receded, and that our national solvency has been freed from immediate

361

peril. We are also cheered by a confident feeling that, no matter how much we are abused by our opponents, if we do our duty faithfully and without fear, we shall get fair play from the British people.

There has been an Election lately in the United States which we have all watched with unflagging attention. For me, I must admit it has been painful to see so many of my best friends over there and comrades in war and peace fighting one another with all the ardour which we associate with party politics and democracy. Nothing like that could have happened under the Soviets or their satellite states. There all is presented with glacial decorum. One party only is allowed, and majorities are presented of 98 per cent. What I always wonder at is how the remaining 2 per cent are persuaded to deny their votes to the mighty oligarchy who hold their lives and every detail of their daily life in its grasp. Are they rewarded, or are they punished, and if punished, does this take place beforehand or afterwards? After all, it would be a very serious thing if any of these elections produced a hundred per cent result. That might easily lead the capitalist world to doubt whether actually all had been fair and square. They might even suggest that the whole performance was humbug, enforced by iron discipline. Personally I prefer the kind of thing that happens at British and American Elections, even though I must admit there ought, in both countries, to be some lucid intervals between them.

At any rate there was one thing about the American Election which gave us great comfort here and throughout the Commonwealths who together are partners in the English-speaking world. Both the candidates were the finest figures American public life could present. Both were worthy of the highest traditions of the Great Republic which is now so valiantly sustaining the freedom of the world. With full confidence I express, in your name here tonight, our salutations to General Eisenhower and our assurance that, to the utmost limit of our strength, we will work with him for those great causes which we have guarded and cherished in ever greater unity as the generations have rolled by.

I did not wonder at all that the President-Elect, in the brief period before his inauguration, wished to visit Korea to view the scene with his own experienced and discerning eye. There is no doubt that the absorption of so large a proportion of American and United Nations resources in the Far East is to the advantage of Moscow and of the Communist Movement as a whole. That was why the Kremlin ordered the original aggression to begin; and that is why (after President Truman had effectively marshalled the United Nations to repel it) the so-called 'truce talks' have been dragged out over more than a year.

It is a convenient way of dispersing the strength of the free world and preventing, or at least delaying, the building up of a secure defence against the subjugation of Western Europe.

For these reasons I have always been anxious to bring the conflict in Korea to an end as speedily as possible and to keep it within the strictest limits while it lasts. That is my view today, but there is one thing it is never worthwhile doing. That is to purchase peace at the price of dishonour. It would be dishonour to send thousands of helpless prisoners-of-war back by force to be massacred by a Chinese Communist Government which boasts that it has actually rid itself of two millions of its own people. All history shows that such bargains, though they may afford a momentary relief, have to be paid for on a far larger scale later on. Every kind of reasonable proposal has been made by the Allies and there can be no doubt that it has so far been the policy of Moscow, for reasons which are obvious, to prevent an agreement from being reached. All these are matters of grave concern. I turn to another scene.

A year ago, in the closing days of the late Government and following on the retreat from Abadan, our forces in Egypt were subjected to an outbreak of murderous attacks at the instigation of the Wafd Party led by Nahas Pasha. The Socialist Government ordered strong reinforcements to the Canal Zone and resisted these unprovoked outrages. They also put forward the statesmanlike conception of a four-power approach to Egypt in which Britain, the United States, France and Turkey should share with Egypt in the protection of the world interests involved in maintaining the freedom of the famous waterway of the Suez Canal. We continued the policy of our predecessors and after a few months the terrorist campaign—in which the Egyptian Army did not join—was quelled.

In July there was a revolution in Egypt rather similar to that of the young Turks in Turkey many years ago, as a result of which a distinguished Egyptian soldier became, for the time being, virtually a military dictator. I have visited Egypt at frequent intervals under varying circumstances during the last fifty-four years. I am bound to say that I felt much sympathy with the new hope aroused by General Neguib, that the shocking condition of the Egyptian peasantry under the corrupt rule of former Egyptian Governments would be definitely improved. We are anxious to help the new Government and to negotiate with them on friendly terms. We understand their point of view and we hope they will understand ours.

We are not in Egypt for imperialist motives or self-seeking mastery or advantage, but in the common interests of all nations and to discharge what has become an international rather than a national responsibility, and we have no intention of being turned from our duty. I hope indeed that negotiations may reach a happy conclusion, as they may well do if only they are inspired by a sense of mutual responsibility and seek the preservation of interests most important to the peace and safety, not only of Egypt, but of the whole anxious area of the Middle East.

There is another country I must mention at this moment. Those of us who have been Zionists since the days of the Balfour Declaration know what a heavy loss Israel has sustained in the death of its President, Dr Chaim Weizmann. Here was a man whose fame and fidelity were respected throughout the free world, whose son was killed fighting for us in the late war, and who, it may be rightly claimed, led his people back into their promised land, where we have seen them invincibly established as a free and sovereign State.

All our safety and the hopes of bringing the world—gradually, it may well have to be—out of its present oppressive and ruinous plight, rest upon the preservation of friendship, alliance, and growing unity between Great Britain and her Commonwealths and the USA. In what is called NATO—the North Atlantic Treaty Organization—of which Lord Ismay is the Secretary General—we have the most effective instrument ever prepared to resist aggression in the Western hemisphere. We have also the Council of Europe. NATO embraces all active, living movements towards the unity of the free nations of Europe, in which I have always felt the hopes of a lasting peace reside.

The organization of NATO does not exclude the Mediterranean and here we are very glad to welcome during the year the membership of Greece and of Turkey. Both these ancient and virile races have repudiated the Communist conception of society. I am very glad to remember the help I was instrumental in winning for the Greeks during the great crisis of their fate in the winter of 1944. I had the pleasure only the other day of receiving the Prime Minister of Turkey, and of learning from that strong-minded statesman of the fearless outlook of modern Turkey and of their readiness to play a full part in our general organization of defence.

Six years have passed since I said at Zurich that France should take Germany by the hand and lead her back into the family of nations, and thus end the thousand-years' quarrel which has torn Europe to pieces and finally plunged the whole world twice over into slaughter and havoc. There can be no effective defence of European culture and freedom unless a new Germany, resolved to set itself free from the ghastly crimes of Hitlerism, plays a strong and effective part in our system. Any man in Germany or France or Britain who tries to hamper or delay that healing process is guilty of undermining the foundations upon which the salvation of all mankind from war and tyranny depends.

Every addition to the strength of NATO increases the deterrents against aggression on which our hopes and convictions stand. It is for this that our Foreign Secretary, Mr Eden, strives, as did Mr Bevin before him. It was for this that General Eisenhower, under President Truman's administration, undertook his solemn task in Europe, to which General Ridgway, our new and trusted commander, has now succeeded. It is to this that Mr Schuman, the Foreign Minister of France, and the German Chancellor, Dr Adenauer, have devoted their remarkable wisdom and their courage. Time alone can prove whether final success will reward these earnest, faithful efforts. Terrible would be the accountability of those in any country who, for petty, narrow, or selfish ends, weakened the common cause by stirring bygone passions, hates and tragedies.

A year ago I said here, in this famous Guildhall, that Britain stood erect, calm, resolute, and independent. What report should I make tonight? Surely it is that we have gained both in strength and in purpose. Britain is loyal to her faith: to her belief in the principles of the United Nations and in the dignity of the individual: and to her determination to see, with all her Allies, a true and lasting settlement among the nations. With this faith, and in this high companionship, we shall march forward undaunted by danger, unwearied by toil.

# MOTION OF CENSURE

A SPEECH TO THE HOUSE OF COMMONS
4 DECEMBER 1952

---

14 *November—Egyptian Cabinet issue a decree conferring supreme powers on General Neguib for six months.*

24 *November—The Marquess of Salisbury becomes Lord President of the Council, Viscount Swinton Secretary of State for Commonwealth Relations, and Lord Woolton, who has been seriously ill, Chancellor of the Duchy of Lancaster.*

4 *December—The Prime Minister announces in the House of Commons that expenditure on defence production is to be curtailed.*

---

[4 *December* 1952

I have today to deal with a Motion of censure, and therefore I hope I shall be pardoned if I do not confine myself entirely to the uncontroversial methods which I usually practice. Let me in the first place begin by offering my congratulations to the Leader of the Opposition who left the sharp, harsh language of the Motion behind and launched out into a general parade of all those topics which are usually a subject of discussion in our constituencies. Taking all that he said together, one must feel that he made a scathing denunciation of the Government, and I earnestly hope that that may be considered sufficient and that he will not be left at the post, as it were, when the right hon Gentleman the Member for Ebbw Vale [Mr Bevan] resumes his role of virtuous indignation reinforced with the abuse for which he is celebrated.

It is a remarkable fact that, if we look at the terms of the Motion, the first occasion for ten months in which the Opposition have moved a formal Motion against the present Government it is on terms of a purely technical matter in the conduct of the House, and which has no bearing whatever upon the daily lives of the people or the march of events. No censure is urged on the manner in which the Government conduct their affairs in these anxious times either at home or abroad, and Her Majesty's Government may congratulate themselves upon the success of their administration. The country has no reason to rejoice on the feeble, barren absence of constructive thought on the part of the Opposition.

MR C. R. ATTLEE (Walthamstow, West): May I remind the right hon Gentleman that only a few weeks ago we were on the debate on the Queen's Speech. Therefore, it would be inappropriate to cover the ground we amply covered then.

THE PRIME MINISTER: I should have thought that, in view of the interval that has occurred, the right hon Gentleman might well have thought of some variants to the general indictment which we all remember he threw upon us then. I am quite sure the right hon Gentleman did his best, and he had every reason to do his best. We shall have the opportunity of seeing how this works out before we get to the end of the day. I should like to look back a little on the course of events in order rightly to judge this Motion on the Paper. On Tuesday last we were expecting a strong, vigorous debate upon the Steel Bill. At the end of Questions, when we were about to take this important discussion, the Adjournment of the House was moved about a tragic incident in Kenya and, after some vehement discussion, this was permitted by Mr Speaker.

I was sorry that the Opposition should have concentrated upon this single point in the difficult and harrowing scene in East Africa. I thought I made a fair and reasonable offer to the Opposition, namely, to give them a whole day for the debate on East Africa. It would have protected the Second Reading of the Steel Bill from violent interruption, which would have been so much better than focusing public attention by debate and by as it then seemed a Division on party lines upon the action of two or three young police officers who, with only twenty native police, were confronted with 2,000 tribesmen with long knives. Upon the nerve and decision of these officers at a critical moment much depended. Had they not acted with resolution, the whole detachment of police would have been torn to pieces, even if they had fired every bullet they possessed. When there is such a state of affairs as exists in Kenya, it would be most dangerous to undermine the confidence of subordinate officers.

MR R. T. PAGET (Northampton): Is a discussion of events in Kenya in order on this Motion?

MR DEPUTY-SPEAKER [SIR CHARLES MACANDREW]: I thought the opening speech was fairly wide. I did not stop it, and I do not see any reason to stop this now.

THE PRIME MINISTER: I am only discussing this particular episode in Kenya in order to draw the attention of the House to what actually happened before the proceedings on Tuesday night. I am giving the House my own feelings at the time. When there is such a state of affairs as in Kenya, I thought myself that, if there were a debate and Division on this matter, we might rupture and break the nerve of these young people, and we might well find that great disasters and bloodshed would follow. Not only might there be a massacre, but the whole structure of Government might be weakened. All the settlers throughout this scattered country would be in mortal peril. [*Interruption.*] Hon Members opposite will give me credit for not being afraid of interruptions or noise. It even would be much easier to be shouted down continually or booed down, because I have not the slightest doubt I could obtain publicity for any remarks I wish to make, even if they are not audible in the House. It was this desire to debate the matter which made us make what I thought was a generous offer of a whole day's debate. However, the Opposition persisted and obtained the Adjournment. Then we came to the Steel Bill—I am showing the background in which the count was sought—which we have been told was so important—a terrible Bill of reaction. But what happened? There could have hardly been a greater contrast between the House excited in the arguments about the Adjournment on the Kenya episode and the scene at the Second Reading of the Steel Bill. Not only had the debate been wantonly disturbed and interrupted by the Opposition——

Mr John Hynd (Sheffield, Attercliffe): Am I correct in understanding that the debate was interrupted in order to discuss Kenya because the Chair considered that that was an urgent matter of vital public importance, and in that case is not the right hon Gentleman criticizing the Chair?

Mr Deputy-Speaker: It was not I who gave the decision, and I do not think the right hon Gentleman was criticizing the Chair.

Mr Sydney Silverman (Nelson and Colne): The right hon Gentleman has just said in the hearing of all of us that the interruption to which he refers, namely, the debate on the special adjournment of the House under Standing Order No. 9, was a wanton interruption. If it were a wanton interruption, the reflection would not be upon my right hon Friends but upon the Chair which allowed the wanton Motion to be moved.

Mr James Griffiths (Llanelly) *rose*——

Mr Deputy-Speaker: Let me take one at a time. It is the House that gives permission.

Hon Members: No.

Mr J. Griffiths: Further to that point of order. Is it not a fact that on that day, when I moved the Adjournment of the House and Mr Speaker accepted it, the Colonial Secretary himself said the matter was important? He made a statement to the House on that Tuesday in reply to a Private Notice Question, because it was of urgent public importance.

MR DEPUTY-SPEAKER: I think that that is a different incident.

THE PRIME MINISTER: I am certainly not making any reflection at all upon the Chair.

MR SILVERMAN: Then withdraw the word 'wanton'.

THE PRIME MINISTER: I will not withdraw the word 'wanton' or any other word I use.

MR SILVERMAN: On a point of order. The right hon Gentleman has said that he will not withdraw the word 'wanton'—[HON MEMBERS: 'Under the hon Gentleman's instructions.']—although it is perfectly clear that, under the Ruling you have just given, Sir, the word 'wanton' could only be an attack on the Chair. [HON MEMBERS: 'Nonsense.'] There is only one occupant of the Chair, and I understand it to be you, Sir, and not the dozen or so answering Members opposite. The point I put to you is this, that to call that Motion or debate 'wanton' is a reflection on the Chair, without whose permission the Motion could not have been moved, and if that is so, I suggest to you that it is your duty in the Chair in this House to keep every Member of the House strictly within the rules of order even if it be the Prime Minister himself, and not to discriminate between Members. [HON MEMBERS: 'Oh!'] Therefore, I say it is your duty—I submit to you with respect—to call upon the Prime Minister to withdraw the offending word.

MR DEPUTY-SPEAKER: If my duty is at fault it will be discussed on Monday. I do not want to say anything about that now. In order to to raise a Motion under Standing Order No. 9 a Member has to get the leave of the House, which he got, and that is all I have to say on the matter.

MR ATTLEE: Further to that Ruling. It is quite true that he has to get the leave of the House, but it is Mr Speaker who says whether it is a matter of definite urgent public importance. That is a ruling as to the nature of the subject.

MR DEPUTY-SPEAKER: That is how it arises, but I do not see that 'wanton' is necessarily directed to that.

MR F. BESWICK (Uxbridge): Do I understand it to be your Ruling, Mr Deputy-Speaker, that Mr Speaker would give permission for a debate in this House which can be properly described as a 'wanton' subject?

MR DEPUTY-SPEAKER: Mr Speaker allowed the matter because it was urgent, public and definite. The Prime Minister did not use the word against Mr Speaker at all. He used it against the subject.

MR JACK JONES (Rotherham): Not only did he refuse to withdraw the word 'wanton', but the Prime Minister went on to say nor would he withdraw any other word he used. May I have an assurance that while we on these back benches are confined to the rules of the House the Prime Minister shall not have rules of his own?

MR DEPUTY-SPEAKER: If the Prime Minister uses unparliamentary words I shall stop him.

THE PRIME MINISTER: I hope I shall be allowed a measure of free speech. I thought it was perfectly understood that the Chair interpreted the rules of the House. Those who put these rules into motion, and those who, when opportunity is given to them, cry for action—they are the ones who take the actual responsibility. And it is to them, and to them alone, the word 'wanton' applies. I have got a lot to say, and I shall have to keep the House several hours if we go on at this rate. Nothing will induce me to be frustrated in unfolding the argument— not even sham points of order.

Let me recall the House to the point I had reached in the argument. I said that the Adjournment of the House was given, that the debate on the Iron and Steel Bill, which, we had been told, was very important indeed—[HON MEMBERS: 'Who said so?']—was to be interrupted at 7 p.m. We could not have had a greater contrast between the House, excited by the Adjournment on the Kenya episode, and the scene at the beginning of the Second Reading of the Iron and Steel Bill. Not only had the debate been interrupted, but it had been made to extend to 1 a.m. instead of ending at 10 p.m. But not only that. There appeared to be a strange lack of interest on the subject on the part of the Opposition.

MR IVOR OWEN THOMAS (The Wrekin): Where were the Prime Minister's men?

THE PRIME MINISTER: Rarely have I seen such a change of mood in the House. The Opposition Members trooped out in all directions, and a quiet, half empty House was left to listen to the debate on a Measure which, we were told, was such a flagrant example of reactionary legislation. Nothing could more clearly vindicate the Government in allocating only two days to the debate on the Second Reading of the Iron and Steel Bill than the lack of interest—and, I may say, of argumentative power—shown throughout the proceedings by the Opposition. [Interruption.] I am going through what happened on Tuesday.

We now reach the Adjournment at 7 p.m. on Kenya. I was very glad that the Opposition, or the responsible Members of it, on second thoughts did not force a party Division on the conduct of those young officers in their terrible ordeal, and that the right hon Gentleman moved to withdraw the Motion. That shows how much better advised he and his colleagues would have been to have accepted my offer—

THE PRIME MINISTER: I have already said that we regret that we did not keep a quorum. I have already explained that the reason was that after the other debate on Kenya had been concluded there was —[*Interruption.*]Well, if hon Gentlemen opposite will not listen I will not interrupt my own speech.

I have gone at some length and in full detail into the sequence of events which led to the count and to the House being counted out against our responsibility, on which the Opposition have based their demand for a Motion of censure, which we have naturally accorded at the earliest possible moment. The consequences of this Socialist misbehaviour involved the House in an exhausting all-night Sitting, which turned out very badly for the Opposition. In a long series of Divisions they were defeated by majorities far outranging the normal and greatly improving the Government's average majority. They were far above the normal or what we received from the electors.

MR I. O. THOMAS: Where was the right hon Gentleman?

THE PRIME MINISTER: I will be perfectly frank with the House. I was better employed in sound slumber on that occasion. I was, of course, paired. If I had not taken some of these precautions I should not have sufficient strength to sustain the ordeal to which I am now being subjected. The Opposition were beaten in this long series of Divisions. They have shown that they do not really regard the denationalization of the iron and steel industry as an important or, indeed, highly controversial Measure, and this will be a valuable guide to us in considering the amount of time to be given to its later stages.

Here let me pay my tribute to the Leader of the House and the Chief Whip, who have been the subject of so much abuse. Both my right hon Friends were in their places at the count, and I have already expressed my regret that a quorum was not maintained. But I repudiate with conviction the charge that the management of Parliamentary business this session, or indeed since the new Parliament met, has been in any way unequal to the very difficult duties entrusted to these two Ministers.

The word 'incompetence' is used in the censure Motion. [An HON MEMBER: 'Wanton incompetence.'] I think that is a contradiction in terms. This rude word is not an expression of opinion which need be treated with the slightest respect. It is only a yelp of anger from men who have been beaten thoroughly in all their manoeuvres however disreputable. Not only have Her Majesty's Government been the victors in over 250 Divisions, but they have had throughout these Divisions a majority almost double what it is on paper. Is that incompetence?

When this Parliament first met, just over a year ago, the Opposition challenged us twice on Amendments to the Address. Our actual majority is only 16. On the first occasion we had a majority of 38, and on the second 37, or more than double. Is that incompetence? In the Division on the Christmas food supplies, we had a majority of 37. Was that incompetence? In February, the Opposition tried a snap Division on an Adjournment debate on the resignation of the Chairman of the Iron and Steel Corporation. Our majority was 47. Is that incompetence? On the question of fares, in April, we had a majority of 44. Was it incompetence that we had a majority of 64 in the debate on food? Was it incompetence that on the Steel Bill we had a majority of 36 a week ago? Was it due to incompetence that the business for last week was finished at the time originally proposed, or that the business for this week will be disposed of with equal precision? On the contrary, our success, which has been the cause of so much anger, is due not only to the competence of the Ministers concerned but to the vigour and exertions of a united party.

The present indications seem to show that public opinion is hardening in favour of Her Majesty's Government. It may well be that this tendency will be strengthened by the exhibitions we are having and by the frustration from which the Socialist Party—or Labour Party, as I call them when I mean to be polite—rent and torn with their bitter internal quarrels, is so obviously suffering. A year ago, their party managers thought that our majority was too small for the Government to have any real expectation of long life or of being able to undo the harm and bear successfully the grievous burden we inherited. It was prophesied by the high expert Socialist authorities that by-elections would soon reduce that majority. Mr Morgan Phillips, whose competence I should be the last to assail, in a broadcast on 2 November of last year said—and I will read this to the house:

> 'If we cannot cut into the Government's majority in by-elections in the next twelve months, I will eat my hat.'

The twelve months are over, so what is going to happen? Let me say that I do not think that such an unpalatable ordeal is needed at a time when the Christmas season is upon us and there will be other things to eat. I have always been an advocate of magnanimity in victory, and so far as the Government and their supporters are concerned, I wish formally to announce that we give Mr Phillips complete release from his obligation. We will not even occupy time in asking whether his mistake was due to his competence or incompetence.

This brings me to another point to which I must draw the attention of the House, namely, the treatment by the Opposition of the mass of routine legislation without which the administration of national affairs would be brought to a stop. Take the Expiring Laws Continuance Bill. I have looked into what has happened since the war. I find that in 1945 1 hour 9 minutes were taken on it; in 1946, 1 hour 21 minutes; in 1947, 1 hour 9 minutes—through all stages; in 1948, 2 hours 51 minutes, and in the second Session in 1948-49, 53 minutes. In 1950-51 the time taken was 2 hours 44 minutes; in 1951-52, 2 hours and 41 minutes—the average of all this being 1 hour and 49 minutes. In this particular Session, we have had to give 14 hours and 33 minutes, or eight times the average for the previous years.

MR ALFRED ROBENS (Blyth): Will the right hon Gentleman look into the history of the Gas Bill?

THE PRIME MINISTER: That is a tempting subject—the Gas Bill. The right hon Gentleman has given great study to it, which he will no doubt benefit by now that he is in opposition.

I wish to speak, if I may, in reply to the Leader of the Opposition, who moved the Motion of censure. He said on the 6 November of last year:

'The Opposition will be vigilant but not factious. We shall not oppose merely for the sake of opposition . . . the Press expect a much higher standard of public service from Socialists than they do from Conservatives. They suggest that it would be quite wrong for anyone in this House to indulge now in the kind of tactics which were indulged in during the last Parliament. They expect something altogether better from us, and they are quite right.'

This was a boast of a much better performance and a much higher standard which was as little fulfilled by the Opposition as were Mr Morgan Phillips's expectations which induced him to undertake such formidable forfeits.

I now come to the Public Works Loans Bill. Here again the time spent in the last six years has been 35 minutes, 46 minutes, 46 minutes, 50 minutes, 21 minutes, and, in 1950-51, 1 hour and 22 minutes, an average of 47 minutes for all that period, the bulk of which we were in Opposition. But on this last occasion, it is 8 hours and 39 minutes, or nearly 12 times the previous average. More time has been spent in this present Session on that Bill than in the previous six. [*Interruption.*] I do not pretend that I have never tried to delay the proceedings of the House, but this is a matter which is designed to affect our conduct of a Bill.

MR ANEURIN BEVAN (Ebbw Vale) *rose*——

THE PRIME MINISTER: Cannot you let your right hon Friend have the afternoon, anyhow? As the right hon Gentleman is so lonely, I will treat him with chivalry.

MR BEVAN: I am very grateful to the right hon Gentleman for

giving way. I just wanted to understand his argument, as I am under an obligation to reply. Is he rebuking his hon Friends behind him for the speeches they made in those debates?

THE PRIME MINISTER: I was not reproaching any of my hon Friends behind me but trying to throw rebukes upon those who are in the wrong this afternoon. It seems to me that it is quite clear that with this process of a handful of Members, unable and unwilling to divide the House, nevertheless delaying the whole process of legislation, they could produce a situation different from any which has hitherto confronted Parliament. The hope of the Opposition is to hold up our de-nationalization Measures. We cannot accept the words of the Motion that the Measures are not related 'to the needs of the nation'. On the contrary, we should never have faced the trouble and burden of this legislation if we were not convinced that not only were we redeeming our pledges—and who would have mocked us if we had not done so?—but that we were notably improving the conditions on which the fertility and prosperity of our trade and production depends.

I am finishing in a minute: I will not keep hon Members under such a vocal strain for too long. I do not want to make them so hoarse that they cannot even continue the debate. But we must now contemplate this vote of censure, and the use of normal rountine business to produce deadlocks, in their larger setting. The abusive language of the right hon Gentleman's Motion, the harsh epithets, may no doubt be dismissed with any attention it deserves, but the vote of censure and the tactics now being employed against Her Majesty's Government in the circumstances I have described must be viewed against the general political background. We have had two General Elections in little more than two years. Each has resulted in Parliamentary majorities far smaller than are required for the convenient course of Parliamentary business. The Standing Committees are no longer the help and relief to the House of Commons that they were. A far greater portion of our business must be conducted in the whole House. That is only one of the factors which adds to the very heavy burden imposed upon Members of all parties, but so far borne, as the figures show, with greater success by Her Majesty's Government. We feel that we are in a definitely stronger position, both in the House and in the country, than we were a year ago, but I cannot feel that it would be in the national interest to have another General Election, even though it would seem that we should improve our position, and not suffer at any future election—and hon Members opposite should pay attention to this—the serious injury which was inflicted upon us by what is now admitted to be the warmonger lie.

The country needs a period of steady, stable administration to recover from its maltreatment, as we say, but anyhow from the extreme exertions and disturbance in the preceding six years; to undo some of the work that was then done and to ward off, as we are trying to do, bankruptcy; and to strengthen and broaden the foundations of peace. I have repeatedly said that we ask to be judged by deeds not words, by results not promises; and time and perseverance are needed for these. We do not believe that it is in the power of the party opposite to prevent us from doing what we conceive to be our duty. If we act, as we shall do, in a resolute manner, we shall make it clear to our opponents that artful dodges and dull methods of delay—[An Hon Member: 'Obstruction.']—I am rather careful about the word obstruction; I have looked it up, but its permissibility has carefully to be considered—cannot bring the House of Commons to a standstill; or else, if that failed, it would be the prelude to a succession of General Elections contrary to the principle of the Quinquennial Act. If we can show that a Government, even with a majority as moderate as our own, can in fact do several years' good and faithful work, we shall have rendered an historic service to Parliamentary government. We are much encouraged by what has happened so far and by the failure of the Opposition to mask their own internal feuds by uniting in hysterical and violent abuse of their opponents. Their conduct throughout this Parliament in our opinion has been reprehensible in a high degree. Far from moving a Motion of censure on Her Majesty's Government, they should shake and shiver in their shoes with shame.

*Note:* The Opposition's Motion of Censure was defeated by a majority of 24.

# COMMONWEALTH ECONOMIC CONFERENCE

A SPEECH TO THE CONFERENCE
11 DECEMBER 1952

---

6 *December—It is announced that General Eisenhower, President-Elect of the United States, has just completed a three-day tour in Korea in fulfilment of his election pledge.*

8 *December—India rejects the latest Anglo-American proposals for the settlement of the Kashmir dispute.*

---

[11 *December* 1952

The business of the Conference is now concluded. The time has come to say farewell to the Prime Ministers and other Ministers who travelled so far from all the continents of the world to contribute their counsel and experience towards solution of our common problems. Sir Chintaman Deshmukh, who made such a notable contribution to your deliberations, has already had to return to Delhi. The others will be leaving in the course of the next few days.

Though I have not been able to preside at your full meetings here, I have followed your proceedings with close interest. I am greatly impressed by the amount of solid hard work that has been done and by the results achieved. I have no doubt that the Conference has been a great success. I do not think that any of us would wish this afternoon to go over the many problems dealt with at the Conference and described in the communique. But I may perhaps record three broad impressions which it has made on my mind.

First, it was right for us to take stock of our position now—seven years after the end of the war—seven years of transition and physical recovery from war, political tension, economic change and difficulty. It was necessary and timely to look forward now in hope of moving towards more stable economic conditions and to decide what broad courses the 600 million people of the Commonwealth should follow in the years ahead.

Secondly, it seems to me that the discussions in this Conference were marked by a striking degree of frankness and common sense. Difficulties have not been shirked or glossed over with comfortable words. In discussion of our internal financial problems we have had a most valuable interchange of views. This frank disclosure of difficulties, doubts and aspirations gives us a far greater understanding of each others' aims and policies. It is bound to make our co-operation in the future more easy and more fruitful. For our part, we shall do our best to continue to keep other Commonwealth Governments in close touch with the development of our thought on our common economic problems.

Finally, let me say that consultation of this kind between partners is a source of strength. It is fully consonant with the close ties which we must all have, in economic as well as political matters, with other great trading nations—particularly the United States and the leading countries of Europe. Our next step will be to enter upon discussions with them in the hope that conditions can be established which will enable the free nations to go forward together to build a world of expanded trade, wise development, and fuller economic opportunities for all free peoples.